N⬤T

Not For Tourists Guide to
SAN FRANCISCO

Get more on
notfortourists.com

Keep connected with:
Twitter:
twitter/notfortourists

Facebook:
facebook/notfortourists

iPhone App:
nftiphone.com

www.notfortourists.com

Not For Tourists, Inc

Skyhorse Publishing

designed by:
Not For Tourists, Inc
NFT™—Not For Tourists™ Guide to San Francisco
www.notfortourists.com

Publisher	**Production Manager**
Skyhorse Publishing	Aaron Schielke
Creative Direction and Information Design	**Graphic Design and Production**
Jane Pirone	Aaron Schielke
Director	**Information Systems Manager**
Stuart Farr	Juan Molinari
Managing Editor	
Scott Sendrow	

Printed in China
Print ISBN: 978-1-63450-145-3 $18.99
Ebook ISBN: 978-1-5107-0024-6
ISSN 2163-9140
Copyright © 2015 by Not For Tourists, Inc.
13th Edition

Every effort has been made to ensure that the information in this book is as up-to-date as possible at press time. However, many details are liable to change—as we have learned.
Not For Tourists cannot accept responsibility for any consequences arising from the use of this book.

Not For Tourists does not solicit individuals, organizations, or businesses for listings inclusion in our guides, nor do we accept payment for inclusion into the editorial portion of our book; the advertising sections, however, are exempt from this policy. We always welcome communications from anyone regarding ANYTHING having to do with our books; please visit us on our website at www.notfortourists.com for appropriate contact information.

www.skyhorsepublishing.com

10 9 8 7 6 5 4 3 2 1

Dear NFT User,

If you've just bought this book and are opening it for the first time, we want to thank you for your business and support. We at Not For Tourists believe that this guide is the urban manual to San Francisco that no friend or loved one should be without. This map-based guidebook organizes SF into 40 neighborhoods with details about all of the essentials: restaurants, nightlife, shopping, landmarks, transit options, and all the practical information you need to get by. Not only is the NFT Guide to SF chock full of useful facts but we've also engineered it to fit neatly in your pocket.

If you're standing a bookstore figuring out whether to buy this book, we beseech you: please buy this book. Don't just stand there memorizing facts or details: stay with us a while, take us home, make us a part of your family. Check out the rest of the book for the latest in listings, maps, tips, and all-around expert NFT guidance. We've got our team of local writers and scourges-about-town back to let you know what's going on, and where—all in a compact, sharp-looking volume that's easy to check when you're going from place to place.

Speaking of keeping things mobile, check out our city-by-city iPhone apps, crammed with thousands of listings, or the website (www.notfortourists.com). Both provide you with up-to-the-minute tips, the minute you want them. We're also on Twitter (@notfortourists) and Facebook: send us a message or just drop by to say hello.

Here's hoping you find what you need in the fog…

—Jane, Scott, et al.

Driving Map and Bay Area Map
foldout, last page

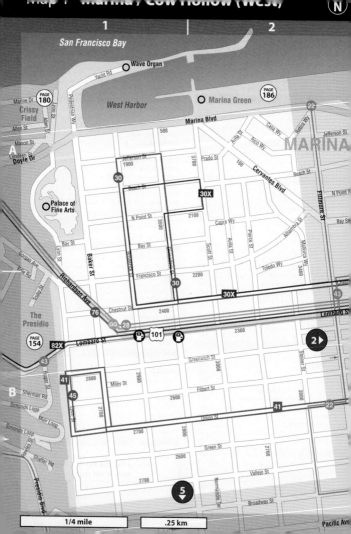

Flanked by the Presidio to the west and the bay to the north, this neighborhood has some of the best sea-level strolling and views in the city, particularly from Marina Boulevard along the shore of Marina Green. Main drags Chestnut Street and Union Street offer shopping and a mix of bars and restaurants. Busy Lombard Street has motels, drugstores, fast food, and other necessities.

○ Landmarks

- **Marina Green** •
  Marina Blvd btwn Scott St & Webster St
  Fly a kite with the Golden Gate in the background.
- **Palace of Fine Arts Theatre** • 3301 Lyon St
  415-567-6642
  Designed for the 1915 World's Fair by Bernard Maybeck, the Roman ruin's grandeur is strikingly beautiful.
- **The Wave Organ** • Yacht Rd
  Trippy ocean-powered musical instrument.

Bars

- **Bin 38** • 3232 Scott St
  415-567-3838
  Comfy new wine bar.
- **The Final Final** • 2990 Baker St
  415-931-7800
  Sports bar off the beaten path.
- **Liverpool Lil's** • 2942 Lyon St
  415-921-6664
  Quiet, comfy little pub tucked away by the Presidio. NFT fave.
- **Marina Lounge** • 2138 Chestnut St
  415-922-1475
  Marina dive.
- **Nectar Wine Lounge** • 3330 Steiner St
  415-345-1377
  Stylish wine bar. Flights and small bites.

Map 1

Marina / Cow Hollow (West)

🍴 Restaurants

- **A16** • 2355 Chestnut St
  415-771-2216 • $$$$
  Rustic Italian, great pizzas, vintage foosball table. Nice wines.
- **Ace Wasabi's Rock and Roll Sushi** •
  3339 Steiner St
  415-567-4903 • $$$$
  Lively sushi bar. Bingo at 6:30.
- **Amici's East Coast Pizzeria** • 2200 Lombard St
  415-885-4500 • $$
  Thin crust pizzas, with vegan and gluten-free options.
- **Baker Street Bistro** • 2953 Baker St
  415-931-1475 • $$$
  Casual, quaint, French.
- **Barney's Gourmet Hamburgers** •
  3344 Steiner St
  415-563-0307 • $$
  Good burgers. Take the kids.
- **Bistro Aix** • 3340 Steiner St
  415-202-0100 • $$$$
  Mediterranean- and French-inspired bistro with a cozy heated patio.
- **Blue Barn** • 2105 Chestnut St
  415-441-3232 • $$
  Cozy spot with carefully-sourced salads and sandwiches, popular but pricey.
- **Circa** • 2001 Chestnut St
  415-351-0175 • $$$
  Popular, LOUD bar and grill.
- **Dragon Well** • 2142 Chestnut St
  415-474-6888 • $$$
  Cheap modern Chinese.
- **The Grove** • 2250 Chestnut St
  415-474-4843 • $$
  Cozy, laptop-friendly café.
- **Home Plate** • 2274 Lombard St
  415-922-4663 • $
  Complimentary scones. The only Marina freebie.
- **International House of Pancakes** •
  2299 Lombard St
  415-921-4004 • $$
  Where else can you get pancakes and eggs at 3 am?
- **Isa** • 3324 Steiner St
  415-567-9588 • $$$$$
  Excellent small plates and charming heated patio.

- **Izzy's Steak and Chops** • 3345 Steiner St
  415-563-0487 • $$$$
  Casual steakhouse. Don't miss the creamed spinach and Izzy's potatoes.
- **Liverpool Lil's** • 2942 Lyon St
  415-921-6664 • $$
  Quiet, comfy little pub tucked away by the Presidio.
- **Los Hermanos** • 2026 Chestnut St
  415-921-5790 • $
  Simple, friendly, unfussy tacos and burritos.
- **Mamacita** • 2317 Chestnut St
  415-346-8494 • $$
  Mexican for the trendy set.
- **Mel's Drive-In** • 2165 Lombard St
  415-921-2867 • $$
  Diner food, great for kids. Anybody see *American Graffiti*?
- **Mezes** • 2373 Chestnut St
  415-409-7111 • $$$
  Popular Marina Greek.
- **Original Buffalo Wings** • 2499 Lombard St
  415-931-8181 • $
  Lunchtime specials are reasonable value for the Lombard motel crowd.
- **Pluto's** • 3258 Scott St
  415-775-8867 • $$
  Made-to-order salads are the key attraction.
- **RISTOBAR** • 2300 Chestnut St
  415-923-6464 • $$
  Northern Italian food and gelato, wine bar, café, pastry shop.
- **Ristorante Parma** • 3314 Steiner St
  415-567-0500 • $$$
  Casual Italian. Try the carbonara.
- **Rose's Café** • 2298 Union St
  415-775-2200 • $$$
  Charming Italian-style café. Breakfast, lunch, and dinner. Great for sidewalk dining.
- **Squat and Gobble** • 2263 Chestnut St
  415-441-2200 • $$
  Sizeable menu and a nice patio out back.
- **Terzo** • 3011 Steiner St
  415-441-3200 • $$$
  Ever-changing, always-enticing menu of Mediterranean small plates.
- **The Tipsy Pig** • 2231 Chestnut St
  415-292-2300 • $$$
  Raucous gastropub with incredible bacon-infused mac and cheese.
- **Yukol Place Thai Cuisine** • 2380 Lombard St
  415-922-1599 • $$
  Neighborhood Thai.

hrongs of twenty-something professionals bar hop along lively Chestnut treet. Shoppers will find old standbys like **Lucky Brand** as well as a reckling of unique boutiques. For dinner on the fancy side, **Isa** is a good et. For something different, hit **Liverpool Lil's** pub next to the Presidio ates.

🛍Shopping

- **Apple Store** • 2125 Chestnut St
  415-848-4445
  iParadise for Mac fanatics.
- **Benefit** • 2219 Chestnut St
  415-567-1173
  Cosmetics galore.
- **Books Inc.** • 2251 Chestnut St
  415-931-3633
  Books and magazines.
- **Chadwick's of London** • 2068 Chestnut St
  415-775-3423
  Pricey Italian Lingerie.
- **City Optix** • 2154 Chestnut St
  415-921-1188
  Cool eyewear.

- **Fiori** • 2314 Chestnut St
  415-346-1100
  Beautiful flowers.
- **Fleet Feet** • 2076 Chestnut St
  415-921-7188
  Running shoes and clothes.
- **Lucca Delicatessen** • 2120 Chestnut St
  415-921-7873
  Good Italian deli and staples.
- **Lucky Brand** • 2301 Chestnut St
  415-749-3750
  Jeans and casual wear.
- **Marine Layer** • 2209 Chestnut St
  415-346-2400
  Ridiculously soft, high-quality t-shirts.

Map 2
22 | 5 | 6 | 7 | 8
9 | 10 | 11 | 12 | 13

Life is simply fabulous—and clean—in the Marina and Cow Hollow, SF's enclave for young adult professionals. "Marina types" is an insult in all other parts of the city but the people here could care less. **Fort Mason**, a onetime military outpost, is now a cultural destination with museums, experimental theater, and acres of open space.

○ Landmarks

• **Fort Mason Center** •
Buchanan St & Marina Blvd
415-345-7500
Former military base. Now houses small galleries, museums, and restaurants.

• **Octagon House** • 2645 Gough St
415-441-7512
Fengshui a la Orson Fowler in 1861: octagonal houses provide a healthful living environment. Now a museum for colonial decorative arts.

🍸 Bars

• **Balboa Cafe** • 3199 Fillmore St
415-921-3944
Historic upscale pub.

• **Bar None** • 1980 Union St
415-409-4469
Union Street pub with beer pong.

• **Black Magic Voodoo Lounge** •
1400 Lombard St
415-931-8711
The voodoo that they do so well is a spell made with Absinthe.

• **The Brazen Head** • 3166 Buchanan St
415-921-7600
Low-key marina bar serving food 'til late.

• **Bus Stop** • 1901 Union St
415-567-6905
Casual Cow Hollow hangout.

• **City Tavern** • 3200 Fillmore St
415-567-0918
Good for afternoon sidewalk drinkin'.

• **Comet Club** • 3111 Fillmore St
415-567-5589
Good spot for the last round.

• **HiFi** • 2125 Lombard St
415-345-8663
Marina club with velvet paintings and disco balls.

• **Horseshoe Tavern** • 2024 Chestnut St
415-346-1430
Sports bar.

• **Kelley's Tavern** • 3231 Fillmore St
415-567-7181
Chic Irish pub, if that's possible.

• **Lightning Tavern** • 1875 Union St
415-704-1875
Down pitchers of cocktails in a glass-enclosed patio with TVs.

• **MatrixFillmore** • 3138 Fillmore St
415-563-4180
Shiny happy people doing key bumps in the bathroom.

• **Mauna Loa** • 3009 Fillmore St
415-563-5137
Low-key dive, with a pool table.

• **Ottimista** • 1838 Union St
415-674-8400
European wine bar. Serves brunch.

• **Silver Clouds** • 1994 Lombard St
415-922-1977
The regular drunken Marina crowd, only singing.

Map 2

Restaurants

- **Alegrias Spanish Restaurant** •
2018 Lombard St
415-929-8888 • $$$
Specialities from Campania; great pizza.
- **Balboa Cafe** • 3199 Fillmore St
415-921-3944 • $$$$
Fresh California fare in a clubby setting.
Owned by Mayor Gavin Newsom.
- **Betelnut** • 2030 Union St
415-929-8855 • $$$$
Popular contemporary Asian cuisine. Prepare
to wait.
- **Boboquivari's** • 1450 Lombard St
415-441-8880 • $$$$$
Steak and crab. Outlandish décor.
- **The Brazen Head** • 3166 Buchanan St
415-921-7600 • $$$$
Low-key Marina bar serving food til' late.
- **Eastside West** • 3154 Fillmore St
415-885-4000 • $$$
Seafood, live music, and swanky bar scene.
- **Gamine** • 2223 Union St
415-771-7771 • $$
Cozy French resto, get the oozy gambozola.
- **Greens Restaurant** • Ft Mason
415-771-6222 • $$$$
Imaginative vegetarian cuisine; great views.
- **Helmand Palace** • 2424 Van Ness Ave
415-345-0072 • $$
Pleasant Afghan restaurant—order the kaddo,
baked pumpkin.
- **Jake's Steaks** • 3301 Buchanan St
415-922-2211 • $
Artery-busting cheesesteaks with onion rings
and waffle fries.

- **La Boulange** • 1909 Union St
415-440-4450 • $$
Exceptional French bakery.
- **La Cucina** • 2136 Union St
415-921-4500 • $$
Diner. Great for breakfast.
- **Lite Bite** • 1796 Union St
415-931-5483 • $
Healthy to-go options labeled with calorie
counts.
- **Mas Sake** • 2030 Lombard St
415-440-1505 • $$
California-influenced sushi; party atmosphere.
- **The Matterhorn Swiss Restaurant** •
2323 Van Ness Ave
415-885-6116 • $$$$
Fondue and other Swiss goodies.
- **Osha Thai** • 2033 Union St
415-567-6742 • $$
Modern, trendy atmosphere for modern Thai.
- **Pacific Catch** • 2027 Chestnut St
415-440-1950 • $$
The wasabi bowls are worth a try.
- **Pane e Vino** • 1715 Union St
415-346-2111 • $$$$
A new location for an old favorite. Italian.
- **Perry's** • 1944 Union St
415-922-9022 • $$
An institution and classic bar and grill. Go for
brunch!
- **Roam Artisan Burgers** • 1785 Union St
415-440-7626 • $$
Grass-fed beef, bison, and even elk burgers.
- **Zushi Puzzle** • 1910 Lombard St
415-931-9319 • $$$
Immaculate sushi, best enjoyed at the bar.

Cow Hollow's stylish main drag is Union Street, brimming with boutiques, salons, trendy restaurants, and pickup bars. Like Chestnut Street in the Marina, it's an ideal destination for preening, strolling, window shopping, and flirting over the evening's first lemon drop (especially at **Betelnut Pejiu Wu**, the **Balboa**, or **Eastside West**).

🛍Shopping

- **Ambiance** • 1864 Union St
  415-923-9797
  All the hip local girls shop here.
- **American Apparel** • 2174 Union St
  415-440-3220
  Brightly colored, sweatshop-free basics.
- **Artesanias** • 1711 Greenwich St
  415-922-2783
  Excellent furniture store. Locally owned.
  Owners extremely helpful.
- **Canyon Beachwear** • 1728 Union St
  415-885-5070
  All bikinis, all the time.
- **Chan's Trains & Hobbies** • 2450 Van Ness Ave
  415-885-2899
  Model trains and all the fixings for the kid in
  all of us.
- **CocoaBella Chocolates** • 2102 Union St
  415-931-6213
  Fabulous compendium of world-wide
  designer chocolates.
- **The Enchanted Crystal** • 1895 Union St
  415-885-1335
  Exquisite jewelry, art, and crystal.

- **Hideo Wakamatsu** • 1980 Union St
  415-255-3029
  Suitcases so divine, you won't want to check
  them.
- **Jest Jewels** • 1869 Union St
  415-563-8839
  Accessories and gifts for girls.
- **Krimsa** • 2190 Union St
  415-441-4321
  Beautiful handmade rugs, from one-of-a-kind
  Oriental to modern.
- **Lush** • 2116 Union St
  415-921-5874
  Funky and fresh handmade soaps.
- **Mingle** • 1815 Union St
  415-674-8811
  Women's and men's clothing from emerging
  designers.
- **Mudpie** • 2185 Fillmore St
  415-771-9262
  Nice clothes for kids.
- **PlumpJack Wines** • 3201 Fillmore St
  415-346-9870
  Great wines at great prices.
- **Real Food Co.** • 3060 Fillmore St
  415-567-6900
  Neighborhood market for organic foods.

Map 3 • **Russian Hill / Fisherman's Wharf**

1
2

PAGE
164

Fisherman's
Wharf

Pier 43

Pier 43 1/2

Musée
Méchanique

The Embarcadero

F
47

Jefferson St

Beach St

400

2600

A

San Francisco
Maritime
National
Historical
Park

National Maritime
Museum

PAGE
158

Ghirardelli
Square

3100

PH

Del Monte
Cannery

N Point St

10

82X

2500

NORTH
WATERFRONT

49
10

GG

Polk St

Larkin St

Bergen Pl

30

700

600

Columbus Ave

P

PM

Bay St

Vandewater St

82X

19

N View Ct

Bay St

Francisco St

Bret Harte Ter

Leavenworth St

800

Francisco St

Houston St

Water St

2300

Bimbo's
365 Club

2

47

Colusa Ter

San Francisco
Art Institute

GG

Chestnut St

Montclair Ter

800

76

Lombard St

2500

Geo
Sterling
Park

PH

Lombard
Street

RUSSIAN

1000

30X

Greenard Ter

Greenwich St

Alice Marble
Tennis Court

Southard Pl

HILL

Roach St

Redfield Aly

Valparaiso St

Filbert St

101

Filbert St

Allen St

Hastings Ter Haven St

900

45 41

4

Larkin St

Eastman Pl

Sharp Pl Hamlet St

Macondray Ln

Taylor St

Macondray Lane

1000

Leavenworth St

Florence St

Valejo Steps

49

Green St

2100

White St

1800

GG

Bonita St

Vallejo St

7

Glover St

30X

19

Bernard St

Salmon St

1/4 mile
.25 km

Join your sweetheart in a romp through romantic Russian Hill. Steep, tree-lined hills inhabited by old-money families give way to leafy enclaves offering unbeatable views of the city and the Bay. Down along the waterfront, tourists and buskers entertain each other at **Fisherman's Wharf**, **Ghirardelli Square**, and the **Cannery at Del Monte Square**.

◯ Landmarks

- **Alice Marble Tennis Court** •
  Greenwich St & Hyde St
  Russian Hill-top courts named after the 1930s US tennis star.
- **Bimbo's 365 Club** • 1025 Columbus Ave
  415-474-0365
  Plush music venue with a swanky vibe.
- **Del Monte Cannery** • 2801 Leavenworth St
  415-771-3112
  What was once the biggest peach cannery in the world is now a big ol' tourist trap.
- **Fisherman's Wharf** •
  Embarcadero b/w Aquatic Park & Pier 39
  Tacky tourist trap, but the sea lions love it. Historic boats, fresh crabs, the ferry to Alcatraz, etc.
- **Ghirardelli Square** • 900 North Point St
  415-474-3938
  Site of the original Ghirardelli chocolate factory; touristy shops and cafés.
- **Lombard Street** •
  Lombard St btwn Hyde St & Leavenworth St
  Known as "the world's crookedest street," it is packed with tourist cars on weekends, but fun to ride down on a bike!
- **Macondray Lane** •
  Jones St btwn Green St & Union St
  Hidden gem on Russian Hill. Influenced Armistead Maupin's "Barbary Lane" in *Tales of the City*. No cars allowed.
- **Musee Mecanique** • Fisherman's Wharf
  415-346-2000
  Fun and creepy.
- **National Maritime Museum** • 900 Beach St
  415-561-6662
  Museum of everything seaworthy—ship models, figureheads, maritime paintings, photos, and artifacts. Free.
- **San Francisco Art Institute** • 800 Chestnut St
  415-771-7020
  Spanish mission-style building with Diego Rivera mural.
- **Vallejo Steps** • Vallejo St & Mason St
  Sweat the 167 steps and 45-degree slope, and you will be rewarded with views of Coit Tower and Bay Bridge.

▼ Bars

- **Bimbo's 365 Club** • 1025 Columbus Ave
  415-474-0365
  Topless mermaids.
- **The Buccaneer** • 2155 Polk St
  415-673-8023
  Arrrr! Free pool and cheap prices.
- **Bullit** • 2209 Polk St
  415-268-0140
  Weekend crowds flirt over Fernet (on tap!) and tater tots.
- **Cresta's 2211 Club** • 2211 Polk St
  415-673-2211
  Friendly and cozy neighborhood saloon.
- **Fiddler's Green** • 1333 Columbus Ave
  415-441-9758
  Irish bar, tiny downstairs, dance area on second floor.
- **Greens Sports Bar** • 2239 Polk St
  415-775-4287
  Great sports bar with tons of TVs.
- **Kennedy's Irish Pub & Indian Curry House** •
  1040 Columbus Ave
  415-441-8855
  Hookahs and Tandoori and Foosball and Guiness, oh my.
- **La Rocca's Corner** • 957 Columbus Ave
  415-674-1266
  Old Italian bar. Louis Prima-era jukebox.
- **Tonic** • 2360 Polk St
  415-771-5535
  Dim corner lounge fit for happy hour in Russian Hill.

🍴 Restaurants

- **Aux Delices** • 2327 Polk St
  415-928-4977 • $$
  Consistently good, budget-friendly Vietnamese.
- **Bistro Boudin** • 160 Jefferson St
  415-351-5561 • $$
  Watch the bakers kneading dough, or try clam
  chowder in sourdough bowls.
- **The Buena Vista** • 2765 Hyde St
  415-474-5044 • $
  Sometimes you need a view with your Irish coffee.
- **Frascati** • 1901 Hyde St
  415-928-1406 • $$$$
  Neighborhoody and friendly.
- **Gary Danko** • 800 North Point St
  415-749-2060 • $$$$$
  The best of the big names. Sophisticated California
  cuisine.
- **Grandeho's Kamekyo** • 2721 Hyde St
  415-673-6828 • $$$$
  Great sushi.
- **In-N-Out Burger** • 333 Jefferson St
  800-786-1000 • $
  Legendary fast food burgers. Double double with
  cheese, please.
- **Kara's Cupcakes** • 900 North Point St
  415 563-2223 • $
  Frosted cupcakes, beautifully presented.
- **La Boulange** • 2300 Polk St
  415-345-1107 • $$
  Exceptional French bakery.
- **La Folie** • 2316 Polk St
  415-776-5577 • $$$$$
  One of the greats. California-French.
- **Lemongrass Thai Cuisine** • 2348 Polk St
  415-346-1818 • $$
  Order the prawn pumpkin curry in this cozy Thai
  joint.

- **Leopold's** • 2400 Polk St
  415-474-2000 • $$
  Bright, bustling "Alpine" tavern for beer, schnitzel,
  and Linzer Torte.
- **Luella** • 1896 Hyde St
  415-674-4343 • $$$$$
  Sleek but cozy interior showcases Mediterranean
  flavors.
- **Nick's Crispy Tacos** • 1500 Broadway
  415-409-8226 • $
  Fabulous fresh fish tacos, but burritos are sub-par.
- **Okoze Sushi** • 1207 Union St
  415-567-3397 • $$$
  A stylish, cozy neighborhood spot for slightly
  pricey fish.
- **Pesce** • 2227 Polk St
  415-928-8025 • $$$$
  Venetian-style small plates.
- **Polker's** • 2226 Polk St
  415-885-1000 • $
  Gourmet burgers and weekend brunch.
- **Scoma's** • Pier 47
  415-771-4383 • $$$$
  Classic touristy San Francisco seafood. Try the crab
  sandwich.
- **Swensen's Ice Cream** • 1999 Hyde St
  415-775-6818 • $
  Landmark ice cream shop right off the cable car
  route.
- **Za Pizza** • 1919 Hyde St
  415-771-3100 • $
  Great hole-in-the-wall thin crust pizza place. They
  deliver, too.
- **Zarzuela** • 2000 Hyde St
  415-346-0800 • $$$
  Authentic Spanish tapas.

ead to Hyde and Polk Streets for the eclectic mix of cafés, restaurants, outiques, and bars. On both streets, outposts for the posh set mingle with ngtime local businesses. On sunny days, grab an ice cream from wensen's and watch tourist-packed cable cars grind to and from the harf below.

Shopping

- **Atelier des Modistes** • 1903 Hyde St
  415-775-0545
  Custom-made evening and bridal gowns. By appointment only.
- **The Candy Store** • 1507 Vallejo St
  415-921-8000
  Quality chocolate and old-fashioned jars of candy. Very sweet indeed.
- **Cole Hardware** • 2254 Polk St
  415-674-8913
  Committed to helping the community!
- **Ghirardelli Square** • 900 North Point St
  415-474-3938
  Site of the original Ghirardelli chocolate factory; touristy shops and cafés.

- **Patagonia** • 770 North Point St
  415-771-2050
  Adventure gear for outdoor enthusiasts or fakers.
- **Russian Hill Bookstore** • 2234 Polk St
  415-929-0997
  Greeting cards for every occasion. Used books too.
- **Smoke Signals** • 2223 Polk St
  415-292-6025
  International magazine stand.
- **William Cross Wine Merchants** • 2253 Polk St
  415-346-1314
  Great little wine shop on Russian Hill. Don't miss the tasting bar in the back.

With its lively cafés, dark watering holes, and bookish bona fides, locals and tourists alike always have a favorite spot they keep coming back to in North Beach. With strong Italian roots and **City Lights Bookstore**—whose owner put the Beat writers on the literary map—the area's narrow alleys and hectic thoroughfares teem with people night and day. Parking is a nightmare and weekend nights attract the drunken masses on Broadway and friendly locals at places off the main strip like **Grant & Green Saloon**.

O Landmarks

- **Balclutha** • Pier 41
415-561-7000
A square-rigged ship that's over one hundred years old, but still a beaut.
- **Coit Tower** • 1 Telegraph Hill Blvd
415-362-0808
Art deco memorial on Telegraph Hill, built in 1933 and funded by Lilie Hitchcock-Coit. Stellar WPA murals and great views.
- **Condor Club** • 560 Broadway
415-781-8222
Birthplace of world's first topless and bottomless entertainment.
- **Exploratorium** • Pier 15
415-528-4444
Experimental hands-on museum of science, art, and human perception.
- **Filbert Steps** • Filbert St & Sansome St
Telegraph Hill stairway amidst gardens and residences. A flock of wild parrots lives in the trees here.
- **Joe DiMaggio Playground** • 651 Lombard St
The playground where the Yankee Clipper learned to play ball.
- **St. Peter and Paul's Church** • 666 Filbert St
415-421-0809
Washington Square's Romanesque Catholic church. Masses in English, Italian, and Chinese.

Bars

- **15 Romolo** • 15 Romolo Pl
415-398-1359
Blue velvet and candlelight. Tiny. Great jukebox.
- **Bamboo Hut** • 479 Broadway St
415-989-8555
Tiki bar amongst the strip clubs.
- **Broadway Studios** • 435 Broadway
415-291-0333
Everything from blues to burlesque.
- **Gino and Carlo** • 548 Green St
415-421-0896
1940s bar in the heart of North Beach. Pool table, pinball, serves Italian food.

- **Grant & Green Saloon** • 1371 Grant Ave
415-693-9565
North Beach classic, good live blues.
- **Hawaii West** • 729 Vallejo St
415-362-3220
North Beach island dive.
- **La Trappe** • 800 Greenwich St
415-440-8727
Over 200 beers and tasty, Belgian food.
- **Northstar Café** • 1560 Powell St
415-397-0577
Free popcorn and 80s music on the jukebox.
- **O'Reilly's** • 622 Green St
415-989-6222
Traditional Irish pub.
- **Penthouse** • 412 Broadway Ave
415-391-2800
Decidedly politically incorrect Mad Men vibe.
- **Pier 23** •
415-362-5125
Live music, great deck, on the water.
- **The Red Jack Saloon** • 131 Bay St
415-989-0700
New England-style bar.
- **Rogue Ales Public House** • 673 Union St
415-362-7880
If 44 ales on tap doesn't grab you, the menu is enormous and very tasty.
- **Rosewood** • 732 Broadway
415-951-4886
A gem of a hideaway in burnished wood.
- **The Saloon** • 1232 Grant Ave
415-989-7666
North Beach institution, great live music.
- **Savoy Tivoli** • 1434 Grant Ave
415-362-7023
Good for an afternoon beer or wine, or pool game, in a touristy setting.
- **Sip Bar & Lounge** • 787 Broadway
415-699-6545
Chill spot to sip and quip. Don't forget to tip.
- **Tony Nik's** • 1534 Stockton St
415-693-0990
Cool retro cocktail lounge.

Restaurants

- **A. Cavalli & Co.** • 1441 Stockton St
415-421-4219 • $
North Beach mainstay for caffe e dolci.
- **Burger Meister** • 759 Columbus Ave
415-296-9907 • $$
Juicy half-pound Niman Ranch burgers. Fine
onion rings.
- **Buster's** • 366 Columbus Ave
415-392-2800 • $
Cheesesteaks for the midnight munchies.
- **Butterfly** • Pier 33 & Bay St
415-864-8999 • $$$$
Trendy average tapas.
- **Café Jacqueline** • 1454 Grant Ave
415-981-5565 • $$$$$
Romantic—and they only serve souffle.
- **Caffe Sport** • 574 Green St
415-981-1251 • $$
Old school Sicilian, family style and family run.
- **Capp's Corner** • 1600 Powell St
415-989-2589 • $$
Bare-bones Italian.
- **COI** • 373 Broadway
415-393-9000 • $$$$
Inventive global cuisine in four or eleven
courses.
- **Coqueta** • Pier 5, Embarcadero Dr
415-704-8866 • $$$
Chiarello's waterfront experiment with
Spanish cuisine.
- **Da Flora** • 701 Columbus Ave
415-981-4664 • $$
Beautifully crafted Italian soul food; meltingly
good gnocchi.
- **Firenze by Night** • 1429 Stockton St
415-392-8485 • $$$
Old-school Italian by day.
- **Forbes Island** • I Dock
415-951-4900 • $$$
Nemo-esque island getaway a few yards off
Fisherman's Wharf.

- **Golden Boy Pizza** • 542 Green St
415-982-9738 • $$
Great cheap pizza.
- **Henry's Hunan** • 924 Sansome St
415-956-7727 • $$
Get Diana's Meat Pie—gloriously greasy!
- **Hillstone** • 1800 Montgomery St
415-392-9280 • $$
Nice American grill. Great cocktails.
- **The House** • 1230 Grant Ave
415-986-8612 • $$$
Asian fusion extraordinaire in a North Beach
nook.
- **Ideale Restaurant** • 1315 Grant Ave
415-391-4129 • $$$$
Modern Roman trattoria.
- **Il Fornaio** • 1265 Battery St
415-986-0100 • $$$$
Italian. Shhh, don't tell anyone about the patio
for brunch.
- **Il Pollaio** • 555 Columbus Ave
415-362-7727 • $$
Neighborhood nook with roast chicken and
carafes of red wine.
- **International House Of Pancakes** •
200 Beach St
415-837-0221 • $
Breakfast 24/7 for the Fisherman's Wharf crew.
- **L'Osteria del Forno** • 519 Columbus Ave
415-982-1124 • $$$
Tiny and everything is cooked in the wood
oven.
- **La Boulange** • 543 Columbus Ave
415-399-0714 • $
Ahhh…Paris.
- **Mama's** • 1701 Stockton St
415-362-6421 • $$
Outstanding breakfast. Go early.
- **Mario's Bohemian Cigar Store Cafe** •
566 Columbus Ave
415-362-0536 • $
Focaccia sandwiches, Italian sodas, and a
Washington Square view.

North Beach / Telegraph Hill

Map 4

ld-school favorites **Caffe Trieste**, **Gino & Carlo**, **Mara's Bakery**, and orth Beach palaces. Boutiques dot Grant Street up the hill. At dusk, try a leisurely roll through dog-friendly Washington Square Park.

- **Mo's** • 1322 Grant Ave
415-788-3779 • $$
Really good burgers.
- **North Beach Pizza** • 1462 Grant Ave
415-433-2444 • $$
Good local chain pizza.
- **North Beach Restaurant** • 1512 Stockton St
415-392-1700 • $$$$
Authentic Italian fare. Watch for mob-esque clientele and proprietors.
- **Panta Rei** • 431 Columbus Ave
415-591-0900 • $$$
Italian.
- **Park Tavern** • 1652 Stockton St
415-989-7300 • $$$
Sprawling, casual-chic brasserie for any occasion; don't miss the deviled eggs.
- **Penthouse** • 412 Broadway Ave
415-391-2800 • $$$
Strippers with a side of steak.
- **Pier 23** •
415-362-5125 • $$
Seafood, margaritas, music, and an outdoor patio overlooking the bay.
- **Piperade** • 1015 Battery St
415-391-2555 • $$$
Really good Basque.
- **Rose Pistola** • 532 Columbus Ave
415-399-0499 • $$$$$
Popular family-style Ligurian.
- **The Stinking Rose** • 325 Columbus Ave
415-781-7673 • $$$
Garlic everything, including the ice cream.
- **Sushi Hunter** • 1701 Powell St
415-291-9268 • $$
Great all-you-can-eat sushi.
- **Trattoria Contadina** • 1800 Mason St
415-982-5728 • $$$$
More good, basic Italian.
- **Victoria Pastry Co.** • 1362 Stockton St
415-781-2015 • $
One of the city's oldest bakeries. Try the cakes and tiramisu.

Shopping

- **101 Music** • 1414 Grant Ave
415-392-6369
Vintage vinyl for serious collectors.
- **A-B Fits** • 1519 Grant Ave
415-982-5726
Jeans from all over the world.
- **Alla Prima Lingerie** • 1420 Grant Ave
415-397-4077
Dreamy lingerie.
- **Biordi** • 412 Columbus Ave
415-392-8096
Imported Italian handmade Majolica pottery.
- **Eastwind** • 1435 Stockton St
415-772-5888
Chinese and Asian culture and medicine books.
- **Goorin Bros. Hat Shop** • 1612 Stockton St
415-402-0454
Add some style to your noggin.
- **Graffeo Coffee** • 735 Columbus Ave
415-986-2420
The coffee that makes North Beach smell so good.
- **Liguria Bakery** • 1700 Stockton St
415-421-3786
Focaccia!
- **Lola of North Beach** • 1415 Grant Ave
415-781-1817
Cute cards, quirky gifts, and custom printing.
- **Mara's Italian Pastry** • 503 Columbus Ave
415-397-9435
Maybe the best Italian bakery in the city.
- **Mee Mee Bakery** • 1328 Stockton St
415-362-3204
Ask nicely, and they"ll show you the old fortune cookie machine. Very cool.
- **Rosalie's New Looks** • 1222 Sutter St
415-771-8814
Hair-dos and wigs reminiscent of the '50s and '60s.
- **Schein & Schein** • 1435 Grant Ave
415-399-8882
Fabulous den of curiosities.

Map 5 · Pacific Heights/Western Addition

The Presidio

PAGE 154

Lyon Street Stairs

Mrs. Doubtfire House

Alta Plaza Park

PACIFIC HEIGHTS

California St

KPOO Mural

Hamilton Rec Ctr

The Fillmore

Kimball Playground

St. John Coltrane African Orthodox Church

WESTERN ADDITION

Terra Vista Ave

Turk St

Golden Gate Ave

McAllister St

Fulton St

The Painted Ladies

Alamo Square

HAIGHT ASHBURY

1/4 mile   25 km

Aside from boasting the city's most manicured mansions, Pac Heights is also home to one of the steepest hills (Fillmore between Green and Broadway), scenic vistas at **Alta Plaza Park**, and the **Lyon Street Stairs**. Down in the Western Addition, the ragged charm of old Victorians mingle with public housing that looks more like ski chalets than projects, but you definitely want to stay on the main drags at night.

○ Landmarks

- **Alamo Square** • Fulton St & Scott St
  One of the most picture-perfect sights in the city.
- **Alta Plaza Park** • Clay St & Steiner St
  Tennis courts top this park terrace with several steep staircases leading up from the street.
- **The Fillmore** • 1805 Geary Blvd
  415-346-3000
  Part of Bill Graham's entertainment empire. Have a red apple from the bucket at the entrance, it's a Fillmore tradition.
- **KPOO Mural** • Steiner St & Post St
  Tribute to one of the first Black non-commercial radio stations.
- **Lyon Street Stairs** • Green St & Lyon St
  Scenic flight of stairs guaranteed to make you sweat.
- **Mrs. Doubtfire House** • 2640 Steiner St
  The house where the 1993 comedy hit was filmed.
- **The Painted Ladies** • 720 Steiner St
  Famous row of Victorian houses in pastel colors juxtaposed against the SF cityscape.
- **St. John Coltrane African Orthodox Church** • 1286 Fillmore St
  Jazz-inspired services and a John Coltrane memorial.

▼ Bars

- **Bar 821** • 821 Divisadero St
  The bubbles tickle my nose.
- **Boom Boom Room** • 1601 Fillmore St
  415-673-8000
  Great live music every night, mostly blues.
- **The Fillmore** • 1805 Geary Blvd
  415-346-3000
  Legendary music venue. Purple chandeliers and free apples.
- **Fly Bar** • 762 Divisadero St
  415-931-4359
  Sake cocktails.
- **Frankie's Bohemian Café** • 1862 Divisadero St
  415-567-7899
  Beer bar, pub food.
- **Harry's Bar** • 2020 Fillmore St
  415-921-1000
  Harry's serves a Kobe burger, while Turiaf serves Kobe. Boo-ya.
- **Lion Pub** • 2062 Divisadero St
  415-567-6565
  Free appetizers and great music.
- **Rasselas Jazz Club** • 1534 Fillmore St
  415-346-8696
  A Jazz club. On Fillmore. And all is right with the Universe.
- **Yoshi's** • 1330 Fillmore St
  415-655-5600
  Nothing says jazz like Japanese fusion.

Map 5

Pacific Heights / Western Addition

Restaurants

- **B Patisserie** • 2821 California St
  415-440-1700 • $
  Amazing pastries, including the kouign-amann specialty.
- **Blue Jay Café** • 919 Divisadero St
  415-926-8657 • $$
  Down-home comfort food for ersatz Confederates.
- **Café Abir** • 1300 Fulton St
  415-567-6503 • $$
  Classy renovation includes new menu items.
- **Candybar** • 1335 Fulton St
  415-673-7078 • $$
  Wine and desserts. Pricier than the name would suggest.
- **Cheese Steak Shop** • 1716 Divisadero St
  415-346 3712 • $
  Outstanding cheese steaks. Philly's best export since Rocky Balboa.
- **Dino's** • 2101 Fillmore St
  415-922-4700 • $
  Tasty Pac Heights pizza joint.
- **Dosa** • 1700 Fillmore St
  415-441-3672 • $$$
  South Indian crepes and a Mark Bright wine list.
- **The Elite Café** • 2049 Fillmore St
  415-673-5483 • $$$$
  Cajun and Creole food with a great bar.
- **Eliza's** • 2877 California St
  415-621-4819 • $$$
  Healthy modern Chinese.
- **Ella's** • 500 Presidio Ave
  415-441-5669 • $$$
  A weekend brunch institution. Prepare to wait.
- **Florio** • 1915 Fillmore St
  415-775-4300 • $$
  Cozy French/Italian. Great atmosphere.
- **Fresca** • 2114 Fillmore St
  415-447-2668 • $$$$
  Tasty Peruvian.
- **Garibaldis** • 347 Presidio Ave
  415-563-8841 • $$$$$
  California Cuisine and an upscale local crowd.
- **Godzila Sushi** • 1800 Divisadero St
  415-931-1773 • $$
  Packed place for sushi in Pac Heights.

- **The Grove** • 2016 Fillmore St
  415-474-1419 • $$
  Cozy, laptop-friendly café.
- **Jackson Fillmore Trattoria** • 2506 Fillmore St
  415-346-5288 • $$$$
  A Pac Heights favorite for casual Italian.
- **King Lee's** • 1426 Fillmore St
  415-563-8882 • $
  Good delivery option.
- **La Mediterranee** • 2210 Fillmore St
  415-921-2956 • $$
  Cozy Middle Eastern.
- **Little Star Pizza** • 846 Divisadero St
  415-441-1118 • $$
  SF-specialized versions of both thick and thin crust; good jukebox.
- **Noah's New York Bagels** • 2213 Fillmore St
  415-441-5396 • $
  To go with your Saturday morning coffee.
- **SPQR** • 1911 Fillmore St
  415-771-7779 • $$$
  Roman inspired osteria for the upper-Fillmore set.
- **State Bird Provisions** • 1529 Fillmore St
  415-795-1272 • $$$
  Unusual creations served dim sum-style.
- **Stelladoro Pizza** • 808 Divisadero St
  415-928-4454 • $
  Decent slice near The Independent.
- **Takara** • 22 Peace Plaza
  415-921-2000 • $$
  Great bet for standard Japanese.
- **Ten-Ichi** • 2235 Fillmore St
  415-346-3477 • $$$
  Homestyle Japanese and sushi.
- **Tony's Cable Car Restaurant** •
  2500 Geary Blvd
  415-931-2416 • $
  Great signage, outdoor seating, cheap prices, and Tony himself.
- **Tortilla Heights** • 1750 Divisadero St
  415-346-4531 • $$
  Best (and cheapest) of the upscale taquerias in the neighborhood.
- **Woodhouse Fish Co.** • 1914 Fillmore St
  415-437-2722 • $$
  It's crabtastic.

Pacific Heights / Western Addition

Map 5

llmore Street flows from a trendy boutique and restaurant belt in the
orth to don't-leave-anything-in-the-car around Geary Boulevard. In
change for living dangerously, that area is top notch in musical choices
th the classic **Fillmore Auditorium** and blues venue **Boom Boom
oom.** The single-screen **Clay Theatre** shows great independent films.

Shopping

- **Benefit** • 2117 Fillmore St
415-567-0242
Cosmetics galore.
- **Brown Eyed Girl** • 2999 Washington St
415-409-0214
Women's shop in converted Victorian.
- **Crossroads Trading Co.** • 1901 Fillmore St
415-775-8885
Used clothes. Buy and sell.
- **George** • 2512 Sacramento St
415-441-0564
Priviledged pet supplies.
- **Gimme Shoes** • 2358 Fillmore St
415-441-3040
Top-notch, hip shoes.
- **Goodwill Boutique** • 1669 Fillmore St
415-354-8570
Good resource for costume creations.
- **Heidi Says Collections** • 2426 Fillmore St
415-749-0655
Friendly designer boutique.
- **In Water Flowers** • 2132 Fillmore St
415-359-1232
Flowers with attitude.
- **Juicy News** • 2453 Fillmore St
415-441-3051
Newsstand and smoothies.
- **Jurlique** • 2136 Fillmore St
415-346-7881
Gorgeous Australian skin care.
- **Katsura Garden** • 1825 Post St
415-931-6209
Whimsical plants and fresh oxygen.
- **Kiehl's** • 1971 Fillmore St
415-359-9260
Skin care nirvana!
- **L'Occitane** • 2207 Fillmore St
415-563-6600
Wonderful French soaps.

- **La Boulange** • 2325 Pine St
415-440-0356
Excellent breads, pastries, and desserts.
- **March** • 3075 Sacramento St
415-931-7433
Deluxe kitchen supplies and housewares for
the cozy home.
- **Marcus Bookstore** • 1712 Fillmore St
415-346-4222
African-American history, culture, and
thought.
- **Margaret O'Leary** • 2400 Fillmore St
415-771-9982
Rustic, urban, locally-made clothes.
- **Narumi** • 1902 Fillmore St
415-346-8629
Decoratives and gifts from Japan.
- **Nest** • 2300 Fillmore St
415-292-6199
French-inspired gifts and things.
- **Paper Source** • 1925 Fillmore St
415-409-7710
All kinds of paper for all kinds of things.
- **The Perish Trust** • 728 Divisadero St
415-555-5555
Collected antiques and Americana, curated to
make something new.
- **Sue Fisher King** • 3067 Sacramento St
415-922-7276
Top-notch bath, bedroom, tabletop, and home
furnishings.
- **Sunhee Moon** • 1833 Fillmore St
415-928-1800
A clothing boutique almost too chic for Pacific
Heights.
- **Toujours** • 2484 Sacramento St
415-346-3988
Entertain your lingerie fantasy.
- **Zinc Details** • 1905 Fillmore St
415-776-2100
Clean, contemporary home furnishings.

Map 6 • **Pacific Heights / Japantown**

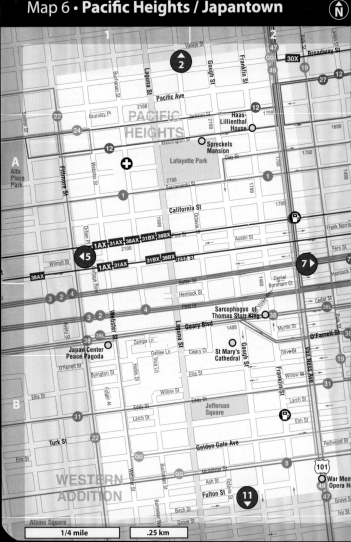

Dogs, children, and sunbathers love Lafayette Park, the crown of this part of Pacific Heights. **The Japan Center Peace Pagoda** anchors the few blocks that make up Japantown. Sluggish Van Ness Avenue marks the eastern border of the neighborhood. The modern interior of **St. Mary's Cathedral** makes for a study of light's visible spectrum.

Landmarks

Cathedral of Saint Mary of the Assumption •
1111 Gough St
415-567-2020
Modern funky-looking cathedral with a hyperbolic paraboloid that forms a cross. Designed by Peter Luigi Nervi in 1971.
Haas-Lilienthal House • 2007 Franklin St
415-441-3000
Queen Anne 1886 classic with added turrets and towers for extravagant ornamentation.
Japan Center Peace Pagoda •
Geary Blvd & Webster St
Five-tiered structure designed by Yoshiro Taniguchi.
Sarcophagus of Thomas Starr King •
Geary Blvd & Franklin St
The only public sarcophagus in the city.
Spreckels Mansion • 2080 Washington St
1912 Spreckels family home, an example of a shift from late Victorian to neoclassical. Now owned by Danielle Steele.

Bars

Crimson Lounge • 687 McAllister St
415-673-9353
Dark, red, and sexy for your next private party.
Route 101 • 1332 Van Ness Ave
415-474-6092
Decent jukebox, a motley crowd and two pool tables.

Restaurants

Baker & Banker • 1701 Octavia St
415-351-2500 • $$$
Cinnamon buns to go, or cozy and sophisticated spot for date night.
Harris' • 2100 Van Ness Ave
415-673-1888 • $$$$$
Steak house serving California-grown beef.
House of Prime Rib • 1906 Van Ness Ave
415-885-4605 • $$$$$
Beef and martini fest.

Iroha • 1728 Buchanan St
415-922-0321 • $$
Small, busy Japanese.
Juban • 1581 Webster St
415-776-5822 • $$$
Grill it yourself Japanese.
Korea House • 1620 Post St
415-563-1388 • $$$
Popular Korean.
May's Coffee Shop • 1737 Post St
415-346-4020 • $
Japanese tea, pastries, and sweets.
Mel's Drive-In • 1050 Van Ness Ave
415-292-6357 • $$
Diner food, great for kids. Anybody see *American Graffiti*?
Mifune • 1737 Post St
415-922-0337 • $$
Casual Japanese noodles.
Sapporo-Ya • 1581 Webster St
415-563-7400 • $$
Ramen noodles.
Tommy's Joynt • 1101 Geary Blvd
415-775-4216 • $
Carved meats, Buffalo meatball sandwiches and beer on tap. SF institution.

Shopping

Books Inc. • 601 Van Ness Ave
415-776-1111
Plenty of store events!
Kinokuniya Books • 1581 Webster St
415-567-7625
75,000 Japanese and English books and mags.
Reliquary • 544 Hayes St
415-431-4000
Vintage wares and new designs.
Rosebowl Florist & Wine Shop •
601 Van Ness Ave
415-474-1114
Offerings from boutique wineries and custom arrangements, too.
Whole Foods Market • 1765 California St
415-674-0500
Great produce, meats, fish, and cheese.

elegant hotels with commanding views, old money old-timers, and prominent landmarks define Nob Hill. Nearby, Chinatown's hectic streets hold islands of calm, like pungent Chinese herb shop streets, bakeries where you'll probably have to use sign language to order your meat-filled dumpling (but will be amazed by how much food a dollar buys) and trinket shops that all sell pretty much the same inexpensive chotchkes. Union Square is bordered by bustling department stores as well as the gritty but soulful Tenderloin.

Landmarks

450 Sutter Building • 450 Sutter St
26-story Art Deco masterpiece by renowned architect Timothy Pfleuger.

Asian Art Museum • 200 Larkin St
415-581-3500
Extensive Asian art collection in the old Beaux Arts style library building—a little claustrophobic in the galleries, but well worth your time.

Bohemian Club • 624 Taylor St
415-885-2440
Club for rich republicans who like to get freaky-deaky in the woods.

Chambord Apartments • 1298 Sacramento St
James Francis Dunn's 1921 Gaudi-esque building evokes the art and design of fin-de-siecle Paris.

City Hall • 1 Dr Carlton B Goodlet Pl
415-701-2311
Administrative offices and art exhibits inside. The most earthquake-retrofitted National Landmark.

Civic Center •
Grove St btwn Franklin St & Leavenworth St
Includes City Hall, Court House, state and federal buildings, the main library, Asian Art Museum, Davies Symphony Hall, War Memorial Opera House, Bill Graham Civic Auditorium. Whew!

Fleur de Lys • 777 Sutter St
415-673-7779
High-end French cuisine in one of the most romantic dining rooms in SF.

GLIDE • 330 Ellis St
415-674-6000
Uplifting all-inclusive Sunday services led by Reverend Cecil Williams and a full chorus.

Golden Gate Fortune Cookie Company •
56 Ross Alley
415-781-3956
Dimly-lit business in the oldest alley in SF. A bag of 40 cookies is a bargain at $3, or buy the "unfortunate" flat disks.

Grace Cathedral • 1100 California St
415-749-6300
Grand Episcopalian cathedral on Nob Hill.

Great American Music Hall • 859 O'Farrell St
415-885-0750
Grand, ornate venue in a gritty neighborhood.

Heart of the City Farmers Market • Market St btwn 7th & 8th St
415-558-9455
Shopping for cheap fruits and veggies alongside downtown crazies on Wednesdays and Sundays at the UN Plaza.

Heart Sculpture • Post St & Powell St
The heart Tony Bennett left in San Francisco.

The Huntington Hotel • 1075 California St
415-474-5400
Old luxury hotel reminiscent of a bygone era of San Francisco.

Masonic Auditorium • 1111 California St
415-776-7457
Theater on top of Nob Hill, seats about 2,000. Excellent acoustics. Exhibits downstairs.

Melvin M. Swig Interfaith Memorial Labyrinth •
California St & Taylor St
Tune out the trolly bells at this circular labyrinth at Grace Cathedral, which offers a place for rest and meditation.

Ocean Aquarium • 120 Cedar St
415-771-3206
For piranhas go elsewhere; these are friendly fish to look at and purchase.

Pacific Union Club • 1000 California St
415-775-1234
Private men's club. Former home to James C. Flood. Brownstone built in 1885 and survivor of the 1906 earthquake and fire.

Powell St Cable Car Turnaround •
Powell St & Market St
Gawk at the tourists who think you have to stand in line to take a cable car.

San Francisco Main Library • 100 Larkin St
415-557-4400
Very modern, very organized public library.

Union Square • Powell St & Geary St
The epicenter of downtown shopping, anchored by department giant Macy's.

Map 7

🍸 Bars

- **Aunt Charlie's Lounge** • 133 Turk St
  415-441-2922
  Gay drag shows.
- **Big 4 Restaurant** • 1075 California St
  415-771-1140
  Classy, clubby, elegant San Francisco.
- **Bigfoot Lodge** • 1750 Polk St
  415-440-2355
  Find your inner cub scout over campground-themed cocktails.
- **Blur** • 1121 Polk St
  415-567-1918
  Laid back boozin'. Unlimited lollipops on the house.
- **Bourbon & Branch** • 501 Jones St
  415-346-1735
  Speakeasy where the entrance is clandestine and requires a password.
- **The Brown Jug Saloon** • 496 Eddy St
  415-501-0327
  Mellow Tenderloin dive. Pool table, pinball, jukebox.
- **Burritt Room + Tavern** • 417 Stockton St
  415-400-0561
  Ask around for this hidden speakeasy.
- **Cantina** • 580 Sutter St
  415-398-0195
  Pisco sours, caipirinhas, other great cocktails.
- **The Cellar** • 685 Sutter St
  415-441-5678
  Hip-hop and '80s tunes.
- **Chelsea Place** • 641 Bush St
  415-989-2524
  Darts, jukebox, fireplace.
- **The Cinch** • 1723 Polk St
  415-776-4162
  Gay and western.
- **Divas Nightclub and Bar** • 1081 Post St
  415-474-3482
  Lots of lovely special ladies at this 3-story nightclub.
- **Edinburgh Castle** • 950 Geary St
  415-885-4074
  Great divey Scottish bar.
- **Great American Music Hall** • 859 O' Farrell St
  415-885-0750
  Grand, ornate venue in a gritty neighborhood.

- **Ha-Ra Club** • 875 Geary St
  415-673-3148
  Tenderloin dive. Pool table.
- **Hemlock Tavern** • 1131 Polk St
  415-923-0925
  Live music.
- **Hi-Lo Club** • 1423 Polk St
  Dark, low-key den for good cocktail; hard-to-spot entrance.
- **High Tide** • 600 Geary St
  415-771-3145
  You've been here before, you just don't remember.
- **The Hyde Out** • 1068 Hyde St
  415-441-1914
  Dive. Sit upstairs by the window. Eat free popcorn.
- **Le Colonial** • 20 Cosmo Pl
  415-931-3600
  Vietnamese restaurant and bar. Hit the upstairs lounge.
- **Lefty O'Doul's** • 333 Geary St
  415-982-8900
  Hofbrau, baseball and AM Gold: The Holy Trinity of piano bars.
- **Lush Lounge** • 1221 Polk St
  415-771-2022
  Cool mixed crowd, good happy hour, and oatmeal cookie martinis.
- **Mezzanine** • 444 Jessie St
  415-625-8880
  New huge dance club, DJs can be hit or miss.
- **Mr. Smith's** • 34 7th St
  415-355-9991
  Three-level club with DJs.
- **Owl Tree** • 601 Post St
  415-359-1600
  Who, who decorated this place? Hmm.
- **Playland Bar** • 1351 Polk St
  415-440-7529
  Drinks in homage to our city's defunct amusement park.
- **R Bar** • 1176 Sutter St
  415-567-7441
  Neighborhood watering hole.
- **Red Devil Lounge** • 1695 Polk St
  415-921-1695
  Popular Russian Hill bar. Live music.

general, the closer you are to the top of Nob Hill or Union Square, the
zier the shops and services. The theater district and Tenderloin to the
st is a sometimes seedy grab bag of bare-bones food spots, nightclubs,
sidential hotels, rare booksellers, drug deals, and liquor stores.

Redwood Room • 495 Geary St
415-929-2372
Upscale trendy hotel bar for the beautiful
people.

Ruby Skye • 420 Mason St
415-693-0777
Terribly hip and trendy dance club.

Shanghai Kelly's • 2064 Polk St
415-771-3300
Laid back Russian Hill saloon.

Slide • 430 Mason St
415-421-1916
Speakeasy style, nightclub lines, and an actual
slide.

Soluna • 272 McAllister St
415-621-2200
Great food and drink, reasonably priced.

The Starlight Room • 450 Powell St
415-395-8595
Swanky cocktails and dancing with a view.

Swig • 561 Geary St
415-931-7292
LOTS of whiskey. Emerge Art on Wednesdays.

Tonga Room & Hurricane Bar • 950 Mason St
415-772-5278
Tiki bar with dancing and thunderstorms. You
can't beat it.

Top of the Mark • 1 Nob Hill
415-616-6940
Swanky drinkin' and dancin'. Expensive and
touristy.

Tradition • 441 Jones St
415-474-2284
Dark woods, private booths ("snugs"), and
barrel-aged spirits.

Tunnel Top • 601 Bush St
415-722-6620
Perched above the Stockton Tunnel, good
mojitos.

The Warfield • 982 Market St
415-345-0900
Legendary live music venue.

Whiskey Thieves • 839 Geary St
415-506-8331
Kleptomaniac smoker's bar stocks a zillion
whiskeys.

Zeki's Bar • 1319 California St
415-928-0677
Cozy pub near Fillmore. Fireplace and pool
table.

Restaurants

A La Turca • 869 Geary St
415-345-1011 • $$
Turkish delights, bare-bones décor.

Acquerello • 1722 Sacramento St
415-567-5432 • $$$$$
Good, swanky Italian.

Allegro Romano • 1701 Jones St
415-928-4002 • $$$$
Simple, neighborhood, tablecloth Italian.

Ananda Fuara • 1298 Market St
415-621-1994 • $
Veggie/vegan menu, sarong-wearing staff.

The Bagelry • 2139 Polk St
415-441-3003 • $
Local fresh-baked bagels.

Beard Papa • 865 Market St
415-978-9972 • $
Cream puffs in the basement of the Westfield
Center.

The Bell Tower • 1900 Polk St
415-567-9596 • $$
Friendly neighborhood grub and cocktails.
Seats outside when sunny.

Big 4 Restaurant • 1075 California St
415-771-1140 • $$$$$
Classy, clubby, elegant San Francisco.

Biscuits and Blues • 401 Mason St
415-292-2583 • $$$
Southern cookin' and live music nightly.

Brenda's French Soul Food • 652 Polk St
415-345-8100 • $$
Gumbo"s great, but beignets are better. Worth
the wait.

Campton Place • 340 Stockton St
415-955-5555 • $$$$$
Fancy Union Square dining for the ladies who
lunch, or a romantic date.

Canteen • 817 Sutter St
415-928-8870 • $$$$
Bijou space, creative Californian menu.

Chutney • 511 Jones St
415-931-5541 • $
Best Indian food around. Don't go for the
atmosphere.

Co Nam • 1653 Polk St
415-292-6161 • $$
Sleek, narrow space serving up banh mi,
claypots, and chill music.

Map 7

22 5 6 7 8
9 10 11 12 13

- **Cocotte** • 1521 Hyde St
415-292-4415 • $$$
Rotisserie chicken and French bistro classics.
- **Colibri** • 438 Geary St
415-440-2737 • $$$
Mexican tapas and fruity margaritas.
- **Crustacean** • 1475 Polk St
415-776-2722 • $$$$$
Vietnamese roasted crab and garlic noodles.
- **Dottie's True Blue Café** • 28 6th St
415-885-2767 • $$
Even Mark Ruffalo eats breakfast here.
Seriously. We ate next to him.
- **Dunya** • 1609 Polk St
415-400-5770 • $$
Casual, low-lit spot for mezze platters, lamb
burgers, and wine.
- **Farallon** • 450 Post St
415-956-6969 • $$$$$
Superb seafood and a cool aquatic décor.
- **farmerbrown** • 25 Mason St
415-409-3276 • $$
Neo-soul food with a hip vibe and ingredients
from local farmers.
- **Fifth Floor** • 12 4th St
415-348-1555 • $$$$$
Fancy and elegant.
- **Fleur de Lys** • 777 Sutter St
415-673-7779 • $$$$$
High-end French cuisine in one of the most
romantic dining rooms in SF.
- **Fly** • 1085 Sutter St
415-441-4232 • $$$
Artsy destination for New American fare.
- **Golden Era** • 572 O'Farrell St
415-673-3136 • $$
Vegetarian and vegan Asian dishes on the
cheap.
- **Grand Café** • 501 Geary St
415-292-0101 • $$$
French fare in Belle Epoque surroundings at
the Monaco Hotel.
- **HanaZEN** • 115 Cyril Magnin St
415-421-2101 • $$$
Straightforward sushi and solid bento boxes
are great for lunch.

- **Hyde Street Seafood House & Raw Bar** •
1509 Hyde St
415-931-3474 • $$
Oysters at happy hour…where do we sign?
- **Jasper's Corner Tap** • 401 Taylor St
415-775-7979 • $$
Gastropub-sportsbar for hand-crafted cocktails,
local brews, and comfort food.
- **Katana-Ya** • 430 Geary St
415-771-1280 • $
A bowl of bliss in a bustling downtown spot.
- **Kuleto's** • 221 Powell St
415-397-7720 • $$$$
Perfect Northern Italian after the theater or
shopping in Union Square.
- **Le Colonial** • 20 Cosmo Pl
415-931-3600 • $$$$
Upscale, trendy, Vietnamese.
- **Lotta's Bakery** • 1720 Polk St
415-359-9039 • $
Great all-American bakery. Try the
gingerbread.
- **Lucky Creation** • 854 Washington St
415-989-0818 • $
Very small, family-owned and operated all-
vegetarian Chinese.
- **Mangosteen** • 601 Larkin St
415-776-3999 • $$
Popular garlic noodle and bun dishes in Little
Saigon.
- **Masa's** • 648 Bush St
415-989-7154 • $$$$$
Classic San Francisco. Another one of the
greats.
- **Mayes Oyster House** • 1233 Polk St
415-885-1233 • $$$
Oysters by day, clubbing by night.
- **Millennium** • 580 Geary St
415-345-3900 • $$$$$
Fancy vegan and organic everything.
- **Morty's** • 280 Golden Gate Ave
415-567-3354 • $
UC Hastings law students munch sandwiches
while dodging Tenderloin transients.
- **Nook** • 1500 Hyde St
415-447-4100 • $$
Café by day. Lounge by night.

Map 7

ttie's True Blue Café does breakfast about as well as anyone and enda's French Soul Food has great beignets. **Big 4** at the Huntington tel and **Swan Oyster Depot** are two mainstays, and **Fleur de Lys** and mpton Place are both splurge-worthy. **Shalimar** and **Tai Chi** are some od inexpensive options.

- **Olive Bar and Restaurant** • 743 Larkin St
415-776-9814 • $$
Artsy lounge serving tasty small plates and gourmet pizzas.
- **Pakwan** • 501 O'Farrell St
415-776-0160 • $
Indian. Bare bones, cheap, and good.
- **Pearl's Deluxe Burgers** • 708 Post St
415-409-6120 • $
Burgers, fries, and milkshakes. Deluxe and delightful.
- **Piccadilly Fish & Chips** • 1348 Polk St
415-771-6477 • $
Oy mates! Bloody good fish-and-chips.
- **Postrio** • 545 Post St
415-776-7825 • $$$$$
Wolfgang Puck's place. Still going after more than a decade.
- **Ristorante Milano** • 1448 Pacific Ave
415-673-2961 • $$$$
The gnocchi here has its own fan club.
- **The Rotunda** • 150 Stockton St
415-249-2720 • $$$
Grab a cocktail at the bar to ease your shopping pain.
- **Saha** • 1075 Sutter St
415-345-9457 • $$$
Outstanding Arabic fusion inside the Carlton hotel.
- **Saigon Sandwich** • 560 Larkin St
415-474-5698 • $
Wallet-friendly French-Vietnamese sandwiches bursting with flavor and spice.
- **Scala's Bistro** • 432 Powell St
415-395-8555 • $$$$
Classic Union Square bistro—and it's open late! Great atmosphere.
- **Sears Fine Food** • 439 Powell St
415-986-0700 • $$
A Union Square breakfast institution.
- **Shalimar** • 532 Jones St
415-928-0333 • $$
Excellent, cheap, bare bones Indian.

- **Show Dogs** • 1020 Market St
415-558-9560 • $
Upscale sausage marks Mid-Market's revival.
- **Straits** • 845 Market St
415-668-1783 • $$$
High-end Singaporean in the giant Westfield. Atmosphere a bit busy, loud.
- **Street** • 2141 Polk St
415-775-1055 • $$
Sturdy food, real drinks. No reservations.
- **Sushi Rapture** • 1400 Leavenworth St
415-359-1388 • $$
Rapturously good tiny sushi spot atop Nob Hill.
- **Swan Oyster Depot** • 1517 Polk St
415-673-1101 • $$
A tiny seafood and oyster institution. Seats 18 at the counter. Open 8-5:30, closed Sundays.
- **Tai Chi Restaurant** • 2031 Polk St
415-441-6758 • $
Delicious. Healthy. Chinese. Take Out. Crazy-ass cheap.
- **Taqueria Cancun** • 1003 Market St
415-864-6773 • $
Gigantic burritos.
- **Thai Spice** • 1730 Polk St
415-775-4777 • $$
One of the better Thai places on Polk Street.
- **Tout Sweet** • 170 O'Farrell St
415-385-1679 • $$
French-inspired patisserie.
- **U-Lee Restaurant** • 1468 Hyde St
415-771-9774 • $
Don't leave without trying the potstickers.
- **Upcider** • 1160 Polk St
415-931-1797 • $$
Ciders and sliders, while looking down on Polk.
- **Venticello** • 1257 Taylor St
415-922-2545 • $$$$$
Italian. Oozes Nob Hill charm.
- **Victor's Pizza** • 1411 Polk St
415-885-1660 • $
New York-style pizza and calzones. One of the best.

Map 7

🛍 Shopping

- **Alessi** • 424 Sutter St
  415-434-0403
  Playful italian housewares.
- **Apple Store** • 1 Stockton St
  415-392-0202
  The building looks like an iBook.
- **Argonaut Book Shop** • 786 Sutter St
  415-474-9067
  California history, the West, and Americana.
- **Blick Art Materials** • 979 Market St
  415-441-6075
  Art supplies and helpful staff.
- **Cheese Plus** • 2001 Polk St
  415-921-2001
  Cheese and hard-to-find specialty gourmet foods.
- **City Discount** • 1542 Polk St
  415-771-4649
  Affordable kitchen and housewares.
- **Clarion Music Center** • 816 Sacramento St
  415-391-1317
  Array of quality exotic musical instruments.

- **CocoaBella Chocolates** • 845 Market St
  415-896-5222
  Various assortments of international artisan chocolates.
- **Cris** • 2056 Polk St
  415-474-1191
  Top-drawer consignment shop.
- **DSW Designer Shoe Warehouse** • 400 Post St
  415-956-3453
  Pile 'em high, sell 'em cheap.
- **Foot Worship** • 1214 Sutter St
  415-921-3668
  Where else can you find glow-in-the-dark 6" Lucite heels?
- **Ghirardelli** • 42 Stockton St
  415-397-3030
  Don't miss out on this SF sweet treat.
- **Good Vibrations** • 1620 Polk St
  415-345-0400
  A clean, well-lighted place for sex toys.
- **Goodwill Boutique** • 822 Geary St
  415-922-0405
  If you want to dress as Screetch from SBTB for Halloween, you're all set.

Map 7

ot Worship is great for shoes while thrift shopping at **Out of the Closet**
nefits AIDS research. **Lombardi** does sports gear and duds, and for art
pplies it's **Blick Art Materials.**

- **Kayo Books** • 814 Post St
  415-749-0554
  Vintage paperbacks from the '40s through the
  '70s and esoteric books of all persuasions.
- **L'Occitane** • 865 Market St
  415-856-0213
  Wonderful French soaps.
- **Lombardi Sports** • 1600 Jackson St
  415-771-0600
  Basic sporting goods.
- **Lush** • 240 Powell St
  415-693-9633
  Funky and fresh handmade soaps.
- **The North Face** • 180 Post St
  415-433-3223
  High-performance outdoor gear.
- **One Half** • 1837 Polk St
  415-775-1416
  Books, dinnerware, cosmetics, and everything
  in between at half the retail price.
- **Out of the Closet** • 1498 Polk St
  415-771-1503
  Great thrift store benefiting AIDS research.

- **Picnic** • 1808 Polk St
  415-346-6556
  Unique gifts, clothing and jewelry, many local
  designers.
- **Pink** • 255 Post St
  415-421-2022
  Beautiful button-downs.
- **Public Barber Salon** • 571 Geary St
  415-441-8599
  Affordable and awesome cuts.
- **Rasputin Music & DVDs** • 69 Powell St
  415-834-0267
  New and used music.
- **Real Food Co.** • 2140 Polk St
  415-673-7420
  Neighborhood market for organic foods.
- **Velvet da Vinci** • 2015 Polk St
  415-441-0109
  Exquisite collectors' jewelry and art.
- **Westfield San Francisco Centre** • 865
  Market St
  415-495-5656
  The beautiful old facade hides the mallrats
  from view.

Map 3

With the **Ferry Building**'s popular **farmers market** and **AT&T Park**'s success, development dollars funnel into South Beach along the Embarcadero in the form of condos. During the daytime, the Financial District teems with workers scurrying around the **Transamerica Pyramid** and other historic buildings.

⭕ Landmarks

- **Bank of America Building** • 555 California St
761-feet-tall. Really cool views from the hokey Carnelian Room upstairs.
- **City Lights** • 261 Columbus Ave
415-362-8193
Ferlinghetti's baby and a mecca for 1950s Beat scene. Check out the poetry room upstairs.
- **Cupid's Span** • Folsom St & The Embarcadero
The giant bow and arrow on the Embarcadero by Claes Oldenburg and Coosje van Bruggen.
- **Embarcadero Center** • 301 Clay St
415-772-0700
Fancy-pants retail and office district.
- **Ferry Building** • Market St & The Embarcadero
415-983-8030
Gathering of local farmers and artisan producers, creating a foodie community in the 1850s-erected building.
- **Hallidie Building** • 130 Sutter St
Early modern architecture; first glass-curtain wall building in America, 1918.
- **Historic Interpretive Signage Project** •
The Embarcadero & King St
Twenty-two bronze plaques tell the story of the waterfront in a span of 2.5 miles.
- **Hunter-Dulin Building** • 111 Sutter St
The city's most gorgeous Deco skyscraper. Check out the lobby.
- **Justin Herman Plaza** •
Market St & The Embarcadero
A good place to meet for a protest, or better yet Critical Mass. Downtown types rendezvous here for lunch.
- **Lotta's Fountain** •
Kearny St btwn Geary Blvd & Market St
Meeting point for separated families during the 1906 earthquake.
- **One Rincon Hill** • 489 Harrison St
415-744-8886
Tallest residential structure west of the Mississippi.
- **Portsmouth Square** •
Kearny St btwn Clay St & Washington St
Chinatown's living room and center of social activity. Also the site of California's first public school.
- **Rincon Center** • 121 Spear St
415-777-4100
Controversial California history depicted in nearly thirty murals at this post office-turned-popular downtown lunch spot.

- **Sea Change Sculpture** • 2nd St & Townsend St
Bright-red stainless steel sculpture on the Embarcadero by abstract expressionist Mark di Suvero.
- **Sentinel Building** • 916 Kearny St
Francis Ford Coppola bought this 1905 green copper flatiron from the Kingston Trio in the 1970s, and has used it for his film company since.
- **SFMOMA** • 151 3rd St
415-357-4000
Mario Botta-designed modern art museum. Check out the new rooftop sculpture garden.
- **Sing Chong and Sing Fat Buildings** •
California St & Grant Ave
Great examples of Chinese pagoda-style architecture, built in 1908.
- **South Park** • Brannan St & 2nd St
Local riche in the 1870s and dotcom royalty in the 1990s live around this oval SOMA park.
- **Spec's Twelve Adler Museum Cafe** •
12 William Saroyan Pl
415-421-4112
Eclectic, bohemian bar hidden in a tiny nook off Columbus.
- **Transamerica Pyramid** • 600 Montgomery St
San Francisco's tallest (853') and most distinctive building, built by William Pereira in 1972.
- **Transamerica Redwood Park** •
600 Montgomery St
Relax among cute, baby redwoods.
- **Tree Sculpture** • 747 Howard St
415-974-4000
Hand-carved from a single NoCal redwood tree, this sculpture scales the staircase of Moscone Center West.
- **V.C. Morris Gift Shop** • 140 Maiden Ln
1948 Frank Lloyd Wright-designed building with interior spiral.
- **Vaillancourt Fountain** • 1 Market St
It's that weird fountain sculpture thing at Embarcadero 4. Herb Caen hated it and most of San Francisco still does.
- **Vesuvio** • 255 Columbus Ave
415-362-3370
Old Beat hang-out.
- **Yerba Buena Center for the Arts** •
701 Mission St
415-978-2787
Fumikiko Maki-designed exhibition and performance space.

Map 8

Bars

- **111 Minna Gallery** • 111 Minna St
415-974-1719
Bar-cum-gallery. It's all about Wednesday after work.
- **BIX** • 56 Gold St
415-433-6300
Remarkable martinis, beautiful bar.
- **The Bubble Lounge** • 714 Montgomery St
415-434-4204
Our outpost of the New York champagne bar.
- **Buddha Bar** • 901 Grant Ave
415-362-1792
Chinatown classic.
- **Cigar Bar and Grill** • 850 Montgomery St
415-398-0850
Feels like Havana circa 1945—or at least how we imagine it.
- **Dave's** • 29 3rd St
415-495-6726
Quite possibly the diviest dive that ever dived.
- **EZ5** • 684 Commercial St
415-362-9321
Hip Chinatown meets Pac-Man. DJs spin house to hip-hop.
- **Harrington's Bar & Grill** • 245 Front St
415-392-7595
Stop here for snacks and a pint after work.
- **The Hidden Vine** • 408 Merchant St
415-674-3567
Delightful little wine bar with an unusual selection.
- **House of Shields** • 39 New Montgomery St
415-975-8651
Financial crowd decompressor.
- **The Irish Bank** • 10 Mark Ln
415-788-7152
Financial district watering hole.
- **Jillian's** • 175 4th St
415-369-6100
Play some pool after a flick at the Metreon.
- **Kate O'Briens** • 579 Howard St
415-882-7240
Average busy Irish pub.
- **L'Amour Nightclub** • 600 Jackson St
415-781-5224
Chinese karaoke, gold-digging cocktail waitresses, spotty service. Awesome.
- **Li Po Cocktail Lounge** • 916 Grant Ave
415-982-0072
Cool Chinatown dive.

- **Local Edition** • 691 Market St
415-795-1375
Swank, spacious underground lounge with red banquettes and retro cocktails.
- **The Lusty Lady** • 1033 Kearny St
415-391-3991
The girls in this peep show are unionized, like Norma Rae, only naked.
- **Mr. Bing's** • 201 Columbus Ave
415-362-1545
Liar's dice is not a game for pussies.
- **Pete's Tavern** • 128 King St
415-817-5040
Eat, drink, and cheer on the Giants.
- **The Pied Piper Bar & Grill** •
2 New Montgomery St
415-546-5089
Maxfield Parrish's Pied Piper mural dominates this lush, lovely lounge.
- **Press Club** • 20 Yerba Buena Ln
415-744-5000
Elegant downstairs lounge for an after-work flight of California wine.
- **Punch Line** • 444 Battery St
415-397-7573
Top-notch comedy in Embarcadero Center.
- **Raven** • 1151 Folsom St
415-431-1151
Edgar Allan Poe-themed bar; lounge, dance, or watch music videos.
- **Rickhouse** • 246 Kearny St
415-398-2827
Dim, cavernous place for cocktails in the Financial District.
- **The Royal Exchange** • 301 Sacramento St
415-956-1710
Financial district pub.
- **Spec's Twelve Adler Museum Cafe** •
12 William Saroyan Pl
415-421-4112
Eclectic, bohemian bar hidden in a tiny nook off Columbus.
- **Sugar Cafe** • 679 Sutter St
415-441-5678
This schizophrenic little minx is coffee by day and booze at night.
- **Sutter Station** • 554 Market St
415-434-4768
The ultimate commuter dive bar.
- **Temple** • 540 Howard St
415-978-9942
White lounge, dimlit dining, dancing in the dark, and Buddha.
- **Thirsty Bear** • 661 Howard St
415-974-0905
Brew pub and tapas by Moscone.

A coffee shop or a big-bank ATM is most certainly on every corner, and there is no shortage of happy hour bars. For downtown lunch enjoyment there are hole-in-the-walls and fancy restaurants for all, whether a Downtown full-timer, a Moscone Center convention attendee, or a visitor to **SFMOMA** on free first Tuesday of the month.

• **Tosca Cafe** • 242 Columbus Ave
415-986-9651
Italian opera on the juke, Tom Waits sightings, classic red booths…pretty much heaven.
• **Upstairs Bar & Lounge** • 181 3rd St
415-817-7836
If you're stuck at the Moscone Center. In the W Hotel.
• **Vesuvio** • 255 Columbus Ave
415-362-3370
North Beach literati bar.
• **Zeke's** • 600 3rd St
415-392-5311
Have a beer before they charge you double at the ball park.

Restaurants

• **21st Amendment** • 563 2nd St
415-369-0900 • $$$
Grab a microbrew and a burger before the game.
• **5A5 Steak Lounge** • 244 Jackson St
415-989-2539 • $$$
Expensive steaks in a Vegas-style setting.
• **Alfred's Steakhouse** • 659 Merchant St
415-781-7058 • $$$$
Great, old-world steakhouse.
• **Americano** • 8 Mission St
415-278-3777 • $$$
Enjoy Italian while gazing at the Bay Bridge. In the Hotel Vitale.
• **B & M Mei Sing Restaurant** • 62 2nd St
415-777-9530 • $
Whole fried fish includes tasty intact eyeballs.
• **B44** • 44 Belden Pl
415-986-6287 • $$$$
Catalan and great paella.
• **Baladie Gourmet Café** • 337 Kearny St
415-989-6629 • $
Delicious, huge pita pockets; you can eat one for lunch AND dinner.
• **Banana House** • 321 Kearny St
415-981-9090 • $$
Thai for lunch. Try the pumpkin curry with tofu.
• **Barbacco** • 220 California St
415-955-1919 • $$$
Lively trattoria serving small plates—don't miss the Brussels sprouts.
• **Benu** • 22 Hawthorne St
415-685-4860 • $$$$
Ultra-creative tasting menus worthy of a very special occasion.

• **BIX** • 56 Gold St
415-433-6300 • $$$$$
First-rate martinis. The food's OK.
• **Bocadillos** • 710 Montgomery St
415-982-2622 • $$
Delicious, moderately priced Basque restaurant.
• **Boulevard** • 1 Mission St
415-543-6084 • $$$$
Wonderful, classic, San Francisco institution.
• **Boxed Foods Company** • 245 Kearny St
415-981-9376 • $
Fresh. Organic-oriented. Not too cheap. Decent eats.
• **Brandy Ho's Hunan Food** •
217 Columbus Ave
415-788-7527 • $$$
Popular Hunan Chinese restaurant.
• **Brickhouse Café and Saloon** • 426 Brannan St
415-369-0222 • $
Fresh, casual, American fare from friendly folks.
• **Brindisi Cucina di Mare** • 88 Belden Pl
415-593-8000 • $$$$
Southern Italian.
• **The Butler And The Chef Bistro** •
155 S Park St
415-896-2075 • $$
An unexpected Gallic treat in SOMA— delicious Croque Monsieurs.
• **Café Bastille** • 22 Belden Pl
415-986-5673 • $$$
Popular French bistro downtown with outdoor seating.
• **Cafe Claude** • 7 Claude Ln
415-392-3505 • $$
Live jazz on weekends, fabulous fries, full bar.
• **Cafe de la Presse** • 352 Grant Ave
415-398-2680 • $$
French brasserie/cafe with sidewalk tables for post-shopping people-watching.
• **Cafe Venue** • 218 Montgomery St
415-989-1144 • $
Quick service and a wide array of sandwich and salad options.
• **Cafe Venue** • 70 Leidesdorff St
415-576-1144 • $
Quick service and a wide array of salad and sandwich options.
• **Cafe Venue** • 215 Fremont St
415-357-1144 • $
Quick service and a wide array of salads and sandwiches.
• **Caffe Centro** • 102 S Park St
415-882-1500 • $
Popular coffee and lunchspot for nearby businesses.

- **Caffe Macaroni** • 59 Columbus Ave
415-956-9737 • $
Authentic Neapolitan restaurant-trattoria.
- **Chaya Brasserie** • 132 The Embarcadero
415-777-8688 • $$$
Trendy Franco-Japanese fusion. Good drinks and sushi, too.
- **Chef Jia's** • 925 Kearny St
415-398-1626 • $
Avoid the line next door and check this place out.
- **Ciao Bella Gelato** • 1 Ferry Building
415-834-9330 • $
From Cabernet to Amaretto, these sweet flavors are sensational.
- **Comstock Saloon** • 155 Columbus Ave
415-617-0071 • $$
Upscale Tuscan fare that never disappoints.
- **Cotogna** • 490 Pacific Ave
415-775-8508 • $$$
You can never go wrong with the raviolo di ricotta.
- **Crossroads Café** • 699 Delancey St
415-512-5111 • $
Part café, part bookstore; serves thick sandwiches and eclectic tapas.
- **Delica** • 1 Ferry Building
415-834-0344 • $$
Sleek Japanese deli. Take-out only.
- **Fleur de Sel** • 308 Kearny St
415-956-5005 • $
Natural, fresh ingredients for upscale deli fare.
- **Globe** • 290 Pacific Ave
415-391-4132 • $$$$
Casual California cuisine. Open late.
- **Golden Flower Vietnamese Restaurant** •
667 Jackson St
415-433-6469 • $
A decent bowl of pho in Chinatown.
- **Golden Star Vietnamese Restaurant** •
11 Walter U Lum Pl
415-398-1215 • $
Best spot to get pho'ed up near Chinatown.
- **Hard Water** • Pier 3, Embarcadero Dr
415-392-3021 • $$$
Raw bar and rare bourbon on the waterfront.
- **Henry's Hunan** • 110 Natoma St
415-546-4999 • $$
Get Diana's Meat Pie—gloriously greasy!
- **Hog Island Oyster Bar** • 1 Ferry Building
415-391-7117 • $$$
Excellent oyster bar with a view.

- **House of Nanking** • 919 Kearny St
415-421-1429 • $$
Legendary cheap Chinese.
- **Il Cane Rosso** • 1 Ferry Building
415-391-7599 • $$
Sandwiches from the rotisserie.
- **Jai Yun** • 680 Clay St
415-981-7438 • $$$$$
Wonderful Chinatown dive. No menu, let the chef choose your meal.
- **Koh Samui and the Monkey** • 415 Brannan St
415-369-0007 • $$
Thai. No monkey meat.
- **Kokkari Estiatorio** • 200 Jackson St
415-981-0983 • $$$$$
Comfortable, glamorous Greek.
- **Le Central Bistro** • 453 Bush St
415-391-2233 • $$$$
Clubby lunch scene.
- **Local Restaurant and Wine Merchant** •
330 1st St
415-777-4200 • $$
Wood-fired pizzas and a Mark Bright wine list.
- **MarketBar** • 1 Ferry Building
415-434-1100 • $$$
California cuisine, great cocktails, huge sidewalk patio.
- **Mel's Drive-In** • 801 Mission St
415-227-0793 • $$
Diner food, great for kids. Anybody see *American Graffiti*?
- **Michael Mina** • 252 California St
415-397-9222 • $$$$$
New American cuisine from famed chef.
- **Mijita** • 1 Ferry Building
415-399-0814 • $$
Una cocina mexicana—get the queso fundido!
- **Mixt Greens** • 560 Mission St
415-296-8009 • $
Save the world. Eat a salad.
- **MoMo's** • 760 2nd St
415-227-8660 • $$$$
Fun American grill across form the ballpark. Great bar.
- **Naan-N-Curry** • 533 Jackson St
415-693-0499 • $$
Indian on the cheap.
- **One Market** • 1 Market St
415-777-5577 • $$$$$
Consistently good.
- **Out the Door** • 1 Ferry Building
415-321-3740 • $
Slanted Door's take-out counter.

Financial District / SOMA

Map 8

Perbacco comes as advertised and **The Slanted Door** is worth it. Meanwhile, **Sam's Grill** and **Tadich Grill** are two classics. **R&G Lounge** is a great inexpensive option. Possibly the greatest Chinese experience in all the land is **House of Nanking** in Chinatown, where you'll consider yourself lucky to wait in line only to be rushed out, with the best fried rice you've ever eaten in between.

- **Ozumo** • 161 Steuart St
415-882-1333 • $$$$$
High-end Japanese fare overlooking the waterfront. Excellent sake selection.
- **Paladar Cafe Cubano** • 329 Kearny St
415-398-4899 • $$
Excellent lunch option for downtown office slaves.
- **Pazzia Caffe & Pizzeria** • 337 3rd St
415-512-1693 • $$$
Homemade pasta down the street from SF MOMA.
- **Perbacco** • 230 California St
415-955-0663 • $$$$
Hip Northern Italian perfect for a date or party.
- **Plouf** • 40 Belden Pl
415-986-6491 • $$$$
French cuisine. Try the mussels.
- **Quince** • 470 Pacific Ave
415-775-8500 • $$$$$
Sophisticated, intimate, and Italian-inspired.
- **R&G Lounge** • 631 Kearny St
415-982-7877 • $$$
Cantonese favorite of in-town Hong Kongers.
- **Red's Java House** • Pier 30 & Bryant St
415-777-5626 • $
Cheap burgers and dogs by the bay.
- **RN74** • 301 Mission St
415-543-7474 • $$$$
A must-visit for serious foodies.
- **Saison** • 178 Townsend St
415-828-7990 • $$$$
Elegant and quality-obsessed, serving one multi-course menu nightly.
- **Salt House** • 545 Mission St
415-543-8900 • $$$$
Superb contemporary cuisine.
- **Sam's Grill** • 374 Bush St
415-421-0594 • $$$
Classic American grill since 1867.
- **San Buena Taco Truck** • 2598 Harrison St
415-559-6127 • $
Tacos de lengua rock!
- **Sens** • 4 Embarcadero Center
415-362-0645 • $$
Join the happy hour crowd on the patio.
- **The Sentinel** • 37 New Montgomery St
415-284-9960 • $
FiDi lunch fave—must try the meatball sandwich!
- **The Slanted Door** • 1 Ferry Building
415-861-8032 • $$$$$
First-rate Vietnamese. Make a reservation.

- **South Park Café** • 108 S Park St
415-495-7275 • $$$$
Distinguished, casual French.
- **Sushirrito** • 59 New Montgomery St
415-495-7655 • $
Burrito-size sushi rolls! Brilliant, and worth the line.
- **Sweet Joanna's Café** • 101 Howard St
415-974-6822 • $
Tasty sandwiches and macaroons.
- **Tadich Grill** • 240 California St
415-391-1849 • $$$$
Legendary old-world seafood.
- **The Toaster Oven** • 145 2nd St
415-243-0222 • $
Warm toasty goodness!
- **The Toaster Oven** • 201 Spear St
415-537-1111 • $
Warm toasty goodness!
- **The Toaster Oven** • 3 Embarcadero Center
415-421-0111 • $
Warm toasty goodness!
- **Tommaso's** • 1042 Kearny St
415-398-9696 • $$
Best pizza in North Beach since 1935.
- **Town Hall** • 342 Howard St
415-908-3900 • $$$$$
Wildly popular modern American food.
- **Tres** • 130 Townsend St
415-227-0500 • $$
Casual, hip spot for Mexican with top-notch tequila menu. Good for groups.
- **Tropisueño** • 75 Yerba Buena Ln
415-243-0299 • $
Chic Mission style burritos if that makes any sense.
- **Waterbar** • 399 Embarcadero Dr
415-284-9922 • $$$
Ultra-fresh seafood and happy hours oyster specials.
- **Wayfare Tavern** • 558 Sacramento St
415-772-9060 • $$$
Addictive popovers kick off a high-end comfort meal.
- **What's Up Dog!** • 28 Trinity Pl
$
Hot dog stand with mini-donuts for the lunchtime crowd.
- **Yank Sing** • 101 Spear St
415-781-1111 • $$$$
Terrific dim sum.
- **Zare at Fly Trap** • 606 Folsom St
415-243-0580 • $$$$
Northern Italian and Southern French.

Map 3   22 5 6 7 8   9 10 11 12 13

🛍 Shopping

- **A.G. Ferrari Foods** • 688 Mission St
415-344-0644
Italian foods and wine and wonderful deli items.
- **Acme Bread** • 1 Ferry Building
415-288-2978
Premier high-end bakery.
- **Adolph Gasser** • 181 2nd St
415-495-3852
One of the best camera stores in town.
- **Ambassador Toys** • 2 Embarcadero Center
415-345-8697
Great toys and books for junior.
- **American Apparel** • 363 Grant Ave
415-296-1555
Brightly colored, sweatshop-free basics.
- **Bastille** • 66 Kearny St
415-951-0210
Trendy designers a la Acne, Band of Outsiders, James Perse.
- **Camper** • 39 Grant Ave
415-296-1005
Funky urban shoes.
- **City Lights** • 261 Columbus Ave
415-362-8193
Ferlinghetti's store with fab poetry section.
- **The Container Store** • 26 4th St
415-777-9755
Organizational superstore.

- **Cowgirl Creamery** • 1 Ferry Building
415-362-9354
Yummy, stinky cheese.
- **Discount Camera** • 33 Kearny St
415-392-1100
One of the other best camera stores in town.
- **Eastern Bakery** • 720 Grant Ave
415-433-7973
Moon cakes and BBQ pork buns. If they"re good enough for Bill Clinton…
- **Far West Fungi** • 1 Ferry Building
415-989-9090
Mushrooms. (Not the magic kind.)
- **Ferry Plaza Wine Merchant** • 1 Ferry Building
415-391-9400
Wine and spirits.
- **Fiona's Sweetshoppe** • 214 Sutter St
415-399-9992
Scrumptious sweets from all over the world.
- **Fog City News** • 455 Market St
415-543-7400
The stationery/chocolate/magazine store that could.
- **Frog Hollow Farm** • 1 Ferry Building
415-445-0990
Organic urban farmstand.
- **Golden Gate Bakery** • 1029 Grant Ave
415-781-2627
The best egg tarts.
- **Goorin Bros. Hat Shop** • 111 Geary St
415-362-0036
Add some style to your noggin.

Financial District / SOMA

Map 8

San Francisco is one of the great literary cities, and **City Lights** is a national treasure. If you're looking for photography supplies, try **Adolph Gasser**, **Photographers Supply** or **Discount Camera**. Hit up **Camper** for shoes.

- **Gump's** • 135 Post St
  415-982-1616
  Very upscale home décor.
- **Hermes** • 125 Grant Ave
  415-391-7200
  Loud scarves and Birkin bags.
- **Hog Island Oyster Bar** • 1 Ferry Building
  415-391-7117
  Look for a pearl.
- **Japonesque Gallery** • 824 Montgomery St
  415-391-8860
  Authentic Japanese art and antiques.
- **Jeffrey's Toys** • 685 Market St
  415-546-6551
  No. Not the Giraffe. This is an independent
  joint for kids of all ages.
- **Jeremy's** • 2 S Park St
  415-882-4929
  Cheap designer clothing.
- **Katz Bagels** • 606 Mission St
  415-512-1570
  Also great pizza!
- **Loehmann's** • 222 Sutter St
  415-982-3215
  Designer shopping at a discount.
- **Ma Maison** • 592 3rd St
  415-777-5370
  Francophlic trove of imported dinnerware and
  household knicknacks.
- **Marina Morrison** • 30 Maiden Ln
  415-984-9360
  Quintessential bridal salon.
- **Miette** • 1 Ferry Building
  415-837-0300
  Sweet pastries.

- **Photographers Supply** • 436 Bryant St
  415-495-8640
  Not quite B&H, but good.
- **Recchiuti** • 1 Ferry Building
  415-834-9494
  Carefully crafted chocolate and confections
  you"ll crave.
- **Red Blossom Tea Company** • 831 Grant Ave
  415-395-0868
  Assortment of premium teas from the Far East.
- **Stonehouse California Olive Oil** •
  1 The Embarcadero
  415-765-0405
  Olive oil plus tasting rooms!
- **Sur La Table** • 1 Ferry Building
  415-262-9970
  Remarkable kitchen stuff.
- **Teuscher** • 307 Sutter St
  415-834-0850
  Celebrated Swiss chocolate store speciallizing
  in truffles.
- **Torso Vintages** • 272 Sutter St
  415-391-1166
  Luxury vintage that you can afford.
- **Under One Roof** • 50 Post St
  415-503-2300
  Support a good cause by buying that special
  something.
- **William Stout Architectural Books** •
  804 Montgomery St
  415-391-6757
  Architecture, art, furniture, and landscaping
  books.

Hippies and anything free left the Haight when the housing prices soared. Expect to find gutter punk teens panhandling and selling eighths of oregano shake. Fashionable boutiques and expensive vintage clothing shops abound. Nearby Cole Valley is a fully self sufficient neighborhood where community is strong and locals go for a quiet meal.

O Landmarks

- **Buena Vista Park •**
  Haight St & Buena Vista Ave E
  A labyrinth of paved paths in SF's oldest park.
- **Charles Manson's House •** 636 Cole St
  SF "family" recruiting grounds.
- **Grateful Dead House •** 710 Ashbury St
  Corner of Haight and Ashbury, circa-1890s
  Cranston-Keenan building. We miss you Jerry.
- **Haight-Ashbury •** Haight St & Ashbury St
  1960s hippie haven and early home to the
  Grateful Dead. Great Victorians, cool shops,
  disillusioned youth, and drugs.

🍸 Bars

- **The Alembic Bar •** 1725 Haight St
  415-666-0822
  Home crafted cocktails (try a Ladyslipper) and
  local brews.
- **Aub Zam Zam •** 1633 Haight St
  415-861-2545
  Funky stylish interior. Crowded on weekends.
- **Club Deluxe •** 1511 Haight St
  415-552-6949
  Art deco swing-era lounge.
- **Finnegan's Wake •** 937 Cole St
  415-731-6119
  Cole Valley dive with ping-pong.
- **Gold Cane Cocktail Lounge •** 1569 Haight St
  415-626-1112
  Cheapest drinks in town and bartenders as
  toasted as you.
- **Hobson's Choice •** 1601 Haight St
  415-621-5859
  Victorian décor and rum drinks.
- **The Kezar Pub •** 770 Stanyan St
  415-386-9292
  Sports bar.
- **Magnolia Gastropub and Brewery •**
  1398 Haight St
  415-864-7468
  Quality handmade beers with hippie names.
  Kitchen open late.
- **Martin Macks Gastro Pub •** 1568 Haight St
  415-861-1586
  Haight Street pub showing Gaelic futbol in the
  early mornings.
- **Milk Bar •** 1840 Haight St
  415-387-6455
  DJs spin hip-hop, funk, and retro grooves.
- **Murio's Trophy Room •** 1811 Haight St
  415-752-2971
  Great rock and roll dive.
- **Trax •** 1437 Haight St
  415-864-4213
  Gay and straight in the Haight.

Map 9
Haight Ashbury / Cole Valley

Restaurants

- **1428 Haight** • 1428 Haight St
  415-864-8484 • $$
  Eggs, omelettes, crepes, sandwiches.
- **Best of Thai Noodle** • 1418 Haight St
  415-552-3534 • $
  Sticky rice with mangos fulfills any late night sweets craving.
- **Blue Front Café** • 1430 Haight St
  415-252-5917 • $
  Middle Eastern café with killer lemonade.
- **Burger Meister** • 86 Carl St
  415-566-1274 • $$
  Large burgers, also hot dogs and cheesesteaks. Cash only.
- **Cha Cha Cha** • 1801 Haight St
  415-386-7670 • $$$
  Popular Caribbean-style tapas. Be ready to wait.
- **The Citrus Club** • 1790 Haight St
  415-387-6366 • $$
  Popular Asian noodle dishes with California twist. Try the chicken noodle soup.
- **Escape From New York Pizza** • 1737 Haight St
  415-668-5577 • $
  Big, cheap slices not just to soak up the booze.
- **Grandeho's Kamekyo** • 943 Cole St
  415-759-8428 • $$$$
  Great sushi.
- **Home Service Market** • 1700 Hayes St
  415-346-7000 • $
  Off-the-radar spot serves off-the-hook sandwiches.
- **La Boulange** • 1000 Cole St
  415-242-2442 • $$
  Café with excellent baked goods.
- **North Beach Pizza** • 800 Stanyan St
  415-751-2300 • $$
  Good local chain pizza.
- **Padrecito** • 901 Cole St
  415-742-5505 • $$$
  Upscale Mexican, great guacamole.
- **Panhandle Pizza** • 2077 Hayes St
  415-750-0400 • $$$
  Eclectic toppings such as soy cheese, clams, and eggplant.
- **Parada 22** • 1805 Haight St
  415-750-1111 • $$
  One of the only Puerto Rican restaurants in SF.
- **People's Cafe** • 1419 Haight St
  415-553-8842 • $
  Spacious, mellow space for coffee and casual meals.
- **Ploy II** • 1770 Haight St
  415-387-9224 • $$
  A second floor Thai secret.
- **Pork Store Café** • 1451 Haight St
  415-864-6981 • $$
  Greasy breakfast joint.
- **Red Victorian** • 1665 Haight St
  415-864-1978 • $
  Reminisce about the summer of love while eating quiche.
- **Siam Lotus Thai** • 1705 Haight St
  415-933-8031 • $
  Solid Thai food for the Haight.
- **Zazie** • 941 Cole St
  415-564-5332 • $$$
  Brunch is a Cole Valley tradition here.

Shopping

- **Ambiance** • 1458 Haight St
  415-552-5095
  All the hip local girls shop here.
- **American Apparel** • 1615 Haight St
  415-431-4028
  Brightly colored sweatshop-free threads.
- **Amoeba Music** • 1855 Haight St
  415-831-1200
  Huge music store, new and used. Frequent free live shows!
- **Ashbury Tobacco Center** • 1524 Haight St
  415-552-5556
  Water pipe is the legal term.
- **Buffalo Exchange** • 1555 Haight St
  415-431-7733
  Vintage and thrift wear.
- **Cal Surplus** • 1541 Haight St
  415-861-0404
  Patches with your name on it and army surplus kinds of things.
- **Ceiba Records** • 1364 Haight St
  415-437-9598
  Future fashions, digital arts, and music.

side from vestiges of the '60s, shopping is the draw. Hunt for records at **moeba Music** and scour the vintage racks at **La Rosa** or **Static**. Then elebrate your finds with a very cheap drink at **Gold Cane** or something ncier at **Alembic**.

- **City Optix** • 1685 Haight St
  415-626-1188
  Cool eyewear.
- **Cold Steel America** • 1783 Haight St
  415-933-7233
  Glow-in-the-dark nipple ring anyone?
- **Cole Hardware** • 956 Cole St
  415-753-2653
  For all your hardware needs, shop local.
- **Crossroads Trading Co.** • 1519 Haight St
  415-355-0555
  Used clothes. Buy and sell.
- **Discount Fabrics** • 2315 Irving St
  415-418-7602
  A little dingy, but fabric people go nuts for this place.
- **FTC** • 1632 Haight St
  415-626-0663
  Skateboards and clothes.
- **Haight Ashbury Music Center** •
  1540 Haight St
  415-863-7327
  Guitars, drums, flutes, and all your music needs.
- **Haight Ashbury Tattoo and Piercing** •
  1525 Haight St
  415-431-2218
  Tattoos, body manipulation, and general oddness.
- **Held Over** • 1543 Haight St
  415-864-0818
  Add it to the vintage store loop.
- **Ideele** • 1600 Haight St
  415-431-8836
  Cool cute clothes on the (fairly) cheap.
- **John Fluevog** • 1697 Haight St
  415-436-9784
  Crazy. Comfy. Cool.
- **Kidrobot** • 1512 Haight St
  415-487-9000
  Funky, Asian pop-inspired toys.
- **La Rosa Vintage** • 1711 Haight St
  415-668-3744
  Fine vintage clothing.
- **Mendel's Art Supplies** • 1556 Haight St
  415-621-1287
  Art supplies and far out fabrics.
- **New York Apparel** • 1772 Haight St
  415-786-8076
  Strippers get dancer discounts on all foxy 'fits.

- **Occasions Boutique** • 858 Cole St
  415-731-0153
  Beauty products, candles, and scents.
- **Pharmaca** • 925 Cole St
  415-661-1216
  Natural medicine pharmacy, supplements, and pure skincare products.
- **Piedmont Boutique** • 1452 Haight St
  415-864-8075
  The ultimate source for custom-made hats, feather boas, wigs, and other fancy trashy stuff.
- **Ruby** • 1431 Haight St
  415-550-8052
  This cute boutique, named after owner"s dog, has gifts galore.
- **Say Cheese** • 856 Cole St
  415-665-5020
  One of the best specialty cheese shops in the city. Wine and other epicurean delights as well.
- **SFO Snowboarding** • 1630 Haight St
  415-626-1141
  Rip the pow-pow.
- **Shoe Biz II** • 1553 Haight St
  415-861-3933
  Hard to find and alternative-style shoes. Yes, there really are three on Haight.
- **Skates on Haight** • 1818 Haight St
  415-752-8375
  Skating and Nor-cal gear.
- **Static Vintage Clothing** • 1764 Haight St
  415-422-0046
  Well-picked, moderately expensive pieces spanning half a century.
- **Super Shoe Biz** • 1420 Haight St
  415-861-0313
  Hard to find and alternative-style shoes. Yes, there really are three on Haight.
- **Urban Mercantile** • 85 Carl St
  415-643-6372
  Eclectic gifts and housewares.
- **Wasteland** • 1660 Haight St
  415-863-3150
  Super cool vintage clothes.
- **X Generation 2** • 1401 Haight St
  415-863-6040
  Hip, trendy, sparkly T's and sexy little dresses.

Map 10 · **Castro / Lower Haight**

Rainbow flags, leather bars, older guys letting it all hang out by going completely nude, daddies and their sugar boys dancing it up at the Café—that's just the side of the Castro that is living up to the racy reputation. The other side of the Castro is intensely political—this is where gay rights pioneers like the late Harvey Milk added impetus to a movement that's still in the headlines today, and where activists mobilized against the AIDS epidemic and made the disease part of the national dialogue when most people wanted to write it off as the "gay cancer."

◯ Landmarks

- **Abner Phelps House** • 1111 Oak St
  Oldest house in SF, built by Colonel Phelps in 1850 and since relocated three times.
- **Café du Nord** • 2170 Market St
  415-861-5016
  Though it gets big musical acts, it still maintains a lounge atmosphere. Also check out the Swedish American Club upstairs.
- **Castro Theatre** • 429 Castro St
  415-621-6120
  Beautiful old-fashioned art deco theater for movies and special programs.
- **Corona Heights** •
  Roosevelt Way & Museum Way
  Hilltop park dominated by native chert formations and 360-degree views.
- **DMV** • 1377 Fell St
  800-777-0133
  Good spot to mention while giving directions.
- **Dolores Park** • Dolores St & 18th St
  415-554-9529
  The sunniest spot in the city (and great tennis courts!).
- **Duboce Bikeway Mural** •
  Duboce btwn Market St & Church St
  Celebrates the car-free public space of bikeway behind the "super" Safeway, sponsored by the SF Bicycle Coalition.
- **Harvey Milk Memorial Plaza** • 400 Castro St
  Castro Street plaza built in memory of Harvey Milk.
- **Harvey's** • 500 Castro St
  415-431-4278
  Bar and Castro Street institution at the former site of the Elephant Walk and the 1979 White Night riots.
- **Market St. Railway Mural** • 300 Church St
  Depicts sweeping birds-eye view of Market Street through different eras and historical events in harmonious colors.
- **Mission Dolores** • 3321 16th St
  415-621-8203
  1776 Spanish mission and Catholic church.
- **Randall Museum** • 199 Museum Way
  415-554-9600
  Petting zoo, earthquake exhibit, and model trains!
- **Randall Museum Dog Run** •
  Roosevelt Way & Museum Way
  Home of the Chihuahua Cha Cha.

🍸 Bars

- **Blackbird** • 2124 Market St
  415-503-0630
  Thank you Blackbird, caw caw!
- **Café du Nord** • 2170 Market St
  415-861-5016
  Excellent live music, pool tables. Former speakeasy.
- **Café Flore** • 2298 Market St
  415-621-8579
  Open air café. Great for an afternoon beer or wine and Castro people watching.
- **Club Waziema** • 543 Divisadero St
  415-346-6641
  Stiff drinks and Ethiopian food.
- **Harvey's** • 500 Castro St
  415-431-4278
  A Castro institution. Considered touristy by the locals.
- **The Independent** • 628 Divisadero St
  415-771-1421
  Ideal live music venue. Great staff and stiff drinks.
- **Last Call Bar** • 3988 18th St
  415-861-1310
  A row of bar stools complete this local gay dive.
- **Lucky 13** • 2140 Market St
  415-487-1313
  Rocker bar. Great beer selection. Award winning jukebox and pool table.
- **Mad Dog in the Fog** • 530 Haight St
  415-626-7279
  Great beer bar. Your dog is welcome on the patio.
- **Madrone Art Bar** • 500 Divisadero St
  415-241-0202
  Chill neighborhood art lounge.
- **The Midnight Sun** • 4067 18th St
  415-861-4186
  Gay bar with big TVs and sitcoms.
- **The Mint** • 1942 Market St
  415-626-4726
  Karaoke! Gay and straight.
- **Mojo Bicycle Cafe** • 639 Divisadero St
  415-440-2370
  Get your bike fixed while you swill a brew.
- **Molotov's** • 582 Haight St
  415-558-8019
  The quintessential dive of Lower Haight, punk rockers and all.

Map 10

- **Nickies** • 466 Haight St
415-255-0300
Dancing, DJ, food and drink—no mixed drinks.
- **The Page** • 298 Divisadero St
415-255-6101
Young, hip crowd with a neighborhood bar
feel.
- **Pilsner Inn** • 225 Church St
415-621-7058
Gay bar with a pool table, darts, and pinball.
- **Q Bar** • 456 Castro St
415-864-2877
Castro Street bar with small dance floor and
front patio smoking.
- **San Francisco Badlands** • 4121 18th St
415-626-9320
Gay dance bar.
- **Toad Hall** • 4146 18th St
415-621-2811
Like a nightly gay fiesta with Top 40 music and
a happening back patio.
- **Toronado** • 547 Haight St
415-863-2276
THE BEST beer selection in the city.
- **Twin Peaks Tavern** • 401 Castro St
415-864-9470
One of the oldest gay bars in the Castro.
- **Uva Enoteca** • 568 Haight St
415-829-2024
All Italian wine bar, an instant classic.
- **Vinyl Coffee & Wine Bar** • 359 Divisadero St
415-621-4132
Casual wine bar on an up-and-coming block.
- **Woods Cerveceria** • 3801 18th St
415-273-9295
Beer infused with yerba mate for a kick.

🍴 Restaurants

- **Alamo Square Seafood Grill** • 803 Fillmore St
415-440-2828 • $$$
Carefully prepared seafood, no corkage fee
on Weds.
- **Anchor Oyster Bar** • 579 Castro St
415-431-3990 • $$$
Get the crab cakes.
- **Axum Café** • 698 Haight St
415-252-7912 • $$
Ethiopian. Eat with your fingers.
- **Bar Crudo** • 655 Divisadero St
415-409-0679 • $$$
Amazing raw bar that never disappoints.

- **Bi-Rite Creamery** • 3692 18th St
415-626-5600 • $
Gourmet ice cream. Long lines. High prices.
Worth every penny.
- **Burger Meister** • 138 Church St
415-437-2874 • $$
Two-hand burgers, a little pricey.
- **Café du Soleil** • 200 Fillmore St
415-934-8637 • $
Charming, rustic French café.
- **Café Flore** • 2298 Market St
415-621-8579 • $
Great people-watching.
- **Canela** • 2272 Market St
415-552-3000 • $$$
Spanish-inspired tapas in the Castro.
- **Catch** • 2362 Market St
415-431-5000 • $$$$
Seafood and California-style cuisine. Live
piano and a patio.
- **Cathay Express Restaurant** • 720 14th St
415-431-3229 • $
Cheap bastards chow down on chow mein.
- **Chow** • 215 Church St
415-552-2469 • $$$
Good, affordable home-cookin'.
- **Club Waziema** • 543 Divisadero St
415-346-6641 • $$
Stiff drinks and Ethiopian food.
- **Crepevine** • 216 Church St
415-431-4646 • $
Fresh food and big selection, but the items
add up.
- **CuCo's** • 488 Haight St
415-863-4906 • $
Salvadorean, plantain burrito in town.
- **Eiji** • 317 Sanchez St
415-558-8149 • $$
Cute, tiny, yummy spot. Get the homemade
tofu.
- **El Castillito** • 136 Church St
415-621-3428 • $
Substitute fresh avocado for guac.
- **Fable** • 558 Castro St
415-590-2404 • $$
Whimsical setting (antler lights, Aesop-
inspired art) for hearty classics.
- **Fork Cafe** • 469 Castro St
415-553-6633 • $$
Community-centric place that donates to local
charities; indoor/outdoor seating.
- **Indian Oven** • 233 Fillmore St
415-626-1628 • $$$
Above-average Indian.

The Castro supplies one of the biggest assets of a sleepless city: 24-hour food (**Orphan Andy's**, **Sparky's**). Local live music is fresh at **Café du Nord** and the brave can make their own music with karaoke at **The Mint**. Lower Haight is brunch central at **Kate's Kitchen** and **Café du Soleil** by morning and beer heaven at **Toronado** by night.

- **Jay's Cheesesteak** • 553 Divisadero St
  415-771-5104 • $
  Philly-style cheesesteaks.
- **Kasa Indian Eatery** • 4001 18th St
  415-621-6940 • $$
  Homestyle Indian using local produce + food truck.
- **Kate's Kitchen** • 471 Haight St
  415-626-3984 • $$
  Breakfast and lunch with a Southern edge.
- **La Fajita Grill** • 2312 Market St
  415-796-2818 • $
  Lesser known, but solid Mexican. Great chips.
- **La Mediterranee** • 288 Noe St
  415-431-7210 • $$
  Cozy Middle Eastern.
- **The Little Chihuahua** • 292 Divisadero St
  415-255-8225 • $
  Health conscious Mexican using Niman Ranch and Petaluma Poultry products.
- **Love N Haight Deli** • 553 Haight St
  415-252-8190 • $
  Vegetarian deli sandwiches, some with fake meat.
- **M&L Market** • 691 14th St
  415-431-7044 • $
  Choose your bread first: a.k.a Mae's Sandwich Shop.
- **Marcello's Pizza** • 420 Castro St
  415-863-3900 • $
  A quick slice across from the Castro Theater.
- **Maven** • 598 Haight St
  415-829-7982 • $$
  Candlelight, redwood tables, impressive cocktails, and a living garden wall.
- **Memphis Minnie's BBQ Joint** • 576 Haight St
  415-864-7675 • $$
  Casual barbecue and sake menu (seriously).
- **Metro Caffe** • 247 Fillmore St
  415-621-9536 • $
  Pint-sized joint for good, greasy cheesesteaks and burgers.
- **Mission Beach Cafe** • 198 Guerrero
  415-861-0198 • $$
  Upscale cafe where Paris meets casual San Francisco.
- **Nickies** • 466 Haight St
  415-255-0300 • $$
  Dancing, DJ, food and drink—no mixed drinks.
- **Nizario's Pizza** • 4077 18th St
  415-487-0777 • $
  Decent, at least when you're drunk.
- **NOPA** • 560 Divisadero St
  415-864-8643 • $$$
  Airy, sexy room serves late.

- **Nopalito** • 306 Broderick St
  415-437-0303 • $$
  Mexican kitchen serving totopos (terrific!) and house-made popsicles.
- **Oakside Cafe** • 1195 Oak St
  415-437-1985 • $
  Open super early, great space for studying.
- **Orphan Andy's** • 3991 17th St
  415-864-9795 • $
  Burgers, scrambles, and drag queens 24 hours a day.
- **Poesia** • 4072 18th St
  415-252-9325 • $$
  Homey Italian food with La Dolce Vita projected silently on the wall.
- **Red Jade Restaurant** • 245 Church St
  415-621-3020 • $
  Indulge in hot crab rangoons and generous Chinese dishes.
- **Rosamunde Sausage Grill** • 545 Haight St
  415-437-6851 • $
  Gourmet sausage joint.
- **Rotee** • 400 Haight St
  415-552-8309 • $
  Tucked at the end of the Lower Haight strip, it's fast and good Indian food.
- **Samovar Tea Lounge** • 498 Sanchez St
  415-626-4700 • $$
  Tea lounge that also serves breakfast.
- **The Sausage Factory** • 517 Castro St
  415-626-1250 • $$
  Hearty Italian in the Castro.
- **Sparky's** • 242 Church St
  415-626-8666 • $
  Open 24 hours for all your alcohol absorbing needs.
- **Starbelly** • 3583 16th St
  415-252-7500 • $$
  Taking Cali comfort food to new levels with Mediterranean flourishes.
- **Sushi Time** • 2275 Market St
  415-552-2280 • $$
  Tiny gem hidden downstairs in mini strip mall.
- **Thep Phanom** • 400 Waller St
  415-431-2526 • $$
  Thai food at its finest.
- **Woodhouse Fish Co.** • 2073 Market St
  415-437-2722 • $$
  It's crabtastic.
- **Zadin** • 4039 18th St
  415-626-2260 • $$
  Warm, softly lit space for pho and gluten-free Vietnamese.
- **Ziryab** • 528 Divisadero St
  415-522-0800 • $$
  Good Middle Eastern food and desserts.

Map 1
9 10 11 12 13
29 14 15 16 17

Shopping

- **A.G. Ferrari Foods** • 468 Castro St
415-255-6590
Italian foods and wine and wonderful deli items.
- **B Parlor** • 782 Haight St
415-255-8554
Never hard to get an appointment.
- **Best In Show** • 545 Castro St
415-864-7387
Find that special bone for Rover.
- **Books & Bookshelves** • 99 Sanchez St
415-621-3761
Exactly what the name says, plus a precious poetry collection.
- **Books Inc.** • 2275 Market St
415-864-6777
The Castro's only full service general bookstore! Events galore!
- **Citizen** • 489 Castro St
415-575-3560
Hip men's clothes.
- **Cliff's Variety Store** • 479 Castro St
415-431-5365
Excellent hardware store.
- **Comix Experience** • 305 Divisadero St
415-863-9258
Are you experienced?
- **Cookin'** • 339 Divisadero St
415-861-1854
Huge, disorganized selection of professional cookware.

- **Costumes on Haight** • 735 Haight St
415-621-1356
Huge and funky selection of costumes for all budgets, all the time.
- **Crossroads Trading Co.** • 2123 Market St
415-552-8740
Used clothes.
- **DeLessio Market and Bakery** •
302 Broderick St
415-552-8077
Fancypants market sells wonderful prepared food.
- **Edo Salon & Gallery** • 631 Haight St
415-861-0131
Hair salon. Straight out of Tokyo (Edo).
- **Falletti Foods** • 308 Broderick St
415-626-4400
Locally grown produce and specialty gourmet items.
- **Faye's Video & Espresso Bar** • 3614 18th St
415-522-0434
Small, cool, video joint that also serves coffee.
- **Gamescape** • 333 Divisadero St
415-621-4263
All kinds of board games.
- **Golden Produce** • 172 Church St
415-431-1536
The name says it all.
- **Groove Merchant Records** • 687 Haight St
415-252-5766
Desirable vinyl in a groovy neighborhood.

y **Thep Phanom** for Thai, **Chow** for a down-home diner, and **NOPA** just ecause it feels right. While **Harvest Market** is a healthyish store, horough **Bread And Pastry** makes everyone happy. **Streetlight ecords**, **Groove Merchant Records** and **Jack's Record Cellar** are all great ecord stores.

- **Harvest Ranch Market** • 2285 Market St
  415-626-0805
  Amazing soup and salad bar. Vegetarian-friendly.
- **ImaginKnit** • 3897 18th St
  415-621-6642
  Get your yarn, fancy and plain. Helpful staff!
- **Jack's Record Cellar** • 254 Scott St
  415-431-3047
  Rare 78s and offbeat vinyl.
- **L'Occitane** • 556 Castro St
  415-621-4668
  Wonderful French soaps.
- **Life** • 604 Haight St
  415-252-9312
  Lovely assortment of fragrant oils, candles and incense.
- **Mickey's Monkey** • 218 Pierce St
  415-864-0693
  Used furniture and knick knacks.
- **Needles and Pens** • 3253 16th St
  415-255-1534
  Zines and other punk rock things.
- **Other Shop** • 327 Divisadero St
  415-621-5424
  Retro furnishings.
- **Photoworks San Francisco** • 2077 Market St
  415-626-6800
  Go from digital to print in a matter of seconds.
- **Rolo** • 2351 Market St
  415-578-7139
  Hip men's clothes.

- **Salon Baobao** • 2041 Market St
  415-626-6806
  Ask for the latest haircut in this mod salon.
- **Sam's Smoke Shop** • 250 Divisadero St
  415-865-1678
  Family-owned head shop.
- **Streetlight Records** • 2350 Market St
  888-396-2350
  New, used, and rare music.
- **Sui Generis** • 2265 Market St
  415-437-2265
  Consignment boutique for men.
- **Swirl on Castro** • 572 Castro St
  415-864-2262
  Features fine wines, books and local art.
- **Tan Bella** • 2185 Market St
  415-522-1234
  Award-winning spray and UV tanning from friendly, stylish salon.
- **Thorough Bread And Pastry** • 248 Church St
  415-558-0690
  Adorable bakery; tasty treats.
- **Tim's Market** • 667 Fillmore St
  415-552-6830
  Smokes, nutter butters, and alcohol.
- **Upper Playground** • 220 Fillmore St
  415-861-1960
  Gallery, Fifty24SF, urban clothing, and used music.
- **Zip Zap Hair** • 245 Fillmore St
  415-621-1671
  Super stylists and service.

Map 11 • **Hayes Valley / The Mission**

's two great neighborhoods in one—slightly more fashionable Hayes Valley to the north of Market and the beginning of the Mission to the south. This area has tons of mass transit, highway on/off ramps, festivals, parades, old buildings, new lofts, and everything else thrown in. You won't be bored.

Landmarks

The Armory • 1800 Mission St
415-677-0456
Former military base, now the HQ for fetish company Kink.

The Bike Kitchen • 650 Florida St
415-647-2453
A do-it-yourself bicycle repair and resource shop run entirely by volunteers.

Clarion Alley • 17th St & Valencia St
Alley of vibrant, socially conscious community street art. Bring your camera.

Global Exchange • 2017 Mission St
415-255-7296
Activism headquarters for fair trade. Volunteers always needed, and rooftop has great views on Friday beer day.

Hayes Green •
Octavia Blvd btwn Hayes St & Fell St
Newest green area to go along with Octavia Boulevard freeway exit in the heart of Hayes Valley.

MaestraPeace Mural • 18th St & Valencia St
Mural by 7 women painters depicting women at work, play, etc. on the side of the Women's Center Building.

Mission Police Station • 630 Valencia St
415-558-5400
Seven Dancing Stones in the lobby are arranged in form of Pleiades constellation, telling myths of the native Oholone Indians.

San Francisco Opera • 301 Van Ness Ave
415-864-3330
Second largest opera company in America.

San Francisco Symphony • 201 Van Ness Ave
415-864-6000
Seen the likes of Stravinsky and Metallica.

Street Quotes • Mission St & 14th St
Sidewalk dialogue in blue stencils.

Bars

500 Club • 500 Guerrero St
415-861-2500
Fine Mission dive. We love the sign.

Absinthe • 398 Hayes St
415-551-1590
Have a minty Ginger Rogers with your fries.

Amnesia • 853 Valencia St
415-970-0012
Beer, wine, and lots of red light.

Beauty Bar • 2299 Mission St
415-285-0323
Be beautiful or get beautiful after a couple of drinks.

Bender's Bar and Grill • 806 S Van Ness Ave
415-824-1800
Weird Fish, PBR and punk rock. Bring your Taz tat.

Blondie's Bar and No Grill • 540 Valencia St
415-864-2419
Big blondes and even bigger…martinis.

Butter • 354 11th St
415-863-5964
House music, PBR, WWF on big screen, and tater tots.

Casanova Lounge • 527 Valencia St
415-863-9328
Swanky lounge with cozy couches and dim red lighting.

Dalva • 3121 16th St
415-252-7740
Nice Mission lounge. Candlelight and sangria. Check out the jukebox!

Dear Mom • 2700 16th St
415-644-8445
Strong pours and bar food that's a class above.

DNA Lounge • 375 11th St
415-626-1409
ABC wants to shut them down for lewd behavior. Yeah lewd behavior.

Double Dutch • 3192 16th St
415-373-1042
Post-modern old-school hip-hop vibe.

Double Play • 2401 16th St
415-621-9859
Old time San Francisco sports bar. Giants and Seals memorabilia.

Dr Teeth & the Electric Mayhem •
2323 Mission St
415-285-2380
Tater tots, Jameson on tap, Tuesday trivia. Often insanely crowded.

Elbo Room • 647 Valencia St
415-552-7788
Legendary alternative live music joint.

Elixir • 3200 16th St
415-552-1633
Corner pub with lots of beers on tap.

Esta Noche • 3079 16th St
415-861-5757
Bisexuals and drag queens.

The Homestead • 2301 Folsom St
415-282-4663
Ask the bartender to play Yahtzee.

Map

9 10 11 12 13
29 14 15 16 17

- **Kilowatt** • 3160 16th St
415-861-2595
Great trashy place to get trashed. Dogs
allowed.
- **Lexington Club** • 3464 19th St
415-863-2052
Cozy lesbian bar.
- **Little Baobab** • 3372 19th St
415-643-3558
Hybrid nightclub and Caribbean-Creole
restaurant.
- **Martuni's** • 4 Valencia St
415-241-0205
Show tunes anyone? Great piano bar, mostly
gay crowd.
- **Nihon Whisky Lounge** • 1779 Folsom St
415-552-4400
For well-heeled lovers of the brownest of the
brown liquors.
- **Orbit Room** • 1900 Market St
415-252-9525
Café atmosphere, great Mojitos.
- **Phoenix Irish Bar** • 811 Valencia St
415-695-1811
Irish bar and restaurant.
- **Place Pigalle** • 520 Hayes St
415-552-2671
Low-key watering hole for the locals of Hayes
Valley.
- **Rickshaw Stop** • 155 Fell St
415-861-2011
Eclectic live music, cheap eats, and real
rickshaws.
- **Rite Spot Cafe** • 2099 Folsom St
415-552-6066
Funky piano bar/grub pub that is Rite, tight
and out of sight.
- **Roxie Theater** • 3117 16th St
415-863-1087
Get out of the multiplex and into this
charismatic theater.
- **Skylark** • 3089 16th St
415-621-9294
Mission watering hole.
- **Slim's** • 333 11th St
415-255-0333
Big name live music.
- **Southern Pacific Brewing** • 620 Treat Ave
415-341-0152
Massive bar, brewery, and beer-inspired pub
fare.
- **Sugar Lounge** • 377 Hayes St
415-255-7144
Happy hour cocktails and food for free—
enough said.

- **Thieves Tavern** • 496 14th St
415-252-9082
Beers, bicycle enthusiasts and (pool) balls.
- **Truck** • 1900 Folsom St
415-252-0306
Rough and scruff live up to this LGBT pit-stop.
- **Uptown** • 200 Capp St
415-861-8231
Cool Mission dive.
- **Wish Bar & Lounge** • 1539 Folsom St
415-431-1661
Intimate lounge.
- **Zeitgeist** • 199 Valencia St
415-255-7505
Biker bar with a big yard.

🍴 Restaurants

- **1601 Bar & Kitchen** • 1601 Howard St
415-552-1601 • $$
Modern French fare with a touch of Sri Lankan
- **The Abbot's Cellar** • 742 Valencia St
415-626-8700 • $$$
Dedicated to pairing craft beers with Californi
cuisine.
- **Absinthe** • 398 Hayes St
415-551-1590 • $$$$$
French brasserie with great cocktails. Open
late.
- **Andalu** • 3198 16th St
415-621-2211 • $$$$
Eclectic small plates.
- **Arinell Pizza** • 509 Valencia St
415-255-1303 • $
Thin-crust New York-style pizza with punk roc
atmosphere.
- **Bar Agricole** • 355 11th St
415-355-9400 • $$$
Artisinal cocktails and farm-fresh eats.
- **Bar Jules** • 609 Hayes St
415-621-5482 • $$$
Menu changes every day, has brunch.
- **Bar Tartine** • 561 Valencia St
415-487-1600 • $$
Upscale spin-off of popular French bakery.
- **Basil Canteen** • 1489 Folsom St
415-552-3963 • $$
Atypical Thai restaurant, serving fusion dishes
and cocktails.
- **Big Lantern** • 3170 16th St
415-863-8100 • $$
Specializes in dim sum and mock meats.

'll never go hungry, whether you've got $5 or $500 to spend on food—everything from **Pancho Villa** and **Limon** to **Delfina** and **Slow Club** and dozens of places in between. Shopping is equally stellar—from the fashionable shops on Hayes to Valencia institutions such as **826 Valencia**, **Paxton Gate**, and **Good Vibrations**.

Blowfish Sushi • 2170 Bryant St
415-285-3848 • $$$$
Upscale sushi, cocktails, and electronic beats.

The Blue Muse • 370 Grove St
415-701-9888 • $$$
Reopened in new location, popular with opera crowd.

Boxing Room • 399 Grove St
415-430-6590 • $$
The best food from New Orleans the city has to offer.

Burger Joint • 807 Valencia St
415-824-3494 • $$
Jetsons-like burger joint.

Cafe Taboo • 600 York St
415-341-1188 • $$
Neighborhood feastery serving breakfast all day.

Caffe Delle Stelle • 395 Hayes St
415-252-1110 • $$$
Cozy, simple Italian.

Canto do Brasil • 41 Franklin St
415-626-8727 • $$
Brazilian ambience in the heart of SF.

Central Kitchen • 3000 20th St
415-826-7004 • $$$$
Locally sourced, ever-evolving menu in casual cosetting.

Cha Cha Cha • 2327 Mission St
415-842-1502 • $$$
Caribbean spiced tapas.

Cha-Ya Vegetarian Japanese Restaurant •
762 Valencia St
415-252-7825 • $$$$
Not just vegetarian, it's vegan too.

Chez Spencer • 82 14th St
415-864-2191 • $$$$
Pricey French.

Christopher Elbow Artisanal Chocolates •
401 Hayes St
415-355-1105 • $$$
Gourmet chocolate, need we say more?

Commonwealth • 2224 Mission St
415-355-1500 • $$$
Subtle molecular gastronomy, open kitchen, disco ball.

Craftsman & Wolves • 746 Valencia St
415-913-7713 • $$$
Pricey, delectable baked goods, attractively arranged.

Dante's Weird Fish • 2193 Mission St
415-863-4744 • $$
Sustainably farmed fish at unfishlike prices. Holy moley.

• **DeLessio Market and Bakery** •
1695 Market St
415-552-5559 • $$
Bakery, buffet and hot lunch by the pound.

• **Delfina** • 3621 18th St
415-552-4055 • $$$$
Exceptional Italian. If we ever get in we'll like it.

• **Destino** • 1815 Market St
415-552-4451 • $$$$
Nuevo Latino bistro.

• **Domo** • 511 Laguna St
415-861-8887 • $$
Very very very tiny. Great sushi.

• **Double Decker** • 465 Grove St
415-552-8042 • $
Spicy chicken wings are a big hit.

• **El Toro Taqueria** • 598 Valencia St
415-431-3351 • $$
Fantastic tacos and burritos.

• **Espetus Churrascaria** • 1686 Market St
415-552-8792 • $$$$$
Brazilian steakhouse, all-you-can-eat roasted meats served on swords.

• **Farina** • 3560 18th St
415-565-0360 • $$
Interesting decor, solid Italian food, but early close hours for dinner on weekends.

• **Flipper's** • 482 Hayes St
415-552-8880 • $
Neighborhood favorite with outdoor seating.

• **Frances** • 3870 17th St
415-621-3870 • $$$
Maple-laced bacon beignets.

• **Go Getters Pizza** • 69 Gough St
415-621-1401 • $
Go Get 'Em! Em's shitty pizza.

• **Hayes Street Grill** • 320 Hayes St
415-863-5545 • $$$
Good, basic seafood—popular with the symphony crowd.

• **Hotel Biron** • 45 Rose St
415-703-0403 • $$
Get a cheese platter and an unusual grape wine by the glass.

• **Irma's Pampanga Restaurant** • 2901 16th St
415-626-6688 • $
Cafeteria-style Filipino restaurant made with love.

• **It's Tops Coffee Shop** • 1801 Market St
415-431-6395 • $$
Basic greasy spoon that's great for breakfast.

• **Jardiniere** • 300 Grove St
415-861-5555 • $$$$$
High-end California-French fare.

Map 1

9 10 11 12 13
29 14 15 16 17

- **Kenny's Restaurant** • 518 S Van Ness Ave
415-621-8902 • $
Greasy spoon, with breakfasts as cheap as chips.
- **La Cumbre Taqueria** • 515 Valencia St
415-863-8205 • $
Classic longstanding taqueria.
- **La Oaxaquena** • 2128 Mission St
415-621-5446 • $
Try the tlayuda—a large tortilla slathered in toppings.
- **Limon Rotisserie** • 524 Valencia St
415-252-0918 • $$$$
Modest, popular Peruvian. Try the ceviche.
- **Little Star Pizza** • 400 Valencia St
415-551-7827 • $$
Deep dish or thin crust and a variety of toppings.
- **Local Mission Eatery** • 3111 24th St
415-655-3422 • $$
Local farmers, vendors, and artisans.
- **Locanda** • 557 Valencia St
415-863-6800 • $$$
Lively, Rome-inspired osteria serving housemade pasta and offal.
- **Lolinda** • 2518 Mission St
415-550-6970 • $$$
Argentinian steakhouse in former Medjool space. Roof with a view.
- **Luna Park** • 694 Valencia St
415-553-8584 • $$$
Casual, moderately-priced American food. Try the make-your-own 'smores for dessert!
- **Manora's Thai Cuisine** • 1600 Folsom St
415-861-6224 • $$$
Above average Thai.
- **Maverick** • 3316 17th St
415-863-3061 • $$
Southern comfort food.
- **Minako** • 2154 Mission St
415-864-1888 • $$
Homey Japanese.
- **Mission Chinese Food** • 2234 Mission St
415-863-2800 • $$
Creative, Americanized Chinese food.
- **Mission Dispatch** • 1975 Bryant St
$
A changing cast of food trucks for lunch.
- **Moishe's Pippic** • 425 Hayes St
415-431-2440 • $$
Jewish-style deli.
- **Momi Toby's Revolution Café** • 528 Laguna St
415-400-5689 • $
Great spot for an afternoon Chimay or coffee.

- **The Monk's Kettle** • 3141 16th St
415-865-9523 • $$
Tasty, filling pub grub.
- **Nojo** • 231 Franklin St
415-896-4587 • $
Japanese-style skewers, sake, and shochu.
- **Pakwan** • 3182 16th St
415-255-2440 • $
Indian. Bare bones, cheap, and good.
- **Pancho Villa Taqueria** • 3071 16th St
415-864-8840 • $
Try the prawn quesadilla.
- **Patxi's Chicago Pizza** • 511 Hayes St
415-558-9991 • $$
They let you order while you wait.
- **Pauline's Pizza Pie** • 260 Valencia St
415-552-2050 • $$
Wild and wonderful California 'za.
- **Picaro** • 3120 16th St
415-431-4089 • $$
Authentic Spanish tapas. Good sangria.
- **Pizzeria Delfina** • 3611 18th St
415-437-6800 • $$
Absurdly popular. Absurdly tasty.
- **Poc-Chuc** • 2886 16th St
415-558-1583 • $$
Mayan fusion in the heart of the Mission.
- **Pork Store Café** • 3122 16th St
415-626-5523 • $$
Greasy breakfast joint.
- **Puerto Alegre** • 546 Valencia St
415-255-8201 • $$
Popular standard Mexican.
- **Radish** • 3465 19th St
415-834-5441 • $$
Gluten-free, eclectic American menu with Southern touches.
- **Range** • 842 Valencia St
415-282-8283 • $$$
Inventive California cuisine.
- **Rich Table** • 199 Gough St
415-355-9085 • $$$
Casually elegant. Come for sardine potato chips and pasta.
- **The Sage Cafe** • 340 Grove St
415-252-9887 • $
Best watermelon juice in town.
- **Samovar Tea Lounge** • 297 Page St
415-861-0303 • $$
A (pricey) assortment of teas in a cozy atmosphere.
- **Slow Club** • 2501 Mariposa St
415-241-9390 • $$$$
Cool supper-club vibe.

nako is organic Japanese, **Manora**'s Thai is yum, and **Luna Park** is a nsistent favorite, but **Zuni Café**'s roasted chicken is sublime, even elatory, and San Francisco's restaurant scene will be forever indebted to ly Rodgers.

Stacks • 501 Hayes St
415-241-9011 • $$
Don't hate it because it's a chain—the pancakes are great.

Sunflower Restaurant • 3111 16th St
415-626-5022 • $
Two locations with an attached kitchen, Vietnamese food.

Suppenkuche • 525 Laguna St
415-252-9289 • $$$
Authentic German food and great beers.

Taqueria Cancun • 2288 Mission St
415-252-9560 • $
Gigantic burritos.

Taqueria El Buen Sabor • 699 Valencia St
415-552-8816 • $
Good tofu burritos, but otherwise average.

Tartine Bakery • 600 Guerrero St
415-487-2600 • $$
Great French café.

Tokyo Go Go • 3174 16th St
415-864-2288 • $$$$
Handroll happy hour. Super yummy. Cucumber gimlet. Creative sushi.

Truly Mediterranean • 3109 16th St
415-252-7482 • $
Quick Mediterranean take-out. Falafel, shawarma, hummus, and baba ghanoush.

Una Pizza Napoletana • 210 11th St
415-861-3444 • $$
Pizza-only resto with oven in the dining room.

Universal Café • 2814 19th St
415-821-4608 • $$$
Warm, sleek, California cuisine. Excellent for brunch.

Walzwerk • 381 S Van Ness Ave
415-551-7181 • $$
Hearty German grub and excellent beer.

West of Pecos • 550 Valencia St
415-252-7000 • $$
Tex-Mex on huge plates for hungry rustlers.

The WestWood • 1152 Valencia St
415-641-1350 • $$
Specializing in pork belly.

Woodward's Garden • 1700 Mission St
415-621-7122 • $$$$$
Cozy and discreet.

Yamo • 3406 18th St
415-553-8911 • $
Friendly, raucous, cheap, and tasty.

Zuni Café • 1658 Market St
415-552-2522 • $$$$$
An institution—and there's so much more than the sublime roasted chicken.

🛍 Shopping

- **826 Valencia** • 826 Valencia St
  415-642-5905
  Writing center and pirate supplies. Thank you, Dave Eggers.
- **Alla Prima Lingerie** • 539 Hayes St
  415-864-8180
  Dreamy lingerie.
- **The Apartment** • 3469 18th St
  415-255-1100
  Eclectic, interesting furniture; vintage artefacts; awesome exterior mural.
- **Arlequin Wine Merchant** • 384 Hayes St
  415-863-1104
  Specialty wine shop.
- **Azalea Boutique** • 411 Hayes St
  415-861-9888
  Eclectic boutique and nail bar for men and women.
- **Bell Jar** • 3187 16th St
  415-626-1749
  Darling items for your home and body. Fall in love.
- **Bi-Rite Market** • 3639 18th St
  415-241-9760
  Small, good, old grocery store.
- **Black And Blue Tattoo** • 381 Guerrero St
  415-626-0770
  Impressive, female-centric tattoo, cutting, and branding shop.
- **Borderland Books** • 866 Valencia St
  415-824-8203
  Sci-fi, fantasy, and horror.
- **Botanica Yoruba** • 3423 19th St
  415-826-4967
  Fulfilling your Santeria, Lucumi, Palo, and Ifa needs.
- **Bulo Shoes** • 418 Hayes St
  415-255-4939
  Fashionable footwear for women.
- **Claudia Kussano** • 591 Guerrero St
  415-671-0769
  Unique, contemporary jewelry from local designer.
- **Clothes Contact** • 473 Valencia St
  415-621-3212
  Vintage clothing sold by the pound.
- **Community Thrift Store** • 623 Valencia St
  415-861-4910
  Proceeds go to the charity of your choice.

- **Currents** • 911 Valencia St
415-648-2015
Soap and stuff.
- **Dark Garden** • 321 Linden St
415-431-7684
Custom-made corsets, bridal gowns, and bras.
- **DeLessio Market and Bakery** •
1695 Market St
415-552-5559
Bakery, buffet, and hot lunch by the pound.
- **Density** • 593 Valencia St
415-552-2249
Hipster threads for men and women, with
great service.
- **Discount Fabrics** • 2170 Cesar Chavez St
415-685-4064
Family-owned for three decades. Event
planning as well.
- **Dish Boutique** • 541 Hayes St
415-252-5997
Women's clothing with simple, feminine styles.
- **Evelyn's** • 2088 Oakdale Ave
415-255-1815
Antique Chinese furniture.
- **F. Dorian** • 370 Hayes St
415-861-3191
Step into creativity.
- **Five and Diamond** • 510 Valencia St
415-255-9747
Like stepping onto the set of a Western movie
with Malcolm McLaren as art director.
- **Flax** • 1699 Market St
415-552-2355
Excellent art and craft supplies for all kinds
of projects.
- **Flight 001** • 525 Hayes St
415-487-1001
Hip travel store with everything you need
to carry everything you want, everywhere
you go.
- **Gimme Shoes** • 416 Hayes St
415-864-0691
Top-notch, hip shoes.

- **Good Vibrations** • 603 Valencia St
415-522-5460
A clean, well-lit place for sex toys.
- **Harrington Galleries** • 599 Valencia St
415-861-7300
Vast space full of unusual old and new home
furnishings.
- **Idol Vintage** • 3162 16th St
415-255-9959
Vintage clothing store, specializing in the '60s,
'70s, and '80s.
- **Katz Bagels** • 3147 16th St
415-552-9050
Great lox schmear and quick service.
- **Lava 9** • 542 Hayes St
415-552-6468
Animal coats.
- **Lavish** • 508 Hayes St
415-565-0540
Vintage décor, home, bath, jewelry, women's
clothing, and baby gifts.
- **Lost Art Salon** • 245 S Van Ness Ave
415-861-1530
Like prowling through an eccentric aunt's
private gallery.
- **Miette** • 449 Octavia St
415-626-6221
Old-fashioned sweet shop in Hayes Valley.
- **The Mission Statement** • 3458 18th St
415-255-7457
New co-op featuring clothing from up-and-
coming SF designers.
- **Mission Thrift** • 2330 Mission St
415-821-9560
Keep this one on the DL.
- **Monument** • 573 Valencia St
415-861-9800
High class and high priced gorgeous furniture
designs.
- **Multikulti** • 539 Valencia St
415-437-1718
Hotbed of kooky accessories, including the
best tights in town!

dow shop on Hayes Street. For your home, there's **Monument**, rrington Galleries, and **Propeller**. Go to **Box Dog Bicycles** for your e. At **Clothes Contact** you can buy clothes by the pound. Oh, and the ice eam at **Bi-Rite Creamery** is great.

Nomads • 556 Hayes St
415-864-5692
Trendy men's clothing.

Paxton Gate • 824 Valencia St
415-824-1872
Taxidermy, fossils, and other things once living.

Paxton Gate's Curiosities For Kids •
766 Valencia St
415-252-9990
Ignite your kids' imaginations with old fashioned 'n' fun delights.

Propeller • 555 Hayes St
415-701-7767
Innovative furniture and home accessories.

Rainbow Grocery • 1745 Folsom St
415-863-0620
Best natural, organic, vegetarian-focused food market in town, not just for hippies anymore.

Residents Apparel Gallery (RAG) •
541 Octavia St
415-621-7718
Clothing by young, local designers.

Retrospect Furniture • 1649 Market St
415-863-7414
Fine vintage furniture.

The San Francisco Chocolate Factory •
286 12th St
415-677-9194
Free samples!

Schauplatz • 791 Valencia St
415-864-5665
Reasonably priced, colorful, vintage awesomeness. Great finds galore.

Self Edge • 714 Valencia St
415-558-0658
Denim specialists with a global eye and designer prices.

• **Shoe Biz** • 877 Valencia St
415-550-8655
Their shoes are the business!

• **Sports Authority** • 1690 Folsom St
415-734-9373
Sports apparel and gear.

• **Steven Alan** • 445 Hayes St
415-558-8944
Classic designs, jewelry, and handbags.

• **Sunhee Moon** • 3167 16th St
415-355-1800
A clothing boutique almost too chic for the Mission District.

• **Taylor / Monroe** • 448 Grove St
415-252-9723
Haven for hipsters and fresh haircuts in Hayes Valley.

• **Therapy** • 545 Valencia St
415-865-0981
Hip clothing and magnets of cat butts.

• **Thrift Town** • 2101 Mission St
415-861-1132
Thift-y emporium.

• **Timbuk2** • 506 Hayes St
415-252-9860
Not for your average bike messenger.

• **True Sake** • 560 Hayes St
415-355-9555
Sake shop.

• **The Voyager Shop** • 365 Valencia St
415-779-2712
Treasures from ocean gear to books.

• **Weston Wear** • 569 Valencia St
415-621-1480
Smart clothes for smart women.

• **Zeni** • 567 Hayes St
415-864-0154
Hip boutique for men and women.

• **Zoe Bikini** • 3386 18th St
415-421-4551
The latest and greatest in custom bikinis.

Map 1

The former industrial district of Soma is now dotted by spacious dot-com startups and hip restaurants where tech workers grab a quick lunch. The not-long-for-this-world witty sculpture **Defenestration** features apartment furniture freeze-framed in mid-suicide, and marks a city seam where urban tenements meet industrial glamour. **Anchor Brewing Company** still makes amazing beer in small batches.

◯ Landmarks

- **Anchor Brewing Company** •
  1705 Mariposa St
  415-863-8350
  Call for info about the free brewery tours of this SF institution.
- **Defenestration** • Howard St & 6th St
  That great empty building south of Market with furniture and home appliances stuck all over the outside of it. Brian Goggin created it in 1997.
- **Marriott View Lounge** • 55 4th St
  415-896-1600
  The steep drink prices you're paying at the roof lounge are really for the magnificent 180-degree view.
- **Metreon Mall** • 135 4th St
  415-369-6000
  Shopping complex frequented for movies and virtual bowling.
- **Mint Plaza** • Jessie St & Mint St
  A new public open space, the plaza is an urban haven for art exhibits, live music, and small festivals.
- **San Francisco Flower Mart** • 640 Brannan St
  415-392-7944
  The best place to buy flowers—open to the public after 10 am.

◯ Bars

- **1015 Folsom** • 1015 Folsom St
  415-431-1200
  Club scene.
- **Asia SF** • 201 9th St
  415-255-2742
  Gender illusionists. Go for the entertainment.
- **Brainwash Cafe & Laundromat** •
  1122 Folsom St
  415-255-4866
  Laundry, cocktails, live music.
- **Cat Club** • 1190 Folsom St
  415-703-8964
  DJ dance club.

- **The Chieftain Irish Pub & Restaurant** •
  198 5th St
  415-615-0916
  Irish pub. 20 beers on tap.
- **City Beer** • 1168 Folsom St
  415-503-1033
  The proverbial candy store for kids who like to drink beer and wine.
- **Club 93** • 93 9th St
  415-952-0207
  You're a long way from home, yuppie boy.
- **Connecticut Yankee** • 100 Connecticut St
  415-552-4440
  New England-style sports bar.
- **The End Up** • 401 6th St
  415-646-0999
  An institution and notorious for the Sunday T dance. Watch for theme nights.
- **Hole in the Wall Saloon** • 1369 Folsom St
  415-431-4695
  Neighborhood SoMa gay dive with cheap drinks and horny daddies.
- **The Holy Cow!** • 1535 Folsom St
  415-621-6087
  Holy Cow! There are a lot of bridge and tunnelers here.
- **Hotel Utah Saloon** • 500 4th St
  415-546-6300
  Serving up suds since 1908. Intimate live music venue.
- **Il Pirata** • 2007 16th St
  415-626-2626
  Italian restaurant and bar. Mermaid murals.
- **Mars Bar & Restaurant** • 798 Brannan St
  415-621-6277
  Jetsons-like lounge.
- **Mighty** • 119 Utah St
  415-762-0151
  Spacious dance club with rotating DJs.
- **The Stud** • 399 9th St
  415-863-6623
  Infamous gay club.
- **Thee Parkside** • 1600 17th St
  415-252-1330
  Punk garage haven. Good bloody Marys.

Map 12

SOMA / Potrero Hill (North)

Restaurants

- **54 Mint** • 16 Mint Plaza
  415-543-5100 • $$$
  Warm welcome, wow wine list, pretty people, perfect pasta!
- **AK Subs** • 397 8th St
  415-241-9600 • $
  SoMa sub-sandwich shop serving delicious deli meats.
- **Asia SF** • 201 9th St
  415-255-2742 • $$$$
  Anything but a "drag," the waitstaff are as stunning as they are entertaining.
- **Basil Thai** • 1175 Folsom St
  415-552-8999 • $$
  A taste of Thailand in SOMA.
- **Brainwash Cafe & Laundromat** •
  1122 Folsom St
  415-255-4866 • $
  Eat food, drink coffee, and do laundry.
- **Cafe Venue** • 67 5th St
  415-546-1144 • $
  Quick service and a wide array of salads and sandwiches.
- **Chez Maman** • 1453 18th St
  415-824-7166 • $$$
  Casual French brunch in a charming, pocket-sized space.
- **The Chieftain Irish Pub & Restaurant** •
  198 5th St
  415-615-0916 • $$
  Classic Irish pub with food to match.
- **Custom Burger** •
  121 7th St
  415-252-2634 • $
  Pick your own meat and toppings at this contemporary burger joint.

- **Dos Pinas** • 251 Rhode Island St
  415-252-8220 • $
  Loud and lively taqueria with $2 Coronas on Fridays.
- **Goat Hill Pizza** • 300 Connecticut St
  415-641-1440 • $$
  Monday neighborhood night in P-hill: $8 AYCE.
- **Grab 'N Go** • 480 6th St
  415-553-6666 • $
  Vietnamese done fast 'n cheap.
- **Heaven's Dog** • 1148 Mission St
  415-863-6008 • $$
  Enjoy a Chinese fusion meal as dog portraitures hover over your shoulder.
- **Henry's Hunan** • 1016 Bryant St
  415-861-5808 • $
  Get Diana's Meat Pie—gloriously greasy!
- **Restaurant LuLu** • 816 Folsom St
  415-495-5775 • $$$$
  Wood-fired oven and grill fare served family-style.
- **Sally's** • 300 De Haro St
  415-626-6006 • $
  Honkin' big omelets, strong coffee.
- **Sunflower Restaurant** • 288 Connecticut St
  415-861-2336 • $
  Potrero Hill location of Mission favorite.
- **Triptych** • 1155 Folsom St
  415-703-0557 • $$$
  Mediterranean with California twist in artsy, industrial setting.
- **What's Up Dog!** • 300 De Haro St
  $
  Hot dog stand: chili cheese, Chicago, veggie.
- **Wolfe's Lunch** • 1220 16th St
  415-621-3684 • $
  Korean BBQ, omelets, burgers and sushi. Located at the corner of a three-way intersection.
- **Zero Zero** • 826 Folsom St
  415-348-8800 • $$
  Swanky bi-level space for thin-crust pizza and Italian.

he sun always shines on the Hill, but the bar scene is better in its shadow.
sit **Hotel Utah** and channel your inner Barbary Coast longshoreman.
ighty makes industrial space pulsate with beats demanding you get
otloose. At the incline to Potrero, shopping gets serious and food
ecomes cuisine.

🛍 Shopping

City Beer • 1168 Folsom St
415-503-1033
The proverbial candy store for kids who like to
drink beer and wine.
General Bead • 637 Minna St
415-255-2323
Beads, beads, beads. Best selection in town.
Levi's Store • 815 Market St
415-501-0100
Flagship store with design-your-own jeans
technology.
Out of the Closet • 1295 Folsom St
415-558-7176
Great thrift store benefiting AIDS research.
Podesta Baldocchi • 410 Harriet St
415-346-1300
A San Francisco institution for elegant flowers.

• **REI** • 840 Brannan St
415-934-1938
Outdoor gear co-op.
• **Rolo** • 1301 Howard St
415-578-7139
Hip men's clothes.
• **San Francisco Flower Mart** • 640 Brannan St
415-392-7944
THE wholesale flower market. Opens to the
public at 10 am.
• **SF Design Center** • 2 Henry Adams St
415-490-5800
Browse contemporary furnishings from top
designers.
• **Trader Joe's** • 555 9th St
415-863-1292
Affordable specialty foods.

Map 13 · **Mission Beach**

81X

1

2

45
30
81X

AT&T Park
PAGE
199

8

82X
80X

N

76

McCovey
Cove

Pier 46B

Pier 48C

South
Beach
Harbor

Brannan St.

47
10

CalTrain
Depot 4th &
King

Bluxome St.

China Basin St.

Pier 48

19th St.

King St.

Berry St.

T

Mission Rock
Terminal

A

Mission Creek

Channel St.

15

Owens St.

Mission Rock

12

1000

4th St.

Mission Rock St.

China Basin St.

Pier 52

3rd St.

**MISSION
BAY**

Illinois St.

Pier 54

Pier

14X

Owens St.

7th St.

6th St.

UCSF
Mission Bay

Alameda St.

El Dorado St.

Michigan St.

T

15

16th St.

Pier 66

Hubbell St.

500

17th St.

B

Daggett St.

280

Mariposa

1900

Central Basin

Missouri St.

Texas St.

Mississippi St.

Pennsylvania Ave.

Iowa St.

Mariposa St.

Indiana St.

Minnesota St.

Tennessee St.

18th St.

**POTRERO
HILL**

600

600

22

609

19th St.

22

Port of SF
Northern Cargo Terminals

53

16

House featured
in the movie
Pacific Heights

20th St.

17

20th St.

1/4 mile

.25 km

Map
10 11 12 13
14 15 16 17

On game day Giants fans on their way to **AT&T Park** make the area feel more like a big festival than a neighborhood. If you can't score tickets, stop in at one of the many sports bars just steps from the stadium and you're guaranteed a good time. Baseball is by far the most popular spectator sport in San Francisco—people love it that the players are as quirky and colorful as the locals.

Landmarks

- **AT&T Park** • 24 Willie Mays Plaza
  415-972-2000
  Ball games and concerts. Best place to catch a homerun: on the bay in a kayak.
- **House featured in the movie Pacific Heights** •
  1243 19th St
  Film location of the 1990 movie with Michael Keaton and Melanie Griffith.

Bars

- **Bottom of the Hill** • 1233 17th St
  415-626-4455
  Great live music of all kinds.
- **Café Cocomo** • 650 Indiana St
  415-410-4012
  Salsa club with thrice-weekly dance lessons.
- **The Ramp** • 855 Terry Francois St
  415-621-2378
  Hit the deck on Saturday/Sunday afternoons.

Restaurants

- **Aperto** • 1434 18th St
  415-252-1625 • $$$
  Cute, unpretentious Italian.
- **Chez Papa Bistrot** • 1401 18th St
  415-824-8205 • $$
  Where the homesick French dine.
- **Fringale** • 570 4th St
  415-543-0573 • $$$$
  Excellent French.
- **Hazel's Kitchen** • 1319 18th St
  415-647-7941 • $
  Tiny sandwich joint with a couple of street-front tables.
- **Moshi Moshi** • 2092 3rd St
  415-861-8285 • $$
  Hidden sushi place with tangy miso dressing.
- **Primo Patio Cafe** • 214 Townsend St
  415-957-1129 • $
  Great, affordable local hole-in-the-wall Caribbean food.
- **The Ramp** • 855 Terry Francois St
  415-621-2378 • $$
  Simple food with a great deck. Go on a sunny day.

Shopping

- **ARCH** • 99 Missouri St
  415-433-2724
  They sell cool quirky gifts, too.
- **Christopher's Books** • 1400 18th St
  415-255-8802
  Neighborhood bookshop.
- **Collage Gallery** • 1345 18th St
  415-282-4401
  Crafts for the home by Bay Area artists.
- **K&L Wine Merchants** • 638 4th St
  415-896-1734
  The best wine shop in town. Great selection, including old and rare wines.
- **Ruby Wine** • 1419 18th St
  415-401-7708
  Wine, beer, and gourmet treats.

Protected from the fog by Twin Peaks on one side and the Mission on the other, Noe Valley's clear weather and nicer homes attract a proud population of young families, lesbians, and well-heeled ex-hippies. The *Noe Valley Voice* dishes out the inside scoop on the neighborhood.

Landmarks

Sparky • 20th St & Church St
From this hydrant "came a stream of water allowing the firemen to save the Mission district" in 1906. Annually painted gold by admirers.

Bars

• **The Dubliner** • 3838 24th St
415-826-2279
Casual local Irish bar.
• **Noe's Bar** • 1199 Church St
415-282-4007
Sports bar.
• **Valley Tavern** • 4054 24th St
415-285-0674
Check out the beer garden in back.

Map 14 29 15 16 17 31 32 35 36 3

Restaurants

- **Bacco** • 737 Diamond St
  415-282-4969 • $$$$
  Cozy neighborhood Italian.
- **Barney's Gourmet Hamburgers** •
  4138 24th St
  415-282-7770 • $$
  Good burgers. Better onion rings. Take the kids.
- **Chloe's Café** • 1399 Church St
  415-648-4116 • $$
  Popular Noe Valley brunch spot.
- **Choice Yakiniku** • 5214 Diamond Heights Blvd
  415-206-9755 • $$
  Hole-in-the-wall with friendly service, low prices and wide selection.
- **Eric's Restaurant** • 1500 Church St
  415-282-0919 • $$
  American-Chinese joint serving up fresh dishes, fast.
- **Fattoush** • 1361 Church St
  415-641-0678 • $$$
  Hearty, authentic Middle eastern grub in low-key setting.

- **Firefly** • 4288 24th St
  415-821-7652 • $$$$
  Fantastic, warm, and cozy home-style restaurant.
- **Fresca** • 3945 24th St
  415-695-0549 • $$$$
  Tasty Peruvian.
- **Hamano Sushi** • 1332 Castro St
  415-826-0825 • $$$$
  Neighborhood Japanese.
- **Happy Donuts** • 3801 24th St
  415-285-5890 • $
  Bear claws rule.
- **Incanto** • 1550 Church St
  415-641-4500 • $$$$$
  Fantastic neighborhood Italian.
- **Le Zinc** • 4063 24th St
  415-647-9400 • $$$$
  Parisian-style bistro.
- **Lovejoy's Tea Room** • 1351 Church St
  415-648-5895 • $$
  Classic British tearoom.
- **Pasta Pomodoro** • 4000 24th St
  415-920-9904 • $$
  Fast cheap pasta.
- **Savor** • 3913 24th St
  415-282-0344 • $$
  Crepes, omeletes, frittata, and sandwiches. A brunch favorite.

...u should be able to find everything you need on either 24th Avenue or ...urch Street. Highlights include the **Noe Valley Farmers Market**, ...ggey's Hardware, **PlumpJack Wines**, **Savor** (brunch), **Lovejoy's Tea** ...om, and **Noe Valley Bakery**. It's all good.

Shopping

24th Street Cheese Co. • 3893 24th St
415-821-6658
Gourmet cheese shop.
Ambiance • 3979 24th St
415-647-7144
All the hip local girls shop here.
Astrid's Rabat Shoes • 3909 24th St
415-282-7400
Go see Ronnie if you need some comfort
(shoes).
Church Nails • 1211 Church St
No frills service; bank balance-friendly.
Flowers of the Valley • 4077 24th St
415-970-0579
Long lasting and affordable bouquets.
Holey Bagel • 3872 24th St
415-647-3334
For non-New York bagels, Holey"s are damn
decent.
Joshua Simon • 3915 24th St
415-821-1068
Women's clothes. Normal to plus sizes.
Just for Fun • 3982 24th St
415-285-4068
Whimsical gifts and stationery.

• **Lehr's German Specialties** • 1581 Church St
415-282-6803
All things German.
• **Noe Valley Bakery** • 4073 24th St
415-550-1405
Artisan breads, tasty pastries, and seasonal
loaves.
• **Noe Valley Pet** • 1451 Church St
415-282-7385
Only the best for your pup.
• **PlumpJack Wines** • 4011 24th St
415-282-3841
Great wines at great prices.
• **Rabat** • 4001 24th St
415-282-7861
Women's urban wear, shoes, and accessories.
• **See Jane Run** • 3910 24th St
415-401-8338
Women's athletic gear.
• **Shoe Biz** • 3810 24th St
415-821-2528
Their shoes are the business!
• **Wink SF** • 4107 24th St
415-401-8881
Quirky gifts from around the globe.
• **Xela Imports** • 3925 24th St
415-695-1323
Super selection of sterling silver jewelry.

Map 15 • **Mission**　　N

One of the city's sunniest neighborhoods is also one of its most diverse and dynamic, as post-college neophytes rub shoulders with recent Latin American immigrants. Gentrification, love it or hate it, has made a neighborhood that has historically been the first stop for newcomers to this country into the ultimate go-to for a night of drinking and dining.

Landmarks

- **Balmy Alley** • Balmy St btwn 24th & 25th St
Every garage door in this narrow passage is an artistic statement.

Bars

- **The Attic Club** • 3336 24th St
415-643-3376
Mellow hole in the wall.
- **Bruno's** • 2389 Mission St
415-643-5200
Old-time Mission supper club. Live music.
- **Doc's Clock** • 2575 Mission St
415-824-3627
Mission hipster bar with shuffle board.
- **Dovre Club** • 1498 Valencia St
415-285-4169
Outer Mission dive bar.
- **Foreign Cinema** • 2534 Mission St
415-648-7600
Cool outdoor (and indoor) dining and cocktails where you can catch a talkie in the courtyard.
- **Latin American Club** • 3286 22nd St
415-647-2732
Kick back Mission bar. Pool table.
- **The Liberties** • 998 Guerrero St
415-282-6789
Neighborhood Irish pub and grub.
- **Lone Palm** • 3394 22nd St
415-648-0109
Laid back sleek Mission dive.
- **Make-Out Room** • 3225 22nd St
415-647-2888
Great divey local, alternative live music.
- **Mission Bar** • 2695 Mission St
415-647-2300
The sign says it all: BAR.
- **The Napper Tandy** • 3200 24th St
415-550-7510
Irish dive pub with Wednesday quiz night and Saturday karaoke.
- **The Phone Booth** • 1398 S Van Ness Ave
415-648-4683
Tiny and authentic Mission dive.
- **Pop's** • 2800 24th St
415-401-7677
Pacman, pool, friends, and the neighborhood sketchballs.

- **Red Poppy Art House** • 2698 Folsom St
415-826-2402
Artists' studios, gallery, classroom, performance space. Small and unpretentious.
- **Savanna Jazz** • 2937 Mission St
415-285-3369
New jazz club in the Mission with Afro-Caribbean food.
- **St Vincent** • 1270 Valencia St
415-285-1200
100 well-priced hand-picked wines.

Restaurants

- **Atlas Café** • 3049 20th St
415-648-1047 • $
Hipster café with soups, sandwiches, and wireless access.
- **Beretta** • 1199 Valencia St
415-695-1199 • $$$
Cocktails, thin-crust pizza & Italian comfort food.
- **Big Mouth Burger** • 3392 24th St
415-821-4821 • $
Solid burgers cooked to order. Good fries too.
- **Boogaloos** • 3296 22nd St
415-824-4088 • $
Breakfast joint for the hip and hungover.
- **The Dark Horse Inn** • 942 Geneva Ave
415-469-5508 • $$
Local/craft beer & wine and original pub grub.
- **Dosa** • 995 Valencia St
415-642-3672 • $$
South Indian fare. Mostly vegetarian.
- **El Farolito** • 2779 Mission St
415-824-7877 • $
Looks like a dive, but the tacos and burritos taste like a dream.
- **El Mahajual** • 1142 Valencia St
415-821-7514 • $
Family run Salvadorian-Colombian restaurant.
- **El Metate** • 2406 Bryant St
415-641-7209 • $
Neighborhood gem. Fresh grilled veggie tacos.
- **El Nuevo Frutilandia** • 3077 24th St
415-648-2958 • $$
Zesty Cuban and Puerto Rican. A portal to the Carribean.
- **El Valenciano Restaurant and Bar** •
1153 Valencia St
415-826-9561 • $$
Salsa dancing, Spanish food, and a gi-normous tequila selection.

Map

29 14 **15** 16 17
31 32 35 36 3

- **flour + water** • 2401 Harrison St
  415-826-7000 • $$$
  Modern and classic interpretations to pasta
  and pizza in the Italian bistro.
- **Foreign Cinema** • 2534 Mission St
  415-648-7600 • $$$$
  Cool outdoor (and indoor) dining where you
  can catch a talkie in the courtyard.
- **Garcon** • 1101 Valencia St
  415-401-8959 • $$$
  Friendly French bistro.
- **Herbivore** • 983 Valencia St
  415-826-5657 • $$
  Good, clean, cheap vegetarian.
- **Jay's Cheesesteak** • 3285 21st St
  415-285-5200 • $
  Philly-style cheesesteak.
- **La Espiga De Oro** • 2916 24th St
  415-826-1363 • $
  Top-notch burritos plus extras like tamales,
  pupusas and chicharrones.
- **La Taqueria** • 2889 Mission St
  415-285-7117 • $$
  Good tacos, burritos.
- **Local's Corner** • 2500 Bryant St
  415-800-7945 • $$
  First-rate seafood and California fare.
- **Lolo** • 3230 22nd St
  415-643-5656 • $$
  Turkish-Mexican.
- **Mission Pie** • 2901 Mission St
  415-282-1500 • $
  Sustainable responsibly produced pies and
  social change.
- **Old Jerusalem Restaurant** • 2976 Mission St
  415-642-5958 • $$
  Tasty falafel served by stylish Israeli guys.
- **Papalote** • 3409 24th St
  415-970-8815 • $
  Vegetarian-accommodating Mission taqueria.
- **Pete's Barbeque** • 2399 Mission St
  415-826-1009 • $
  Reliable rotisserie chicken and baked potatoes.

- **Phat Philly** • 3388 24th St
  415-550-7428 • $
  Cheesesteaks with Kobe beef and Amoroso
  rolls. Regular is 7", Phat is 12".
- **Revolution Café** • 3248 22nd St
  415-642-0474 • $
  Bohemian-style cafe/bar with sidewalk patio
  and live music.
- **Roosevelt Tamale Parlor** • 2817 24th St
  415-824-2600 • $$
  Recent make over has dulled the spice.
- **San Jalisco** • 901 S Van Ness Ave
  415-648-8383 • $$
  Popular Mexican brunch.
- **Schmidt's** • 2400 Folsom St
  415-401-0200 • $$
  A delicious new German place for lunch in
  the Mission.
- **Serrano's Pizza** • 3274 21st St
  415-695-1615 • $
  Fresh-made slices, so call ahead.
- **Sidewalk Juice** • 3287 21st St
  415-932-6221 • $
  Smooth Travels.
- **St Vincent** • 1270 Valencia St
  415-285-1200 • $$$
  100 well-priced hand-picked wines.
- **St. Francis Fountain** • 2801 24th St
  415-826-4210 • $
  Good sundaes but no more homemade candy.
- **Taqueria Guadalajara** • 3146 24th St
  415-642-4892 • $
  Skip the lines, savor the flavor. Home of atomic
  habanero salsa.
- **Udupi Palace** • 1007 Valencia St
  415-970-8000 • $$
  Huge dosas; delicious South Indian food at
  equally tasty prices.
- **Velvet Cantina** • 3349 23rd St
  415-648-4142 • $
  Clever desserts.

...querias proliferate here, with 24th Street host to some of the best in the ...ty, including **El Farolito** (open very late) and **La Espiga de Oro**. Coffee is ...uge here, too: try **Ritual**, **Sugarlump**, and **Atlas**. **Aquarius Records** and ...og Eared Books** are de rigueur shopping. **Humphry Slocombe** is ice ...ream heaven.

🛍 Shopping

- **Aquarius Records** • 1055 Valencia St
  415-647-2272
  Independent record shop with all types of music.
- **Arizmendi Bakery** • 1268 Valencia St
  415-826-9218
  Worker-owned cooperative specializing in pastries, breads, and pizza.
- **Back To The Picture** • 934 Valencia St
  415-826-2321
  Custom picture framing for locals in the know.
- **Buffalo Exchange** • 1210 Valencia St
  415-647-8332
  Buy and sell, thrifty.
- **Casa Bonampak** • 1051 Valencia St
  415-642-4079
  Traditional Mexican arts and crafts celebrated in this colorful store.
- **Casa Lucas Market** • 2934 24th St
  415-826-4334
  Latino produce market.
- **Dema** • 1038 Valencia St
  415-206-0500
  60s-inspired threads.
- **Dianda's Italian American Pastry** •
  2883 Mission St
  415-647-5469
  Try their sicilian cookies, tres leches, rum, pineapple, or napoleon cakes!
- **Dog Eared Books** • 900 Valencia St
  415-282-1901
  New and used books, with good local zines.
- **Dynamo Donuts** • 2760 24th St
  415-920-1978
  Three words: maple bacon donuts.
- **Fabric 8** • 3318 22nd St
  415-647-5888
  Rad urban art, plus hip-hop stylings from independent designers.
- **Gravel & Gold** • 3266 21st St
  415-552-0112
  Enjoy handmade creations from local California artists.
- **Gypsy Honeymoon** • 1266 Valencia St
  415-821-1713
  Beautiful, vintage, unique furniture, nick-nacks, and oddities.

- **Hair Candy Salon** • 3387 22nd St
  415-550-8238
  Cosy, creative and (literally) cutting edge.
- **Humphry Slocombe** • 2790 Harrison St
  415-550-6971
  Breakfast done right: (ice) cream (and bourbon) with your cornflakes.
- **Janet Moyer Landscaping** • 1031 Valencia St
  415-821-3760
  By appointment only, high end garden landscaping.
- **Laku** • 1069 Valencia St
  415-695-1462
  Oddball collection of old-timey clothes, nick-nacks, and oddities.
- **Lucca Ravioli** • 1100 Valencia St
  415-647-5581
  Old-fashioned Italian deli.
- **Modern Times Bookstore** • 2919 24th St
  415-282-9246
  Progressive bookstore.
- **Press: Works on Paper** • 3108 24th St
  415-913-7156
  The art of paper, bound and unbound.
- **Retro Fit** • 910 Valencia St
  415-550-1530
  Vintage used clothes and remakes of old t-shirts.
- **Ruby Gallery** • 3602 20th St
  415-550-8052
  This cute boutique, named after owner"s dog, has gifts galore.
- **Scarlet Sage Herb Co.** • 1193 Valencia St
  415-821-0997
- **Streetwise Skate Shop** • 981 Geneva Ave
  415-585-2500
  Relaxed atmosphere, good deals & good people.
- **The Touch** • 2221 Mission St
  415-550-2640
  Mid-century furniture with random curiosities and a retro vibe.
- **Valencia Whole Foods** • 999 Valencia St
  415-285-0231
  Pricey but delicious organic produce, salads, snacks and frozen meals.
- **Vanilla Saffron Imports** • 949 Valencia St
  415-648-8990
  Providers of vanilla and saffron-related products for 30 years!

Map 16 · **Potrero Hill (Southwest)**

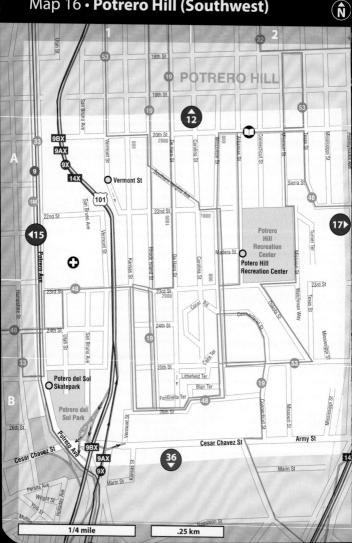

This part of Potrero Hill is predominantly residential, but it's worth an urban hike here up 20th Street to Connecticut or Missouri Streets to take in the postcard-perfect views of downtown and the Bay. The weather here is some of the best in San Francisco, so pickup ball games are often in play at the **Potrero Hill Rec Center**.

O Landmarks

- **Potrero del Sol/La Raza Skate Park** •
  25th St & Utah St
  SF's newest skatepark.
- **Potrero Hill Recreation Center** •
  801 Arkansas St
  See the old OJ Simpson mural, where as a kid The Juice once ran loose.
- **Vermont St** • 20th St & Vermont St
  The actual crookedest street in SF; steeper than Lombard!

Shopping

- **Good Life Grocery** • 1524 20th St
  415-282-9204
  Friendly neighborhood market.

A former working-class/industrial neighborhood in the midst of transformation, this area will look completely different in five years. The impetus for change is largely due to the new Third Street Light Rail and the trickle-down effect of the Mission Bay improvement projects taking place nearby. For the time being, though, there's still not much here.

Bars

- **Dogpatch Saloon** • 2496 3rd St
  415-643-8592
  Comfy bar. Beers on tap.
- **Yield Wine Bar** • 2490 3rd St
  415-401-8984
  Don't it make your red wine green.

Shopping

- **Pro Camera** • 1405 Minnesota St
  415-282-7368
  Camera rentals.

Restaurants

- **Hard Knox Café** • 2526 3rd St
  415-648-3770 • $
  Simple, cheap soul food.
- **Just For You Café** • 732 22nd St
  415-647-3033 • $
  All the breakfast standards, plus beignets.
- **Mr. and Mrs. Miscellaneous** • 699 22nd St
  415-970-0750 • $
  Black sesame, Earl Grey, or salted mango? Ice cream, that is…
- **Piccino** • 1001 Minnesota St
  415-824-4224 • $$
  Excellent flatbread style pizza, salads, and cafe fare. Great for lunch. Miniscule seating.
- **Serpentine** • 2495 3rd St
  415-252-2000 • $$
  Noisy, popular, hip—come for burgers or brunch.

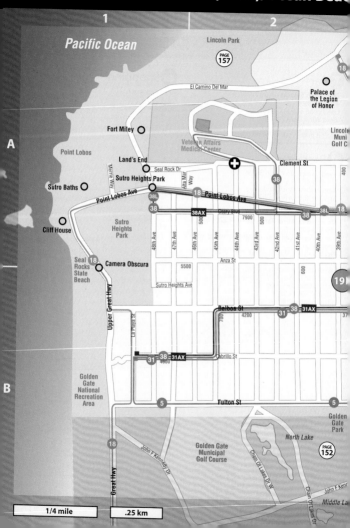

Map 18 **Outer Richmond (West)/Ocean Beach**

1

2

Pacific Ocean

Lincoln Park

PAGE 157

18

El Camino Del Mar

Palace of
the Legion
of Honor

Fort Miley

Point Lobos

Veteran Affairs
Medical Center

Land's End

Lincoln
Muni
Golf C

A

Seal Rock Dr

Clement St

Sutro Heights Park

38

Sutro Baths

Point Lobos Ave

18 **Point Lobos Ave**

400

38L

Merrie Way

Alta Mar Way

38L 18

Cliff House

Point Lobos Ave

38

38AX

Geary Blvd

7900

500

38

Sutro
Heights
Park

500

48th Ave

47th Ave

46th Ave

45th Ave

44th Ave

43rd Ave

42nd Ave

41st Ave

40th Ave

39th Ave

Seal
Rocks
State
Beach

18

Camera Obscura

5500

Anza St

600

19

Sutro Heights Ave

Balboa St

38 31AX

Upper Great Hwy

La Playa St

700

4200

31

37

38 31AX

B

Cabrillo St

31

4800

Golden
Gate
National
Recreation
Area

5

Fulton St

5

Golden
Gate
Park

Great Hwy

John F Kennedy Dr

North Lake

18

Golden
Gate
Municipal
Golf Course

PAGE 152

Chain Of Lakes Dr W

John F Kenn

Chain Of Lakes Dr E

Middle L

1/4 mile

.25 km

Residential and mellow, the periphery of this area is home to some of the city's most regal spots. The **Sutro Baths** ruins echo a bygone time. Stately in form and locale, the **Palace of the Legion of Honor** brims with art from a bygone time. Just north of Ocean Beach is **Cliff House**, a perfect-view brunch spot.

Landmarks

- **Camera Obscura** •
  1096 Point Lobos
  415-750-0415
  Based on a 15th-century Da Vinci invention. Giant camera provides 360-degree views of Seal Rock.
- **Cliff House** • 1090 Point Lobos
  415-386-3330
  Originally built in 1863, then again in 1896,1909, and 2005, it currently houses touristy restaurants and bars with great ocean views.
- **Fort Miley** • El Camino Del Mar & Clement St
  SFSU Adventure Rope Courses at the ruins of old defense batteries.
- **Legion of Honor** • 100 34th Ave
  415-750-3600
  Our prettiest museum. Ancient, European, and decorative arts.
- **Sutro Baths** • Great Hwy & Point Lobos Ave
  Ruins of Alfred Sutro's massive indoor swimming pool complex, 1896.
- **Sutro Heights Park** •
  Point Lobos Ave & 48th Ave
  Ruins of Mayor Alfred Sutro's clifftop mansion.

Restaurants

- **Al-Masri** • 4031 Balboa St
  415-876-2300 • $$$$
  Authentic Egyptian.
- **Beach Chalet** • 1000 Great Hwy
  415-386-8439 • $$$
  Brewpub with a view of Ocean Beach.
- **Hakka Restaurant** • 4401 Cabrillo St
  415-876-6898 • $
  Best postickers in the 'hood.
- **Hunan Cafe 2** • 4450 Cabrillo St
  415-751-1283 • $
  Great neighborhood Chinese with delivery.
- **KL Restaurant** • 4401 Balboa St
  415-666-9928 • $$
  Authentic Chinese, specializes in seafood.
- **Louis'** • 902 Point Lobos Ave
  415-387-6330 • $$
  Cheaper breakfast and better view than Cliff House next door.
- **Seal Rock Inn** • 545 Point Lobos Ave
  415-752-8000 • $$
  "Friendly underwater theme" and view make up for so-so food.
- **Yu Zen** • 4036 Balboa St
  415-386-9800 • $
  Good sushi, good price.

Map 19 • **Outer Richmond (East) / Seacliff** (N)

1

2

Pacific Ocean

South Bay

China Beach

PAGE 185

Gibson Rd

Sea Cliff Ave

Scenic Way

El Camino Del Mar

Golden Gate National Recreation Area

McLaren Ave

W Cla

El Camino Del Mar

Lake St

200

A

PAGE 157

Lincoln Park
Golf Course

Lake St

2800

Sea View Ter

California St

1AX

29

20

18

Legion of Honor Dr

18

300

Marvel
Ct

400

2

Clement St
2700

400

31st Ave

32nd Ave

1

Geary Blvd

38L 18

7000

500

38AX

38L 38

500

25th Ave

24th Ave

38

39th Ave

38th Ave

37th Ave

36th Ave

35th Ave

34th Ave

33rd Ave

30th Ave

29th Ave

28th Ave

27th Ave

26th Ave

400 Ave

38

Shore View Ave

400

Anza St
3600

600

4400

600

2

George
Washington
Park

B

38

31AX

Balboa St

31

RICHMOND

3700

700

31st Ave

700

2800

29

Cabrillo St

25th Ave

Fulton St

Spreckels Lake Dr

30th Ave

Golden Gate Park

PAGE 152

Marx Meadow Dr

1/4 mile

.25 km

eacliff is old money, and that money buys you a mansion with a ridge view. Lincoln Park also has beautiful views (and they're free). Walk from the park's public golf course down to the Lands End Coastal Trail for a dramatic stroll complete with stunning scenery, or find hidden China Beach.

Landmarks

Lincoln Park Golf Course •
34th Ave & Clement St
415-759-3700
Public golf course, built in 1908. Stellar views.

Bars

Tee Off Bar & Grill •
3129 Clement St
415-752-5439
Dive bar with strong drinks and pool table.
Trad'r Sam • 6150 Geary Blvd
415-221-0773
Unpretentious tiki bar.

Restaurants

Bill's Place • 2315 Clement St
415-221-5262 • $
Big burgers, sit at the bar with locals.
Chino's Taqueria • 3416 Balboa St
415-668-9956 • $
Good burrito.
Drunken Sushi • 2311 Clement St
415-876-2311 • $$
Open late, cute servers, pretty sushi.
El Mansour • 3119 Clement St
415-751-2312 • $$$
Moroccan cuisine mixed with belly dancing in the Outer Richmond.
Jang Soo BBQ • 6314 Geary Blvd
415-831-8282 • $$
Very good Korean BBQ. Friendly and clean.

- **Oyaji Restaurant** •
  3123 Clement St
  415-379-3604 • $$
  Very good sushi.
- **Pacific Café** • 7000 Geary Blvd
  415-387-7091 • $$$
  If there's a wait they'll give you a free glass of wine.
- **Pizzetta 211** • 211 23rd Ave
  415-379-9880 • $
  Vera pizza napolitana.
- **Simple Pleasures Café** •
  3434 Balboa St
  415-387-4022 • $
  Have a cup of joe, play a game, argue politics.
- **The Sweet House** • 3512 Balboa St
  415-876-1388 • $
  Bubble tea, taro smoothies.
- **Zephyr Cafe** • 3643 Balboa St
  415-221-6063 • $
  Huge coffeehouse, low on atmosphere.

Shopping

- **AK Meats** • 2346 Clement St
  415-933-6328
  Butcher shop with cracking pastrami sandwiches.
- **Gaslight & Shadows Antiques** •
  2335 Clement St
  415-387-0633
  Rare yet affordable antiques.

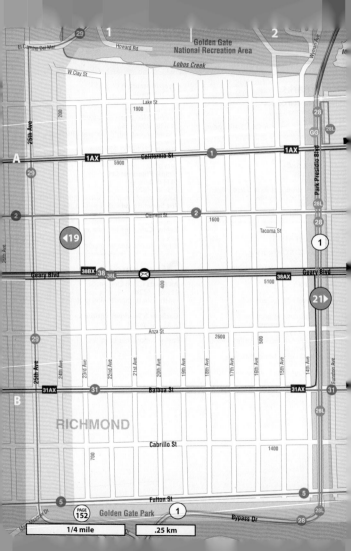

Geary is where the action is in this ethnically diverse zone. Avoid problematic parking by taking the 38-Geary (the most-used city bus). Geary and 25th is the center of the SF Russian immigrant community; score pierogi at a grocery and shop for cheap fruits and veggies at the plentiful Asian markets.

🍸 Bars

- **Blarney Stone** • 5625 Geary Blvd
415-386-9914
Irish sports bar. Darts.
- **Tommy's Mexican Restaurant** •
5929 Geary Blvd
415-387-4747
Legendary margaritas!

🍴 Restaurants

- **Aziza** • 5800 Geary Blvd
415-752-2222 • $$$$
Modern versions of Moroccan classics.
- **Cafe Enchante** • 6157 Geary Blvd
415-251-9136 • $
Parisian-themed cafe.
- **Creations Dessert** • 5217 Geary Blvd
415-668-8812 • $
Mmmm—I want some glutinous rice balls.
- **Kabuto Sushi** • 5121 Geary Blvd
415-752-5652 • $$$$
Fresh, consistent sushi.
- **Khan Toke Thai House** • 5937 Geary Blvd
415-668-6654 • $$$
Thai with a garden.
- **Kitaro** • 5723 Geary Blvd
415-386-2777 • $$
Satisfies the sushi craving. Go for the rolls.
- **La Vie** • 5830 Geary Blvd
415-668-8080 • $$$
Tasty Vietnamese.
- **Lou's Cafe** • 5017 Geary Blvd
415-379-4429 • $
Creative sandwiches and friendly service.
- **Mescolanza** • 2221 Clement St
415-668-2221 • $$$
Wonderful neighborhood Italian.
- **Tia Margarita** • 300 19th Ave
415-752-9274 • $$$
Traditional Northern Mexican food.
- **Tommy's Mexican Restaurant** •
5929 Geary Blvd
415-387-4747 • $$$
Terrific tequila, fair food.
- **Ton Kiang** • 5821 Geary Blvd
415-387-8273 • $$$
Authentic Chinese and good dim sum.

🛍 Shopping

- **Blackwell's Wines & Spirits** • 5620 Geary Blvd
415-386-9463
Best Scotch/bourbon selection around.
- **Hobby Company of San Francisco** •
5150 Geary Blvd
415-386-2802
Independent source for craft and hobby supplies.
- **Kawaii Corner** • 5406 Geary Blvd
415-666-3826
Sanrio and San-X cuteness.
- **Purple Skunk** • 6037 Geary Blvd
415-668-7905
Skate, surf, and snowboard gear.
- **San Francisco Brewcraft** • 1555 Clement St
415-751-9338
Everything you need to make beer!

Map 21 • **Inner Richmond**

This neighborhood has grown to be one of the city's premier eating and drinking destinations, so always allow extra time for parking. Lower rents have brought an influx of the young and hip looking for their San Francisco Days. Bordered by GGP to the south and the Presidio and Mountain Lake Park to the north, outdoor activities (and fog) abound.

Landmarks

- **Congregation Emanu-El** • 2 Lake St
  415-751-2535
  Jewish temple built in a Byzantine-Roman fusion style.

Bars

- **540 Club** • 540 Clement St
  415-752-7276
  Classic local dive showcasing art, DJs, and irreverent theme parties.
- **Abbey Tavern** • 4100 Geary Blvd
  415-221-7767
  Irish pub and sports bar. Live music and TVs.
- **The Bitter End** • 441 Clement St
  415-221-9538
  Cozy, neighborhood Irish bar. Fireplace, pool tables, pinball, darts.
- **Buckshot Restaurant, Bar and Gameroom** • 3848 Geary Blvd
  415-831-8838
  Get shots and play some shuffleboard!
- **Dirty Trix Saloon** • 408 Clement St
  415-387-1400
  Pub.
- **Ireland's 32** • 3920 Geary Blvd
  415-386-6173
  Irish pub and live music.
- **Neck of the Woods** • 406 Clement St
  415-387-6343
  Live music for a fratty crew.
- **The Plough and the Stars** • 116 Clement St
  415-751-1122
  More Irish than a head of cabbage…and the body of potato.
- **Would You Believe?** • 4652 Geary Blvd
  415-752-7444
  A bit weird. Not as weird as the name, but still…weird.

Map 2
...ond

🍴 Restaurants

- **B Star Bar** • 127 Clement St
  415-933-9900 • $$$
  Burma Superstar offshoot, takes reservations.
- **Bella Trattoria** • 3854 Geary Blvd
  415-221-0305 • $$$
  Friendly neighborhood Italian.
- **Boudin** • 399 10th Ave
  415-221-1210 • $
  Bread bowl anybody?
- **Brother's** • 4128 Geary Blvd
  415-387-7991 • $$$
  Cook-it-at-your-table Korean.
- **Burma Superstar** • 309 Clement St
  415-387-2147 • $$
  OMG! The hype is totally justified.
- **Cafe Bunn Mi** • 417 Clement St
  415-668-8908 • $
  Simple Vietnamese sandwiches.
- **Cafe La Flore** • 1032 Clement St
  415-386-2814 • $
  French-press coffee and homemade soups.
- **Caffe del Sole** • 4342 California St
  415-386-1800 • $
  Great coffee and cheap Italian eats.
- **Chapeau!** • 126 Clement St
  415-750-9787 • $$$$$
  Great neighborhood French.
- **Cinderella Russian Bakery and Café** •
  436 Balboa St
  415-751-9690 • $$
  Yummy desserts and traditional Russian
  dishes.
- **Eats** • 50 Clement St
  415-751-8000 • $
  Fresh juices, salads, sammies.

- **Giorgio's Pizza** • 151 Clement St
  415-668-1266 • $$
  Great pizza.
- **Katia's Russian Tea Room** • 600 5th Ave
  415-668-9292 • $$$
  Traditional Russian tea room and restaurant.
- **King of Thai** • 346 Clement St
  415-831-9953 • $$
  Standard neighborhood Thai.
- **King of Thai** • 639 Clement St
  415-752-5198 • $$
  Standard neighborhood Thai that sets the
  standard.
- **Le Soleil** • 133 Clement St
  415-668-4848 • $$$
  Casual, clean-tasting Vietnamese.
- **Little Vietnam Café** • 309 6th Ave
  415-876-0283 • $
  Cheap and tasty sandwiches.
- **Mai's Vietnamese Restaurant** •
  316 Clement St
  415-221-3046 • $$
  Classic, traditional Vietnamese institution.
- **Mandalay** • 4348 California St
  415-386-3895 • $$
  Southeast Asian cuisine.
- **Nizario's Pizza** • 3840 Geary Blvd
  415-752-7777 • $$
  Hot and cheap + good beer.
- **Q** • 225 Clement St
  415-752-2298 • $$$
  Funky American comfort food.
- **The Richmond** • 615 Balboa St
  415-379-8988 • $$$
  Cozy local spot offering attentive service and
  top-notch food.
- **Spices I** • 294 8th Ave
  415-752-8884 • $$
  Stinky tofu, flaming red oil = yum.

s all here, everything from coffee shops, liquor stores, hardware stores,
okstores (**Green Apple**), and pet shops to several Irish pubs, rock 'n roll
ves (**540 Club**), organic juice bars, and some of the city's best ethnic
teries—**Burma Superstar**, **Spices I & II**, **Cinderella Russian Bakery** and
other's Korean BBQ.

9

23 24 25 29

Map

- **Spices II** • 291 6th Ave
  415-752-8885 • $
  Funky little Szechuan café. Good chow, cheap.
- **Star India** • 3721 Geary Blvd
  415-668-4466 • $$
  Great buffet.
- **Sushi Bistro** • 445 Balboa St
  415-933-7100 • $$
  Mellow vibe, amazing combos, decent service.
- **Tanuki Sushi** • 4419 California St
  415-752-5740 • $$
  Inexpensive and fresh sushi.
- **Tawan's Thai** • 4403 Geary Blvd
  415-751-5175 • $
  When they say "hot," take them seriously.
- **To Hyang** • 3815 Geary Blvd
  415-688-8186 • $$
  Best Korean in the Bay.
- **Tong Palace** • 933 Clement St
  415-668-3988 • $$
  Cantonese standby.
- **Toy Boat Dessert Café** • 401 Clement St
  415-751-7505 • $
  25-cent rocking horse and vintage toys keep
  kiddies busy.
- **Troya** • 349 Clement St
  415-379-6000 • $$
  Turkish deliciousness.
- **Uncle Boy's** • 245 Balboa St
  415-742-4468 • $
  Fab neighborhood burger joint.
- **Velo Rouge Café** • 798 Arguello Blvd
  415-752-7799 • $
  Biker-friendly café along the Arguello bike
  path.
- **Wing Lee Bakery** • 503 Clement St
  415-668-9481 • $
  Dim sum.

🛍 Shopping

- **April in Paris** • 55 Clement St
  415-750-9910
  Leather goods and purses by appointment
  only.
- **Arguello Supermarket** • 782 Arguello Blvd
  415-751-5121
  Get the turkey on dutch crunch sandwich!
- **First Korean Market** • 4625 Geary Blvd
  415-221-2565
  Kimchi, bulgogi, shumai ad nauseum.
- **Green Apple Books** • 506 Clement St
  415-387-2272
  Get lost in here for hours, literally.
- **Heroes Club: The Art of Toys** •
  840 Clement St
  415-387-4552
  Sci-fi and anime action figures.
- **Kamei Restaurant Supply** • 547 Clement St
  415-666-3699
  Cheap things for the chef.
- **Kumquat Art** • 147 Clement St
  415-752-2140
  Local art and jewelry.
- **Park Life** • 220 Clement St
  415-386-7275
  Retail and art gallery. Kitschy and cool
  gadgets.
- **Richmond New May Wah Supermarket** •
  707 Clement St
  415-221-9826
  Large Asian grocery saves a scouring of
  Chinatown.
- **Schubert's Bakery** • 521 Clement St
  415-752-1580
  Exquisitely crafted cakes.
- **Sloat Garden Center** • 327 3rd Ave
  415-752-1614
  All kinds of plants and gardening supplies.
- **Super Tokio** • 251 Clement St
  415-668-1118
  Your source for Asian junk food.

Map 22 • Presidio Heights / Laurel Heights

PRESIDIO

Golden Gate
National Recreation Area
PAGE
154

West Pacific Ave.
Roos House
Jackson St   3400

Washington St   200
Clay St   3500
Sacramento St

PRESIDIO HEIGHTS

California St
1BX   1AX   3300

Mayfair Dr
Heather Ave
Iris Ave
Manzanita Ave
Laurel St   1AX — 31AX
                                  31BX
                                  1AX — 31AX
                                  31BX

Euclid Ave
Palm Ave
Jordan Ave
Commonwealth Ave
Parker Ave
Spruce St
Cook St
Blake St
Collins St
Emerson St
Wood St
Lupine Ave
Masonic Ave
5

21

Bridge
Theater
Geary Blvd
31AX 38AX 38BX   3000
Sonora Ln
Leona Ter
43
GG

Neptune Society of
Northern California
Almaden Ct
Loraine Ct
Stanyan St 100
Beaumont Ave
Anza St
Ewing Ter
John Way
O'Farrell St
Vega St
Anza

University of
San Francisco
Lone Mountain Ter
Parker Ave
Beaumont Ave
31BX
Blood Centers of
the Pacific Fountain

Edward St
Rossi Ave

31 31BX
Golden Gate Ave
Temescal Ter
Chabot Ter
Kittredge Ter
Turk St
Joseph Ter
Tamalpais Ter
Annapolis Ter
Golden Gate Ave
43

Golden Gate Ave
Paramount Ter
Parsons St
Willard St
University of
San Francisco
Loyola Ter
Heřman Ter
Aldebaran Ter

McAllister St
McAllister St
St Ignatius
Church
Fulton St   1800

Jefferson
Airplane
House
PAGE
152
5 9
Grove St
Ashbury St
Clayton St
21

1/4 mile   .25 km

This upscale part of the city features distinctive neighborhoods. Mansions border the Presidio in the Pacific Heights section (visit the **Roos House**), while Laurel Heights, south of California Street, is a quiet mix of apartments and town houses. Hike up to the University of San Francisco perched high on the hill for 360-degree views.

O Landmarks

- **Blood Centers of the Pacific Fountain** •
  270 Masonic Ave
  415-567-6400
  Most consistently-flowing, unnaturally-blue fountain in the city.
- **Bridge Theater** • 3010 Geary Blvd
  415-267-4893
  1939 Art Deco theater showing indie and foreign films.
- **Jefferson Airplane House** • 2400 Fulton St
  Mortuary turned music mansion.
- **Neptune Society of Northern California—San Francisco** • 1 Loraine Ct
  415-771-0717
  Neoclassical building and repository of burial ashes, including remains of prominent San Francisco figures.
- **Roos House** • 3500 Jackson St
  Classic Bernard Maybeck house in Pacific Heights.
- **St. Ignatius Church** • 650 Parker Ave
  415-422-2188
  Jesuit Baroque architecture parish in its fifth incarnation, now on University of San Francisco campus.

Bars

- **Pig & Whistle** • 2801 Geary Blvd
  415-885-4779
  Cozy pub where Guiness is poured the right way.

Restaurants

- **Lucky Penny** • 2670 Geary Blvd
  415-921-0836 • $
  If you weren't already going to barf at 3 am…
- **Magic Flute Garden Ristorante** •
  3673 Sacramento St
  415-922-1225 • $$
  Hidden neighborhood brunch spot.
- **Mel's Drive-In** • 3355 Geary Blvd
  415-387-2255 • $$
  Diner food, great for kids. Anybody see
  American Graffiti?
- **Osteria** • 3277 Sacramento St
  415-771-5030 • $$
  Quiet neighborhood Italian. Jammed.

- **Pancho's Salsa Bar & Grill** • 3440 Geary Blvd
  415-387-8226 • $
  Really good non-authentic Mexican food.
- **Papalote** • 1777 Fulton St
  415-776-0106 • $
  Healthy enough burritos.
- **Rigolo** • 3465 California St
  415-876-7777 • $$
  French bakery café with great breakfast menu.
- **Sociale** • 3665 Sacramento St
  415-921-3200 • $$$$
  Upscale, casual patio dining.
- **Spruce** • 3640 Sacramento St
  415-931-5100 • $$$$
  Cal-French splurge spot.
- **Twilight Cafe** • 2600 McAllister St
  415-386-6115 • $
  The BEST hummus and super-friendly service.

fornia and Sacramento Streets are the destination for boutique pping and specialty foods. Try **Bryan's** for excellent meat and fish. ary Boulevard has the ethnic-shopping bargains—and, of course, **Pig &** istle.

Shopping

A.G. Ferrari Foods • 3490 California St
415-923-4470
Italian food and wine and wonderful deli items.

Bedroom Outlet • 2901 Geary Blvd
415-387-7892
Need a mattress? Friendly service, family run, great prices.

Books Inc. • 3515 California St
415-221-3666
Great store events!

Bryan's Quality Meats • 3473 California St
415-752-3430
Best place to buy meat, fish, and poultry in San Francisco.

- **Button Down** • 3415 Sacramento St
415-563-1311
Beautiful and pricey clothing for men and women.
- **Day One** • 3490 California St
415-440-3291
Strollers, slings, books, bottles, breastpumps, and parent classes.
- **The Grocery Store** • 3625 Sacramento St
415-928-3615
High-end casual women's clothes.
- **Kendall Wilkinson** • 3419 Sacramento St
415-409-2299
Upscale homewares and furniture.
- **Mom's the Word** • 3385 Sacramento St
415-441-8261
Funky maternity clothes.
- **Trader Joe's** • 3 Masonic Ave
415-346-9964
Affordable specialty foods.

ear-round, hardcore surfers hold ground (and water) at Ocean Beach, while bikers and joggers frequent the seaside paths on the Great Highway. The eternal fog gives the residential Outer Sunset a stigma that is refuted by sunny beach days during Indian Summer. Residents here like to live on the edge—of the contiguous United States, that is.

Bars

- **Flanahan's Pub** • 3805 Noriega St
  415-665-2424
  Serious dive bar for serious drinkers who get seriously drunk.
- **Pittsburgh's Pub** • 4207 Judah St
  415-664-3926
  The single most frightening bar ever. You MUST go.

Restaurants

- **El Beach Burrito** • 3914 Judah St
  415-731-2004 • $
  Burritos.
- **Java Beach** • 1396 La Playa St
  415-665-5282 • $
  Beachfront café with strong coffee and large subs. Bring a windbreaker.
- **Outerlands** • 4001 Judah St
  415-661-6140 • $$
  A warm oasis of bread and soup.
- **Pisces** • 3414 Judah St
  415-564-2233 • $$$
  Cheaper than downtown food, better than SOMA food.
- **The Pizza Place on Noriega** • 3901 Noriega St
  415-759-5752 • $
  Surfside pies: The Spicoli comes with double-cheese and sausage.
- **Polly Ann Ice Cream** • 3138 Noriega St
  415-664-2472 • $
  Asian-themed frozen fare. Try the durian, if you dare.
- **Sea Breeze Café** • 3940 Judah St
  415-242-6022 • $
  Almost perfect neighborhood diner.
- **Thanh Long** • 4101 Judah St
  415-665-1146 • $$$$$
  Vietnamese roasted crab and garlic noodles.

Shopping

- **General Store** • 4035 Judah St
  415-682-0600
  Beautifully curated one-of-a-kind home things.
- **The Last Straw** • 4540 Irving St
  415-566-4692
  Local artisan jewelry.
- **Other Avenues** • 3930 Judah St
  415-661-7475
  Highest concentration of hippies outside the Haight.

This gridded neighborhood—"The Avenues"—houses much of San Francisco's middle class (and shrouds them in fog during the summer). Many of the family homes were built after World War II by Henry Doelger, who favored uniformity. Some residents have even been known to try their keys on the wrong house.

🍸 Bars

- **Chug Pub** • 1849 Lincoln Way
  415-242-9930
  Have a hankering for an easy lay? Check out the Dub.
- **Durty Nelly's** • 2328 Irving St
  415-664-2555
  Irish pub with a fireplace.
- **The Taco Shop @ Underdogs** • 1824 Irving St
  415-566-8700
  Because watching sports without tacos would be stupid.

🍴 Restaurants

- **Café Bakery** • 1365 Noriega St
  415-661-6116 • $
  Hungry and poor? Get a BBQ pork bun.
- **Chabaa Thai** • 2123 Irving St
  415-753-3347 • $
  Homey Thai haven.
- **Izakaya Sozai** • 1500 Irving St
  415-742-5122 • $$
  Japanese small plates.
- **Marnee Thai** • 2225 Irving St
  415-665-9500 • $$$
  Above-average Thai.
- **Shangri-La** • 2026 Irving St
  415-731-2548 • $$
  Vegetarian Chinese.
- **Sunrise Deli** • 2115 Irving St
  415-664-8210 • $
  Homey Palestinian deli. Really fresh falafel.
- **Underdog** • 1634 Irving St
  415-665-8881 • $
  Kid-friendly vegan hot dogs.

🛍 Shopping

- **The Hard Wear Store** • 2401 Irving St
  415-682-9565
  Ocean Beach hoodies and Sunset tee-shirts. Represent.
- **Sunset Music** • 2311 Irving St
  415-731-1725
  Everything a brilliant musician needs, and lessons for the not-so brilliant.
- **Sunset Soccer Supply** • 3401 Irving St
  415-753-2666
  Everything soccer.
- **Wonderful Foods Co.** • 2035 Irving St
  415-731-6889
  Snack foods, candy, and tapioca drinks here.

Map 25 • **Inner Sunset / Golden Gate Heights**

UCSF's proximity guarantees a young-ish crowd, bars, and ample cheap food, but simultaneously keeps things quiet—cozy side streets and reliable fog make it easy to stay in and study. Runners and picnickers love the short jaunt to Golden Gate Park's trails and meadows.

🍸 Bars

- **Blackthorn** • 834 Irving St
  415-564-6626
  Cozy Irish pub. Darts.
- **Fireside Bar** • 603 Irving St
  415-731-6433
  Yes, this dive bar does have a working fireplace.

- **The Little Shamrock** • 807 Lincoln Way
  415-661-0060
  Must love Guinness and darts.
- **Mucky Duck** • 1315 9th Ave
  415-661-4340
  Ugly people and dartboards. England in SF.
- **Yancy's Saloon** • 734 Irving St
  415-665-6551
  Sports-y Sunset bar.

Restaurants

- **Arizmendi Bakery** • 1331 9th Ave
  415-566-3117 • $
  Fresh bread and gourmet pizza. Cheeseboard's sister co-op.
- **Art's Cafe** • 747 Irving St
  415-665-7440 • $$
  The hashbrown sandwich will cure any hangover.
- **Baan Thai House** • 534 Irving St
  415-519-2858 • $$
  Modern, cool Cal-Thai spot.
- **Crepevine** • 624 Irving St
  415-681-5858 • $
  Crepes for any time of day.
- **Ebisu** • 1283 9th Ave
  415-566-1770 • $$$$
  Quality sushi.
- **Enjoy Vegetarian Restaurant** •
  754 Kirkham St
  415-682-0826 • $$
  Unpretentious Chinese for herbivores.
- **Gordo Taqueria** • 1239 9th Ave
  415-566-6011 • $
  Rock-solid burritos, fantastic take-out salsa.
- **Hahn's Hibachi** • 535 Irving St
  415-731-3721 • $$
  Pile o' Pork and Meat Mountain say it all.
- **Hotei** • 1290 9th Ave
  415-753-6045 • $$
  Friendly Japanese with great soba and udon noodles.
- **Howard's** • 1309 9th Ave
  415-564-4723 • $
  Breakfast 'til 3 pm.
- **Irving Street Cafe** • 716 Irving St
  415-661-1366 • $
  Cheap breakfasts, good hash browns.
- **Kazu Sushi** • 841 Irving St
  415-681-5539 • $$
  Fresh sushi and cold sake.
- **Kiki** • 1269 9th Ave
  415-661-5522 • $
  Cheap sushi that will make you smile.
- **Koo** • 408 Irving St
  415-731-7077 • $$$
  Upscale sushi pleasures.
- **Lavash** • 511 Irving St
  415-664-5555 • $$
  For your fast-food Persian fix.
- **Manna** • 845 Irving St
  415-665-5969 • $
  Homestyle Korean.
- **Marnee Thai** • 1243 9th Ave
  415-731-9999 • $$$
  This location is roomier and the food's just as good.
- **Milano Pizzeria** • 1330 9th Ave
  415-665-3773 • $
  Pizza place for pizza placeophiles.
- **Naan-N-Curry** • 642 Irving St
  415-664-7225 • $
  Indian on the cheap.
- **New Eritrea Restaurant** • 907 Irving St
  415-681-1288 • $$
  Warm and friendly staff.
- **Nopalito** • 1224 9th Ave
  415-233-9966 • $$
  Upscale Mexican regional food.
- **Pacific Catch** • 1200 9th Ave
  415-504-6905 • $$
  Try the Hawaiian Poke and sweet potato fries.
- **Park Chow** • 1240 9th Ave
  415-665-9912 • $$
  American comfort food with a great atmosphere.
- **Pasion** • 737 Irving St
  415-742-5727 • $$
  Sexy Peruvian.
- **Peasant Pies** • 1039 Irving St
  415-731-1978 • $
  Fresh hand-held pies. Savory and sweet. Meal + dessert.
- **Pluto's** • 627 Irving St
  415-753-8867 • $$
  Made-to-order salads are the key attraction.
- **San Tung Chinese Restaurant** • 1031 Irving St
  415-242-0828 • $$
  Sino chicken wings.
- **Yumma's** • 721 Irving St
  415-682-0762 • $
  Fast Mediterranean-gyros, shawarma, hummus, etc.
- **Yummy Yummy** • 1015 Irving St
  415-566-4722 • $
  Casual pho and Vietnamese hang.

Map 25

e action is on 9th Avenue and Irving Street. Try **Ebisu** for sushi and **izmendi Bakery** for superb scones. Get a buzz at the **Beanery** or play unken backgammon at **The Little Shamrock**. For shopping, check out **shbone**'s novelty knick-knacks. Parking here is scarce—try Bowling een Drive across Lincoln Way.

🛍 Shopping

- **Alaya** • 1256 9th Ave
  415-731-2681
  Hip and casual women's clothing.
- **Amazing Fantasy** • 650 Irving St
  415-681-4344
  For the serious collector.
- **Andronico's** • 1200 Irving St
  415-661-3220
  Another good spot for fancy groceries.
- **Cheese Boutique** • 1298 12th Ave
  415-566-3155
  Nice little cheese shop.
- **Crossroads Trading Co.** • 630 Irving St
  415-681-0100
  Mecca of re-sale clothing.
- **The Great Overland Book Company** •
  345 Judah St
  415-664-0126
  General used, California history.

- **Holy Gelato!** • 1392 9th Ave
  415-681-3061
  Biodegradable containers!
- **Irving Variety** • 647 Irving St
  415-731-1286
  Endearing garage-sale charm.
- **Le Video** • 1231 9th Ave
  415-566-3606
  Offers a huge selection of eclectic movie rentals.
- **Misdirections Magic Shop** • 1236 9th Ave
  415-566-2180
  All the magic anyone needs.
- **On the Run** • 1310 9th Ave
  415-665-5311
  Orthopedic foot heaven.
- **Wishbone** • 601 Irving St
  415-242-5540
  Eclectic items for personal and home use.

The **San Francisco Zoo** is the main attraction in this part of town, and the daily penguin feedings at 10:30 and 3:30 are all the rage. Taraval Street along the Metro L line has some action, but the urban landscape becomes almost entirely residential as the road approaches ocean sand. The **Doggie Diner Head** suspended at Sloat and 45th adds a hallucinatory touch to a quiet corner of the city.

Landmarks

- **Doggie Diner Head** • Sloat Blvd at 45th Ave
  Head of fast food chain mascot, now SF landmark.
- **San Francisco Zoo** • 1 Zoo Rd
  415-753-7080
  250 species spread out over 100 acres along Great Highway.

Bars

- **The Riptide** • 3639 Taraval St
  415-681-8433
  Last great bar before the ocean.

Restaurants

- **Bashful Bull Too** • 3600 Taraval St
  415-759-8112 • $
  Breakfast basics.
- **Java Beach at the Zoo** • 2650 Sloat Blvd
  415-731-2965 • $
  Peckish after the beach or zoo? Here's your spot.
- **North Beach Pizza** • 3054 Taraval St
  415-242-9100 • $$
  Good local chain pizza.
- **Old Mandarin Islamic** • 3132 Vicente St
  415-564-3481 •
  Muslim Chinese food, specializing in hot pot.
- **Sunset's Best Seafood Restaurant** •
  3060 Taraval St
  415-681-2899 • $$
  Excellent Chinese seafood.

Shopping

- **Aqua Surf Shop** • 2830 Sloat Blvd
  415-242-9283
  Boards and gear.
- **Sloat Garden Center** • 2700 Sloat Blvd
  415-566-4415
  All kinds of plants and gardening supplies.
- **Sunset Supermarket** • 2801 Vicente St
  415-504-8188
  Quintessential Asian supermarket.

This is a quiet and modest neighborhood with **Stern Grove** at its heart. During summer Sundays, the area is jammed with people going to the Grove's free concerts. Parking is usually decent in affluent neighboring St. Francis Wood.

⭕ Landmarks

- **Sigmund Stern Grove** • 19th Ave & Sloat Blvd
  415-252-6252
  Free concerts in the summer, Sundays at 2 pm.
- **Stonestown Galleria** • 3251 20th Ave
  415-564-8848
  Large shopping center.

🍸 Bars

- **Costello's Four Deuces** • 2319 Taraval St
  415-566-9122
  Your wild Irish rose is here, drunk off her ass, singing karaoke.
- **Grandma's Saloon** • 1016 Taraval St
  415-665-7892
  Local dive for those seeking to destroy their livers.
- **Shannon Arms** • 915 Taraval St
  415-665-1223
  Fog, fights, frat boys, and fiddles.

🍴 Restaurants

- **Eight Immortals** • 1433 Taraval St
  415-731-5515 • $$
  Good neighborhood Chinese restaurant.
- **El Burrito Express** • 1601 Taraval St
  415-566-8300 • $
  Small burrito shop.
- **King of Thai** • 1541 Taraval St
  415-682-9958 • $$
  Standard neighborhood Thai.
- **Kingdom of Dumpling** • 1713 Taraval St
  415-566-6143 • $
  No-frills hole in the wall for dumplings.
- **Ming's Diner** • 2129 Taraval St
  415-242-0811 • $$
  Chinese.
- **Ristorante Marcello** • 2100 Taraval St
  415-665-1430 • $$
  Like a North Beach refugee cooling it in the Sunset.
- **Shin Toe Bul Yi** • 2001 Taraval St
  415-566-9221 • $
  Friendly neighborhood Korean place.
- **The Spot Lounge** • 2325 Taraval St
  415-564-4464 •
  Pan-Asian fusion.
- **Szechuan Taste** • 917 Taraval St
  415-681-8383 • $
  Super-cheap, spicy Chinese.

🛍 Shopping

- **Apple Store** • 3251 20th Ave
  415-571-2780
  iParadise for Mac fanatics.
- **Bella Blue** • 549 Taraval St
  415-702-9470
  Exquisite kids threads.
- **L'Occitane** • 3251 20th Ave
  415-665-2863
  Wonderful French soaps.
- **Marco Polo Italian Ice Cream** •
  1447 Taraval St
  415-731-2833
  Tropical flavors.
- **Stonestown Galleria** • 3251 20th Ave
  415-564-8848
  120 stores in this urban mall.

1/2 mile   .5 km

San Francisco State University, Lake Merced (great for running, biking, and boating), and the renovated **Harding Park Golf Course** dominate this area. **Fort Funston** is also nearby; take your puppy for play dates above the beach and watch the hang gliders. Aside from college parties, the area is quiet at night.

◯ Landmarks

- **Fort Funston** • Skyline Blvd & John Muir Dr
415-561-4323
Cliffside view of coast—excellent hang-gliding and hiking.

🍴 Restaurants

- **Xiao Long** • 250 West Portal
415-753-5678 • $
Spicy dry-fried chicken.

Forest Hill and Twin Peaks are posh, hilltop, residential islands with big lots and lots of green. Smack dab in the middle of the city, the epic view from Twin Peaks can be the best in town—but strong winds often bring in thick fog in the evening. Look for enticing stair walks to really explore all the nooks and crannies of this area.

○ Landmarks

- **Seward Street Slides** •
  Douglass St & Seward St
  Make like you're 12! Bring some cardboard.
- **Sutro Tower** • 250 Palo Alto Ave
  Giant antenna in a wealthy 'hood.
- **Tank Hill** • Twin Peaks Blvd & Crown Terrace
  Hilltop park. Look into people's backyards 300'
  below, and view both bridges.
- **Twin Peaks** • Twin Peaks Blvd
  City's geographical center, arguably the best
  nightime panoramic view.
- **UCSF Parnassus Campus Library** •
  530 Parnassus Ave
  415-476-2334
  Best views of any university library in the
  world (from the ocean to downtown). Public
  admission.

Restaurants

- **Lime Tree** • 450 Irving St
  415-665-1415 • $
  It's cheap and good, but don't come here in
  a hurry.
- **Pomelo** • 92 Judah St
  415-731-6175 • $$$
  Rice, noodle, and grain dishes with global flair.
- **Tower Burger** • 729 Portola Dr
  415-504-6340 • $$
  Niman Ranch beef burgers and Mitchell's ice
  cream shakes.
- **The Yellow Submarine** • 503 Irving St
  415-681-5652 • $
  Very decent East-Coast-style subs.

Hop the K-L and M MUNI Metro and head through the tunnel. The "Main Street" is a classic, somewhat lost in time strip of shops and restaurants catering to the quiet, laid-back middle class residents. To the south is the exclusive, mansion-studded enclave of St. Francis Wood.

🍸 Bars

- **Philosopher's Club** • 824 Ulloa St
  415-753-0599
  After a few drinks all the women look like Simone de Beauvoir.
- **Que Syrah** • 230 W Portal Ave
  415-731-7000
  A place you can imagine even Doris Day getting drunk.

🍴 Restaurants

- **Ambrosia Bakery** • 2605 Ocean Ave
  415-334-5305 • $
  Princess cake and mousse cake—next question?
- **Bullshead Restaurant** • 840 Ulloa St
  415-665-4350 • $$
  The buffalo head over the door should give you a clue.
- **Bursa** • 60 W Portal Ave
  415-564-4006 • $$
  Turkish food makes you glad for meat.
- **Chouchou** • 400 Dewey Blvd
  415-242-0960 • $$$
  Cozy French bistro with Provencal feel.
- **El Toreador** • 50 W Portal Ave
  415-566-2673 • $$
  Standard Mexican, very friendly.
- **Fresca** • 24 W Portal Ave
  415-759-8087 • $$$$
  Tasty Peruvian.
- **Manor Coffee Shop** • 321 W Portal Ave
  415-661-2468 • $$
  Diner food, good for breakfast.
- **Market & Rye** • 68 W Portal Ave
  415-564-5950 • $$
  Signature "Salted Rye" bread; sandwiches require knife.
- **Mozzarella di Bufala** • 69 W Portal Ave
  415-661-8900 • $$
  Pizza and Brazilian food, together at last.
- **Rain Tree Café** • 118 W Portal Ave
  415-242-9000 • $$
  Standard café menu. No frills, no crowds.
- **Roti Indian Bistro** • 53 W Portal Ave
  415-665-7684 • $$$
  A feast of authentic, refined Indian cuisine in warm setting.
- **Submarine Center** • 820 Ulloa St
  415-564-1455 • $
  Best sandwiches in town.

🛍 Shopping

- **Ambassador Toys** • 186 W Portal Ave
  415-759-8697
  Global games for kids.
- **Goodwill Boutique** • 61 W Portal Ave
  415-665-6304
  Isn't that an oxymoron?
- **Growing Up** • 240 W Portal Ave
  415-661-6304
  Books and toys for kids.
- **Guerra Quality Meats** • 490 Taraval St
  415-564-0585
  Meat straight from the beast. Butchers straight from Italy.
- **Simply Bella** • 159 W Portal Ave
  415-661-1777
  Fun and stylish Euro-design, clothes, shoes, and accessories.
- **Two Cats Comic Book Store** • 320 W Portal Ave
  415-566-8190
  Anime, sci-fi, and more with knowledgeable and keen staff.

Standing tall at nearly 1000 feet, Mt Davidson is the highest point in the city. Covered in eucalyptus and blackberry on the sea-side and dry grass to the east, a 103-foot-high controversial giant cross commemorating the Armenian genocide tops the hill—you'll recognize it from *Dirty Harry*. In between here and Glen Canyon is a residential neighborhood spilling down the hillside.

Landmarks

• **Mount Davidson Cross** • 125 Dalewood Way
Controversial symbol embodied in a 103'
concrete and steel structure inaugurated
by FDR.

Restaurants

• **Shanghai Dumpling King** •
696 Monterey Blvd
415-387-2088 • $
Fast. Hot. Delicious.

Map
27 30 31 32 35
28 33 34 38

hough adjacent, these neighborhoods are worlds apart in vibe and weather. Diamond Heights, with its boxier, modern, ho-hum apartments and homes, is requently foggy but offers stellar views. Sunny Glen Park, in the valley below, s a friendly "village" with narrow, winding streets, charming restaurants, cafes, ookshops as well as enchanting, older homes. BART and the multi-use Glen anyon Park are close to both.

Landmarks

Children's Art at Glen Canyon • Glen Canyon
Freaky public art.
Sunnyside Conservatory • 236 Monterey Blvd
Nature unleashed on an old Victorian.

Bars

Glen Park Station • 2816 Diamond St
415-333-4633
Neighborhood bar.

Restaurants

• **Alice's** • 1599 Sanchez St
415-282-8999 • $$
Chinese. Similar to Eric's.
• **Chenery Park** • 683 Chenery St
415-337-8537 • $$$$
Chic American food.
Joe's Cable Car • 4320 Mission St
415-334-6699 • $$$
"Joe grinds his own fresh chuck daily."
La Ciccia • 291 30th St
415-550-8114 • $$
Sardinian take on Italian fare.
La Corneta Taqueria • 2834 Diamond St
415-469-8757 • $$
Great tacos and burritos.
• **Le P'tit Laurent** • 699 Chenery St
415-334-3235 • $$$
Classic French bistro.
• **Noeteca** • 1551 Dolores St
415-824-5524 • $$
Comfortable and familiar neighborhood spot;
rustic, yet classy.

• **Pomelo** • 1793 Church St
415-285-2257 • $$$
Rice, noodle, and grain dishes with global flair.
• **Pop's Sandwich Shop** • 737 Portola Dr
415-681-9501 • $
"Free Bird" Thanksgiving dinner in a bun.
• **Regent Thai** • 1700 Church St
415-643-5893 • $$
Above average Thai at ridiculously cheap
prices.
• **Spicy Bite** • 3501 Mission St
415-647-4036 • $$
Rockin' chicken masala with Bollywood movies
playing in background.
• **Tyger's** • 2798 Diamond St
415-239-4060 • $
Busy breakfast joint on the weekends.

Shopping

• **Canyon Market** • 2815 Diamond St
415-586-9999
Gourmet supermarket with prices to match.
• **Cheese Boutique** • 666 Chenery St
415-333-3390
Cheese, cheese, cheese!
• **Manila Oriental Market** • 4175 Mission St
415-337-7272
Buy live frogs, fresh fish, and oriental treats in
this Outer Mission Asian.
• **Thrillhouse Records** • 3422 Mission St
No Phone
Non-profit, volunteer-run, punk rock record
and 'zine store.

Ingleside Terraces, to the west, is more upscale; in Ingleside proper you're more likely to see single-family homes and street corners decorated with discarded mattresses and swirls of garbage floating around. It's still relatively safe, though—just not particularly exciting, although changes are afoot on Ocean Avenue.

O Landmarks

• **Ingleside Terraces Sundial** •
Borica St & Entrada Ct
Massive 28' white sundial erected in 1913 to lure young families to developments south of the city center commotion.

 Bars

• **The Ave** • 1607 Ocean Ave
415-587-6645
Proudly serving the Champagne of Beers for 2 bucks a pop.

Restaurants

• **Yama Sushi** • 850 Holloway Ave
415-333-2889 • $$
This corner's been cursed before, but we've got a winner.

San Francisco City College is the main player in this sleepy residential, working-class neighborhood. A collection of various high schools contributes to the demographic, which includes Balboa Park and the BART station. With I-280 and some large thoroughfares, Oceanview (which doesn't really have an ocean view) is a well-connected transit hub.

Restaurants

- **Beep's Burgers** • 1051 Ocean Ave
  415-584-2650 • $$
  Throwback drive-in with meaty burgers and thick-cut fries.
- **Java Creperie** • 1125 Ocean Ave
  415-333-3771 • $
  Great coffee and sandwiches near City College.
- **Reinas Restaurant** • 5479 Mission St
  415-585-7694 • $
  Great pupusas, crappy service.

Map 35

Tucked away beneath Bernal Heights Park and its commanding views of downtown and the Bay, Bernal Heights is perhaps San Francisco's best-kept neighborhood secret. Cortland Avenue has everything a lazy afternoon-into-evening could require: bookshops, hair salons, gourmet restaurants, and even an overgrown back-yard beer garden. Nice.

○ Landmarks

- **Alemany Farmers Market** • 100 Alemany Blvd
  415-647-9423
  Oldest in town. Mixed crowd on Saturdays in the sunny colorful parking lot supporting family-owned farms.

▼ Bars

- **3300 Club** • 3300 Mission St
  415-826-6886
  Poetry readings.
- **El Rio** • 3158 Mission St
  415-282-3325
  Latin dive, racially and sexually mixed.
- **The Knockout** • 3223 Mission St
  415-550-6994
  Pretty people, cheap drinks— "Let the good times roll!"
- **Roccapulco** • 3140 Mission St
  415-648-6611
  One of the oldest Latin clubs in town, great for salsa.
- **Stray Bar** • 309 Cortland Ave
  415-821-9263
  The make-out room is in back. Own it.
- **Vino Rosso** • 629 Cortland Ave
  415-647-1268
  Mamma mia! That's a spicy meatball.
- **Wild Side West** • 424 Cortland Ave
  415-647-3099
  Western and Victorian, but not country. Fireplace. Check out the backyard.

Restaurants

- **Angkor Borei** • 3741 Mission St
  415-550-8417 • $$
  Neighborhood Cambodian.
- **Baby Blues BBQ** • 3149 Mission St
  415-896-4250 • $$
  Order the Mason-Dixon, chicken and Memphis ribs.
- **The Blue Plate** • 3218 Mission St
  415-282-6777 • $$$$
  Great, cozy, American food.
- **El Patio** • 3193 Mission St
  415-641-5056 • $
  Salvadoran pupusas.
- **El Zocalo** • 3230 Mission St
  415-282-2572 • $
  Edible flowers, plantains times infinity.
- **Emmy's Spaghetti Shack** • 18 Virginia Ave
  415-206-2086 • $$$
  The specialty is spaghetti and meatballs, just like it sounds.
- **The Front Porch** • 65 29th St
  415-695-7800 • $$$
  Gastropub simple fare with Caribbean influence.
- **Goood Frikin' Chicken** • 10 29th St
  415-970-2428 • $
  Yummy chicken and mac 'n' cheese.
- **Hillside Supper Club** • 300 Precita Ave
  415-285-6005 • $$$$
  Successful pop-up leveraged Kickstarter to open brick & mortar restaurant.
- **Jasmine Tea House** • 3253 Mission St
  415-826-6288 • $$
  Nothing fancy, but you'll crave it later.
- **The Liberty Café** • 410 Cortland Ave
  415-695-8777 • $$$
  Wonderful neighborhood restaurant serving home-style food.
- **Little Nepal** • 925 Cortland Ave
  415-643-3881 • $$$
  Go crazy with Tandoori at this Nepali café.
- **Mitchell's Ice Cream** • 688 San Jose Ave
  415-648-2300 • $
  City favorite. Scooping exotic flavors since the '50s.
- **Moki's Sushi & Pacific Grill** • 615 Cortland Ave
  415-970-9336 • $$$
  Creative sushi with a Hawaiian twist.
- **Taqueria Cancun** • 3211 Mission St
  415-550-1414 • $
  The food here's good.
- **Zante Pizza & Indian Cuisine** •
  3489 Mission St
  415-821-3949 • $$
  Naan bread pizzas with Indian toppings.

Ber

rnal brims with restaurants for every taste and budget: from gourmet
mfort food at **The Blue Plate** to **Taqueria Cancun** or **Zante Pizza &**
dian Cuisine. After dinner, treat yourself to some tropical ice cream at
itchell's, see live music at **El Rio**, or tie one on at the lesbian-friendly **Wild**
de West.

🛍 Shopping

- **Alemany Flea Market** • 100 Alemany Blvd
415-647-2043
Spend your Sunday finding antique treasures
at this popular flea.
- **Badger Books** • 401 Cortland Ave
415-648-5331
New and used books to buy or trade.
- **Bernal Beast** • 509 Cortland Ave
415-643-7800
Pet supplies and grooming.
- **Big Lots** • 3333 Mission St
415-648-5256
Discount goods, no ambiance, great deals on
staples and housewares.
- **Chloe's Closet** • 451 Cortland Ave
415-642-3300
Hand-me downs for the only child.
- **Cole Hardware** • 3312 Mission St
415-647-8700
Committed to helping the community.

- **The Cottage Bakery** • 410 Cortland Ave
415-695-1311
Bread pudding at a cottage bakery can't be
missed.
- **East & West Gourmet Afghan Foods** •
108 Medburn St
925-687-0817
Bolani: flat bread with spinach, lentil and
hummus. Nice.
- **Heartfelt** • 436 Cortland Ave
415-648-1380
Cute and gifty things you don't really need.
- **Sandbox Bakery** • 833 Cortland Ave
415-642-8580
For those not so concerned with calories.
- **Succulence Life and Garden** •
402 Cortland Ave
415-282-2212
Succulent plants galore, garden goodies and
stylized plantings.

(123)

ne new-ish 3rd St MUNI T Light Rail Line has made this neighborhood
more accessible, and revitalization has continued apace, although the
ea can still be sketchy at night. The **Bayview Opera House** hosts
ultural events, community gatherings, films, classes, and other artistic
roductions.

Landmarks

Bayview Opera House • 4705 3rd St
415-824-0386
Performing arts training for kids.
Flora Grubb Gardens • 1634 Jerrold Ave
415-626-7256
8,000-square foot, solar-paneled building
housing many a flowering plant.

Bars

Sundance Saloon • 550 Barneveld Ave
415-820-1403
Bay Area's premier LGBT country western
dance spot.

Restaurants

- **Bonanza Restaurant** • 16 Toland St
  415-647-2227 • $$
  An oasis; jukebox, heavy pours and plenty of
  parking.
- **Breakfast At Tiffany's** • 2499 San Bruno Ave
  415-468-0977 • $
  Hole-in-the-wall with diverse clientele & big
  portions; yum.
- **Frisco Fried** • 5176 3rd St
  415-822-1517 • $$
  Sassy soul food; finger lickin' fried chicken
  and waffles.
- **La Laguna** • 3906 3rd St
  415-401-9420 • $
  Cavernous taqueria with extensive menu.
- **The Old Clam House** • 299 Bayshore Blvd
  415-826-4880 • $$$
  Old School Seafood. Est. 1861.
- **Radio Africa & Kitchen** • 4800 3rd St
  415-420-2486 • $$$
  African-influenced farm-to-table cuisine.
- **Sam Jordan's Bar** • 4004 3rd St
  415-282-4003 • $$
  Large racks of ribs, friendly crowd and stiff
  drinks.
- **Soo Fong** • 3801 3rd St
  415-285-2828 • $
  Decent Chinese in Bayview Plaza shopping
  center.

Shopping

- **San Francisco Wholesale Produce Market** •
  2095 Jerrold Ave
  415-550-4495
  More than 30 vendors on a 25-acre facility.
- **SCRAP (Scrounger's Center for
  Reusable Art Parts)** • 801 Toland St
  415-647-1746
  Scroungers Center for Reusable Art Parts.

working shipyard and the site of the US's first dry dock, this area is a curious mix of industry and open space. Bayfront access for fishing and kayaking and trails for biking make this area an unusual urban gem. Recent attempts to revitalize this economically challenged sector of the city have been bumpy, but artists flock here for cheap studios and the gritty ambiance.

Landmarks

Hilltop Park Skate Bowl • Hilltop Park
"The Dish." Classic 70s skateboard saucer

Bars

Speakeasy Ales & Lagers • 1195 Evans Ave
415-642-3371
Independent microbrewery.

Restaurants

• **Wok-In Cafeteria** • 50 Mendell St
415-550-7200 • $
Cheap, all-you-can-eat Chinese buffet open for lunch only.

Shopping

• **Building REsources** • 701 Amador St
415-285-7814
Non-profit building salvage emporium.

The neighborhood where Jerry Garcia grew up is one of the city's up-and-coming quarters. Accessible by BART, and often sunny when the fog rolls in, Mission Street is chock-full of Asian, Latino and Old SF shops and restaurants. McLaren Park is a huge, untapped resource and the new Crocker Amazon turf soccer fields are like a Central American fiesta on Saturdays.

Landmarks

- **Crocker Amazon Skate Park** •
1600 Geneva Ave
Single large skateboard bowl.

Bars

Broken Record • 1166 Geneva Ave
415-963-1713
Outer Mission chill spot with great food.
Geneva Pub • 1196 Geneva Ave
415-452-9913
Comfy smoky vibe, mostly Asian crowd.

Restaurants

- **Beijing Restaurant** • 1801 Alemany Blvd
415-333-8182 • $$
Authentic, zesty fare, free parking and free delivery.
- **North Beach Pizza** • 4787 Mission St
415-586-1400 • $$
Good local chain pizza.

Shopping

- **Casa Lucas** • 4555 Mission St
415-334-9747
Cheap produce, cheeses, etc. in this Latin American market.
- **El Chico Produce No 2** • 4600 Mission St
415-587-6025
Fresh and cheap Mexican produce and groceries.

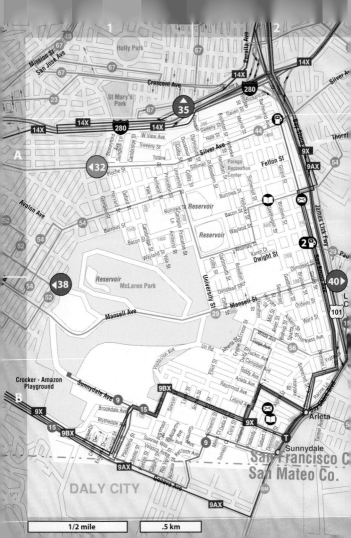

Respite from fog makes this hilly area appealing, and modest, somewhat affordable homes have attracted the most diverse population in the city, from new immigrants to young families looking for starter homes.

Restaurants

- **Hawaiian Drive Inn** • 2600 San Bruno Ave
  415-656-0998 • $$$
  Authentic island-style lunch plates, BBQ and some Aloha.

- **Imperial Garden Seafood Restaurant** • 2626 San Bruno Ave
  415-468-9333 • $$
  Dim Sum, a bit grungy, nothing to rave about but often packed.

- **Queens Louisiana Po' Boy Cafe** • 3030 San Bruno Ave
  415-656-0711 • $$
  Unique stuffed Louisiana style sandwiches and Crescent City specialties.

Map 4

The MUNI 3rd Street Rail Line has made this area more accessible, but it is still not a great lure for out of towners. Artists thrive here and the windsurfers congregate off Candlestick Point. "Croix de Candlestick" buttons are a thing of the distant past, the Giants having long since left **Candlestick Park**, and now that the 49ers have decamped to Santa Clara, there's little left to capture your imagination save for a remarkable YouTube clip of Dwight Clark's "The Catch."

○ Landmarks

• **Candlestick Point State Recreation Area** •
Carroll Ave & Arelious Walker Dr
415-671-0145
Windsurfing, picnicking, community gardens.

Bars

• **Monte Carlo** • 1705 Yosemite Ave
415-822-7338
Mardi Gras year round.

Restaurants

• **B&J 1/4 lb Burgers** • 6202 3rd St
415-467-4560 • $
Former drive-in with handmade no-swearing signs.
• **El Azteca Taqueria** • 5298 3rd St
415-822-1460 • $
Heaviest burritos in town. Try the steak and ham.
• **Limon Rotisserie** • 5800 3rd St
415-926-5665 • $$
Lomo saltado and chicha morada, while listening to Latin lounge music.

Shopping

• **Leeling Import & Export** • 5534 3rd St
415-822-4082
Underground oil painting shop with an abundance of deals. Owner paints as you browse.

EL CERRITO

KENSINGTON

Sunset View Cemetery

Summit Reservoir

Charles Lee Tilden Regional Park

El Cerrito Plaza

Fairmount Ave

Canyon Rd

Grizzly Peak Blvd

Lake Anza

San Pablo Ave

Key Route Blvd

Contra Costa Co

Alameda Co

Colusa Ave

Arlington Ave

Marin Ave

Albany Hill Park

Solano Ave

Tilden Regional F Golf Cour

ALBANY

Marin Ave

Sutter St

Spruce St

Golden Gate Fields Racetrack

University of California

Hopkins St

Berkeley (East)

PAGE 138

Gilman St

Cedar St

Oxford St

San Pablo Ave

80

580

North Berkeley

University Ave

Berkeley

UC Berkeley

PAGE 170

Bancroft Wy

Durant Ave

Clark Ke Campus

Berkeley Marina

6th St

123

Berkeley (West)

PAGE 136

Dwight Wy

Grove St

Sacramento St

Grove Park

Shattuck Ave

13

College Ave

Aquatic Park

San Pablo Park

Ashby Ave

Ashby

Telegraph Ave

Claremont Ave

Alcatraz Ave

Adeline St

Rockridge

San Francisco Bay

Stanford Ave

Broadway

Powell St

24

EMERYVILLE

OAKLAND

1 mile

1 km

Overview

The city of Berkeley, famous for its university and seismically sensitive land, has a long history of community activism. And while the memory of radical ideas still permeates the air, as you get closer to the center and its many academic establishments (besides the UC, there are also the Graduate Theological Union, Vista Community College, and various vocational schools), you're now more likely to encounter a Starbucks than a protest. Shattuck Avenue, the commercial street that runs the length of the city, hosts a staggering array of restaurants and bars (but beware: prices increase as you move further north). Telegraph Avenue, extending southward from campus, is where the out-of-towners shop, the punks beg, and the freshmen scat. Most of the properties in North Berkeley are occupied by studious grad students who don't even have time to enjoy their fabulous views; West Berkeley is a residential mecca; and artistic creativity thrives in gritty South Berkeley. Each neighborhood has a different feel, but the city has an almost unmatched cohesive pride.

Berkeley coffee shops, once hotbeds of activism, have made a seamless transition into 21st-century café culture: Brewed Awakening (1807 Euclid Ave) is filled with students typing papers; at Au Coquelet (2000 University Ave) you can play scrabble and get a hot meal until 1am; at the Free Speech Movement Café (Moffit Undergraduate Library, UC Berkeley Campus) you can learn about Berkeley's most famous social movement and sip a great latte; and you can sit and blog away your concerns at Caffe Strada (2300 College Ave). Visit the original Peet's Coffee & Tea (2124 Vine St) for a strong cup of joe and a taste of a true Berkeley institution.

For cultural experiences, there is no shortage of activity: La Peña (3105 Shattuck Ave) hosts performing arts showcases, poetry slams, and documentaries with a focus on Latin American politics and culture. Next door, Starry Plough slams poetry on Wednesdays over a pint of Guinness. At Ashkenaz (1317 San Pablo Ave) you can rock your body to world and roots music. The Pacific Film Archive, located on campus, screens rare and rediscovered prints of movie classics, new and historic works by great international film directors, restored silent films, and indie fiction and documentaries. On-stage entertainment in this town ranges from neighborhood theater companies like the Shotgun Players and the nationally renowned Berkeley Repertory Theatre to original punk rock at 924 Gilman.

Food

Famous for both its fancy eateries like Chez Panisse, and its cheap on-the-go bites like La Burrita, Berkeley offers the palate variety that mirrors the diversity of the town's population. Visit the Farmers Market (Sat, Tues, Wed, Thurs; check www.ecologycenter.org/fm for locations) for organic veggies, tree-ripened fruits, and handmade artisan breads. Sit on the grass and have delicious mango sticky rice at Thai Temple's popular Sunday Brunch (Russell St & MLK Jr Wy). Order a slice of gourmet vegetarian pizza at The Cheese Board (1504 Shattuck Ave), or try the Chicago-style deep dish at Zachary's (1853 Solano Ave). If you're looking for the perfect sandwich, visit Elmwood Café (2900 College Ave), and don't miss the homemade quiche. While you're at it, ask any of the college kids, and they won't deny: no outing is complete without a cheap, low-fat indulgence at Yogurt Park (2433 Durant Ave).

Outdoors

To get away from the rumble, walk up Euclid Avenue. Extraordinary views of San Francisco across the Bay will accompany you on your stroll. Less than a mile uphill sits the Rose Garden, and then, through the tunnel, you'll discover Cordonices Park's playground and picnic area. If you have a car, explore Tilden Park. Just a bit higher is the expanse of Tilden Park: there's hiking, a golf course, and even Lake Anza with a beach (yes, it's fake). Climbers and sunset-lovers prefer the crags of Indian Rock at the northern end of Shattuck Avenue. For more of the bay's magnificent views, take a relaxing hike or run up the fire trail behind the stadium, past Strawberry Canyon, and pick blackberries on the side of the road (when you get to the bench at the top, continue to Lawrence Berkeley Labs on 1 Cyclotrone Road, or head back down). On the other side of town, you can rollerblade or bike from North Berkeley BART all the way to Richmond on Ohlone Greenway.

How to Get There

With BART stations at Ashby, Downtown, and North Berkeley, and AC Transit running from San Francisco and Oakland, getting to Berkeley on public transportation is easy. However, be aware that BART trains stop running around midnight, and AC Transit service runs on a limited schedule in the late night/early morning hours. If you're arriving by car, exit on University Avenue from I-80 E, or follow Hwy 13 into town from the east. Street parking is tough around campus and on the main drags of Telegraph and Shattuck Avenues, but patience and persistence often pay off. For lot parking, the UC Berkeley parking lots or the Telegraph/Channing Lot (2431 Channing Wy) are always good options, but be sure to get your ticket validated or prices will be steep.

ALBANY

Solano Ave

Golden Gate Fields Racetrack

University of California

Marin Ave

Ramona Ave

Pomona Ave

Key Route Blvd

Santa Fe Ave

Evelyn Ave

Masonic Ave

Francis St

Sonoma Ave

Neilson St

Beverly Pl

Berkeley Skatepark

Harrison St

Dartmouth St

Talbot Ave

Curtis St

Stannage Ave

McGee Ave

Josephine St

Gilman St

Camelia St

Page St

Jones St

Cornell Ave

Stanhope Ave

Kains Ave

Hopkins St

Ada St

Rose St

Vine St

Cedar St

Lincoln St

Virginia St

Francisco St

Deleware St

80

580

6th St

2nd St

123

North Berkeley

Franklin St

Chestnut St

Hearst Ave

Berkeley Wy

Addison St

Spaulding Ave

Jefferson Ave

Sacramento Ave

Bancroft Wy

Roosevelt Ave

McKinley Ave

Grant St

UC Berk

Martin Luther King Jr Wy

Berkeley Marina

University Ave

9th St

7th St

8th St

5th St

4th St

Byron St

10th St

9th St

Curtis St

Acton St

West St

Bonar St

Valley St

Edwards St

Allston Wy

Channing Wy

Dwight Wy

San Pablo Ave

Blake St

Parker St

Carleton St

Derby St

Ward St

California St

McGee Ave

Aquatic Park

Carleton St

Grayson St

Heinz Ave

Anthony St

Potter St

San Pablo Park

Stuart St

Oregon St

Russell St

Julia St

Grove Park

Ashby Ave

Mabel St

Acton St

Dohr St

Stanton St

Tyler St

Prince St

Woolsey St

Fairview St

Harmon St

Ashby

Adeline St

Alcatraz Ave

San Francisco Bay

1/2 mile   .5 km

Festivals & Events

For more information about city-sponsored events, and for individual links for the events listed below, visit www.ci.berkeley.ca.us.

Taste of North Berkeley—Last Tuesday in March. Food and wine fair in the Gourmet Ghetto. 510-540-6444

Cal Day—Saturday in mid-April. Annual UC Berkeley open house for the community; performances, exhibits, lectures, tours, sports events, etc. Contact Visitor Services at 510-642-5215.

Earth Day—Saturday closest to April 22. Festival and Eco-Motion Parade downtown. 510-548-2220.

Berkeley Bay Festival—Saturday in late April or May. Food, music, entertainment, boat tours, and free sailing at the Berkeley Marina. 510-644-8623.

People's Park Anniversary Street Fair & Concert—Late April or early May at the People's Park. 510-644-7729.

Berkeley Arts Festival—First two weeks in May. 510-665-9496.

Fourth of July Celebration—July 4th at the Berkeley Marina. 510-548-5335

Berkeley Kite Festival—Last weekend in July at the Cesar Chavez North Waterfront Park. 510-235-5483.

"How Berkeley Can You Be?" Parade/Festival—Fourth Sunday in September in downtown and North Berkeley. 510-849-4688.

Berkeley Artisans Holiday Open Studios—Four weekends, Thanksgiving into December. 510-845-2612

Off The Grid Street Food Events – Street Food Vendors evening fair; dates and times vary. www.offthegridsf.com

⦾ Landmarks

- **The Berkeley Marina** •
  University Ave & Frontage Rd
- **Berkeley Skate Park** • 5th St & Harrison St

🍸 Bars

- **924 Gilman** • 924 Gilman St
- **Acme Bar & Company** • 2115 San Pablo Ave
- **Albatross Pub** • 1822 San Pablo Ave
- **Ashkenaz** • 1317 San Pablo Ave
- **Lanesplitter** • 2033 San Pablo Ave
- **Missouri Lounge** • 2600 San Pablo Ave
- **Pyramid Alehouse** • 901 Gilman St

🍴 Restaurants

- **900 Grayson** • 900 Grayson St
- **Bette's Oceanview Diner** • 1807 4th St
- **Cactus Taqueria** • 1881 Solano Ave
- **Cafe M** • 1799 4th St
- **Café Rouge** • 1782 4th St
- **Casa Latina** • 1805 San Pablo Ave
- **Everett and Jones** • 1955 San Pablo Ave
- **Gioia Pizzeria** • 1586 Hopkins St
- **Gregoire** • 2109 Cedar St
- **Juan's Place** • 941 Carleton St
- **Kabana** • 1106 University Ave
- **King Tsin** • 1699 Solano Ave
- **Paisan** • 2514 San Pablo Ave
- **Picante** • 1328 6th St
- **Spenger's Fresh Fish Grotto** • 1919 4th St
- **Tacubaya** • 1788 4th St
- **T-Rex Barbecue** • 1300 10th St
- **Vanessa's Bistro** • 1715 Solano Ave
- **Viks Chaat Corner** •2390 4th St
- **Zachary's Pizza** • 1853 Solano Ave
- **Zaki Kabob House** • 1101 San Pablo Ave

🛍Shopping

- **Acme Bread Company** • 1601 San Pablo Ave
- **Berkeley Bowl** • 920 Heinz Ave
- **Berkeley Horticultural Nursery** •
  1310 McGee Ave
- **Fourth Street Shopping District** •
  Cedar St & 4th St
- **The Gardener** • 1836 4th St
- **George** • 1844 4th St
- **La Farine** • 1820 Solano Ave
- **Mignonne** • 2447 San Pablo Ave
- **Monterey Market** • 1550 Hopkins St
- **The North Face Outlet** • 1238 5th St
- **Ohmega Salvage** • 2407 San Pablo Ave
- **Pegasus Books** • 1855 Solano Ave
- **Photolab** • 2235 5th St
- **Sweet Adeline Bakeshop** • 3350 Adeline St
- **Tokyo Fish Market** • 1220 San Pablo Ave
- **Urban Ore** • 900 Murray St

⊙ Landmarks

- **Berkeley Rose Garden** · 1200 Euclid Ave
- **People's Park** · 2556 Haste St

▼ Bars

- **Black Repertory Theatre** · 3201 Adeline St
- **Epic Arts** · 1923 Ashby Ave
- **Jupiter** · 2181 Shattuck Ave
- **La Peña Cultural Center** · 3105 Shattuck Ave
- **The Starry Plough Pub** · 3101 Shattuck Ave
- **Thalassa Bar & Billiards** · 2367 Shattuck Ave
- **Triple Rock Brewery** · 1920 Shattuck Ave

🍴 Restaurants

- **Angeline's Louisana Kitchen** · 2261 Shattuck Ave
- **Blondie's Pizza** · 2340 Telegraph Ave
- **Brazil Café** · 1960 University Ave
- **Cancun Taqueria** · 2134 Allston Wy
- **César** · 1515 Shattuck Ave
- **Cha Am Thai** · 1543 Shattuck Ave
- **The Cheese Board** · 1512 Shattuck Ave
- **Chez Panisse** · 1517 Shattuck Ave
- **Comal** · 2020 Shattuck Ave
- **Crepes Ooh LaLa** · 2125 University Ave
- **Fat Apples** · 1346 Martin Luther King Jr Wy
- **House of Curries** · 2984 College Ave
- **Ippuku** · 2130 Center St
- **Jayakarta** · 2026 University Ave
- **Joshu-ya Brasserie** · 2441 Dwight Way
- **Jupiter** · 2181 Shattuck Ave
- **Kirala** · 2100 Ward St
- **La Burrita** · 1832 Euclid Ave
- **La Note** · 2377 Shattuck Ave
- **Long Life Vegi House** · 2129 University Ave
- **Manpuku** · 2977 College Ave
- **Mitama** · 3201 College Ave
- **PIQ** · 91 Shattuck Sq
- **Revival Bar + Kitchen** · 2102 Shattuck Ave
- **Rick & Ann's Restaurant** · 2922 Domingo Ave
- **Saul's** · 1475 Shattuck Ave
- **Shen Hua** · 2914 College Ave
- **The Smokehouse** · 3155 Telegraph Ave
- **Sushi Ko** · 64 Shattuck Sq
- **Top Dog** · 2534 Durant Ave
- **Trattoria Corso** · 1788 Shattuck Ave
- **Trattoria La Siciliana** · 2993 College Ave
- **Udupi Palace** · 1901 University Ave
- **Wat Mongkolratanaram** · 1911 Russell St
- **Yogurt Park** · 2433 Durant Ave

🛍 Shopping

- **Amoeba Music** · 2455 Telegraph Ave
- **Annapurna** · 2416 Telegraph Ave
- **Berkeley Bowl** · 2020 Oregon St
- **Berkeley Flea Market** · 1937 Ashby Ave
- **Buffalo Exchange** · 2585 Telegraph Ave
- **The Cheese Board Collective** · 1512 Shattuck Ave
- **Crossroads Trading Company** · 2338 Shattuck Ave
- **Jeremy's** · 2967 College Ave
- **Looking Glass Photo** · 1045 Ashby Ave
- **Mars Mercantile** · 2398 Telegraph Ave
- **Moe's Books** · 2476 Telegraph Ave
- **Pegasus Books** · 2349 Shattuck Ave
- **Rasputin Music & DVDs** · 2401 Telegraph Ave
- **Sweet Dreams** · 2901 College Ave
- **Whole Foods Market** · 3000 Telegraph Ave

80

17

PAGE 144

123

Ashby

13

Powell St

Stanford Ave

US Naval
Supply Center

Maritime St

Oakland
Army Base

7th St

W Grand Ave

Peralta St

Oakland West

Mandela Pkwy

Decatur St

Central Ave

Webster St

Naval Airstation
Alameda
Nimitaz Field

Naval
Supply Center
(Alameda
Oakland)

260

PAGE 142

900

19th St/
Oakland

Market St

San Pablo Ave

Martin Luther King Jr Wy

Telegraph Ave

Telegraph Ave

MacArthur

Broadway

Shattuck Ave

Claremont Ave

Rockridge

2

College Ave

College Ave

Claremont
Country Club

Mountain View
Cemetery

Morcom
Rose
Garden

Oakland Ave

Grand Ave

PIEDMONT

Morcom
Amphitheater
of Roses

Oakland Inner Harbor

Downtown Oakland/Lake Merritt

Oakland City
Center/12th St

Lake Merritt

Downtown Oakland /
Lake Merritt

Lake Merritt

Park Blvd

580

OAKLAND

13th Ave

880

Buena Vista Ave

Lincoln Ave

ALAMEDA

61

Grand St

Central Ave

Otis Dr

Park St

Broadway

High St

High St

Foothill Blvd

29th Ave

Fruitvale

Fruitvale Ave

35th Ave

Peralta Hacienda
Historical Park

Lincoln Ave

MacArthur Blvd

San Francisco Bay

BAY FARM
ISLAND

61

Doolittle Dr

San Leandro Bay

Alameda
Municipal
Golf Course

PAGE 210

Oakland
International
Airport

185

San Leandro Blvd

PAGE 200

Coliseum
Complex

Seminary Ave

Foothill Blvd

Seminary

73rd Ave

Coliseum

1 mile

1 km

Overview

San Francisco may be the first place you think of when you hear "city by the bay" but it certainly isn't the only place. Oakland, with its adorable neighborhoods, ethnic diversity, radical history, and eclectic architecture, is as much a destination out here as Brooklyn is in New York City. Travel through Oakland's neighborhoods and you'll find everything from near-ghetto conditions to gentrified warehouse districts, cute bungalow neighborhoods to hillside mansions, city streets, pools, art centers, and a beautiful regional park system in the Oakland hills—perfect for hiking, biking and all things nature.

If you are looking for a day out through some "Oaktown" neighborhoods filled with craftsman bungalows and Victorian homes, boutiques, cafés, bookstores, and the like, try the Rockridge, Temescal, or Piedmont Ave neighborhoods in North Oakland. Check out places like Bittersweet Chocolate Café (everything chocolate), Diesel Books (both in Rockridge), Piedmont Theatre, and Lot 49 (470 49th St), or Bakesale Betty, and Lanesplitter for a unique taste of some of the best Oakland has to offer. Get your art on at Studio One Arts Center (on 45th Street between Broadway and Shafter) where you can find a range of art classes for adults at great prices. For a park-like stroll and a significant history lesson, take the dog for a walk in Mountain View Cemetery (founded in 1863, and designed by none other than Frederick Law Olmsted). Walk by the mansion-like tombs of famous San Franciscans who are the namesakes for such streets as Powell and Stanyan. Famous architect Julia Morgan is buried here alongside common and famous people of all ethnicities, races, and religions.

Oakland's incredible diversity can be found in many of its neighborhoods, including the pan-Asian Chinatown's center at 8th and Webster, the hub of downtown. Since it gets much less tourism than San Francisco's famous Chinatown, this neighborhood has a few less "junk" stores and is perhaps on the more authentic-side. This is the neighborhood to find the best fake-meat restaurants, including the Golden Lotus (on Franklin and 13th), and the Layonna Vegetarian Health Food Market, which sells all the kinds of fake meat you might ever want to try. The Fruitvale neighborhood in East Oakland is home to the cities growing Hispanic community, once named after...you guessed it, fruit orchards. The best Mexican restaurants are Otaez and Mariscos La Costa.

Along International Boulevard between Lake Merritt and Fruitvale are a variety of excellent (and cheap) ethnic restaurants; here you'll find everything from Korean barbecue to carnitas and empanandas. Plan your visit to coincide with the celebrations of Cinco de Mayo or Dia de los Muertos and you'll be in for a real treat.

East of downtown but west of Fruitvale is the hamlet 'hood of Lake Merritt. It is a quick 15-minute walk from downtown, and cozy shops and restaurants can be found tucked away in sloping streets overlooking the water. Looking up at the hills, you can mistake it for a small Mediterranean city. Joggers can be found rounding the lake all day and you'll often see small sail boats, kayaks, and rowboats forging the waters. And once you've made your way around the lake, take a stroll down Lakeshore or Grand Avenues, home to a farmers market every Saturday, and a plethora of restaurants, cafes (check out the workers' co-op Arizmendi Bakery or Walden Pond Books), and shops. Easy Lounge is a perfect place for fresh cocktails post-farmers market. Visit the beautifully restored Grand Lake Theater on a Saturday night to hear the organ played before your movie.

In recent years, downtown Oakland has seen an increase in activity, with notable restaurants, cafés, and cultural centers flourishing along its streets. The Malonga Casquelourd Center, formerly Alice Arts Center, hosts a variety of performances and cultural events. Jack London Square, which used to be a mere tourist trap, is now home to the city's hottest new restaurant, Haven, by star-chef Daniel Patterson. Just east of this area is the city's newer and obtuse warehouse district, where expensive lofts now exist in old warehouses. A loft community of artists, bohemians, intellectuals, and yuppies has colonized the area. You'll find Oakland's best ribs and cornbread at Everett and Jones in Jack London Square and Oakland's best DIY museum/store at Oaklandish (1444 Broadway). Despite what you may have heard, Oakland also has a thriving and varied nightlife scene. While you may want to steer clear of some West Oakland and far East Oakland neighborhoods after dark, the rest of the city can and should be explored. For the upscale set, AIR Lounge (492 9th St) rivals San Francisco's swankiest lounges. Check out Café Van Kleef (1621 Telegraph Ave), the White Horse Bar (the country's second-oldest gay bar) at 6551 Telegraph, and Luka's Taproom & Lounge (2221 Broadway) for a good night out with or without music.

- **Jalisco** · 1721 International Blvd
- **Los Cocos** · 1449 Fruitvale Ave
- **Mariscos La Costa** · 3625 International Blvd
- **Otaez** · 3872 International Blvd
- **Powderface Café** · 3411 E 12th St
- **Taqueria El Farolito** · 3646 International Blvd
- **Quinn's Lighthouse** · 1951 Embarcadero

◯ Landmarks

- **Morcom Rose Garden** · 600 Jean St
- **Peralta Hacienda Historical Park** · 2465 34th Av

▼ Bars

- **Kingman's Lucky Lounge** · 3332 Grand Ave

🍴 Restaurants

- **Brown Sugar Kitchen** · 2534 Mandela Pkwy
- **Camino** · 3917 Grand Ave

🛍 Shopping

- **Mannequin Madness** · 2020 Dennison St
- **Nuherbs** · 3820 Penniman Ave
- **Walden Pond Books** · 3316 Grand Ave

⭘ Landmarks

- **African-American Museum and Library** · 659 14th St
- **Cathedral of Christ the Light** · 180 Grand Ave
- **Children's Fairyland** · 699 Bellevue Ave
- **Creative Growth Art Center** · 355 24th St
- **Malonga Casquelourd Center for the Arts** · 1428 Alice St
- **The Museum of African-American Technology Science Village** · 408 14th St
- **Museum of Children's Art** · 538 9th St
- **Oakland Asian Cultural Center** · 388 9th St
- **Oakland Museum of California** · 1000 Oak St
- **Oakland Public Library—Main Branch** · 125 14th St
- **The Paramount Theatre** · 2025 Broadway St
- **Pro Arts** · Clay St & 2nd St

🍸 Bars

- **AIR Lounge** · 492 9th St
- **Baggy's by the Lake** · 288 E 18th St
- **Café Van Kleef** · 1621 Telegraph Ave
- **Easy Lounge** · 3255 Lakeshore Ave
- **Encuentro** · 550 2nd St
- **Heinold's First and Last Chance** · 48 Webster St
- **Kincaid's** · 1 Franklin St
- **La Estrellita** · 446 E 12th St
- **Luka's Taproom & Lounge** · 2221 Broadway St
- **Radio Bar** · 435 13th St
- **The Ruby Room** · 132 14th St
- **Stork Club** · 2330 Telegraph Ave
- **The Trappist** · 460 8th St
- **Uptown Nightclub** · 1928 Telegraph Ave
- **Yoshi's** · 510 Embarcadero W

🍴 Restaurants

- **Arizmendi** · 3265 Lakeshore Ave
- **Battambang** · 850 Broadway St
- **BC Deli Sandwiches** · 818 Franklin St
- **Boot and Shoe Service** · 3308 Grand Ave
- **Chop Bar** · 247 4th St
- **Duende** · 468 19th St
- **Flora** · 1900 Telegraph Ave
- **Golden Lotus** · 1301 Franklin St
- **Haven** · 44 Webster St
- **Hawker Fare** · 2300 Webster St
- **Holy Land** · 677 Rand Ave
- **House of Chicken & Waffles** · 444 Embarcadero W
- **Kincaid's** · 1 Franklin St
- **Le Cheval** · 1007 Clay St
- **Luka's Taproom & Lounge** · 2221 Broadway St
- **Lynn and Lu's** · 3353 Grand Ave
- **Pho Ga Huong Que Café** · 1228 7th Ave
- **Pican** · 2295 Broadway
- **Plum** · 2214 Broadway
- **Sidebar** · 542 Grand Ave
- **Smart Alec's** · 2355 Telegraph Ave
- **Tamarindo Antojeria** · 468 8th St
- **Yoshi's** · 510 Embarcadero W

🛍 Shopping

- **Bibliomania** · 1816 Telegraph Ave
- **Juniper Tree** · 3303 Lakeshore Ave
- **Layonna Vegetarian Health Food Market** · 443 8th St
- **Oaklandish** · 1444 Broadway
- **Rock, Paper, Scissors Collective** · 430 Orange St

How to Get There

From San Francisco, Highway 80 east over the beautiful Bay Bridge leads to Highways 580, 880, and 980, which go to east, west, and downtown Oakland respectively.

From Contra Costa County, Highway 24 through the Caldecott Tunnel leads to north Oakland.

From the northern part of the East Bay, and from all points east, Highway 80 W leads directly to Oakland.

Almost all entries to Oakland go through the MacArthur Maze. There's terrible commuter traffic, so it's best to avoid it from 7 am to 10 am and 4 pm to 8 pm.

BART and AC Transit have service to Oakland as well. And though you can't ride a bike across the Bay Bridge, Caltran runs a bike shuttle during commute hours between the Transbay Terminal Building in San Francisco and MacArthur BART.

○ Landmarks

- **Mountain View Cemetery** • 5000 Piedmont Ave

▼ Bars

- **Ben & Nick's** • 5612 College Ave
- **Bill McNally's Irish Pub** • 5352 College Ave
- **Cato's Ale House** • 3891 Piedmont Ave
- **Conga Lounge** • 5422 College Ave
- **Egbert Souse's** • 3758 Piedmont Ave
- **George and Walt's** • 5445 College Ave
- **George Kaye's** • 4044 Broadway St
- **Kerry House** • 4092 Piedmont Ave
- **Kona Club** • 4401 Piedmont Ave
- **White Horse Bar** • 6551 Telegraph Ave

▥ Restaurants

- **À Côté** • 5478 College Ave
- **Actual Cafe** • 6334 San Pablo Ave
- **Adesso** • 4395 Piedmont Ave
- **Art's Crab Shak** • 4031 Broadway St
- **Asmara** • 5020 Telegraph Ave
- **Bakesale Betty** • 5098 Telegraph Ave
- **Bar César** • 4039 Piedmont Ave
- **Barlata** • 4901 Telegraph Ave
- **Barney's Gourmet Hamburgers** • 5819 College Ave
- **Bellanico** • 4238 Park Blvd
- **Ben & Nick's** • 5612 College Ave
- **Bucci's** • 6121 Hollis St
- **Burma Superstar** • 4721 Telegraph Ave
- **Café Colucci** • 6427 Telegraph Ave
- **Commis** • 3859 Piedmont Ave
- **Crepevine** • 5600 College Ave
- **Dona Tomas** • 5004 Telegraph Ave
- **Dopo** • 4293 Piedmont Ave
- **Fentons Creamery** • 4226 Piedmont Ave
- **Genova Delicatessen** • 5095 Telegraph Ave
- **Homeroom** • 400 40th St
- **La Calaca Loca** • 5199 Telegraph Ave
- **Lanesplitter** • 4799 Telegraph Ave
- **Little Shin Shin** • 4258 Piedmont Ave
- **Lois the Pie Queen** • 851 60th St
- **Mama's Royal Café** • 4012 Broadway St
- **Nan Yang** • 6048 College Ave
- **Noodle Theory** • 6099 Claremont Ave
- **Oliveto** • 5655 College Ave
- **Pizzaiolo** • 5008 Telegraph Ave
- **Sabuy Sabuy** • 5231 College Ave
- **Soi 4** • 5421 College Ave
- **Southie** • 6311 College Ave
- **Sura** • 4869 Telegraph Ave
- **Wally's Cafe** • 3900 San Pablo Ave
- **Wood Tavern** • 6317 College Ave
- **Zachary's Chicago Pizza** • 5801 College Ave

▣ Shopping

- **Ancient Ways** • 4075 Telegraph Ave
- **Apple Store** • 5656 Bay St
- **Article Pract** • 5010 Telegraph Ave
- **Atomic Garden** • 5453 College Ave
- **Café Mariposa & Bakeshop** • 5427 Telegraph Ave
- **Crossroads Trading Co.** • 5636 College Ave
- **Diesel Bookstore** • 5433 College Ave
- **Fentons Creamery** • 4226 Piedmont Ave
- **Issues** • 20 Glen Ave
- **Itsy Bitsy** • 5520 College Ave
- **Lot 49** • 470 49th St
- **Maison d'Etre** • 5640 College Ave
- **Mariposa** • 5427 Telegraph Ave
- **Pegasus Books** • 5560 College Ave
- **Rockridge Market Hall** • 5655 College Ave
- **Rockridge Rags** • 5711 College Ave
- **Teacake Bake Shop** • 5615 Bay St
- **Trader Joe's** • 5700 Christie Ave

Things to Do

Oakland Museum of California •
1000 Oak St at 10th;
Lake Merritt BART station, 510-238-2200;
www.museumca.org
A wonderful museum dedicated to the art, history, and culture of California.

Joaquin Miller Park
Joaquin Miller Rd (entrance about 1 mile from Highway 13), 510-238-3481; www.oaklandnet.com/parks/facilities/parks_joaquin_miller.asp
A beautiful park in the Oakland Hills, it has some of the oldest redwood groves in the East Bay.

Grand Lake Theatre
3200 Grand Ave (near MacArthur and 580); 510-452-3556;
www.renaissancerialto.com/current/grandlake.htm
This theater, built in 1926, shows first-run movies. The political statements on the marquee are definitely worth driving by for as is the spectacular sign.

Parkway Theatre
1834 Park Blvd, 510-814-2400; www.picturepubpizza.com
California's first speakeasy now shows older movies to movie-goers sitting on large comfy couches and lounge chairs.

Children's Fairyland
699 Bellevue Ave, 510-452-2259; www.fairyland.org/info.html

Amazing playground destination for kids right on Lake Merritt.

Old Oakland Farmers Market
9th St (b/w Broadway & Clay St), 510-745-7100
Every Friday, 8 am–2 pm. Get your fresh fruits, veggies, and prepared foods.

Pro Arts East Bay Open Studios
510-763-4361; www.proartsgallery.org
The East Bay's longest-running and largest open studios event. Take a self-guided tour of hundreds of Oakland artists' studios the first weekends in June.

Woodminster Amphitheatre
3300 Joaquin Miller Rd, 510-531-9597;
www.woodminster.com
This outdoor amphitheater sits deep in the Oakland Hills in Joaquin Miller Park, and has been home to the annual Woodminster Summer Musicals for the last 40 years. Pack a picnic and blanket and visit Oakland's theater under the stars.

General Information

Websites: www.ci.sausalito.ca.us
              www.sausalito.org

Overview

Just over the Golden Gate lies picturesque Sausalito. With a mere 7,500 residents. by most standards it's a small town. However, its numbers swell during the summertime as tourists arrive by the ferryload and day-trippers fill the narrow sidewalks.

Sausalito is a beautiful spot, enjoying unsurpassed views of the city across the bay. The southern part of town along Bridgeway is chockablock with souvenir shops, boutiques, galleries, and overpriced cafés, as well one terrific bar, No Name Bar; the local scene can be found a short walk away on Caledonia Street, which is full of great restaurants like Sushi Ran (107 Caledonia St, 415-332-3620), where you'll find the best sushi in the entire Bay Area, foodies. Sausalito is host to many street fairs and festivals throughout the year, from art shows to chili cook-offs. The town is also home to a unique community of floating homes—approximately 400 houseboats in all—some of them tiny one-room abodes, others magnificent mansions on the water.

How to Get There

Head north on US 101 over the Golden Gate Bridge, and take the first exit (Alexander Ave). Follow Alexander 1.5 miles downhill into town. Better yet, take a ferry: the Blue & Gold Fleet (415-705-5555; www.blueandgoldfleet.com) from Fisherman's Wharf or Golden Gate Ferry (415-455-2000; www.goldengateferry.org) from the Ferry Building in downtown San Francisco. Even better, ride a bike—the ride across the bridge is thrilling (for its views and for its close encounters with tourists on rental bikes), and the descent into Sausalito is fast. Most casual riders prefer to take the ferry back instead of climbing back out.

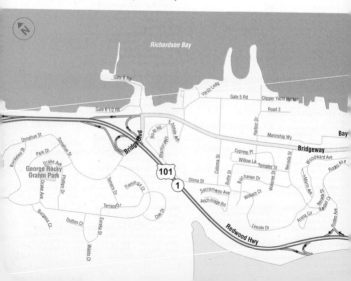

O Landmarks

- **Bay Model Visitor Center** · 2100 Bridgeway

Bars

- **No Name Bar** · 757 Bridgeway
- **Smitty's Bar** · 214 Caledonia St

Restaurants

- **Avatars** · 2656 Bridgeway
- **Feng-Nian** · 2650 Bridgeway
- **Fish.** · 350 Harbor Dr
- **Fred's Coffee Shop** · 1917 Bridgeway
- **Lighthouse Café** · 1311 Bridgeway
- **Poggio** · 777 Bridgeway
- **Sushi Ran** · 107 Caledonia St

Shopping

- **Heath Ceramics** · 400 Gate 5 Rd
- **Mollusk Surf Shop** · 4500 Irving St
- **Sausalito Ferry Company** · 688 Bridgeway

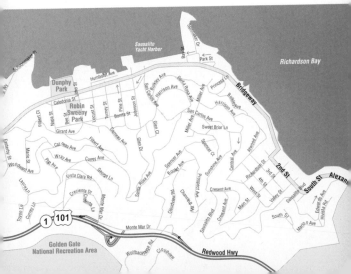

General Information

City Hall: 26 Corte Madera Ave
      Mill Valley, CA 94941
Phone: 415-388-4033
Website: www.cityofmillvalley.org

Overview

Tucked at the foot of Mt. Tamalpais in Marin County, Mill Valley makes a delightful day trip from San Francisco. In its early days, the town's plentiful redwoods provided much of the lumber that built San Francisco. Later on, Mill Valley was famous for its creek-fed canyons and superb hiking as well as "the crookedest railroad in the world," a steam-and-gravity-powered train that connected the town with the top of the mountain and nearby Muir Woods. Although the invasion of the automobile and the great fire of 1929 put the railroad out of business 75 years ago, the town's natural beauty is as seductive as ever.

Downtown Mill Valley is delineated by Throckmorton and Miller Avenues. Depot Plaza and adjacent Lytton Square form the center of the action. Though the town's present reputation rests on the tiny boutiques and galleries that wouldn't seem out of place on Rodeo Drive, there are also quality restaurants nearby. Nightlife is more attractive here than in most shopping meccas, too—the Throckmorton Theater offers theater, music, and performance in a gorgeous old building.

Landmarks

Old Mill Park • Throckmorton Ave & Old Mill St
Outdoor Art Club • 1 W Blithedale Ave

Bars

2 AM Club • 380 Miller Ave

Restaurants

Avatars Punjab Burritos • 15 Madrona St
Buckeye Roadhouse • 15 Shoreline Hwy
Bungalow 44 • 44 E Blithedale Ave
Joe's Taco Lounge • 382 Miller Ave
La Ginestra • 127 Throckmorton Ave
Mama's Royal Café • 393 Miller Ave
Pearl's Phatburgers • 8 E Blithedale Ave
Piazza D'Angelo • 22 Miller Ave

Shopping

· **All Wrapped Up** • 38 Miller Ave
· **Alphadog** • 6 Miller Ave
· **Benefit** • 35 Throckmorton Ave
· **Depot Bookstore & Café** • 87 Throckmorton Ave
· **Margaret O'Leary** • 14 Miller Ave
· **Mill Valley Hat Box** • 118 Throckmorton Ave
· **Mill Valley Market** • 12 Corte Madera Ave
· **Pharmaca** • 230 E Blithedale Ave
· **Tony's Shoe & Luggage Repair** •
   38 Corte Madera Ave
· **Two Neat** • 111 Throckmorton Ave
· **Vintage Wine & Spirits** • 67 Throckmorton Ave
· **Whole Foods Market** • 414 Miller Ave

Landmarks

- **The Old Mill** • Old Mill Park, Throckmorton Ave & Old Mill St • Built in the 1830s and used for 15 years (what you see now is a reconstruction), this landmark is the town's namesake. Mill Valley's beautiful glass-and-redwood library is nearby at the edge of the park.

- **Outdoor Art Club** • 1 W Blithedale Ave • Founded by civic-minded women in 1902 who wanted to preserve Mill Valley's unique natural environment, the Club later became a champion of conservation efforts in surrounding areas as well. Beautifully designed by Bernard Maybeck in a charming garden setting.

Festivals & Events

- **Mill Valley Film Festival** (mid-Oct) • Various venues • The Sequoia Theatre at 25 Throckmorton Avenue is the festival's main venue, but events take place throughout Marin County. The festival is highly regarded with independent film circles and features seminars, panel discussions, and in-person tributes as well as films from around the world. For more information, call 415-383-5256 or visit www.mvff.com.

- **Dipsea Race** (mid-June) • The 7.1-mile course stretching from downtown Mill Valley over Mt. Tamalpais to Stinson Beach includes the grueling 676 Dipsea Steps and is run by 1,500 competitors every summer. This is the second-oldest footrace in the country after the Boston Marathon. For more information, visit www.dipsea.org.

- **Mill Valley Wine & Gourmet Food Tasting** (late June) • Lytton Sq b/w Miller Ave & Sunnyside Ave • Wineries from nearby Napa and Sonoma bring their wares to be sampled alongside the town's delectable food offerings. $30 in advance (or $35 the day of) buys you all the wine you can taste. Visit www.millvalley.org/wine_intro.html to preorder tickets.

- **Concerts in the Plaza** (Summer Thursdays) • Lytton Sq b/w Miller Ave & Sunnyside Ave • Local talent covering a variety of genres entertains the crowds for free.

- **Paint-off in the Plaza** (Late July) • The Ci Arts commission presents the annual paint-c competition in the Plaza. You can go see th artists working beginning at 10 am or check o the finished masterpieces after 3 pm. For mo information visit www.cityofmillvalley.org/boarc art-paint-off.pdf.

- **Mill Valley Fall Arts Festival** (late Sept) • Old M Park, Throckmorton Ave & Old Mill St • Two days art, entertainment, and food among the redwooc Visit www.mvfaf.org for more information.

- **Mountain Play at the Mountain Theatre** (a.k The Cushing Memorial Theatre) (May and June) Mt Tamalpais State Park • This stunning outdo amphitheater seats 3,750 people and has bee the dramatic setting for different plays eve year since 1913; walking the six miles down th mountain after the performance is part of the fu Visit www.mountainplay.org for schedule and tick information.

Outdoors

- **Mt Tamalpais State Park** • Headquarters at 801 Panoramic Hwy • Visit over 50 miles of hiking and biking trails, scenic vistas, and campgrounds. 415-388-2070.

- **Tennessee Beach** • End of Tennessee Valley Trail • Hiking, horseback riding, and picnic tables on the black sand beach. 415-331-1540.

How to Get There

Mill Valley is approximately ten miles north of Sa Francisco across the Golden Gate Bridge. Take 101 the Mill Valley/Stinson Beach exit and head west c what becomes Shoreline Highway. After about a mil veer right at the stoplight by the gas station (left take you onto Highway 1 and over to the coast). The roa becomes Miller Avenue and leads you right into th heart of downtown.

Alternately, take the Tiburon/E Blithedale exit, tw off-ramps along 101 after the Mill Valley/Stinsc Beach exit. Head west and follow your nose for abo three miles. East Blithedale Avenue is the other ma thoroughfare into downtown Mill Valley.

Golden Gate Transit offers minimal bus service to M Valley, mostly serving commuters. Change buses Marin City. Visit www.goldengate.org for more details

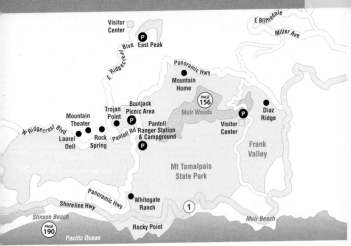

General Information

Address:	801 Panoramic Hwy Mill Valley, CA 94941
Phone:	415-388-2070
Website:	www.parks.ca.gov/?page_id=471 www.friendsofmttam.org
Open:	Daily 7am–sunset year round
Entry:	Free to enter, $8 per car to park, camping costs start at $25

Overview

Easy access from San Francisco makes Marin County's Mt Tamalpais State Park a popular day trip for restless city dwellers and nature lovers. Once thought to be a remnant of an extinct volcano, geologists now believe that Mt Tam was created during millenniums of shifts in the nearby San Andreas Fault. The park's 6,300 acres contain oak woodlands, grassy meadows, chaparral, and even redwoods. These mini-ecosystems are teeming with flora, with more than 750 plant species cataloged thus far. For most visitors, however, the highlight is the panoramic view from the 2,571-foot peak, which (on a clear day) looks out over San Francisco, Ocean Beach, Angel Island, Mt Diablo, the Marin Headlands, and a vast expanse of the Pacific Ocean. On those exceptionally clear days, visibility can extend all the way to the Sierra Nevada mountains (150 miles to the east), and to the Farallon Islands 25 miles offshore. Originally, explorers named the peak La Sierra de Nuestro Padre San Francisco. That proved to be too long, and so the mountain was renamed Tamalpais, a Miwok Indian word. To the locals it's simply (and affectionately) called Mt Tam.

Considered the birthplace of mountain biking, Mt Tam is still a favorite among Bay Area riders. Not all trails are open to cyclists, but there are plenty of twisting and technical roads along the mountain's flank and up to its peak. Hikers can sweat it out on 50 miles of trails within the park (watch out for the prevalent poison oak), which connect to a 200-mile network on adjacent land. The steep trails can be dangerous for both bikers and hikers, so caution is advised. Climbers have an option of four 25- to 45-foot slabs, in the Northern Formation to propel, and geocachers

will be sure to find plenty of hidden treasures throughout the park (www.geocaching.com). Campers who think showering is overrated or are frightened by the sound of a flushing toilet can throw down a bedroll at a first-come, first-serve tent site, or call a few months in advance to reserve one of the 10 rustic cabins (415-388-2070). (The Steep Ravine camp sites and cabins are closed every October.) Day-trippers who enjoy running water can picnic in the Bootjack Picnic Area, which has tables, grills, potable water, and toilets that actually flush.

If it is your first excursion to Mt Tamalpais, you should check out the visitor center on the East Peak Summit. There's also a refreshment stand open daily during the summer. If you're not in the woods to escape civilization, you can use the phones, picnic tables, wireless Internet access (hmmm), and fully accessible restrooms there.

The Mountain Theater (also called The Cushing Memorial Theater) has been in use since the early 1900s. In the 1930s, the Civilian Conservation Corps added seating, improved the stage, and landscaped the area. The stone amphitheater seats 3,750 and stages the Mountain Play each spring, an annual event since 1913.

Practicalities

During the summer months, when the weather heats up and the vegetation dries out, park authorities sometimes close parts of Mt Tam due to the high risk of fire. You can get an update on park closures by calling the Pantoll Ranger Station at 415-388-2070. Depending on the day, you can go through multiple climate changes on the same hike, so be sure to wear layers when at Mt Tam. The temperature difference can be substantial at times, especially during the summer.

How to Get There—Driving

From the south, take Highway 101-North, then take Highway 1 to the Stinson Beach exit and follow signs up the mountain. If you're distracted by the incredible scenery and the curvy roads, then let someone else do the driving so you can enjoy the view without any risk of steering yourself off a cliff. And please watch out for the many cyclists.

General Information

Phone: 415-831-2700
Website: sfrecpark.org/destination/golden-gate-park

Overview

One of the city's finest features, this swath of urban greenery is home to treasures that can surprise and delight even the most jaded San Franciscan. Each Sunday (and Saturdays during the spring and summer months), John F. Kennedy Drive, which snakes through the heart of the park, is closed to auto traffic, so cyclists, joggers, skaters, and even swing dancers have the pavement to themselves.

Bigger than New York City's Central Park, Golden Gate Park takes up 1,013 acres and is about 3 miles long and 1/2-mile wide. William Hammond Hall designed the park in 1870 and chose John McLaren to succeed him in 1887. McLaren worked for fifty years to improve the green by adding trees and plants from all over the world to beautify the vast recreational area. McLaren lived at McLaren Lodge (35), built in 1896, until he died at age 96 in 1943. The park boasts more than fifty ways to spend your day, from buffalo watching (5) and paddle boating (15) to horticultural museums (34) and barbecue pits (12).

Practicalities

If it is summery and sunny in the rest of the city, there is still a chance of dreary mist in the park. Bordered by the fog line of Stanyan Street to the east, Great Highway to the west, Lincoln Way to the south, and Fulton Street to the north, the park is most easily accessed from 19th Avenue. Since parking is often limited, public transportation is the best way to go. For bus, streetcar, and cable car service to Golden Gate Park, take the Muni 5, 7, 16AX, 16BX, 18, 21, 28, 28L, 29, 33, 44, 66, 71, and 71L. The Golden Gate Park Shuttle (it's free!) picks up passengers at 15 locations throughout the park every 15 minutes on weekends and holidays from from 9am-6pm year round. There is also a parking structure just inside the park at 10th Avenue.

Smokers (of all kinds) should note the new city ordinance banning smoking from city parks. Light up here, and you may end up getting fined.

Attractions

The Dutch Windmill (1) is one of two oringally constructed to irrigate the park, and the southern Murphy Windmill (2) opened in April 2012 and is now fully functioning. The M.H. Young Memorial Museum (21), renowned for its vast collection of old and contemporary American art, reopened on October 2005 (50 Hagiwara Tea Garden Dr, 415-750-3600; http://deyoung.famsf.org) after four years of planning and renovations. It's one of the coolest buildings not just in SF, but in America, period. The Sharon Art Studio (31) is a terrific community resource for art classes and education with programs for all ages and abilities (next to the Children's Playground, accessed by Bowling Green Drive between Kennedy and King drives, 415-753-7004; www.sharonartstudio.org). The Buffalo Paddock, created in 1892, has been newly renovated, and the furry residents seem to enjoy the new digs that offer visitors more upfront and personal views of the beasts (5). The California Academy of Sciences has been in the park since 1916, but damage from the 1989 earthquake prompted the Academy to rebuild. Like a phoenix rising from its ashes, the new building, designed by Renzo Piano and touted as the greenest museum in the world, is completed. It features a library, research laboratory, planetarium, aquarium, and natural history museum, but now boasts a rainforest dome and living roof. Fans of Claude, the albino alligator, will be glad to know that he made the move unscathed. Tickets are $34.95 for adults and are $5-$10 less for kids, youth, and seniors. Despite the price tag, the CAS is hugely popular. When you go, expect long lines, but you'll still be able to get in and enjoy yourself. The aquarium has been known get more crowded than a Who concert, especially on Free Days; check www.calacademy.org for more. The new building is located across the Music Concourse (22) from the de Young (21).

Nature

The Conservatory of Flowers (34), the oldest surviving conservatory in the Western Hemisphere, houses huge palm trees, exotic orchids, and water lilies from around the world (JFK Dr, 415-831-2090; www.conservatoryofflowers.org). The Shakespeare Garden (24) is a sweet-smelling tribute to the plants and flowers mentioned in the Bard's poems and plays. The San Francisco Botanical Garden at Strybing Arboretum (18) entices the senses with more than 6,000 plant species (9th Ave and Lincoln Wy, 415-661-1316; www.sfbotanicalgarden.org). The arboretum is located near the Japanese Tea Garden (19), which features Asian foliage. In the middle of Stow Lake (15) is an island called Strawberry Hill (16), which is 428 feet high and makes for a nice city hike.

rchitecture & Sculpture

e Japanese Tea Garden (19) was developed by Makoto
giwara, a famed Japanese landscape designer (who is also
to be the inventor of the fortune cookie), and features a
ditative teahouse, native Japanese and Chinese plants, and
autiful sculptures and bridges. The Conservatory of Flowers (34)
great piece of Victorian architecture modeled after London's
w Gardens. McLaren Lodge (35), built in 1896, is one of the
est Mission-style buildings in San Francisco and it still remains
rgeous sight. The two-story Beach Chalet (2) features some of
most beautiful murals in the city and also houses the park's
center (1000 Great Hwy at Ocean Beach, 415-831-2700;
w.beachchalet.com).

pen Spaces

e your dog to romp in one of the park's two dog runs (11, 37).
st of the picnic tables are first-come, first-serve, but if you've
some meat to heat, reserve a barbecue pit ahead of time at
neer Log Cabin (20) or by calling 415-831-5500.

erformance

concerts, such as the Outside Lands Music & Arts Festival,
held in different meadows throughout the park, as well as
events like Shakespeare in the Park and the sprawling Hardly
ictly Bluegrass Festival. Always free is the big roller boogie held
ery Sunday at 6th Ave. and JFK.

ports

e San Francisco 49ers played in Kezar Stadium (32) from 1946
1970. Now it's used for high school, amateur, and recreational
orts. An archery field lies just north of the public nine-hole
f course (4). The Fly Casting Pools (9) draw aspiring and
pert fishermen alike. The park has two main soccer fields (3,
and pick-up games wherever there is green space. Not to be
out, handball players have their choice of indoor or outdoor
usement (26). The San Francisco Lawn Bowling Club offers
ginner lessons on the Bowling Greens (28) most Wednesdays
d Saturdays at noon (call 415-487-8787 to confirm). If we're
ing to count handball and lawn bowling as sports, why not
ll out your old skates and groove with the roller dancers off
Drive. There are twenty-one tennis courts (33) located at the
tern side of the park, available weekdays on a first-come, first-
ved basis. Reservations for courts are required on weekends
d holidays (415-831-6301). Playing fields and times must be
erved for most team sports. Call 415-831-5510 (for soccer,
tball, baseball, and softball) for pricing and available times.
ere is also a permanent Frisbee golf course located in the park,
ich is internationally celebrated as fun for both experts and

beginners, and is entirely maintained by volunteers. http://www.
sfdiscgolf.org/golden_gate_park/

Landmarks of Golden Gate Park

1. Dutch Windmill & Queen Wilhelmina Tulip Garden
2. Beach Chalet
3. Soccer Fields
4. Golf Course & Clubhouse
5. Bison Paddock
6. Model Yacht Club
7. Equestrian Center & Police Stables
8. Golden Gate Park Stadium Soccer & Polo Fields
9. Anglers Lodge & Fly Casting Pools
10. Playground
11. Dog Run
12. Barbecue Pits
13. Picnic Area
14. Rose Garden
15. Stow Lake Boathouse / Boat Rentals
16. Strawberry Hill
17. Playground
18. Botanical Garden and Strybing Arboretum
19. Japanese Tea Garden
20. Pioneer Log Cabin
21. M.H. de Young Memorial Museum
22. Music Concourse
23. County Fair Building & Horticultural Library
24. Shakespeare Garden
25. Baseball Field
26. Handball Courts
27. De Laveaga Dell & AIDS Memorial Grove
28. Lawn Bowling Greens
29. Carousel
30. Children's Playground
31. Sharon Art Studio
32. Kezar Stadium
33. Tennis Courts
34. Conservatory of Flowers
35. McLaren Lodge
36. Horseshoe Pits
37. Dog Run
38. Official City Tree
39. Park Police Station
40. Murphy Windmill

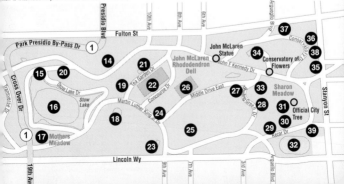

Golden Gate Bridge

Fort Point Rock

Pacific Ocean

Torpedo Wharf

Marine Dr

Fort Point

Long Ave

San Francisco Bay

Marine Dr

Merchant Rd

Lincoln Blvd

Storey Ave

Crissy Field Ave

The Presidio Visitor Center
PAGE 180

Crissy Field

Mason St

Helmut Rock

Lyon St

Langdon Ct

Ralston Ave

Ruckman Ave

Fort Winfield Scott

Washington Blvd

Kobbe Ave

Wright Loop

Sheridan Ave

Lincoln Blvd

San Francisco National Cemetery

Presidio Bowling Center

Moraga

Officer's Club

Visitor Cente

Naumer Rd

Thomas Ave

Arguello Blvd

Baker Beach

Rob Hill Campground

Amatury Loop

Piper Loop

PAGE 183

Lincoln Blvd

Pershing Dr

Shirwell Dr

Pershing Dr

Battery Caulfield Rd

Compton Rd

Washington Blvd

Wedemeyer St

Brown St

(1)

Presidio Golf Course

(P)

W Pacific Ave

Andy Go

Finley Rd

Brooks St

Presidio Trust Facilities

(P)

Public Health Service Hospital

Mountain Lake

7th Ave

6th Ave

5th Ave

Mountain Lake Park

MAP 21

25

Baker Beach Apts

General Information

Website:	www.presidio.gov
	www.nps.gov/prsf
Mailing Address:	Golden Gate National Recreation Area
	Bldg 201, Fort Mason
	San Francisco, CA 94123
Visitor Center:	415-561-4323
Non-Emergency	
Park Police:	415-561-5505
Open:	24 hours a day, year-round
Entry:	Free

Overview

As if a heartbreakingly beautiful location, a trend-setting cultu aesthetic, and endless charming architecture weren't enoug San Franciscans can also boast of having a national park in the city. A former military outpost, the Presidio's 1,491 acres conta more than 500 historic buildings, old coastal defense fortificatio a national cemetery (the only cemetery within San Francisco cit limits), forests, beaches, dramatic coastal bluffs, and miles an miles of trails. It comes as no surprise that everyone jumpe when the base was decommissioned and the land was mad available for development. The Presidio's new tenants are re movers and shakers. Lucasfilm Ltd. operates a 1,500-employe digital arts complex on the site, and the Walt Disney Famil Foundation opened The Walt Disney Family Museum, a museu

Parks & Places • **The Presidio**

military hero finally retired and became a part of the Golden Gate National Recreation Area.

As proof of its historic, scenic, and recreational value, the residential neighborhoods that border the Presidio are some of the more expensive locales in the city. Part of what these residents pay for is easy access to this welcoming chunk of nature—the 11 miles of hiking trails include the Golden Gate Promenade, the Coastal Trail, an ecology trail, and portions of the Bay Area Ridge Trail, the Bay Trail, and the Anza National Historic Trail. 14 miles of paved roads provide smooth—albeit mostly hilly—biking for cyclists. There are also some unpaved parts of the Bay Area Ridge Trail if off-road is more your style. The park also contains numerous sports facilities, including a golf course, bowling alley, tennis courts, athletic fields, and a campground. Baker Beach, the site of the first Burning Man in 1989, features a clothing-optional section, north of the hazardous surf sign (don't get excited: the nudists are mostly old dudes). Offering flat terrain and sweeping views of the Golden Gate, Crissy Field (named for Major Dana H. Crissy, not a Marina chick) is a popular spot for dog walkers, swimmers, bikers, hikers, and kite fliers.

How to Get There—Driving

The Presidio can be reached from the north by crossing the Golden Gate Bridge (Highways 1 and 101); from the east by way of Lombard Street (Highway 101); and from the south via Highway 1.

How to Get There—Mass Transit

San Francisco Municipal Railway (Muni) buses serve the Presidio via the 28, 29, 43, and 76 lines. Bus service from the North Bay to the Golden Gate Bridge toll plaza is available through Golden Gate Transit. Commercial cable car buses are available from Fisherman's Wharf. The Presidio Trust provides free shuttle service within the Presidio and to nearby public transit stops.

💲 Banks

- **First Republic** • 210 Lincoln Blvd

○ Landmarks

- **Andy Goldsworthy Spire** • Bay Ridge Trail near Arguello Blvd
- **Crissy Field** • Mason St
- **Fort Point** • Long Ave & Marine Dr
- **Golden Gate Bridge** • US Hwy 101
- **Presidio Bowling Center** • 93 Moraga Ave
- **Presidio Golf Course** • 300 Finley Rd
- **The Presidio Visitor Center** • temporarily at Bldg 105, Montgomery St
- **Rob Hill Campground** • Washington Blvd & Central Magazine Rd

✉ Post Offices

- **Presidio Station** • 950 Lincoln Blvd, Bldg 210

🏋 Gyms

- **YMCA—Presidio Community** • 63 Funston Ave

🍴 Restaurants

- **Crissy Field Warming Hut** • 983 Marine Dr

🛍 Shopping

- **Sports Basement** • 610 Mason St

dedicated to the animator, in 2009. Twenty-one distinct residential neighborhoods also sprawl over the Presidio—monthly rental options range from $1800 for a one-bedroom apartment to $15,000 for a seven-bedroom house. The Presidio is federal property and does not have to abide by San Francisco laws, such as rent control. Despite the construction and development on the grounds, nothing has marred the beauty of this green-tipped peninsula.

The people of the Ohlone Native American tribe are the first known residents of this land, and the area was named by the Spanish soldiers and missionaries who arrived to conquer and convert in 1776. The Presidio went on to serve as a military post under the flags of Spain, Mexico, and the United States at different points in its military career. It has played a logistical role in every major US military conflict over the last 150 years. In 1994, the old

155

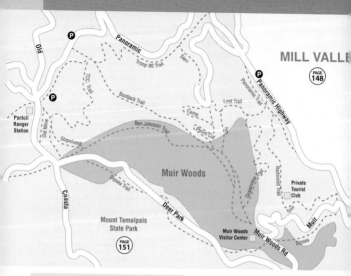

MILL VALLE
PAGE 148

PAGE 151

General Information

Address:	Muir Woods National Monument
	Mill Valley, CA 94941
Phone:	415-388-2596
Website:	http://www.nps.gov/muwo
Hours:	Daily, 8 am to sunset, including holidays.
Admission:	$7 day fee or $20 for an annual pass.

Overview

During California's rapid industrialization and the beginning of the Gold Rush in 1849, Marin County, once covered in redwoods, was spared by development. The land that is now Muir Woods was spared from logging only because of its inaccessibility—and thank God! This sanctuary of old-growth redwood trees is a little piece of heaven. The land was purchased in 1905 by Congressman William Kent, who paid $45,000 for 295 acres of gargantuan redwood trees (they are the tallest trees that grow on earth). To protect his trees, he donated the land to the federal government and President Theodore Roosevelt declared it a national monument in 1908. Although Roosevelt offered to name the area after Kent, the modest congressman decided instead to memorialize conservationist John Muir (thus earning him another gold star in our book).

The monument, which preserves the last redwood forest in the Bay Area, sees about 750,000 visitors annually making weekend parking very difficult. Most visitors stick to the main trail, an easy two-mile round-trip stroll along Redwood Creek; this paved path is accessible for strollers and wheelchairs. Several other dirt trails (totaling six miles) wind their way through the monument, and especially ambitious hikers can connect to an even larger

network of paths on contiguous land in Mt Tamalpais Sta Park. Park rangers lead daily guided walks through the wood it's best to call ahead for scheduling information. The fact tha a place as unspeakably beautiful as Muir Woods can be so clos to a major city like SF just makes life just a bit more bearabl don't you think?

Picnicking is not allowed in Muir Woods, but the Muir Wood Café, which serves sandwiches, salads, and sausages, is locate near the entrance. Pets are prohibited, with the exception o service dogs. Bikes are allowed on designated fire road surrounding Muir Woods. For obvious reasons, smoking is no permitted anywhere near the sacred forest.

How to Get There—Driving

From the south, take Highway 101 N across the Golden Gat Bridge. Exit Highway 1/Stinson Beach (there will be a sig for Muir Woods at this exit) and drive about 0.5 miles. At th stoplight, turn left. Drive about 2.7 miles. At the top of the hil turn right towards Muir Woods/Mount Tamalpais. Follow poste signs to Muir Woods.

How to Get There—Mass Transit

Golden Gate Transit (415-921-5858) offers a free shuttle servic (bus 66) to Muir Woods on summer weekends and holiday From San Francisco, Golden Gate Transit buses 10, 70 and 80 wi take you to the shuttle stop. Bus 63 also runs on weekends an holidays and makes stops at the Mountain Home Inn, Panto Station, and Bootjack on Panoramic Highway. From any of thes stops, it is a one- to two-mile hike down to Muir Woods.

Overview

NFT Maps: 18 & 19

With views of the Golden Gate Bridge and the Marin Headlands, 193-acre Lincoln Park is one of the most spectacular park spaces in San Francisco. It's also probably the only one where visitors can play golf and then stroll over to one of the finest art collections in the country, the Palace of the Legion of Honor.

Originally the site of the Golden Gate cemetery, city commissioners developed Lincoln Park in 1908, turning the Gold Rush graveyard into a posh 18-hole golf course. Many of the corpses were exhumed and moved as the plot was transformed, but hundreds of bodies remain buried beneath this picturesque park.

Practicalities

The park can be easily accessed by car from 34th Avenue or El Camino del Mar. There is parking near the golf course (does this sound like a bad place, anyone?) and the Legion of Honor museum. Muni bus 18 stops right at the Legion of Honor (and anyone with a Muni pass or a bus transfer receives a $2 discount on admission to the museum).

Lincoln Park Golf Course

34th Ave & Clement St; 415-221-9911;
sfrecpark.org/destination/lincoln-park/lincoln-park-golf-course
The par-68 public golf course, where you can play on one of the park's most popular attractions. The layout is not as challenging as the other two public 18-hole courses in town. Harding Park and the Presidio, nor has it benefited from a renovation like the others (even though the course dates back to 1908). The back nine at Lincoln offer challenges for even the most confident golfer, including the 17th hole, a 240-yard par-3 that offers spectacular views of the Golden Gate Bridge. You can make reservations six days ahead of time (415-750-4653). Locals can save $13–14 on green fees by picking up a Resident Golf Card at City Hall. 18 holes cost about $37 on weekdays and $41 on weekends. There is no driving range at Lincoln, but the putting green is a little lumpy, and the pro shop is fully equipped.

Palace of the Legion of Honor

100 34th Ave; 415-750-3600;
http://legionofhonor.famsf.org/

This grand Beaux-Arts building, a ¾-scale replica of Paris's 18th-century Palais de la Légion d'Honneur, houses a notable collection of ancient and European art. The museum was given to San Francisco by the city's grandmother of Art and Culture, Alma de Bretteville Spreckels, who filled it with many sculptures she bought from Rodin himself, including an early cast of *The Thinker*. During construction, music-loving Alma had a Skinner organ built into the structure of the building. The Skinner can be experienced at Public Organ Concerts held Saturdays and Sundays at 4 pm. Hours: Tues–Sun, 9:30 am–5:15 pm. General admission is $10, Seniors are $7, Youth (13–17) $6, and children 12 and under are free, and the first Tuesday of every month is free (though special exhibitions fees still apply). The museum has an excellent café and a well-stocked museum store.

Lincoln Park is also home to George Segal's controversial Holocaust Memorial sculpture, located near the Palace of the Legion of Honor. Installed in 1984, Segal's chilling work depicts a pile of emaciated, dead bodies next to one lone survivor gazing out over the Pacific.

Lands End and the Coastal Trail

www.parksconservancy.org/visit/park-sites/lands-end.html
The newly paved Coastal Trail runs along the cliffside at Lincoln Park, and is hands-down the best way to get out of the city without leaving San Francisco. The trail begins on the east side of the park, where a small platform with benches looks out over the Marin Headlands. If you're coming from the Legion of Honor, just walk straight down through the golf course and you'll hit it. Continue west along the coastline, and the trail eventually reaches Lands End, a rocky outcropping with an odd gravel maze art piece and priceless views of the Golden Gate. There is no food or water along the trail, but if you bring a picnic you can nestle down and eat at one of the secluded rock beaches. If you continue walking (watch out for hardy trail-runners!) you'll end at the brand new Lookout Visitors Center, completely with a newly renovated parking lot (address 680 Point Lobos Avenue, San Francisco, CA 94121.) The visitor center is a treasure trove of information about the Lands End Trail, and is a great jumping off point to explore the other nearby sights, like beautiful Sutro Heights Park, which has a great view of the coast on those exceptional clear days. Below that, in the rocky inlet below the Cliff House, you can find the ruins of Sutro Baths, a giant, heated, seawater swimming complex built in 1896. The structure that housed the Baths was destroyed by a fire in 1966, but the remains of the huge public pools can still be explored. Both places are named after Adolph Sutro, an affluent early citizen and the 24th mayor of San Francisco. Warning—this is a San Francisco trail, and there are hills, and it can be bone-freezing if the fog is in. The best part about it? Crowds are rare.

General Information

NFT Map: 3
Address: 900 North Point St
              San Francisco, CA 94109
Phone: 415-775-5500
Website: www.ghirardellisq.com
Hours: Sun-Thu, 9 am–11pm; Fri–Sat, 9 am–
              midnight

Overview

Right next to Fisherman's Wharf, Ghirardelli Square (pronounced with a hard "g") boasts scores of chocolate-starved travelers every day of the year. Among the tourists, a new creature emerges--the part-time resident. The top floor of the square has been turned into Fairmont Heritage Place, a partial-ownership condominium complex that offers 5 weeks a year of top-of-the-world living. Yes, San Franciscans admit to sometimes visiting the square even when they're not entertaining out-of-towners. When the weather is warm, the big steps facing the bay and Alcatraz offer world-class people-watching opportunities for both tourists and locals.

So who, you ask, is this mysterious Ghirardelli? Domenica "Domingo" Ghirardelli, Italian goldrusher-cum-chocolatier, and his chocolate-loving, entrepreneurial sons bought a block of property on North Point Street in 1893, after two of those many relentless San Francisco fires destroyed his first lot on Jackson Street. By 1915, the North Point Street property featured manufacturing plants, offices, employee housing, and a prominent clock tower. Together, the buildings formed…Ghirardelli Square.

In the 1960s, Ghirardelli Chocolate was purchased by the Golden Grain Macaroni Company and moved across the bay to San Rafael. The new Ghirardelli Square officially opened in 1964. The brick-terraced courtyard of fine shops and restaurants has been granted National Historic Register status. The original 1860 cast-iron chocolate grinder is located in the Lower Plaza, and other chocolate-making equipment still operates on a small scale in the Ghirardelli Chocolate Manufactory. The famous "Ghirardelli" sign, 25 feet tall and 125 feet wide, brightly welcomes ships into the Bay and has become a San Francisco landmark.

Practicalities

Everything at Ghirardelli Square is easy to locate, but if you need help, an information booth is located at Fountain Plaza, which sells souvenirs, film, chocolate, Muni passes and gives out free maps (as if ours aren't enough for you!)

The seven principal buildings that make up the Square are: the Clock Tower, the Mustard Building, the Cocoa Building the Chocolate Building, Woolen Mill, Wurster, and the Power House—all part of the original Ghirardelli factory.

Parking is available at a garage on Beach Street between Larkin at Polk streets. Discounted parking is available with merchant validation. Rates start at $6 for the first hour, going up to $33 maximum for 24 hours. But with all the traffic that comes through here, your best bet is to avoid the parking issue altogether and take public transportation.

Activities

The annual Chocolate Festival, held on the 1st or 2nd weekend in September, features chocolate treats from Ghirardelli Square establishments, as well as prominent restaurants, bakeries, and chocolatiers from around the Bay Area. Not to be missed is the "Earthquake" ice cream sundae-eating contest, where the winner receives his or her weight in Ghirardelli Chocolate.

Holidays are a time for family fun at Ghirardelli Square. On the Fourth of July, there is live musical entertainment and kid-related festivities. Christmas celebrations include the annual Tree Lighting Ceremony in late November, when there are a variety of caroling performances, a local celebrity emcee, and a visit from the Clauses. The 50-foot tree is decorated with, as you've probably guessed, chocolate bars.

Where to Eat Food Besides Chocolate

On the Fountain Plaza you will still find the nostalgic favorite Lori's Diner for your burger and shake needs. McCormick & Kuleto's offers seafood and sea views in the Wurster Building along Beach Street. Wattle Creek Winery caters to the lovers-of-the-grape crowd. And when all the eating and sipping is done, don't forget about dessert. Kara's Cupcakes offers an organic assortment of this ever popular sweet treat. And of course, there is the chocolate. After all, this is Ghirardelli Square. A hot fudge sundae from the Ghirardelli Ice Cream and Chocolate Shop in the Fountain Plaza is a classic, ooey-gooey favorite.

General Information

Map: 4
Address: Pier 15 (on the Embarcadero at Green Street)
             San Francisco, CA 94111
Phone: 415-528-4444
Website: www.exploratorium.edu
Hours: Tues–Sun: 10 am–5 pm. First Thursday of the
             month has After Dark, 6pm–10pm, must be 18
             and older. Closed Monday (except for select
             holidays), Thanksgiving & Christmas Day
Admission: $25 for adults; $19 for youth (6-17), seniors
             (65+), teachers, students, and people with
             disabilities; kids 5 and under are free.

Overview

Want to see what happens to a building during an earthquake? How about charging your body with enough static electricity to give you a Don King 'do? The Exploratorium, located on Pier 15 on the Embarcadero, includes over 650 science, art, and human perception exhibits. Founded in 1969 by Dr. Frank Oppenheimer, who was director until his death in 1985, the Exploratorium is a learning center that combines science and technology with nature and art.

No one is a passive visitor here. Interactive exhibits explore how humans perceive light, color, sound, motion, electricity, heat, language, weather, and more. Don't worry: each exhibit has a "How Does It Work?" card for anyone who can't remember their high school science (yes, we're talking about you). The not-to-be-missed Tactile Dome lets you crawl, climb, and slide through unusual textures in darkness, guided only by touch (which is not that different from a typical night on the town in San Francisco). The experience requires an extra fee with admission and a reservation. The museum also hosts regular film screenings. The Exploratorium has been celebrating an International Geek Holiday of its own creating for over 20 years now. Pi Day, which just happens to fall on Einstein's birthday, occurs on 3/14 at 1:59 pm. It is celebrated with Pi, and also with pie.

Once located in the Palace of Fine Arts, in 2013 the Exploratorium moved to a stunning new facility on San Francisco's waterfront which extends 800 feet over the Bay. It only gets better.

How to Get There—Driving

From the south, take the 101 N towards San Francisco. Take 280 N towards downtown San Francisco. Exit at King Street. Follow King Street past AT&T Park where it becomes the Embarcadero. Continue down the Embarcadero, staying in the middle lane. Pier 15 will be on your right.

From East Bay via the Bay Bridge, take 80 W to San Francisco, crossing the Bay Bridge. Exit at Harrison Street/Embarcadero (this exit is on the left side). At the bottom of the exit, turn right onto Harrison Street. At the end of Harrison Street, take a left onto the Embarcadero. Continue down the Embarcadero, staying in the middle lane. Pier 15 will be on your left.

From the Golden Gate Bridge, take the Marina Boulevard exit, and take Marina Boulevard to Laguna Street, follow Laguna Street to the right for two blocks and turn left onto Bay Street, driving for approximately 1.4 miles, then turn right onto the Embarcadero. Pier 15 will be on your left.

Discounted, validated parking is available at the Embarcadero Center and Levi's Plaza Garage.

How to Get There—Mass Transit

The Exploratorium has convenient access to public transportation. Muni's F Market streetcar stop right in front of the Exploratorium. San Francisco Muni bus lines 2, 6, 14, 21, and 31 stop nearby, as do metro rail lines J, K, L, M, T, and N. Embarcadero BART, Muni stations, and ferry terminals at the Ferry Building are all only a 10-15 minute walk from the Exploratorium..

How to Get There—Biking

It's easy to bike to the Exploratorium. There are lots of public bike racks in the area, as well as Public Bike Work Stations on Piers 15 and 17.

North Building and South Building

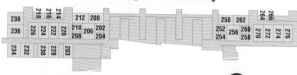

MEZZANINE LEVEL

MAP
8

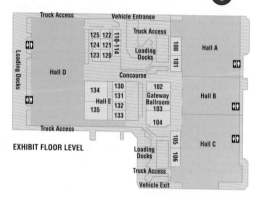

EXHIBIT FLOOR LEVEL

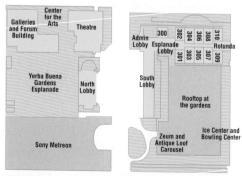

STREET LEVEL

West Building

MAP 8

CK LEVEL   LEVEL 1

LEVEL 2   LEVEL 3

General Information

NFT Map: 8
Address: 747 Howard St,
             San Francisco, CA 94103
Phone: 415-974-4000
Fax: 415-974-4073
Website: http://www.moscone.com/mtgplanners/
             floorplans/index.shtml

Overview

Notice a lot of bag-laden, name-tag-emblazoned people in "business casual" ambling around the streets? They're called conventioneers, and they're a form of wildlife typical to a habitat known as the Moscone Center. The Moscone Center hosts the majority of San Francisco's trade shows, conventions, and corporate banquets. The center is conveniently located in the heart of downtown San Francisco, which affords great dining, shopping, nightlife, and lodging options.

The Moscone complex is composed of three main buildings (Moscone South, Moscone North, and Moscone West) that cover more than twenty acres of building space and 700,000 square feet of exhibit space. All three buildings blend energy-efficient technology and unique designs, including Moscone South's dramatic 16-post-tensioned steel and concrete arches arranged in pairs to support its roof. To maximize light dispersal, large expanses of glass were used for the exterior. Skylights also extend as much natural light as possible. The center has won a series of awards for its environmental efforts, notably the 60,000 square-foot solar panel project on top of Moscone South.

In addition to the ample interior space, the Moscone Center takes great advantage of its outdoor space. On top of Moscone South is the Rooftop at Yerba Buena Gardens. It features a kid's outdoor jungle gym and the Children's Creativity Museum, an educational center that teaches children about technology and the arts with hands-on activities. The complex also features the Yerba Buena Ice

Skating and Bowling Center, a unique 1906 carousel, a café, and concession stands. Across the street, on top of Moscone North, the Yerba Buena Gardens include an expansive grassy knoll and a memorial to Martin Luther King, Jr. To the left and right of the gardens sit the Yerba Buena Center for the Arts and the Metreon respectively—a balancing act of non-profit arts and commercial entertainment.

How to Get There—Driving

Head north on Interstate 101, then take 80 E. Take the Fourth Street exit. Make a left on Bryant, a left on Third, and a left on Howard. The Moscone Center is located on the 700 block of Howard Street. You'll find Moscone South on your left and Moscone North on your right.

Via the Bay Bridge, take the Fremont Street exit to Howard Street and turn left on Howard.

Via the Golden Gate Bridge, take the Lombard Street exit to Van Ness Avenue. Turn right on Van Ness. Travel south to Grove. This will be approximately two miles. Turn left on Grove Street. Continue to Market Street. Cross Market Street and travel south on Eighth Street to Folsom. Turn left on Folsom, left on Third, and left on Howard.

How to Get There—Mass Transit

If you're taking BART or Muni Metro, disembark at the Powell Street Station. Exit to Fourth and Market Streets and turn right onto Fourth. Walk two blocks south to Howard and turn left. The Moscone Center is located on the 700 block of Howard Street. You'll find Moscone South on your right and Moscone North on your left.

If CalTrain is more your speed, get off at Fourth and Townsend. Cross Fourth Street from the train station and catch the 15, 30, or 45 lines. Get off at Third and Folsom. Walk one block north up towards Howard Street. Turn left onto Howard.

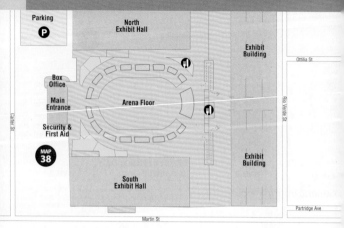

General Information

NFT Map:	38
Address:	2600 Geneva Ave Daly City, CA 94014
Phone:	415-404-4111
Website:	www.cowpalace.com

Overview

There was once a time when stepping on manure in the Cow Palace was a valid concern. The center gained its unusual name from the popular livestock exhibition it once held. After a brief stint as an Army base during World War II, the center has been functioning as a major events arena since the late 1940s. The first athletic event hosted by the Cow Palace was the U.S. Heavyweight Boxing Championship in 1949. Other sports-related shows that followed were roller derby, tennis, wrestling, professional basketball, martial arts, and ice hockey. Of perhaps more interest, the Grateful Dead unveiled the greatest P.A. system ever—the "Wall of Sound"—here in 1974. Today, the Palace hosts political conventions, ice shows, rodeo, Ringling Bros. Barnum & Bailey Circus, the San Francisco Sport & Boat Show, the Golden Gate Kennel Club Dog Show, and the Body Art Expo featuring over 200 artists tattooing and piercing onsite. Though the future of the Cow Palace has been tenuous over the years, thankfully it's here to stay. In fact, the stadium is now home to the professional minor league hockey team, the San Francisco Bulls.

How to Get There—Driving

From the Golden Gate Bridge, follow Hwy 1 (19th Ave) past SF State University. Take the Cow Palace/Alemany Boulevard loop and continue to Alemany Boulevard. Turn left onto Alemany and continue to Geneva Avenue. Turn right onto Geneva and follow the signs. The Cow Palace is on the right. Get on the 9X at Harrison and 5th St and it will take you right there...express-like.

From 101 N, take the Brisbane/Cow Palace exit and go straight to Geneva and turn left. The Cow Palace is located ten blocks up on the left.

From 101 S, take the Cow Palace/Third Street exit and immediately merge to the right onto Bayshore. Follow Bayshore and turn right onto Geneva. The Cow Palace is located ten blocks up on the left.

From 280 N, take the Geneva/Ocean exit and turn right onto Geneva Avenue. Follow for a few miles and the Cow Palace will be on the right.

From 280 S, take the Geneva/Ocean exit and turn left onto Geneva Avenue. Follow for a few miles and the Cow Palace will be on the right.

How to Get There—Mass Transit

Take the San Francisco/Daly City BART line to Balboa Park station. From Balboa Park station, take the 15 Muni bus to the Cow Palace bus stop at Santos Street.

A good alternative to mass transit is the Daly City Cab service. Call 650-992-8865 for taxi transportation to or from the Cow Palace or to schedule taxi pickups at Balboa Park BART station.

General Information

NFT Map:	8
Address:	701 Mission St
	San Francisco, CA 94103
Box Office & Information:	415-978-ARTS (2787)
Website:	www.ybca.org

Overview

Sandwiched between the wacky retail world of the Metreon shopping center and the even wackier world of 20th-century modern art displayed at the SFMOMA, Yerba Buena Center for the Arts is a bright spot in San Francisco's SOMA neighborhood. The Center is comprised of two landmark buildings, both run by the nonprofit center: the Galleries and Forum Building and the Theater.

The YBCA complex features a state-of-the-art 755-seat theater, a 6,700-square-foot space known as the Forum Building, and a 94-seat Screening Room. The Center's galleries present contemporary art exhibits in every medium that are usually worth a look-see. You can visit the Center's website for a schedule of upcoming events, as well as information on current and future gallery exhibitions.

YBCA is located next to the Yerba Buena Gardens Esplanade, a lovely urban oasis that serves as a prime picnicking spot for the downtown lunch crowd. Outdoor live music animates the space from May to October. The Gardens' centerpiece is the 50-foot-high, 20-foot-wide waterfall that leads to the impressive Martin Luther King, Jr. Memorial. Twelve glass sections behind the waterfall are engraved with quotes from Dr. King's writings and speeches. Visit www.yerbabuenagardens.com for more information.

The Gardens include a Butterfly Garden that provides a peaceful habitat for a number of different butterflies, as well as a sanctuary for humans (i.e., weary shoppers, stressed-out cubicle-land refugees, and anyone else seeking urban relief). Oché Wat Té Ou (Reflection), a work that honors the native Ohlone Indians, is a semicircular, wood wall decorated with Ohlone basket designs and set behind a curved pool. The artists created the piece intending for it to be used as a stage for performances by poets, storytellers, and others adept at the oral tradition. The Sister City Gardens feature flowering plants from thirteen of San Francisco's sister cities around the world. Food and drink are available here in stylish surroundings at Samovar Tea Lounge (415-227-9400). The greenspace also has several pieces of sculpture on display, such as Shaking Man, a freaky, life-sized bronze statue of a segmented businessman (he looks like he's been run through a paper shredder and glued back together) extending a handshake to visitors.

Got kids? Head across the street to the Children's Creativity Museum (415-820-3320; www.zeum.org), an art and technology museum for young people. In the same complex, there is an historic carousel, a bowling alley, an ice-skating rink, and a children's play area.

How to Get There—Driving

From the East Bay, take I-80 and exit at Fremont Street. Turn left onto Fremont at the end of the ramp, and another left onto Howard. Turn right on Fifth Street. Follow Fifth to Mission and turn right. Follow Mission to YBCA, between Fourth and Third Streets. From the South Bay, take 101 N and follow signs for I-80 E. Exit on Fourth Street, which will lead to Bryant. Turn left on Third Street. The Theater is on your left at the intersection of Third and Howard. The Galleries and Forum building are on your left at the intersection of Third and Mission. From the North Bay, take 101 S to the Lombard Street exit. Follow Lombard to Van Ness, turning right on Van Ness. Follow Van Ness until you reach Golden Gate then turn left. Golden Gate will take you across Market Street onto Sixth Street. Turn left onto Mission. Follow Mission to YBCA, between Fourth and Third Streets.

How to Get There—Mass Transit

If you're taking BART, exit at the Montgomery Street Station or the Powell Street Station. Muni bus users can take all Market Street lines, as well as 5 Fulton, 9 San Bruno, 14 Mission, 15 Third, 30 Stockton, 38 Geary, or 45 Union. If you're a Muni Metro rider, exit at either the Powell or Montgomery Street Station.

Golden Gate Transit buses 10, 20, 50, 60, 70, and 80 stop on Mission Street at Third Street. The Caltrain stop closest to the YBCA is at Fourth and Townsend Streets.

General Information

NFT Maps:	3 & 4
Address:	Northpoint St b/w Van Ness Ave & Grant St
Phone:	415-391-2000
Website:	www.fishermanswharf.org

Overview

A local's take: Fisherman's Wharf is a tightly encapsulated, overly commercial tourist bubble where every third person is wearing pastel-colored "SF" fleece. Fine—but who cares? Sure, the ubiquitous postcard-and-shot-glass shops make it seem slightly tacky, but the Wharf is not without its hidden charms. After all, the area boasts a rich history, Ghirardelli chocolate, sweeping bay views, holiday celebrations, and quality seafood. Aside from the stigma attached to this place, what's not to like? And one mustn't forget the sea lions. You'll find them basking in all their smelly, noisy glory on the K-dock adjacent to Pier 39. The sea lion population is highest in winter,

when it can grow to as many as 900. During summer months, a stalwart crew of dedicated dock loungers stays behind while the majority of the animals migrate to the Channel Islands.

The Wharf economy is not driven solely by tourism—it's been a continuously functioning fishing port since the days of the California Gold Rush.

Attractions

Alcatraz Cruises is the exclusive operator of ferry service to Alcatraz Island, the prison-turned-museum (415-981-ROCK or 415-981-7625). Trips depart about every half-hour, but sell out quickly in the summer—book as far in advance as possible. To spice it up, take the night tour to the island, or combine the regular tour with a visit to Angel Island for an all-day outing. The Red & White Fleet (Pier 43) has been open since 1892 and takes passengers sailing underneath the Golden Gate Bridge and around Angel Island (415-673-2900). For an aquatic adventure that doesn't require leaving dry land, the Aquarium of the Bay's clear underwater tunnels, tanks, and touch pools ffer a window into the Bay habitat and the its ver 23,000 sea creatures (415-623-5300). Thrill-eekers can perform aerial feats on the Frequent yers bungee trampoline (415-981-6300); soar over an Francisco on a seaplane ride (415-332-4843); r brave Turbo Ride, which uses 3D and hydraulic eats to put you right in the action: a roller coaster, og ride or even smack dab in SpongeBob's square ants. Located at the end of Pier 39 by the Bay, he hand-painted San Francisco Carousel with its ,800 twinkling lights is a hit with kids. Kids of all ges will have bunches of fun at the part-arcade, art-museum Musée Mécanique, Pier 45, especially hose old enough to remember when it was housed t Ocean Beach's Playland at the Beach. And yes, aughing Sal is still there. The Wax Museum (800-39-4305) has Hollywood celebrities, presidents, nd scientists all looking their best—don't miss the useum's Chamber of Horrors.

Shopping

or the most part, the shops surrounding Fisherman's Vharf aren't reason enough for locals to visit (unless ou've got some inexplicable hankering to stock up n kitschy San Fran trinkets). The Anchorage Square 415-775-6000) houses two dozen shops that sell verything from Russian crafts to personalized hats. esidents often brave the crowds here to feast at n-N-Out Burger (333 Jefferson St, 800-786-1000), he chain's only location within city limits. Though lightly more upscale than the Anchorage, The annery (2801 Leavenworth St, 415-771-3112) loesn't offer much in the way of shopping outside of he usual tourist fare. The largest shopping center is ier 39 (2 Beach St, 415-705-5500), with 110 specialty hops. Again, most are only cool if you're a tourist, etween the ages of 12 and 16. At scenic Ghirardelli quare (page 194), galleries, souvenir shops, and a ariety of restaurants surround an attractively laid-ut square. The real attraction here is the chocolate old at the Ghirardelli Ice Cream and Chocolate Shop.

Restaurants

lioto's Restaurant offers great food with a great view #8 Fisherman's Wharf, 415-673-0183). For the penny inchers, free parking is included at the Franciscan rab Restaurant (Pier 43 1/2, 415-362-7733) and coma's (Pier 47, 415-771-4383). Cheap eats can be ad at Joe's Crab Shack (245 Jefferson St, 415-673-266). Another notable restaurant is Pompei's Grotto 340 Jefferson St, 415-776-9265), a family-owned and perated seafood favorite since 1946. No man is an

island, but an exclusive dining experience can be just that. Forbes Island (415-951-4900) is the world's only man-made floating isla and boasts port-holed dining rooms underwater or those overlooking Alcatraz and the Golden Gate Bridge.

Lodging

- **Argonaut Hotel** • 495 Jefferson St • 415-563-0800
- **Best Western Tuscan Inn** • 425 North Point St • 415-561-1100
- **Courtyard by Marriott** • 580 Beach St • 415-775-3800
- **Heritage Marina Hotel** • 2550 Van Ness Ave • 415-776-7500
- **Hilton** • 2620 Jones St • 415-885-4700
- **Holiday Inn** • 1300 Columbus Ave • 1-800-942-7348
- **Hyatt** • 555 North Point St • 415-563-1234
- **Marriott** • 1250 Columbus Ave • 415-775-7555
- **Radisson Hotel** • 250 Beach St • 415-392-6700
- **Sheraton** • 2500 Mason St • 1-888-393-6809
- **Wharf Inn** • 2601 Mason St • 415-673-7411

How to Get There—Driving

From the south, take the 101 N towards San Francisco. Take 280 N towards downtown San Francisco. Exit at King Street. Follow King Street past AT&T Park where it becomes the Embarcadero. Continue down the Embarcadero, staying in the middle lane. Turn left onto Bay Street, right onto Mason Street, then left onto Northpoint Street.

From East Bay via the Bay Bridge, take 80 W to San Francisco, crossing the Bay Bridge. Exit at Harrison Street/Embarcadero (this exit is on the left side). At the bottom of the exit, turn right onto Harrison Street. At the end of Harrison Street, take a left onto the Embarcadero. Continue down the Embarcadero, staying in the middle lane. Turn left onto Bay Street, right onto Mason Street, then left onto Northpoint Street.

How to Get There—Mass Transit

Muni lines 19-Polk, 47-Van Ness, 30-Stockton, 10-Townsend, 15-Third Street, and 39-Coit serve the area. From the shared BART/Muni Embarcadero station, take the F-line streetcar. A fun alternative is the Powell-Hyde cable car to Beach Street or the Powell-Mason cable car to Bay Street.

General Information

NFT Map: 28
Mailing Address: 1600 Holloway Ave
                  San Francisco, CA 94132
Location: 1600 Halloway Ave
                  b/w Cardenas Ave & Varela Ave
Phone: 415-338-1111
Website: www.sfsu.edu
Established: 1899
Present Enrollment: 30,469
Type of School: Public

Overview

Located near the city's posh and sylvan St Francis Wood neighborhood, San Francisco State University's campus is an academic oasis bordered by the Stonestown Shopping Mall to the north, Lake Merced to the west, and tree-lined residential areas south and east. Walk around SFSU's sizeable campus and you'll notice perhaps the school's most admirable trait: an incredibly diverse student body that includes virtually every ethnic group and culture (not to mention age). In fact, SFSU enrolls more international students than any master's degree-granting institution in the country. SFSU ranks tenth in the nation in awarding degrees to minorities.

At SFSU, students don't just learn in classrooms and laboratories—they learn in the Bay Area itself. We sound like we're taking this stuff straight out of their brochure, don't we? But we're not. It's actually true. The school is committed to incorporating learning with service, and SFSU students have always worked to improve city housing projects, bring music instruction to city schools, help immigrants prepare for citizenship tests, and support health care for low income residents.

Tuition

In the 2013-2014 academic year, full-time resident undergraduate students pay $6,500 per year in tuition and fees. Full-time graduate resident students pay $7,716 per year. On-campus room and board costs around an additional $12,500 for the academic year.

Parking

The Lot 20 garage offers general paid public, visitor/guest, and student parking. It's open 24/7 and costs $3 for 2 hours or $6 for the day; exact change is required. The roof level is restricted to staff and faculty weekdays between 7 am and 5 pm. Lot 25 is open daily to the general public from 7 am to 10 pm. For those who bike to campus, the (free!) Bike Barn is open from 7:30 am to 10 pm weekdays and closes at 5 pm on Fridays (note that the Bike Barn is closed when class is not in session).

Cultural Events

In addition to regular music performances and exhibits at the Cesar Chavez Student Center, the University offers a number of annual cultural and arts-related events. Each May, the University's Cinema Department presents its Film Finals Showcase, a one-night gala event showcasing the work of young Bay Area filmmakers. Most of the films in the showcase go on to the national and international film festival circuit. Most performances are free for faculty, staff, and students, and very cheap for community members. The school also hosts community service programs, such as the annual African-American Community Health Fair, usually held in the spring.

Sports

SFSU competes in the NCAA's Division II in 11 different sports, and in the California Collegiate Athletic Association in every sport except wrestling. SFSU currently sponsors men's and women's basketball, cross-country, soccer, track & field, and swimming. Baseball and wrestling have men's teams, while indoor track & field, softball, tennis, and volleyball have women's squads. The varsity teams have piled up 140 NCAA Championship trophies over the years. Intramural leagues, tournaments, and special events exist for students during the academic year. Workout facilities are available in the gym at noon and during certain evening hours for students, faculty, and staff.

Intercollegiate athletics are an integral component of the academic experience at SFSU. On-campus athletic facilities include Cox Stadium, Main Gymnasium, Maloney Field, Stephenson Field, the main pool, and tennis courts. Also, the Gator Conditioning Center is a fitness facility available to all student athletes.

Intramural leagues, tournaments, and special events are offered in the fall and spring semesters. The program consists of men's, women's, and co-ed sports including basketball, volleyball, indoor soccer, swimming, bowling, ultimate Frisbee, water polo, softball, badminton, tennis, and flag football.

Department Contact Info

Undergraduate Studies	415-338-2206
Graduate Studies	415-338-2234
College of Behavioral & Social Studies	415-338-1846
College of Business	415-338-1276
College of Creative Arts	415-338-2467
College of Education	415-338-2687
College of Ethnic Studies	415-338-1693
College of Extended Learning	415-405-7700
College of Health & Human Services	415-338-3326
College of Humanities	415-338-1541
College of Science and Engineering	415-338-1571
Division of Information Technology	415-338-1420
Disability Resource Center	415-338-2472
Interdisciplinary Studies	415-338-6927
Lost and Found	415-338-2306
Recreation Program	415-338-2218
Student Health Center	415-338-1251

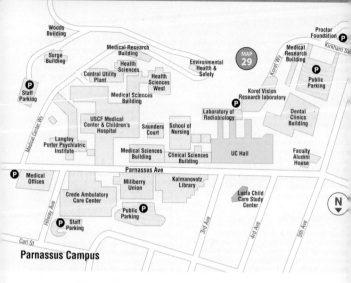

Parnassus Campus

General Information

NFT Map: 29
Mailing Address: The University of California
San Francisco, CA 94143
Parnassus Location: 505 Parnassus Ave
General Phone: 415-476-9000
Website: www.ucsf.edu

Overview

The University of California, San Francisco (UCSF) offers graduate and professional programs in health sciences, education, and patient care, and has been part of the UC system for 138 years. With over 18,000 faculty and staff, the university is the second largest employer in San Francisco. UCSF places a strong emphasis on the diversity of its student body, as well as a commitment to public service amongst its students. The UCSF Homeless Clinic, which provides free medical care to homeless people in San Francisco, is run completely by UCSF

students. They also run a free dental clinic. The Medical Effectiveness Research Center for Diverse Populations (MERC) conducts research on the barriers that impede various ethnic and economic groups' access to quality health care.

UCSF students train at three main teaching hospitals in the city: San Francisco General Hospital, UCSF Mount Zion Medical Center, and the Department of Veterans Affairs Medical Center.

The 43-acre campus at Mission Bay (16th St and Owens St) is the newest addition to UCSF and part of the overall Mission Bay urban development project. In 2003, the first researchers moved into Genentech Hall. By May 2004, 1,200 faculty, staff, and students were working and studying on the campus and, in 15 years, they expect the campus population to grow ninefold. Future plans for the campus include a child-care center, a 1,400-space parking garage, and a 2.2-acre site for a public school. The latest information on the campus may be found at www. ucsf.edu/mission-bay.

University of California, San Francisco

At the main Parnassus Campus, many student services are located in the Millberry Union building (500 Parnassus Ave). There you'll find the bookstore; food services, such as the Courtyard Café, Peet's Coffee Bar, and Panda Express; the Recreation Fitness Center; Golden 1 Credit Union; Reprographics/Quick Copy; conference centers; The Source Computer Services; and faculty housing.

Tuition

Just like at all state schools, tuition at UCSF has risen dramatically in the past couple of years. Some programs saw an increase was as much as 30%, for residents and non-residents alike. There are dozens of programs at UCSF, each with its own tuition rate, so refer to the UCSF website for the most current numbers:http://finaid.ucsf.edu/newly-admitted-students/cost-attendance

Parking

The university's advice when it comes to parking is straightforward: "parking is often difficult at many of our campus locations," reads their website, and we couldn't agree more. There are, however, some limited parking options if public transportation is not an option. Servicing the Parnassus Heights Campus is the Millberry Union Public Garage, located at 500 Parnassus Avenue and Irving Street. The first four hours cost $3 each (totaling $12 for up to four hours). The 24-hour maximum is $24). The Westside/Kirkham Surface Lot is located behind the School of Dentistry at 707 Parnassus Avenue, and the rates are the same as Millberry Union, but are only in effect from 7 am to 6 pm on weekdays. At all other times, a 24-hour flat rate of $2 is in effect. At Beckman/Koret Surface Lot, fees are the same as above, with the same hours as Westside/Kirkham. After 6 pm and on weekends, the lot is for permit parking only.

For parking information at the other four campuses, visit www.campuslifeservices.ucsf.edu/transportation/parking/.

UCSF provides shuttles at some locations on the campuses, including the student apartments on Turk Street, the 16th and Mission BART, and the transportation station at Powell Street.

Sports

UCSF does not have competitive sports teams, but does offer a wide variety of recreational sports including clubs, leagues, and drop-in practices. The Millberry Recreation & Fitness Center is located in Millberry Union, 500 Parnassus Avenue, I Level East. There is also a brand new center, Bakar Fitness & Recreation at Mission Bay, which has both indoor and glamorous rooftop swimming pools.

Department Contact Info

Dentistry 415-476-2737
Graduate Studies 415-476-2310
Nursing.............................. 415-476-1435
Pharmacy............................. 415-476-2732
Physical Therapy (academic).......... 415-476-3147
Physical Therapy (clinic) 415-476-3451
Medicine 415-476-4044

Other Campuses

- **Laurel Heights**
  3333 California St
- **UCSF/Mount Zion Medical Center** ·
  1600 Divisadero St
- **Buchanan Dental Center** ·
  100 Buchanan St
- **San Francisco General Hospital** ·
  1001 Potrero Ave
- **Hunters Point Facility** ·
  900 Palou Ave
- **Veterans Affairs Medical Center** ·
  4150 Clement St
- **Mission Bay** ·
  16th St & Owens St

University of California, Berkeley

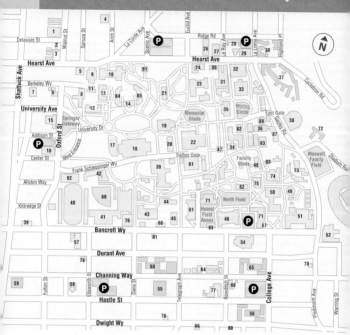

1. Oxford Research Unit
2. Natural Resources Laboratory
3. Insectary
4. McEnerney
5. Barker
6. University Garage
7. UC Press
8. Warren
9. Koshland
10. Tolman
11. Genetics and Plant Biology
12. Mulford
13. Morgan
14. Wellman
15. University Hall/ Visitor Services
16. UC Printing Services
17. Life Sciences
18. Valley Life Sciences
19. Moffitt Library
20. California
21. Haviland
22. Main Library/Bancroft Library

23. McCone Earth Sciences
24. North Gate Hall
25. Etcheverry
26. Soda
27. Cloyne Court
28. Tennis
29. Davis
30. Foothill Student Housing
31. Davis
32. Cory
33. Hearst Mining
34. Birge
35. Evans
36. Latimer
37. Stern
38. Hearst Greek Theatre
39. Career Center
40. Edwards Stadium/Goldman Field
41. Recreational Sports Facility
42. Callaghan
43. Zellerbach
44. Cesar E Chavez Student Center
45. King Student Union
46. Hearst Gym

47. Sather Tower
48. Faculty Club
49. Calvin Laboratory
50. Wurster
51. Law Building
52. International House
53. California Memorial Stadium
54. UC Berkeley Art Museum
55. Haste/Channing Student Housing
56. Residence Halls Unit 2
57. Tang Center/ University Health Services
58. Jones Child Study Center
59. Manville Apartments
60. Residence Halls Unit 3
61. Wheeler
62. Hildebrand
63. Senior Hall
64. Parking and Transit Operations Office
65. Residence Halls Unit 1
66. Dwight Way House
67. Hearst Museum
68. Community Living Office

69. Evans Field
70. Casa Joaquin Murieta
71. Froeber
72. Bowles
73. Haas
74. Minor
75. Hertz
76. Spieker Aquatics Com
77. 2536-38
78. 2298
79. 2427
80. 2600
81. 2440 Bancroft Wy
82. Campbell
83. PFA Thatre
84. Hilgard
85. Giannini
86. Naval Architechture
87. Stanley
88. Donner
89. Banway 2111
90. Eshleman
91. University House
92. Hellman Tennis Court

University of California, Berkeley

General Information

Visitor's Services: 101 Sproul Hall
2200 University Ave
Berkeley, CA 94720

Visitor's Services: 510-623-5215
General Info: 510-642-6000
Website: www.berkeley.edu

Overview

UC Berkeley, or Cal for short, is not only one of the world's leading intellectual centers, but it also has a history of political and social activism that few can rival. The Vietnam War protesters on Sproul Plaza are long gone, but there is no shortage of speaking out on campus. Students are eager to speak their mind on international, local, and social issues, thereby upholding the university's legacy of free speech.

At Berkeley, each department has its own library collection. When the Gardner Stacks of Doe Library, which holds all humanities, arts, and social science-related comes, opened in 1994, the transportation of its 1.5 million volumes was dubbed "the biggest book move west of the Mississippi." Entry into Doe requires a student ID, but visitors unaffiliated with the university can enter the Valley Life Sciences Building Library, where a giant dinosaur replica guards the main hallway. Best views are from the top of the Campanile, from the lounge in 1015 Evans Hall, and from the affiliated Berkeley National Laboratory up the hill. Lectures with guest speakers are usually free and open to the public—call the department of your interest for information on upcoming talks. The Pacific Film Archive and the Berkeley Art Museum on campus have noteworthy exhibits and showcases. The Greek Theatre hosts popular summer concerts.

The campus itself is a beautiful assortment of architectural and historic landmarks scattered amidst green glades and hidden woodsy paths. You can walk across campus in 15 minutes (watch out for bike dismount areas markings—tickets from security are quite common), and if you're late to a meeting on the hour—no worries, as on "Berkeley time," classes start at ten after. The amazing East Bay weather demands hanging out outside. Students cooperate by playing Frisbee on Memorial Glade, bouldering the stone wall at Davis Hall, or seeking out the eccentric markers. They call South Hall the "Mary Poppins Building," as the roof looks like the scene of the chimney sweep's dance; there is a bizarre stain on the stone on Sather Gate that is said to look like Jimi Hendrix. Check out the Free Speech Movement Café off Moffitt Library; plaques and posters there depict the movement's history and origins on campus. (Ironically, back in the 1960s, university authorities were the biggest opponent of the developments.)

Tuition

In the 2012-2013 academic year, undergraduate tuition and fees cost $7,492.75 per semester for California residents, and $18,931.75 per semester for non-residents. Add another average $1,000 per month for room and board (dorms are more expensive than co-op houses around campus, and apartments vary), another $3,000 a year for books, incidentals, and transportation (though full-time students get an Alameda County bus sticker with tuition). Nonetheless, compared to some places that shall remain unnamed where one semester's tuition is more than all this put together, you're still getting yourself a bargain!

Sports

The Golden Bears have many nationally-ranked top-ten teams in various men's and women's sports. For schedules and tickets, visit the Cal athletics website, www.calbears.com. The biggest game of the season is the annual football game against Stanford University, held at the beautiful home stadium every other year. The university also offers a comprehensive intramural and club sports program, and the lap pools and the Recreational Sports Facility are open to students for a nominal fee.

Parking

As in any busy, bustling city, street parking is a total nightmare. Northside is usually more flexible than Southside, but watch for big events such as football games, concerts at the Greek Theatre, and graduations; during high-traffic events, you could be circling the block for hours. Parking on campus requires a permit, and the campus police are vigilant about ticketing non-permit holders. Consider the public lots (Oxford St & Allston Wy, Durant Ave & Telegraph Ave, Bancroft Wy & Telegraph Ave, and Center St & Shattuck Ave). The best thing to do, for your sanity, is to leave the car at home and take BART. Exit at the Downtown Berkeley station, located just a short walk from campus.

Department Contact Info

Undergraduate Admissions.................510-642-3175
Graduate Admissions 510-642-7405
Boalt Hall Law School 510-642-2274
College of Letters & Science 510-642-1483
College of Chemistry......................510-642-5060
College of Engineering.....................510-642-5771
College of Natural Resources 510-642-7171
Graduate School of Education 510-642-5345
Graduate School of Journalism............510-642-3383
Haas School of Business 510-642-1421
The Richard & Rhoda Goldman 510-642-4670
  School of Public Policy
School of Information & 510-642-1464
  Management Systems
School of Optometry.......................510-642-9537
School of Public Health....................510-642-6531
School of Social Welfare~..................510-642-4341

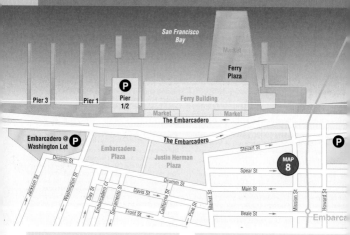

General Information

NFT Map:	8
Address:	One Ferry Building
	San Francisco, CA 94111
Phone:	415-693-0996
Website:	www.ferrybuildingmarketplace.com
Hours:	Mon–Fri: 10 am–6 pm,
	Sat: 9 am–6 pm, Sun: 11 am–5 pm
	Hours for individual businesses may vary

Ferry Plaza Farmers Market

Phone:	415-291-3276
Website:	www.cuesa.org
Hours:	Tues–Thu: 10 am–2 pm (year-round)
	Sat: 8 am–2 pm (year-round)

Ferry Information

> www.goldengateferry.org
> www.baylinkferry.com
> www.sfport.com
> www.blueandgoldfleet.com

Overview

The Ferry Building is a jewel of the San Francisco waterfront and a testament to San Francisco's survivor spirit. In 1898, the Ferry Building opened over the older, wooden Ferry House. Its foundation is the largest for an over-water building. Ferry Building architect A. Page Brown was wise to have used steel to frame the new construction—the structure has survived two major earthquakes, the first in 1906 and the second in 1989. During the '89 earthquake, the neighboring, old Embarcadero freeway crumbled, but the mighty Ferry Building stood firm.

One of our favorite Saturday morning activities is to go down to the recently renovated Ferry Building, grab a cup of coffee, and celebrate our favorite thing…*food*! Saturdays offer two great reasons to visit the Ferry Building: amazing food stores and restaurants inside the Marketplace and the bustling Ferry Plaza Farmers Market outside. Be prepared to battle hoards of tourists and locals for access to the market's fresh, organic produce, beautiful flowers, meat, cheeses, breads, and of course, amazing bay views. Believe us, it's a worthwhile fight.

Oh yeah…the Ferry Building also operates as a ferry terminal. Since well before the building of the Golden Gate and Bay Bridges, the Ferry Building has been an embarkation point for transport to the East Bay, Marin, and Contra Costa County. There are still plenty of ferry commuters that pass through the building, the tide rising at rush hour when the cafés start to fill up. Try a ferry for your next visit to Oakland or Sausalito.

How to Get There—Driving

From the Bay Bridge, take the Main Street/ Embarcadero exit, turn right onto Harrison Street then turn left onto the Embarcadero.

From the Golden Gate Bridge, take the Marina Boulevard exit, and proceed on Marina Boulevard around the Safeway. Turn left onto Bay Street, driving for approximately 2 miles, then turn right onto the Embarcadero.

From the South Bay, take Highway 101 towards the Bay Bridge (I-80), then take the Fourth Street exit and stay right on Bryant Street. Turn left onto the Embarcadero. The alternative is to take Highway 280 towards downtown and take the Sixth Street exit, staying right on Brannan Street. Turn left on the Embarcadero.

Parking

Parking is available in two lots located at the north end of the Ferry Building, at Pier 1/2 and at the Embarcadero & Washington lot directly across from Pier 1/2. IParking garages are also located beneath each of the four Embarcadero Center buildings, accessible via Drumm, Davis, Front and Battery Streets, between Sacramento and Clays streets. On weekends only, you can also park in the 75 Howard Street Garage for a $4 flat rate good for up to four hours from 6 am to 6 pm. Valet parking is also available in front of the building all day Monday– Friday and on weekend evenings. Hey, if you're lucky, you might even hit the jackpot and snag a metered space on the street. Just remember to come with a roll (or two) of quarters.

How to Get There—Mass Transit

The F Market above-ground vintage streetcar line goes right to the Ferry Building. If you're taking the Muni or Bart instead, get off at the Embarcadero stop and take the escalators to Market Street. The Ferry Building is about a block and a half away.

Ferry Building Marketplace Merchants

Bread & Cheese
Acme Bread Company
Cowgirl Creamery's Artisan
  Cheese Shop

Books & Ferry Tickets
Bay Crossings
  (Ferry Tickets, Maps & Guides)
Book Passage
  (Books & Literary Events)

Cafés & Small Eateries
Boulette's Larder
DELICA
Hog Island Oyster Company
Il Cane Rosso
MIJUN
Out the Door

Coffee & Tea
Blue Bottle Coffee
Imperial Tea Court
Peet's Coffee & Tea

Cookware & Tableware
The Gardener
Heath Ceramics
Sur La Table

Farm Produce,
  Flowers & Garden
Alfieri Fruits & Nuts
Beekind—Gifts from the Hive
Benedetta
Farm Fresh to You
Far West Fungi
Ferry Plaza Farmers Market
  (CUESA)
Kingdom of Herbs

Meat, Poultry, & Fish
Boccalone Salumeria
Ferry Plaza Seafood
Golden Gate Meat Company
Hog Island Oyster Company
Prather Ranch Meat Co.
San Francisco Fish Company

Pastry, Ice Cream, & Chocolate
Black Jet Baking Company
Ciao Bella Gelato
Frog Hollow Farm
Mariposa Baking Company
Miette
Recchiuti Confections
Scharffen Berger Chocolate
  Maker

Restaurants
Gott's Roadside
MarketBar
Slanted Door (NFT pick!)

Specialty Grocery
  & Prepared Foods
la Cocina
McEvoy Ranch Olive Oil
el Porteno Empanadas
  Argentinas
Stonehouse California Olive Oil
Village Market

Wine & Spirits
Ferry Plaza Wine Merchant

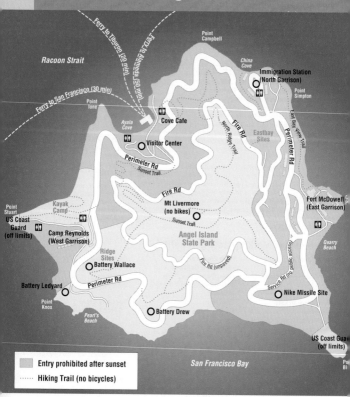

Racoon Strait

Ferry to Tiburon (10 min)

Ferry to Alameda (50 min)

Point Campbell

China Cove

Immigration Station (North Garrison)

Point Simpton

Ferry to San Francisco (30 min)

Point Ione

Ayala Cove

Cove Cafe

North Ridge Trail

Fire Rd

Eastbay Sites

East Bay View Trail

Perimeter Rd

Visitor Center

Perimeter Rd

Sunset Trail

Fire Rd

Mt Livermore (no bikes)

Fire Rd

Sunset Trail

Angel Island State Park

Fire Rd (ungraved)

Service Rd (no public access)

Fort McDowell (East Garrison)

Quarry Beach

Point Stuart

Kayak Camp

US Coast Guard (off limits)

Camp Reynolds (West Garrison)

Ridge Sites

Battery Wallace

Battery Ledyard

Perimeter Rd

Point Knox

Pearl's Beach

Battery Drew

Nike Missile Site

US Coast Gua (off limits)

Po Bl

San Francisco Bay

Entry prohibited after sunset

····· Hiking Trail (no bicycles)

General Information

Phone: 415-435-5390
Website: www.angelisland.org,
            www.angelisland.com
            www.parks.ca.gov/?page_id=468
Hours: 8 am to sunset, year-round
Entry: Free

Overview

Angel Island is the largest island in San Francisco Bay, covering 740 acres. Visitors can now take a guided tour of the newly renovated United States Immigration Station, including the Dentention Barracks. The tours run Wednesday through Sunday at 11 am, 12:30 pm, and 2 pm and costs $7 for adults, $5 for children ages 5-11. It sits as an oasis of natural beauty rich in historical significance, just a ferry ride from the city. Across the centuries, it's been a hunting ground for the Miwok Indians, a Civil War encampment, a quarantine station, a POW camp, and an immigration station referred to as "the Ellis Island of the West." In reality it was quite different, as immigrants (97% Chinese) were detained rather than welcomed at "the Guardian of the Western Gate." During the Cold War it was used as a Nike Missile Base, and by 1963 the entire island had become State of California parkland, with the exception of the Coast Guard stations on Point Blunt and Point Stuart (still in operation).

Practicalities

Tourist season runs from March through November, with all services in full swing on a daily basis. The off-season sees some activity; however, tours and ferries are limited.

Activities

While no dogs, roller blades, skateboards, or scooters are allowed, there is still fun to be had. Over thirteen miles of foot trails and fire roads ring the island, along with eight miles of cycling trails, making for great hiking and biking fun (bring your own or rent on-site). Follow the Perimeter Road to access the historical sights such as the Immigration Station and Fort McDowell, as well as the island's beaches. The sandy shores are not for swimming—these are the same rough, cold waters shared with Alcatraz.

A trail leads up to the 788-foot summit of Mount Livermore (so it's not *quite* a mountain). When the Nike Missile Base was built, the top of the peak was shaved down 15 feet to accommodate a helicopter landing pad and a control booth. The dirt was only pushed over to the side and not removed, and recently the top has been reshaped to its original contours. Here you'll find a panoramic view and, on a clear day, you can see all five Bay Area bridges.

Tours of the historic sights are given by volunteer docents on weekends and holidays. Motorized one-hour TramTours are also presented through the Angel Island Company and feature an audio guide that highlights the island's military and cultural history ($15 for adults, $13.50 for seniors, $10 for juniors, and free for kids 5 & under when seated on your lap). The island's Cove Café, located near the ferry dock, offers sandwiches, soups, coffee, beer, and wine for sale.

When the families, tourists, and commotion depart on that last ferry, the island is yours. Nine campsites are available for reservation at $15–20 a night depending on the time of year (8 people maximum; 800-444-PARK; www.reserveamerica.com). Amenities at each site include barbeques, tables, running water, pit toilets, and food lockers. Pack light and leave the Duraflame in the fireplace as you will have to carry your gear at least two miles to the sites and no wood fires are allowed. Expect to book a weekend site a few months in advance. There is also a slightly more expensive kayak-accessible site (holds up to 20 people) for $30 a night. Sea Trek Kayak (415-332-8494; www.seatrek.com) leads kayak tours around the island. Visit their website for rates and class information.

How to Get There—Ferry

Blue & Gold Fleet
(415-705-8200; www.blueandgoldfleet.com) runs a 15–20 minute ferry service from Fisherman's Wharf to Ayala Cove with one-way tickets that cost $8.50 for adults and $4.50 for children aged 6–12 years.

The Angel Island-Tiburon Ferry
(415-435-2131; www.angelislandferry.com) runs from Tiburon (we kid you not). A round-trip ticket to ride with admission is $13.50 for adults and seniors, $11.50 for children 6–10 years old, $3.50, free for children 2 and younger, and you can even take your bike along for an extra $1 fee.

The Alameda/Oakland Ferry
(510-749-5972; www.eastbayferry.com) runs on summer weekends at a cost of $14.50 for adults, $11.25 for students and seniors, $8.50 for children 5–12 years old, and free for children under five. Visit the respective websites for a detailed operating schedule and don't forget that ferries have abbreviated service during the off-peak season. But that's okay. The San Francisco Bay gets so choppy and sharky in the winter, it's best to stay inland.

How to Get There—Boat

If you're lucky enough to know someone with their own yacht, private slips 30' to 50' are available year-round on a first-come, first-served basis. Fees are changed according to season, with day fees ranging from $10–15 and overnight fees ranging from $15–$20.

Overview

NFT Maps: 10 & 14

Built on top of a cemetery (don't worry, the last body laid to rest here went under way back in 1894), Mission Dolores Park is a popular haunt for locals from surrounding neighborhoods like the Castro, the Mission, and Noe Valley. On clear, sunny days, groups spread out on the grassy hills while dogs romp and children toddle around the playground area. Casual birthday parties and get-togethers commonly occupy picnic tables on the weekends. Outdoor fitness groups, as well as Tai Chi practitioners and personal trainers with clients in tow, are regular early morning fixtures. When temperatures rise in the city, you can expect Dolores Park to be peppered with bikini-clad bodies starved for sun. Park facilities include six public tennis courts, one basketball court, two soccer fields (often unusable after heavy rains), a clubhouse, public restrooms (prepare to hold your nose!), water fountains, and paved pathways frequently used for jogging, walking, and promenading with baby carriages. The children's playground, opened in 2012, is one of the nicest such facilities in the city—at the very least it has one of the best views of any playground we've ever come across..

Established as a city park in 1905, the sloping area takes its name from Mission Dolores, founded by Spanish colonists in 1776. The Mission Dolores buildings still stand near the intersection of Dolores Street and 16th Street and house an active Catholic church. One of the few areas unscathed by the great 1906 earthquake and ensuing fires, the park became the site of a temporary refugee camp for San Franciscans whose homes had been destroyed during the natural disaster.

Directly across the street from the park at Dolores and 18th Street is the popular outdoor spot, the Dolores Park Café. Across the street from the cafe is the Bi-Rite Creamery (3692 18th St) featuring delicious, if pricey, organic, exotic-flavored ice creams—think honey lavender, balsamic strawberry, and brown sugar with ginger caramel swirl.

How to Get There—Driving

Dolores Park is bounded by Dolores, Church, 18th, and 20th Streets. From Highway 101, take the Cesar Chavez West exit. Follow Cesar Chavez to Dolores St. Turn right on Dolores Street. Follow until you reach the park. From the Golden Gate Bridge, follow the signs to downtown San Francisco, which take you along Lombard Street. Turn right on Van Ness Ave and follow to Market Street. Turn right on Market. Turn left on Dolores and follow to the park.

How to Get There—Mass Transit

San Francisco Municipal Railway (Muni) J-Church line stops right in the park as does the 33-Stanyan bus line. Alternatively, you can ride the 26 Valencia bus to the Valencia/16th St stop. Then walk west two blocks and up another two blocks to the park.

General Information

Address: 1 Bear Valley Rd
Pt. Reyes Station, CA 94956
Phone: 415-464-5100
Website: www.nps.gov/pore/
Open: Sunrise till sunset daily, overnight
camping available with a permit,
but post-midnight beach fires and
overnight parking are prohibited

Overview

Point Reyes National Seashore is a lush, dramatically beautiful, 100-square-mile wilderness preserve abundant with beaches, marshes, forests, grazing lands, and a wider array of land, sea, and airborne critters than you can find practically nowhere else. (Twenty-three endangered species and nearly half of North America's bird species hang out on Point Reyes.) Eighty miles and 32,000 acres of undeveloped coastland host elephant seals, sea lions, mountain lions, coho salmon, steelhead trout, sardines, anchovies, and the occasional shark, and the inland forests and grasslands are abundant with deer, rabbit, mink, beaver, a black bear or two, and tule elk, which flourish in their own 2,600-acre reserve at Tomales Point.

The area's first inhabitants were the Coast Miwok, who lived and thrived for thousands of years in over a hundred villages within the Seashore alone. (A re-created Miwok village, Kule Loklo, is open to the public, and every summer the tribe's descendants throw a Big Time festival on the coast that is not unlike the get-togethers of the past, www.kuleloklo. com.) British buccaneer Sir Francis Drake (probably) landed here in 1579, claiming the area for Elizabeth I. During and after the Gold Rush, failed miners turned their attention to the verdant grasslands of West Marin and brought dairy ranching to Point Reyes, still one of the region's defining aspects.

The area became a federally protected National Seashore in 1962, and today Point Reyes is a popular getaway destination for birders, bikers, kayakers, tidepoolers, and anyone who loves the natural abundance of this magical place. Hikers can satisfy their itch with over 147 miles of trails, and four campgrounds are available with picnic tables, food lockers, and charcoal braziers for hike-in camping (no cars allowed; permit required from Bear Valley Visitor Center, 415-464-5100). Whale watching is also popular during migration season (peak times are mid-January and mid-March) and free ranger-led excursions and field seminars are a fun and always informative way to spend an afternoon.

Points of Interest

Bear Valley Visitor Center—Exhibits of both environmental and historical interest as well as an auditorium for educational programs.
Info: 415-464-5100.

Mount Wittenberg—At 1300 feet, this is the highest point on the seashore, with expectedly gorgeous views.

Point Reyes Lighthouse—Situated on a cliff 300 feet above the ocean, this cast-iron tower has saved many a mist-shrouded mariner from shipwreck since 1870 (Point Reyes not only juts 10 miles into the Pacific, it's the second-foggiest spot in North America and the windiest place on the Pacific Coast). Open to the public Thursdays through Mondays. Info: 415-669-1534.

RCA/Marconi Wireless Stations—In 1913 Guglielmo Marconi, the father of wireless radio, commissioned the building of the wireless telegraphy transmitting station in Bolinas and the receiving station in Marshall, the most powerful on the Pacific Rim. It was replaced 20 years later with an Art Deco receiving station. In 2000 park staff and volunteers set about to restore the original RCA/Marconi stations to their original luster.

Miwok Archeological Preserve of Marin—Offers classes in arrow-making, basket-weaving, hide-tanning, flint-knapping, and other time-honored skills. Info: www.mapom.org.

Pierce Dairy Ranch and Morgan Horse Ranch—Working ranches open to the public for self-guided tours. Check out the breeding grounds for America's first horse breed: the Morgan horse.
Info: 415-464-5169.

Point Reyes Bird Observatory—Point Reyes is a birder's paradise, and this is the place to get started. Includes visitor's center and nature trail. Open 365 days a year. Info: www.prbo.org, 707-781-2555.

Five Brooks Stables—Explore the Seashore on horseback. Info: 415-663-1570 or www.fivebrooks.com.

Drake's Bay Family Farms—Stop by for a fresh half-dozen harvested right out of Drakes Estero. Info: 415-669-1149.

Point Reyes Outdoors Sea Kayaking Tours—Get up close and personal with harbor seals and leopard sharks. Kayaking is permitted at Drakes Estero and Limantour Estero from July through February and at Tomales Bay year-round. Info: 415-663-8192 or www.pointreyesoutdoors.com.

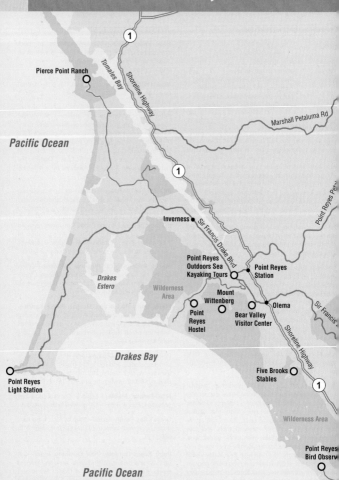

Food, Drink, Etc.

Website: www.cafereyes.net

Drake's Bay Oyster Farm—The best meal in Point Reyes is the farm-fresh oysters you purchase here and grill over a wood fire right on the beach. (Beach fires can only burn pine, almond, or driftwood, and require a permit.) 17171 Sir Francis Drake Blvd, Inverness, CA 94937, 415-669-1149.

Tony's Seafood—Fresh local seafood in a casual roadhouse setting along Tomales Bay. 18863 Highway 1, Marshall, CA 94940, 415-663-1107.

Toby's Feed Barn—A general store that carries hay, tack, and feed for livestock on one side, and fancy jams, country gifts, and souvenirs for visitor-stock on the other. It sits in the center of town and serves as a hangout, hosting the weekly organic farmers market June–Oct. 11250 Highway 1, Point Reyes Station, CA 94956, 415-663-1223, http://www.tobysfeedbarn.com/.

Pine Cone Diner—Diner food taken to an ethereal new level. Fourth & B Sts, Point Reyes Station, CA 94956, 415-663-1536, www.5happy.com/pineconediner/.

Bovine Bakery—The most delectable sticky buns, bear claws, and breadstuffs within at least 100 miles. 11315 Shoreline Highway, Point Reyes Station, CA 94956, 415-663-9420.

Cowgirl Creamery—A wide and excellent array of artisan cheeses made from locally produced organic milk. Fresh produce and picnic items too. 80 Fourth St, Point Reyes Station, CA 94956, 415-663-9335, www.cowgirlcreamery.com.

Station House Café—Serving breakfast, lunch, and dinner everyday except Wednesdays, SHC is a Point Reyes staple. With a wide array of gourmet options from burgers and seafood to pastas, there is something for everyone. 11180 Highway 1, Point Reyes Station, CA 94956, 415.663.1515, www.stationhousecafe.com.

Point Reyes Books—A great small bookstore with good local maps, guides, readings, etc. 11315 State Route 1, Point Reyes Station, CA 94956, 415-663-1542, www.ptreyesbooks.com.

Café Reyes—On the corner as you turn into the 3-block town is this restaurant featuring an outdoor patio, full bar, and big-screen TV, with oversized plates of fresh Mexican and California cuisine. 11101 Highway 1, Point Reyes Station, CA 94956, 415-663-9493.

Accommodations

Point Reyes Hostel—Ideal for the low-cost, big-backpack crowd. 415-663-8811. http://www.norcalhostels.org/reyes/

Other Point Reyes lodging options—www.pointreyes.org/west_marin_point_reyes_lodging.html

How to Get There— Public Transit

West Marin Stagecoach's Route 68 bus runs between San Rafael, Inverness, and Point Reyes Station Mondays through Saturdays. Call 415-526-3239 for schedules. San Rafael is as close as Golden Gate Transit's frequent Route 70 and 80 buses from downtown San Francisco get. Call 511 for schedules.

How to Get There—Driving

Point Reyes National Seashore is 30 miles north of San Francisco along the coast highway. Head across the Golden Gate Bridge and stay on 101 until the Sir Francis Drake-San Anselmo exit. Remain on Sir Francis Drake Boulevard as it meanders for 21 miles through San Anselmo, Fairfax, and West Marin until it ends at Highway 1 in Olema. Go right on Highway 1, continue about 100 yards, and take the first left onto Bear Valley Road. In just under a half mile, go left past the big, red barn to the Bear Valley Visitor Center. Or veer off 101 at the Mount Tamalpais-Stinson Beach exit just past Sausalito and take Highway 1 from there instead; it takes longer, but the scenery is lovely.

General Information

Crissy Field Center: 415-561-7690
Address: 603 Mason St & Halleck St
Presidio, CA 94129
Interim location at 1199 East
Beach, Presidio, CA
Website: www.parksconservancy.org/
visit/park-sites/crissy-field.
html

Overview

Looking out over Crissy Field, it's impossible to tell that from 1919 to 1936 it was an Army Air Corps airstrip. Vast environmental restoration projects (including the planting of 100,000 native plants) have been undertaken with an eye towards heavy human use, and have turned the area into either a mellow ecological showcase or a park on steroids. Either way, Crissy Field has something for everyone.

Crissy Field's 1.5 miles of shoreline are marked by several small beaches, which are shared by windsurfers, waders, and San Franciscans' beloved dogs. Directly behind the shoreline, the Golden

Gate Promenade leads a continuous stream o walkers, runners, and rollerbladers past windswep sand spits, picnic areas, footpaths, huge fields o native bunchgrasses (unsuitable for field sports) and a reconstructed tidal marsh with wildflower and migratory birds. All of the action is framed by postcard views of the Golden Gate Bridge (particularly from Fort Point, directly underneath) sailboats and cargo ships dotting the bay, the wooded hills of the Presidio and Marin Headlands and Angel Island views across the water.

Sunny days, even in the winter, will draw large crowds of locals and tourists alike, but the ample space allows everyone to do their thing in perfect harmony. How very San Francisco.

Amenities

If you're interested in environmental stewardship in an urban environment, the Crissy Field Center (415-561-7752) offers environmental education programming, an activity area, a teaching kitchen, a library, an information center, and a bookstore (415-561-7761). The Crissy Field Center Café (415-561-7756), overlooking the marsh, offers local, organic

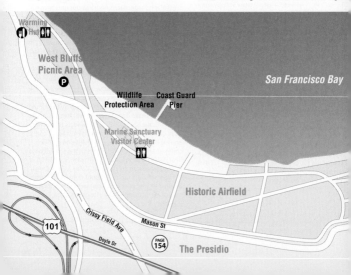

Warming
Hut

West Bluffs
Picnic Area
P

San Francisco Bay

Wildlife   Coast Guard
Protection Area   Pier

Marine Sanctuary
Visitor Center

Historic Airfield

101

Crissy Field Ave   Mason St

Doyle Dr   PAGE 154   **The Presidio**

food with a view. The Center is open everyday from 9 am to 5 pm. Closer to Fort Point is the Warming Hut (415-561-3042), a smaller organic food café and bookstore.

All-terrain wheelchairs are available for rent at the Crissy Field Center. If you're planning on hosting a big group event (50+ people), you'll need to acquire a permit from the National Park Service (415-561-4300).

There are several restrooms around Crissy Field—when you have to go, there are many places to go. See the map below for specific locations, or make friends with a bush.

Activities

Crissy Field is part of the popular bike route that runs from Aquatic Park near Fisherman's Wharf, across Golden Gate Bridge, to the seaside town of Tiburon. Along the Golden Gate Promenade, you can enjoy views of the Golden Gate and boats on the Bay while strolling, jogging, or rollerblading. The strong winds along the bay front make windsurfing, kite-surfing, and flying kites popular activities. The

West Bluffs Picnic Area, next to the Warming Hut, is an excellent place to crash seven-year-olds' birthday parties. Fishing is allowed, but don't try to trap any of the orange Dungeness crabs that use the Bay as a nursery—it's illegal to even touch them.

How to Get There

If you're driving, enter the Presidio from Marina Boulevard as it merges with 101 N toward the Golden Gate Bridge. Parking is available in a lot near East Beach, near the Warming Hut at the west end of Crissy Field, or at the Main Post parking area.

Muni routes 28-19th Avenue, 29-Sunset, and 43-Masonic come directly into the Presidio and drop off at the Main Post parking area, from which you can walk to Crissy Field.

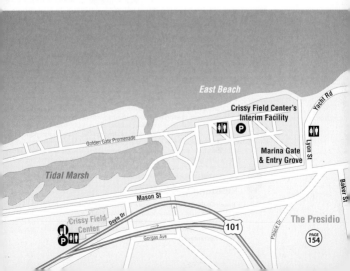

PAGE 154

Golden Gate Park
PAGE 152

General Information

NFT Map:	23 & 26
Park Services:	415-561-4700
Website:	www.nps.gov

Overview

At four miles long, this is the city's largest beach, but cold waters, harsh winds, dangerous rip tides, strong currents, summer fog, and a total absence of lifeguards make it less than a hot spot for beachgoers looking for a little r & r. Many people have drowned here just wading in the water. If that's not enough to keep the bronzed bods out of the salt drink, great white sharks are occasionally spotted in the vicinity. The awesome currents and marine wildlife, however, are no deterrent for Bay Area surfers (pop crooner Chris Isaak is known to be a regular). Despite the blustery weather, this beach is usually filled with joggers, dog walkers, and, on warm days, sunbathers. Bonfires may be lit in special fire rings installed throughout the beach (call the Ocean Beach Hotline for details at 415-561-4741), making it a popular spot for picnicking, cookouts, and nighttime bonfire festivities. Sea lions can be spotted by Seal Rock—that's the big one white-washed in bird shit.

Practicalities

The beach is part of the Golden Gate National Recreation Area, and is free and open to the public at all times. It is conveniently located along the Great Highway, and there are several free parking lots along the road. Although the park service allows dogs on the beach, there is a leash policy to protect the population of endangered western snowy plovers, which inhabit the beach ten months out of the year. To get there, take bus 38-Geary, 31-Balboa, 5-Fulton, or the N-Judah Muni.

Restrooms

Although scarce, there are a few restrooms and changing rooms located along the beach, mostly around the southern end near the zoo, as well as on the residential side of the Great Highway, which parallels the main thoroughfare. Most surfers simply change in and out of their wetsuits right in the parking lot, which only adds to the view at Ocean Beach. Outdoor showers are located at Sloat Boulevard. And nobody will know (or care) if you pee in the ocean.

Sports

This is an extremely popular and scenic spot for surfing, especially during the fall and winter, when the winds die down and the north swells start producing world-class waves. Fledgling surfers take caution—the currents have been known to sweep the unwary out to the mouth of the bay. The beach is also popular for fishing, and the path that runs parallel to the shore and next to the highway is an ideal stretch for walking, running, and biking. Many popular runs end up at the beach (Bay to Breakers on the third Sunday of May every year), and the course of the San Francisco Marathon (July) and the Nike Women's Marathon (October) traverses the stretch from JFK to the zoo and back.

Restaurants & Cafés

- **Beach Chalet Brewery & Restaurant** · 1000 Great Hwy · 415-386-8439
- **Cliff House** (Seafood, American) · 1090 Point Lobos Ave · 415-386-3330
- **Java Beach Café** (American) · 1396 La Playa St · 415-665-5282
- **Louis' Restaurant** (Breakfast, American) · 902 Point Lobos Ave · 415-387-6330
- **Win's Restaurant** (Chinese) · 3040 Taraval St · 415-759-1818

Overview

Nestled between Sea Cliff and the Golden Gate Bridge along the Presidio's western edge, Baker Beach is one of the most popular beaches among locals and tourists alike. In fact, it's one of the most popular urban beaches in the country. Less windy than Ocean Beach, this stretch of sandy real estate is the premier spot for catching some rays, and we're talking serious sun worship here—bathing suits are optional at the northern end of the shore. (The nude area begins near the brown and yellow "Hazardous Surf" sign.) On some days you'll see more gawkers than nudists, but if the weather is particularly warm, be prepared for a major flesh parade.

Although the undertow is extremely dangerous, San Franciscans flock to Baker Beach for the beautiful views, surfing, nude bathing, and hiking trails. But the undertow isn't the only danger here—in 1959, Baker Beach was the site of the Bay Area's first shark attack. There haven't been any there since, however.

The shoreline is dotted with several interesting rock formations, some of which can be climbed, and some of which are rather dangerous to scale, depending on the tide (think slippery surface, jagged rocks, and treacherous slopes). The nearby gun batteries are a great (and safer) spot to explore a bit of local history. Built in 1904 to protect the harbor's minefields, they offer a stellar view of the beach and the bay. Baker Beach also has picnicking facilities with tables and grills at the east end of the parking lot. Beyond the northern tip of Baker Beach and over the rocky hill, is another beach alternately known as North Baker Beach, Golden Gate Bridge Beach, and the Gay Beach—the nudity is more prevalent here, as are various x-rated shenanigans that we'll leave to the imagination.

Activities / Practicalities

Swimming is discouraged, but surfing and boardsailing are very popular at this beach. The surrounding water becomes very deep very quickly, providing a great spot for fishing. Aside from water activities, this beach is famous for its winding hiking trails around the sloping cliffs off the Presidio. The area is filled with indigenous vegetation (including poison oak, so be careful what you touch). There are also rare birds and amazing views. The main trail, called Lands End, is 5.5 miles long and is pretty hilly, so be sure to wear appropriate hiking shoes. Restrooms are located near the parking lot and beach hours are from 9 am to 7 pm during the winter (October to April), and 9 am to 10 pm the rest of the year.

How to Get There

Driving from San Francisco, follow the signs for Baker Beach on Lincoln Boulevard. The beach is located between the Sea Cliff neighborhood and the Golden Gate Bridge. The parking lot on Bowley Street (off Lincoln Boulevard) is free, but fills up very quickly in the summertime. If you must drive, be prepared to look for parking blocks away from the main parking lots. Try your luck by heading north on 25th Avenue to Lincoln Boulevard. Turn right on Lincoln then take the second left on Bowley Street. Take Bowley to Gibson Road and turn right. Gibson will lead you straight to the east parking lot. If you're biking it, there are ample bike racks located around the parking areas. If you'd rather take public transportation, hop on the 29-Sunset Muni bus that stops nearby.

Please note that clothing is required in the parking lot and may only be shed in specified areas.

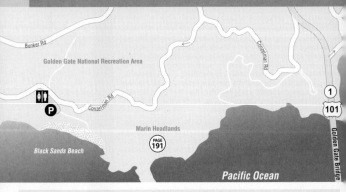

Overview

Just across the Golden Gate Bridge from San Francisco, and (on a clear day) within view of Baker Beach, Black Sands Beach offers a more exclusive retreat for those who enjoy nude sunbathing, magnificent views, and a stretch of sand largely to themselves. This 100-foot-wide beach's black volcanic sand is coarser and harder to walk on than the more traditional sand found on Baker, but the overall vibe at Black Sands is distinctly more casual and low-key. Unlike Baker Beach, Black Sands takes some effort to visit. Parking is limited, off-road vehicles are strictly forbidden, and the steep, poison oak-lined trail leading down to the beach is a challenge. However, once you arrive, the treacherous trek will have been well worth it. Just make sure you stay on the main path—the cliffs are steep and can be dangerous if you veer away from the well-worn trail.

Activities

You won't see many surfers at Black Sands Beach (probably because the trail down is too hard to navigate with a surfboard in hand), but fishing boats do frequent the area. The most popular activities here, however, are nude sunbathing and Frisbee-throwing. If you decide to brave the cold water, note that the beach largely faces the channel between Marin and San Francisco, where currents through the Golden Gate are strong and can be very dangerous.

Amenities / Practicalities

The nearest restaurants, hotels, motels, and other amenities are in Sausalito. There are restrooms in the parking lot and picnic areas along the road that leads away from Black Sands Beach.

How to Get There

Driving directions to trailhead: Cross the Golden Gate Bridge toward Marin and take the Alexander Avenue exit off Highway 101. (The exit will come up quickly on the right as soon as you cross the bridge.) Turn left, away from Sausalito, go through the tunnel that runs under the highway, and then turn right and follow Conzelman Road up to the Marin Headlands. When you come to some old military fortifications, the road becomes one-way and runs steeply downhill (offering amazing views of the Golden Gate). Once the road begins to flatten at about 3.6 miles, look for a small parking area and restrooms on the left. The lot is easy to miss, so keep your eyes peeled. Note: The trailhead at the parking area is blocked by a sign that reads "Trail Closed." Fear not, the rangers have assured us that this posting simply translates to "Trail Not Maintained." Passage is allowed.

There is no public transit available to Black Sands Beach. You can bike into the Marin Headlands, but do so with care, and wear protective gear—the roads there are incredibly steep and potentially dangerous for bikers. A coastal hiking trail passes 100 feet beyond the parking lot.

China Beach / Mile Rock Beach

Overview

NFT Map: 19

Locals originally called this area China Beach, in reference to the Chinese fishermen who docked their junks and camped at this spot during Gold Rush times. It was briefly renamed Phelan Beach after former San Francisco mayor and US Senator James D. Phelan, who was responsible for banning all Chinese immigrants from the beach and the local fishing industry in the 1880s and '90s. Some maps still refer to China Beach as Phelan State Beach, but most locals refer to the quaint patch of shore by its original name. In 1981, a stone marker was placed at the trailhead leading down the steep steps to the beach. Phelan might roll over in his grave to know that the marker celebrates the contributions of the Chinese fishermen to a critical industry and a young city.

China Beach offers great views of the Golden Gate Bridge and the Marin Headlands. A large part of its appeal stems from its unlikely placement—it's tucked into one of the city's most exclusive residential neighborhoods. The beach occupies a small cove bounded by cliffs and overlooked by mansions that enjoy the same stunning views. As with many Bay Area beaches, the unpredictable surf near Baker Beach and China Beach makes swimming risky, so if you do go out, don't go alone. Located west of Baker Beach, between Baker Beach and Land's End, China Beach has changing rooms, barbeque pits, and an enclosed sundeck.

Activities

The beach is small, and visitors mostly sunbathe (clothed) and picnic. Other recreational activities include surfing and fishing. There are some opportunities for rock scrambling at either end of the beach when the tide is low, but caution is advised. For many photographers this is a favorite place to capture iconic images of the Golden Gate Bridge.

Large waves from the northwest provide excellent surfing conditions, but swimming and wading are generally discouraged due to the strong tidal currents. A lifeguard is on duty from April to October, and a ranger is often on-site as well.

Amenities/Practicalities

Restrooms and showers are located in the changing area at China Beach Station, where you'll also find the enclosed sun deck. On Clement Street, facing Lincoln Park, you'll find restaurants and a grocery store to suit all of your dining and picnicking needs.

How to Get There

Driving directions: The beach is accessible from a parking lot at Sea Cliff and 28th Avenues, near El Camino del Mar. A ramp, along with a more direct but steeper trail, leads downhill to the beach.

Mass transit: The Muni 29 bus, which goes to Baker Beach, will drop you off at 25th Avenue and Camino Del Mar. From there, it's about a four-block walk west to Sea Cliff Avenue, then down the slope to the beach.

San Francisco Bay

Golden Gate
Yacht Club

Wave
Organ

MAP
1

East Harbor

St Francis
Yacht Club

Yacht Rd

Harbormaster's
Office

Marina Green Dr

Marina Green

P

West Harbor

Marina Park

Lyon St

Marina Blvd

Cervantes Blvd

Avila W

Rico Wy

Fillmore St

Fillmore St

Jefferson St

Jefferson St

Prado St

Beach St

Overview

Until 1912, the Marina Green area was primarily underwater, its shore dominated by sand dunes, fishermen's hovels, and power plants. After the area was destroyed by the 1906 earthquake, 635 acres were filled with sand, mud, and quake detritus to create the grounds for the 1915 Panama-Pacific International Exposition. Today the area is occupied by three exclusive yacht clubs (are there any other kind?) and a public park. The San Francisco Marina is overseen by the San Francisco Parks & Recreation Department and is composed of two harbors, West Harbor and East Harbor (a.k.a. Gashouse Cove). The Marina Green, a popular spot for locals and tourists alike, separates the two harbors.

The Marina Green is San Francisco's front lawn. A half-mile strip of grass with a seawall on its bayside, the Green is lined with the opulent, glass-fronted mansions of the Marina district with their remarkable views of the Bay. The Green is usually dotted with kite flyers and is sometimes used for organized athletic activities. There's a paved walkway with benches along the seawall, or you can venture out onto the jetty to contemplate the magnificent views of Alcatraz, Russian Hill, and the Golden Gate Bridge.

A controversial proposal to build two new breakwaters in the Bay has created some heat in the community—environmentalists and locals believe that the barriers would disrupt tidal patterns and increase sedimentation and erosion of the shore, not to mention ruining the view of the bay from the Green. The cynics in the group claim that the whole project is orchestrated by the owners of expensive boats who are concerned only with sailing conditions.

One of the Marina's most unique sites is the Wave Organ, located at the end of the jetty on Yacht Road. Part musical instrument, part environmental sculpture, the Wave Organ is made of stones from a demolished cemetery and 25 PVC pipes submerged beneath the jetty. The organ creates music from the movement of the tides of San Francisco Bay.

Boating

The marina has 686 boat slips and houses the St. Francis Yacht Club, the Golden Gate Yacht Club, and City Yachts (10 Marina Blvd, 415-567-8880). At Mean Lower Low Water (MLLW), the depth of the west entrance channel is usually between 10 and 20 feet, while the MLLW in the east channel is between 10 and 15 feet.

The St. Francis Yacht Club (www.stfyc.com) offers guest docking facilities ranging in price from 35¢ to 50¢ per foot per day and $6.50–$26 extra for power hookups. Non-members must present a letter of introduction from their yacht club to gain entry. The VHF radio channels for the St. Francis Yacht Club dockmaster are 68 and 69.

The Golden Gate Yacht Club (www.ggyc.com) also offers reciprocal privileges to members of other yacht clubs. Call 415-346-2628 for info and reservations. Docking rates are $20 per calendar day plus 40¢ per foot over 30 feet. Power hookups cost $5 per day.

No Boat?

Then why not focus on your body? Exercise equipment and a parcourse stop are at the southeast corner of the Green. Good winds also make kite flying a popular activity.

Marina Green is a centerpiece of the chain of waterfront spaces that border the Bay. Fort Mason, a former military reservation, is at the east end and includes a youth hostel. There's a hill to climb and trails to explore before you end up at Aquatic Park and Ghirardelli Square. At the west end of the Green is Crissy Field and the brilliant/sublime Palace of Fine Arts, the only remnant of the Panama-Pacific Exposition. Here you'll find a picturesque duck pond complete with swans, turtles, and the legions who feed them.

Amenities

Restrooms are located near the Harbormaster Building and in Marina Green Park.

The Safeway at the east end of the Green is, believe it or not, a popular singles pickup scene, and there are numerous restaurants and cafés five blocks south along Chestnut Street.

How to Get There

Public Transit: The Muni 22, 28, and 43 bus routes will get you where you want to go. Marina Green Park is located on Marina Boulevard between Scott and Webster streets.

You'll find ample weekday parking along the bay side except for the spaces marked "Permit Parking Only." Parking is hard to come by on weekends, so get to the lots early if you plan on making a day of it.

General Information

NFT Map: 4
Address: Beach St & The Embarcadero
            San Francisco, CA 94119
Phone: 415-705-5500
Websites: www.pier39.com, www.pier39marina.com

Overview

Whether you're there to watch the sea lions, shop, or perhaps catch a ferry to attractions (like Angel Island or Alcatraz), or boats to nearby Sausalito and Tiburon, Pier 39 is your gateway to the San Francisco Bay. It's one of the most popular spots in the city, and on a nice day, a great place to stop as you walk from the Ferry Building and downtown to the wharf (or vice versa).

Keep in mind that Pier 39 is also perhaps the most touristy location in San Francisco. Tourists are a blessing to the city, but they tend to circulate in hermetically sealed environments that focus primarily on capturing their entertainment dollars. While commercialism and the scramble for tourist dollars is the overarching purpose for the 45-acre complex, locals often have opportunities to enjoy live music being performed along the Embarcadero outside the pier or one of the innumerable street performers that swarm the area.

Pier 39 does have something that can appeal to almost anyone. (anyone, that is, without an aversion to strong smells). An entire colony of sea lions has taken up near-permanent encampment on the West Marina side of the Pier 39 harbor atop the wooden floating K-Dock. Although their main activity is sleeping in the sun, there are always plenty of specimens awake and bickering, barking, playing king of the pallet, and otherwise carrying on in typical pinniped fashion. They're a pack of hams, and always draw a good crowd.

While the sea lion faction may dominate, Pier 39 does house a 300-berth marina with slips available for rent and guest docking. The Marina offers a variety of ways to experience the Bay. You can venture out on a sailboat or powerboat, or take a ride on one of the many tour boats that take off from the left side of the pier.

Boating Information

Boaters are welcome to use the guest slips for a few hours during the day, but must make overnight reservations, and pay the overnight price. You can make reservations by phone (415-705-5558) or marine radio (VHF channel 16). Same-day reservations are accepted, provided you call before 5 pm. Utilities include ice, water and electrical hookup, restrooms, private shower rooms, laundry facilities, and pump-a-head. Check in is at noon and check out is at 11:30 am. A key deposit of a $50 credit card authorization is required, and overnight docking fees range from $45 to $60, depending on the size of your vessel.

Rental prices for long-term docking range between $384 a month for a 36' x 13' slip and $618 for a 60' x 20' slip. Visit www.pier39marina.com for more detailed docking information.

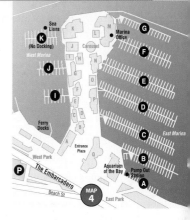

Getting There—Driving

The Pier 39 Marina is located on the San Francisco waterfront, between the two bridges, below Coit Tower. From the East Bay, take the Bay Bridge to SF, exit at Main Street/Embarcadero, turn right on Harrison, go three blocks to the Embarcadero, turn left. Pier 39 is on your right. Driving from the South Bay, take 101 N and follow the signs to the Bay Bridge. Exit at Fourth Street and turn left on Bryant Street to the Embarcadero. Driving from the North Bay, take 101 S, cross the Golden Gate Bridge, exit at Lombard Street, turn left on Van Ness Avenue and right on Bay Street to the Embarcadero.

Parking

Street parking is nearly nonexistent around the pier during the day. The Pier 39 Garage, open 24 hours a day, seven days a week, is located right across from the pier and works in collaboration with Pier 39's full-service restaurants to offer validation discounts for patrons who dine at any of the attraction's 14 major eateries. You can receive 1 hour of free parking at lunch time, and two free validated hours after 6pm for the dinner crowd.

Getting There—Mass Transit

Take BART to the Embarcadero Station. Go upstairs and cross the Embarcadero to the Ferry Building. Once you're in front of the Ferry Building, catch the F-line trolley to Pier 39. The Muni buses that serve the Pier are 10, 15, 39, and 47.

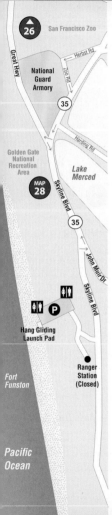

General Information

Phone: 415-561-4323
Website: www.parksconservancy.org/visit/park-sites/fort-funston.html

Overview

Fort Funston is named for Major General Frederick Funston of the US Army who, as Commandant of the Presidio, declared martial law and helped save the city from the great fire that followed the 1906 earthquake. The fort was originally a link in the fortifications surrounding San Francisco. The mortar batteries were decommissioned after WWII and, following a stint as a missile site, the area was handed over to the National Park Service. Today, the park sits on a large bluff overlooking the ocean, with a mile of beach stretching below. The site is largely undeveloped and includes a parking area, trails, dunes, derelict bunkers, and lots of coastal plant life.

The beach is extremely popular with dog owners. Drinking fountains are surrounded by public-use dog bowls and most dogs run off-leash, despite stringent leash laws. In fact, dog owners who frequent Fort Funston even have their own lobbying group, which has clashed with the National Park Service in recent years over enforcement of leash laws and the closure of some areas to protect coastal birds and plants. While enforcement seems lax (particularly on the beach), beware that you could be ticketed if caught letting your dog run free.

Hang gliders (and those of us who like to watch people jumping off cliffs into thin air) are another group of regulars at Fort Funston, as the strong coastal winds make the cliff a prime launching spot. If you want to spectate, the gliders jump off from a launch point near the observation deck by the parking lot, so grab a jacket (the strong winds make the area chilly in all but the warmest weather) and a spot on the sand on one of the many primo viewing spots that line the ridge.

Amenities

Restrooms are located at the northwest and northeast corners of the parking area.

Activities

The beach is clean and pleasant, faced by 150-foot cliffs stretching from the far southern end of Ocean Beach. Most patrons are dog walkers, although families and sunbathers (occasionally nude) are also present, particularly on weekends. The track down to the beach is really a dune face, so be prepared for an arduous walk back up the shifting sands to paved trails on the bluff.

Hang gliders must be licensed and rated H3 to fly at Fort Funston. Access to the site is managed by the Fellow Feathers Hang Gliding Club (www.flyfunston.org); they provide the requisite helmet stickers as well as a mentor program for flyers new to the site.

How to Get There

The entrance to Fort Funston is off Skyline Boulevard (Route 35), half a mile south of John Muir Drive. There is a large parking area adjacent to the hang gliding launch point, observation deck, and trailheads. Some additional, unofficial parking is located along Skyline Boulevard at John Muir Drive, where stairs climb up the dunes and join the trails that lead to the beach. The Muni 18 bus circles Lake Merced, with a stop near the intersection of John Muir Drive and Skyline Boulevard. Look for parked cars and paths on the west side of the intersection before following the stairs up to the paved trails.

General Information

Phone: 650-738-7381
Website: www.parks.ca.gov/?page_id=524

Overview

A mile-long swath of beach running along Highway 1 from Rockaway Point in the north to San Pedro Point in the south, Pacifica State Beach (also called Linda Mar Beach) is as well known for its sunny days as its foggy ones. As the surfers and beachcombers who frequent this area know, there are plenty of both to go around. In general, the spring and summer months bring more fog-filled days, while autumn is the best season to find the sun. Whatever your preference is, check out http://surfline.com for live webcams and weather reports before you go.

In its former life, Pacifica Beach was the domain of the Ohlone Indians, a coastal group of Native Americans who inhabited the area for several thousand years before Spanish explorers arrived in the late 1700s. By 1800, many of the remaining Ohlone had converted to Christianity and gone to work for the missions dotting the California coast.

The area remained largely undeveloped until the Ocean Shore Railroad Company began building tracks to connect San Francisco with Santa Cruz in 1905. After damage from the infamous 1906 earthquake temporarily shut down railroad production, construction continued until the company went under in 1920. The railroad tracks were later paved over to create Highway 1. Even with the new highway in place, the area remained a scattered grouping of small communities until officially becoming a city in 1957. The name Pacifica, which means "peaceful" in Spanish, was chosen through a local contest.

Thanks to the efforts of the Pacifica Land Trust and local residents, Pacifica Beach has grown several acres in recent years. The trust first purchased private land near the beach in 2001. It has since removed houses, concrete, telephone poles, and other debris from the land to make way for landscaped dunes, native plants, and the snowy plover bird population.

In addition to attracting plenty of surfers (the world-famous Mavericks big wave surfing contest is located just south of the beach here), the beach is a favorite getaway for city-dwellers on warm days. Cold water and strong tides make it a less-than-ideal swimming spot, but you can usually see brave visitors taking the plunge anyway. A hiking trail up Pedro Point (look for the trailhead off the parking lot on the southern end of the beach) offers spectacular views. Fishing and clamming are permitted along the beach, as well as dogs on the leash. Facilities include restrooms, showers, and, oddly enough, a Taco Bell (undoubtedly one of the world's most scenic fast food joints).

Accommodations

Pacifica Beach Hotel • 525 Crespi Dr • 650-355-9999
Best Western Lighthouse Hotel • 105 Rockaway Beach Ave • 650-355-6300
Holiday Inn Express Pacifica • 519 Nick Gust Wy • 650-355-5000
Americas Best Value Inn San Francisco/Pacifica • 2160 Francisco Blvd • 650-359-9494

Activities

Plenty of hiking trails snake through the surrounding hills. Mountain biking, bird watching, canning, canoeing, kayaking, paragliding, and golf are all popular activities in the area. The Pacifica Community Skatepark is located at 540 Crespi Drive. The facility provides a much needed practice space for skateboarders and inline skaters. There are also several additional beaches nearby, including Rockaway Beach, Sharp Park Beach, and Grey Whale Cove (nude sunbathing allowed).

How to Get There

Driving:
The beach is about 12 miles south of the city. From San Francisco, take 280 S past the Highway 35/Pacifica exit to the Highway 1/Pacifica exit. Continue five miles south on Highway 1. Go through the stoplight at Crespi Avenue and turn right into the north parking lot. To reach the south lot, continue along Highway 1 until you reach the Linda Mar Boulevard stoplight. There, turn right onto San Pedro Avenue and the lot will be on the right.

Mass Transit:
Take the Samtrans DX bus from the Transbay Terminal to the Crespi or Linda Mar Park & Ride stops in Pacifica. Alternatively, take the BART from San Francisco to the Colma Station and transfer to Samtrans CX. Get off at the Crespi or Linda Mar Park & Ride stops in Pacifica.

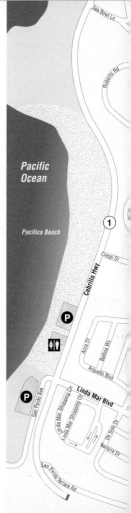

General Information

Website: www.nps.gov/goga/stbe.htm
Open: 9 am until sunset year-round

Overview

In the early 1800s, the area that is now Stinson Beach was a remote site used to raise milk cows. Before a dirt road was built in 1870 to connect the area to Sausalito, it was accessible only by schooner or horseback. Stinson Beach served as a much-needed shelter to refugees from the San Francisco earthquake of 1906. Ten years later, with the opening of the first post office, the area was named Stinson Beach in honor of the largest landowners. Stinson Beach saw an influx of new residents during World War II, and unused land was developed after the war, resulting in the recreation area we know and love today. The beach was incorporated into the Golden Gate Recreation Area in 1972.

Private cottages (some of which can be rented out for a weekend or more) border over half of the 3.5-mile-long beach, while the park itself lines the remainder in a grassy picnic and parking area. This is a family-friendly area, and the park is always filled with big groups combining beach time with BBQs. (Many of the picnic areas are equipped with grills.)

The public alarm system peals at noon and 5 pm daily. Two short blasts mean that everything is under control, and the ominous 15-second blast, roughly translated, means "Get the hell out of here!"

While nudity is accepted at many Bay Area beaches, Stinson isn't one of them, so keep your suit on. Dogs are not permitted on the beach at any time, but alcohol is—provided it is not in a glass bottle and you are over 21. Entrance to the beach is free, but parking is not.

Amenities/Practicalities/ Accommodations

The waterfront areas are manned by lifeguards May through October. Public showers and restrooms are located at the beach entrance. There is a café and grill at the southern end of the paved parking area, and a path near the center that leads out to the highway strip. There are busy picnic areas and BBQ pits in the parking area. Fires are prohibited on the public beach.

The town of Stinson Beach includes cafés with bars, outdoor seating, and sometimes live music. The usual assortment of surf shops, galleries, and trinket shops are packed into about two blocks. Good coffee and baked goods can be found at Greens Restaurant in nearby Fort Mason Center. .

Lodging at Stinson Beach:
• The Sandpiper • 1 Marine Wy • 415-868-1632
• Stinson Beach Motel • 3416 State Rte 1 N • 415-868-1712
• Redwoods Haus B&B • Belvedere &Hwy 1 • 415-868-1034

Activities

Although sunbathing is hardly an athletic event, the Stinso Beach website lists it as a "sporting activity." For those who war to do more than lie down and bake in ultraviolet radiation, Stir son Beach offers hang-gliding, kayaking, and surfing. If you're more terrestrially-bound, there is plenty of hiking and biking t be done, and there are also volleyball nets. There is also a beaut ful trail (of exactly 5 miles) that takes you from the Muir Wooc parking area to the main parking lot of Stinson Beach.

As an alternative, the bohemian enclave of Bolinas sits across th lagoon inlet. There you'll find another impressive beach suitabl for surfing and a small town area, but with fewer amenities tha Stinson. One word of caution: the golden hills that surround her are alive with brambles of poison oak. Stay on the paths unles you're immune to this plant.

How to Get There—Driving

From the south, cross the Golden Gate Bridge and take 101 about 3 miles to the Highway 1/Stinson Beach exit. Follow th signs and enjoy your drive down one of the most scenic high ways in the nation. Stinson Beach is approximately 20 miles fron San Francisco.

If you're after a more scenic route, look for signs to Muir Wooc and Mt Tamalpais State Park while you're traveling along High way 1. Turn right and take Panoramic Highway through the par It will take you back to Highway 1 and ends only blocks sout of Stinson Beach.

Please share the narrow shoulder-less roads with the cyclists. It California law (and the nice thing to do).

How to Get There—Mass Transit

Take Golden Gate 10, 20, or 50 from Transbay Transit Termina Civic Center BART, or Golden Gate Bridge Toll Plaza to Marin Ci Transfer Center. Transfer to Golden Gate bus 63 (available week ends and holidays only).

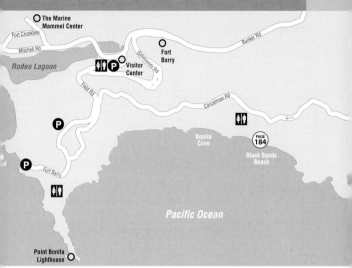

Overview

The best views of San Francisco are only minutes away—across the Golden Gate Bridge and up into the mountains of the Marin Headlands. It's definitely worth following the crowds up Conzelman Road to get an eyeful of San Francisco's spectacular skyline. If you don't keep driving up and over the hill you're missing the majority of what the Marin Headlands have to offer. Once home to the Miwok people, the land was later used by the military (like many of San Francisco's parks) before becoming a part of the Golden Gate National Recreation Area. Keep an eye out as you navigate the steep winding roads—it's not hard to spot the multitude of abandoned bunkers.

Activities

The area is host to numerous trails, suitable for an evening stroll or a grueling workout, depending on your preference. Most trails are open to travelers on foot or bike, and it's a good idea to stop by the ranger station to pick up a map before heading out. The park is home to numerous bird species, and if you keep your eyes peeled you might also catch a glimpse of some of the park's furry wildlife. If you have some time to spend exploring, you can tour the Point Bonita Lighthouse, check out Fort Baker, investigate the Bay Area Discovery Museum, volunteer with the Marine Mammal Center, or visit Muir Woods National Monument. Just don't try to do it all in one day. For more in-

formation on the Marin Headlands (including maps) check out www.nps.gov/goga/marin-headlands.htm, or stop by the Marin Headlands Visitor Center open 9:30 am–4:30 pm daily (closed Thanksgiving and Christmas Day).

Amenities/Practicalities

- Rangers and bathrooms are readily available in the Marin Headlands, but if you're looking for sandwiches or coffee your best bet is to cross back over to the other side of Hwy 101 into Sausalito.

- Trails can be very steep, and cliffs are prone to landslides. Use extreme caution if you decide to veer from the beaten path. That goes double if you are allergic to poison oak.

- Weather can change in a heartbeat. Dress in layers and keep an open mind—even the foggiest of days can be stunning.

- Swimming is not advised anywhere in the Marin Headlands as the currents are very strong and the tides bring drastic changes to shorelines.

How to Get There

Take Hwy 101 North across the Golden Gate Bridge. The second exit after crossing the bridge is the Alexander Ave exit. Take Alexander Ave and follow signs to the Visitor's Center. For the best views, veer right on Conzelman Rd.

General Information

San Francisco Recreation & Parks Dept: 415-831-2700 • Court Lists: sfrecpark.org/recprogram/tennis-program, http://sftenniscourts.com · Golden Gate Park Saturday and Sunday Reservations call: 415-831-6301 on Wed 4–6 pm, Thurs and Fri 9 am–5 pm prior to the coming weekend. After noon on Fri, call Golden Gate Park Tennis Complex at 415-753-7001.

Overview

"Tenez!" ("hold" *en français*) or "Hang on to your racket, I'm about to serve!" (*en anglais*) was the pre-serve cry in royal tennis, and it gave the game its name. Though it seems like everyone in town tries to hold court at one of the 6 centrally-located courts in **Dolores Park (Map 10)**, San Francisco actually has 150 courts in nearly 70 locations around the city. Some of the small parks and hidden courts offer great city views (2 at **Buena Vista (Map 9)**, 2 at **Corona Heights (Map 10)**, 2 at **Alta Plaza (Map 5)**, 1 at **Alamo Square (Map 10)**), and some of the schoolyard parks let you play alongside a pickup basketball game (1 at **Hayes Valley (Map 10)**, 2 at **Hamilton Center (Map 5)**). Golden Gate Park (Page 152) is a safe bet with 21 courts (the most by far at any single location), but reservations are required for weekends. The Dolores Park courts are lamp-lit—perfect for short daylight in winter months, and if you can tough out the competition—are the most popular public courts in town.

Equipment

Super-sports stores like the Sports Basement (see shopping, Map 11 and the Presidio) or Sports Authority (Map 11) have everything you need to start out from rackets to balls to cute little tennis skirts. Extra balls can usually be found at any corner store (look somewhere in a corner behind the cleaning supplies, you may have to blow dust off the lid first).

Tennis Courts

All courts are hard, public, and outdoor, unless otherwise noted. [1]=indoor/outdoor; [2]=private; [3]=clay; [4]=lighted.

Courts	Address	# of Courts	Map
George Moscone	Chestnut St & Buchanan St	4	2
Alice Marble	Greenwich St & Hyde St	3	3
Helen Wills	Broadway & Larkin St	1	3
North Beach	Lombard St & Mason St	3	4
San Francisco Bay Club	150 Greenwich St	2[2,3]	4
Alta Plaza	Jackson St & Steiner St	3	5
Hamilton Recreation	1900 Geary Blvd	2[2]	5
Lafayette Square	Washington St & Laguna St	2	6
Margaret Hayward	Golden Gate Ave & Laguna St	2	6
Chinatown Playground	Sacramento St & Waverly Pl	1	8
Golden Gateway Fitness	370 Drumm St	9[2,3,4]	8
Buena Vista Park	Haight St & Buena Vista Ave	2	9
Grattan	Stanyan St & Alma St	1	9
Alamo Square Park	Hayes St & Steiner St	1	10
Corona Heights Park	States St, near Castro St	2	10
Eureka Valley	Collingwood St b/w 18th St & 19th St	1	10
Hayes Valley	Hayes St & Buchanan St	1	10
Mission Dolores Park	18th St & Dolores St	6[4]	10
Sidney Peixotto	15th St & Roosevelt Wy	2	10
Mission Playground	19th St & Linda St	2	11
Jackson	17th St & Carolina St	1	12
San Francisco Tennis Club	645 5th St	28[1,2,3,4]	13
Douglass Park	26th St & Douglass St	1	14
George Christopher	5210 Diamond Heights Blvd	1	14
Noe Valley Courts	24th St & Douglass St	1	14
Folsom	21st St & Folsom St	1	15
James Jr Rolph	Potrero Ave & Army St	2	18
Potrero Hill	22nd St & Arkansas St	2[4]	16
Cabrillo	38th Ave & Fulton St	1	19
Fulton	27th Ave b/w Fulton St & Cabrillo St	1	19
Margaret O Dupont	30th Ave b/w California St & Clement St	4	19
Rochambeau	24th Ave b/w Lake St & California St	1	19
Argonne	18th Ave b/w Geary Blvd & Anza St	1	20
Richmond	18th Ave b/w Lake St & California St	1	20

Courts	Address	# of Courts	Map
Angelo Rossi	Arguello Blvd & Edward St	3	2
Mountain Lake	12th Ave & Lake St	4	2
Julius Kahn	Spruce St & Pacific Ave	4	2
Laurel Hill	Euclid Ave & Collins St	1	2
West Sunset	39th Ave & Ortega St	4[4]	2
Sunset	28th Ave & Lawton St	2	24
Golden Gate Heights	12th Ave & Rockridge Dr	2	25
John P Murphy	1960 9th Ave	3	25
South Sunset	40th Ave b/w Wawona St & Vicente St	1	26
James B Moffet	26th Ave & Vicente St	4	2
Larsen Park	19th Ave & Vicente St	1	2
McCoppin Square	24th Ave & Taraval St	2	2
Stern Grove Annex	Sloat Blvd b/w 19th Ave & Crestlake Dr	2	2
Junipero Serra	300 Stonecrest Dr	1	2
Midtown Terrace	Clarendon Ave & Olympia Wy	4	24
Aptos	Aptos Ave & Ocean Ave	1	34
West Portal	Clarendon Ave & Olympia Wy	1	3
Miraloma	Omar Wy & Sequoia Wy	1	3
Sunnyside	Forester St & Melrose Ave	1	3
Peter Folger	Chenery St & Elk St	2	3
St Mary's	Murray St & Justin Dr	3	3
Upper Noe	Day St & Sanchez St	1	32
Merced Heights	Byxbee St & Shields St	1	3
Ocean View	Plymouth Ave & Louis St	2[4]	3
Alice Chalmers	Brunswick St & Whittier St	1	3
Balboa	Ocean Ave & San Jose Ave	4	3
Cayuga Park	Cayuga St & Naglee Ave	1	3
Holly Park	Holly Park Cir & Highland Ave	1	3
Joseph Lee	Oakdale Ave & Mendell St	1	3
Youngblood Coleman	Galvez Ave & Mendell St	2	3
Crocker Amazon	Geneva Ave & Moscow St	3	3
Excelsior	Russia Ave & Madrid St	1	3
Francis J Herz	Visitacion Ave & Hahn St	1	3
Louis Sutter	University St & Wayland St	2	34
McLaren Park	Mansell St, near University St	6	3
Portola	Felton St & Holyoke St	2[4]	3
Silver Terrace	Thornton Ave & Bayshore Blvd	1	3
Golden Gate Park	John F Kennedy Dr & Middle Dr E	21[4]	GG

Golf

From nondescript municipal courses to some of the country's most scenic and heralded links, San Francisco's got a course to suit every level of player, even those who don't want to use clubs. At the high end are two of the best courses in the nation—the **San Francisco Golf Club (Map 28)** and the Olympic Club **(Map 7)**, which hosted the US Open in 2012. The SFGC claims only 250 members, which means you'd probably have better luck swimming to shore from Alcatraz than trying to get into this club. For those who do manage to obtain a tee time, it is a truly remarkable experience—the course offers a classic layout with empty fairways and pristine greens. (Yes, we wrote that as if we were one of the lucky few to get a tee time. We weren't.)

While the private courses are some of the most famous, there are numerous public options in and around San Francisco. **The Presidio Golf Course (The Presidio)** has hosted the US Open, and is a much-improved course since the Arnold Palmer Golf Company took over management. There are several interesting par threes on the course, and the 9th and 18th holes are great finishers. The food at the Presidio Café is also some of the best at any golf course in the area, particularly weekend brunch. If you want to play, call early, as tee times are hard to get. Be prepared for a five- to six-hour round on weekends.

Perhaps the most exciting development in San Francisco golf is the renovation of **Harding Park (Map 28)**. The course is ranked the second-best municipal course in the country. The course hosted the 2005 World Golf Championship, which Tiger Woods won when he was still good, and the 2009 President's Cup. Harding is over 80 years old and, like many public courses, fell victim to overlay (160,000 rounds per year) under the management of the Parks & Recreation

Department. Since 2002, however, various agencies have invested roughly $15 million to renovate the course to its former greatness.

There are also several options in San Francisco for golfers looking to save money or avoid crowds. Lincoln Park **(Map 19)** is an inexpensive municipal course boasting terrific views from several holes. Another economical choice is **Glen Eagles (Map 39)**, a nine-hole course that Lee Trevino once described as the hardest nine holes in golf. The course has several unique attributes, including a tree in a bunker on the sixth hole (a 600-plus-yard par five). You may also be treated to some bass-heavy music coming from the adjacent neighborhood on holes four and five.

At the local public courses, the rates for non-residents are roughly double what a resident pays. City residents must have a Resident Card in order to receive a discount. You can apply for a Resident Card at City Hall in room 140. Just take a valid form of ID (driver's license), a copy of a PG&E bill, and $90. Don't fear the bureaucracy; getting a resident card is worth it if you plan to do some golfing. City Hall works smoothly and you can be in and out in 15 minutes. The card pays for itself in a few rounds.

Another great resource for golfing around the bay is the *Golf Guide*, available free at courses and golf shops. It has maps, descriptions, green fees, and anything you want to know about any of the many courses in the region. Check out www.golfguide.org.

If you don't have clubs, take a stroll to the **Golden Gate Park Disc Golf Course (Golden Gate Park)** located along JFK Drive. The park district has recently expanded the course to a full 18-holes. It's free, just bring your Frisbee.

Golf Courses	Address	Phone	Fees	Par	Map
Lincoln Park Golf	34th Ave & Clement St	415-221-9911	$37 Mon–Thurs; $41 Fri–Sun	Par-68, Holes-18	19
Harding Park	99 Harding Rd	415-661-1865	$150 Mon–Thurs; $170 Fri–Sun	Par-72, Holes-18	28
San Francisco Golf Club	Junipero Serra Blvd & Brotherhood Wy	415-469-4122	$50 all times (membership req'd)	Par-71, Holes-18	28
Golden Gate Park	970 47th Ave	415-751-8987	$15 Mon–Thurs; $19 Fri–Sun	Par-27, Holes-9	pg 152
Presidio Golf Course	300 Finley Rd	415-561-4663	$112 Mon–Thurs; $122 Fri–Sun	Par-72, Holes-18	pg 154
Mill Valley	280 Buena Vista Ave	415-388-9982	$17 Mon–Thur; $19 Fri–Sun	Par-33, Holes-9	pg 148
Tilden Park Golf Course	10 Golf Course Dr	510-848-7373	$45 Mon–Thurs; $55 Fri; $65 Sat–Sun	Par-70, Holes-18	pg 138
Lake Chabot Golf Course	11450 Golf Links Rd	510-351-5812	$$		pg 140
Metropolitan Golf Links	10051 Doolittle Dr	510-569-5555	$$$		pg 140
Montclair Golf Course	2477 Monterey Blvd	510-482-0422	$7 Mon–Thurs; $9 for 9 holes, Fri–Sun	Par-27, Holes-9	pg 140
Chuck Corica Golf Complex	1 Clubhouse Memorial Rd	510-747-7800	$28 Mon–Fri, $35 Sat–Sun		n/a
Sharp Park Golf Course	Hwy 1, Sharp Park Rd, Pacifica	650-359-3380	$37 Mon–Thur; $41 Fri–Sat	Par-72	n/a

Note: Quoted fees are for non-residents.

General Information

A great website that details pretty much every imaginable hike in the Bay Area is www.bahiker.com. It is without a doubt the best resource for finding a hike. Here are some of our favorites.

Overview

Built on 42 hills, San Francisco is famous for its steep inclines and excellent vistas (a hill by definition is anything taller than 100 feet or 30 meters). The city's peaks serve as backdrops for car commercials and chase scenes; they fry transmissions and wear out brake pads; and they're the reason the avenues stay drenched in fog while sunbathers lounge in Dolores Park. On a more practical level, sometimes a 40-degree slope is all that stands between you and a clean load of laundry, the Muni stop, or a pint of ice cream from the corner store.

Built on a tumultuous network of fault lines, the hills and mountains give the Bay Area much of its romantic allure. Just outside the city offers an even wider array of hiking options from Mt. Tam to the unspoiled coast of Pt. Reyes and the rugged panoramas of Mt. Diablo and the East Bay Regional Park District.

Since hiking to your morning cup of coffee is an unavoidable fact of life for residents of this fair city, why would anyone deliberately seek out *other* places to break a sweat? Summits within city limits such as Twin Peaks and Inspiration Point actually require little exertion, and their vistas have a way of showing you the city in a whole new light. At Fort Funston, you can embrace your inner Californian and trek barefoot on the beach. And a walk through the redwood cathedral of Muir Woods will leave you feeling uplifted in a way that the Stairmaster or the Lyon Street steps just can't match.

Bay Trail

500 miles when completed, currently 330 miles— varied terrain

Once finished, the Bay Trail will extend over 500 miles through the Bay Area, covering nine counties and 47 cities. This massive route will weave through commercial, residential, rural, and coastal areas, creating scenic haven for bikers, joggers, rollerbladers, and walkers. Aside from the aesthetic appeal of the path, the Bay Trail will provide alternative commute routes for cyclists and link several public transportation systems. The majority of the trail is paved. While some areas will overlap with city sidewalks, others will be more rustic. For more information, visit the official website http://baytrail.abag.ca.gov/.

Crissy Field

Presidio East Beach entrance • 1.65 miles • Easy—flat • Page 180

Formerly a major military post and landing strip, Crissy Field has long been one of the city's most popular recreation destinations. The main trail, which was restored in 1998, weaves through picturesque marshland, dunes, meadows, and shoreline peppered with native flora and fauna. At 3.3 miles out and back, the beautiful scenery and smooth, flat trail distinguish Crissy Field as an ideal place for walking, jogging, biking, rollerblading, and dog walking. But be prepared for gusty winds. Crissy Field can be reached by Muni bus lines 28-19th Ave, 29-Sunset, and 43-Masonic.

Fort Funston

Skyline Blvd & John Muir Dr • 1.52 miles • Easy—some elev. gain • Map 28

A favorite with Bay Area dog-walkers, Fort Funston offers beautiful ocean views, plentiful vegetation, and varied terrain. Sunset Trail, the main thoroughfare, is paved and wheelchair accessible, while other paths are sandy and more suited to sport sandals (or bare feet) than to hiking boots or sneakers. Most trails access the beach and involve some degree of scrambling on dunes (the aptly named Sand Ladder Trail provides steps). When wind conditions are right, Funston is a favorite launching spot for local hang-gliders, who swoop off the bluffs and over the surf below. If you're planning a long walk on the beach, check tide levels before setting out, as high tides can make parts of the beach impassable. To reach the park by car, take Highway 35 to John Muir Drive, and follows signs to the Fort Funston parking lot. For information about group walks, contact the Fort Funston Ranger Station at 415-561-4323.

Glen Canyon

Bosworth St & Elk St • 0.9 miles • Moderate—short but steep • Map 32

Positioned between Glen Canyon Park and Mount Davidson, the steep and gravelly trails in Glen Canyon are mostly used by nearby residents and dog-walkers. Although there is an entrance on Bosworth Street, the entrance off Diamond Heights Boulevard has better parking. Park in the Diamond Heights Shopping Center and take the path through the Christopher Playground. The park may also be accessed by the 44-O'Shaughnessy bus (Elk Street stop) or the Glen Park BART station. The trails are short and riddled with poison oak, but the canyon is rarely crowded and offers some rewarding views.

You'll find some of the best bouldering in San Francisco on the park's interesting rock formations. A hike to the bottom will make you forget that you are in the middle of the City.

Inspiration Point

Arguello Gate Presidio entrance • 1.78 miles • Easy—some hills • Page 154

Located in the Presidio, this trail offers yet another rustic escape from the sights and sounds of the city. Due to the surrounding non-native vegetation and urban development, this area has been dubbed an "ecological island." The Point houses the only serpentine grassland in the entire Golden Gate National Recreation Area, in addition to many other native grasses. The flourishing plant life has much to do with an intensive three-year grassland restoration project which was completed in 1998.

The trail starts near Mountain Lake and continues for 1.78 miles. Yes, there are a few hills (this is San Francisco), but the path is not strenuous. Inspiration Point is dog-friendly, but be sure to observe the National Park Service's strict leash policy.

McLaren Park

Cambridge St & John F Shelly Dr • Easy • Map 39

McLaren is big—317 acres of out-of-the-way hilltop. This multi-faceted park has seven miles of paved trails, which are ideal for walking or jogging. Check out www.bahiker.com/sfhikes/mclaren.html for detailed hike directions in the park. By Muni take the *29 Sunset*, the *52 Excelsior*, or the *54 Felton*.

Mount Davidson Park

Lansdale Ave & Dalewood Wy • 0.5 miles • Easy • Map 31

At 927 feet, Mt Davidson is the city's highest point. The 40-acre park contains numerous paths, but the main trail to the top is short and moderately steep. Views from the top are obstructed by trees and a 103-foot tall concrete memorial cross to the Armenian genocide of 1915. The city of San Francisco was forced to sell the top of the park when residents complained that the gargantuan cross violated the separation of church and state. The peak was also the site of a famous scene from Clint Eastwood's *Dirty Harry* (1971). To get to the park from downtown, take 101 S to 280 W and exit at Monterey Boulevard. There is a small parking area on Portola Drive. Muni bus 36-Teresita conveniently stops right in front of the park. Dogs and bikes are allowed.

Muir Woods National Monument

Mill Valley • Page 148

This Marin County redwood preserve contains some of the most enchanting scenery in the country. Endowed with national monument status in 1908, today it is a quintessential San Francisco stop for tourists and locals alike, and is visited by more than a million people every year. Most visitors just ooh and ahh their way along the main trail, a one-mile wheelchair-accessible loop. Those who want a longer hike can link up with a large network of more strenuous trails (a great, full-day hike is a 5-mile, one-way trail to Stinson Beach). The best times to visit are on weekdays in the early morning, or after 4 pm. Parking at all other times will be an adventure in itself. Dogs, bikes, and picnics are not permitted within the park. To get there by car, cross the Golden Gate Bridge, get off at the first exit, and follow the signs for Muir Woods National Monument. For more information, visit the official website at www.nps.gov/muwo or call the information hotline at 415-388-2596.

Twin Peaks

Twin Peaks Blvd • 0.64 miles • Moderate—some hills • Map 29

Located at the center of the city, the 900-foot Twin Peaks afford incredible panoramic vistas, provided there's no fog creeping down the mountain. If you're seeking solitude, look elsewhere; this is a very touristy area. The entire trail through the hills is short and easily navigated, but some sections are very steep, so wear appropriate footwear. Bring an extra layer, too, since winds up on the peaks can be gusty and frigid. There's a portable toilet but no drinking water, and while the trail is handicapped parking, the peaks themselves are not wheelchair accessible. Dogs are allowed. To get to the trails, travel along Bosworth Street, which becomes O'Shaughnessy Boulevard, heading uphill. Follow O'Shaughnessy to its junction with Portola Drive at the top of the hill. Turn right, then quickly get into the left lane. Make a left turn at the light onto Twin Peaks Boulevard, then continue uphill and park at the first pullout on the left (immediately after the first sharp curve), or in the lot just past the north peak.

On the rare occasion that one actually needs to cool off in San Francisco, there is exactly one public outdoor swimming pool. **Mission Pool (Map 11)** is located at 19th St & Linda St, and is open primarily in the summer (which is a bit comical considering that the summer months are historically the coldest). For those less interested in the sun and more interested in the splashin', there are eight additional (indoor) public pools. Prices range between $1 and $5 depending on your age and whether you are signed up for one of the many swim lessons that are offered. For more information, visit sfrecpark.org/recreation-community-services/aquatics-pools or call 415-831-2747.

For the more serious swimmers, San Francisco offers a variety of experiences which far surpass the monotony of your basic lap swim. Aquatic Park, near Ghirardelli Sqaure, is the spot for lap swimmers undeterred by the Bay's freezing waters. There are two swim clubs—South End, and The Dolphin Club--that have piers at Aquatic Park, complete with warm showers and work out facilities. If you're really interested in swimming in the bay, either of the two groups are great introductions to the healthy environment, but be thoughtful about which club you want to join, because the minute you sign up, you are on the side of one of SF's most fabled rivalries.The truly brave can check out the Alcatraz100 (www.alcatraz100.com). For a donation of just $155, you can get yourself a one-way ticket to Alcatraz Island. Also check out the Annual Alcatraz Invitational, or the Alcatraz Challenge (these and others are easily found through Google). What is it like to traverse this notorious 1.5 miles? In May 2006, Braxton Bilbrey described it as "pretty cool." He was only seven.

Swimming Pools

	Address	Type	Fees	Map
North Beach Pool	1701 Lombard St	Indoor	Adults $5 / kids $1	4
San Francisco Bay Club	150 Greenwich St	Indoor	Membership required	4
Fitness SF	1455 Fillmore St	Indoor	$20/day	5
Hamilton Recreation	1900 Geary Blvd	Indoor	Adults $5 / kids $1	5
Cathedral Hill Plaza Athletic Club	1333 Gough St	Indoor	$15/day	6
Club One	535 Mason St	Indoor	$20/day	7
Olympic Club	524 Post St	Indoor	Membership required	7
Crunch	350 3rd St	Outdoor	$20/day	8
Embarcadero YMCA	169 Steuart St	Indoor	$15/day	8
Bay Club at the Gateway	370 Drumm St	Outdoor	Membership required	8
Equinox	747 Market St	Indoor	Membership required	8
Boy's & Girl's Club	1950 Page St	Indoor	$3/day	9
24 Hour Fitness	1645 Bryant St	Indoor	$15/day	11
Mission Pool	19th St & Linda St	Outdoor	Adults $5 / kids $1	11
Garfield Pool	26th St & Harrison St	Indoor	Adults $5 / kids $1	15
Rossi Pool	600 Arguello Blvd	Indoor	Adults $5 / kids $1	22
Herbst Natatorium	2001 37th Ave	Indoor	$4/day	23
Stonestown YMCA	333 Eucalyptus Dr	Indoor	$12/day	27
Sava Pool	19th Ave & Wawona St	Indoor	Adults $5 / Kids $1	27
24 Hour Fitness	1850 Ocean Ave	Indoor	$15/day	30
Balboa Pool	51 Havelock St	Indoor	Adults $5 / kids $1	34
Coffman Pool	1701 Visitacion Ave	Indoor	Adults $5 / kids $1	39
MLK Jr Pool	5701 3rd St	Indoor	Adults $5 / kids $1	40
Presidio YMCA	1151 Gorgas Ave	Indoor	$15/day	101

All Things Skating

Looking to get outside? The 4.5-mile loop around lush Lake Merced, as well as several miles of pier shoreline along the Embarcadero and the Marina Green, is fairly flat and provides some fantastic views while you skate. For rolling hills and a cardio workout, check out six miles of windswept ocean vistas from the Cliff House to the Zoo (and back) on a paved path along the Great Highway at Ocean Beach. The Midnight Rollers, an organized group made up of hundreds of inline and roller city skaters, meet for their weekly event, known as Friday Night Skate, at 8:30 pm in front of the Ferry Building. From there they take off en masse for a long ride through the city streets to various sites throughout San Francisco. Interested in participating? Call the group's organizer, David Miles, at 415-752-1967 for more details. For other ideas, check out the California Inline Skating Guide (www.caskating.com) and California Outdoor Rollerskating Association (www.cora.org).

Of course, the all-time favorite is Golden Gate Park. Every Sunday, a two-mile section of JFK Boulevard, from Stanyan Street to 19th Avenue, is barricaded off for the exclusive use of pedestrians, skaters, and bikers. Let people roam around on what is usually car territory, and they will take full advantage. Nearly 75,000 people visit the park on the weekend, and a sizeable portion of them are on wheels—this makes navigation of the Park's main arteries that much easier and faster. It's your chance to let loose and roll on the main road as much as you please, but watch out for the speedsters on bikes, tour carriages, skateboarders, and little kids. The roller-dancing area, at JFK Boulevard and 6th Avenue, is a vision of neon spandex, rockin beats, and remarkably bedazzled roller skates. The regulars are welcoming and if you come at the right time on a Sunday afternoon, they will teach you the Thriller dance (RIP MJ). Turn to our Golden Gate Park (pg 188) for other exciting activities and happenings.

For the skateboarder, the cityscape offers a scrumptious plethora of hills, steps and curbs, to ollie, grind, and kick flip. There are a two free public skate parks. Potrero Del Dol (at Rolf park) which is located at 25th and Potrero and the skate park at Crocker-Amazon, (Geneva and Moscow). Both offer bowls, rails, and all the shindig.

The indoor ice rink in Yerba Buena Ice Skating and Bowling Center at 750 Folsom Street (415-820-3532; www.skatebowl.com) has a skating school and private lessons for figure skating and hockey year-round. If you're looking for something a little less structured, public ice skating sessions are offered daily (admission costs $10 for adults, $8 for seniors (55+) and children (6-12), and $6 for toddlers (5 and under) and Military with active ID; $3 skate rental; rental free on Wednesday nights); visit the center's website for an up-to-date public skating schedule. From November to January, have some East Coast fun in a California climate on the outdoor holiday ice rink in the Embarcadero Center ($9.50 adults, $6 senior and children 6 and under; $3.50 skate rental). The Skating Club of San Francisco (www.scsf.org) is for the pros among you.

For skateboard or rollerblade gear, Skates on Haight is the place to go, and it's close to the Park (1818 Haight St, 415-752-8375; www.skatesonhaight.com). Also check out Purple Skunk (5820 Geary Blvd, 415-668-7905; www.purpleskunk.com) or DLX Skateboards & Clothing (1831 Market St, 415-626-5588; www.dlxsf.com). You can pick up ice skating gear at the fully-equipped Yerba Buena Pro Shop (750 Folsom St, 415-820-3521; http://www.skatebowl.com/ice_center/proshop/proshop.htm).

Bowling

Despite the proliferation of Lebowski-esque citizens, bowling options are slim pickings in San Francisco proper. After Japantown Bowl closed down a few years back, bowlers were left with only two options within the city. **Yerba Buena Ice Skating and Bowling Center (Map 8)** is the most accessible via public transportation. But the compact space has only 12 lanes and it fills up fast with teenagers on weekend nights. Another bummer is that they do not regularly serve alcohol or snacks—how the hell are you supposed to bowl without beer and nachos? Worse yet, the lanes are artificial, so you're bowling on plastic, not wood. The alley *does* have "Blacklight Bowling" on Friday and Saturday nights. But who doesn't? **Presidio Bowling Center (The Presidio)** located in Presidio Park, is equally small and family-oriented. Housed in the former Officer's Club, the Presidio can get packed around bowling hour so be prepared to wait for your lanes (or call ahead).

For a full-fledged bowling experience with beer and all the hullabaloo, you've got to head just outside the city. **Sea Bowl** is an old-school bowling operation located in the sleepy hub of Pacifica. **Albany Bowl** is perhaps the finest bowling alley but it is unfortunately located in the East Bay. Situated on San Pablo Avenue, this bowling alley remains popular with students, thugs, and anyone else looking to roll for $1.50/game on Tuesday nights. The place is jam-packed, so show up early unless you want to wait up to an hour for a lane. Pass the time eating in the café (which sells Thai dishes) or "prepping" at the bar. At the **Bel Mateo Bowl** in San Mateo, you can rock out every Friday and Saturday night.

Bowling Alleys	Address	Phone	Fees	Map
Yerba Buena Ice Skating & Bowling Center	750 Folsom St	415-820-3532	Mon-Fri $5-6, Fri after 6 pm and weekends $35-40/lane/hr	8
Presidio Bowling Center	Moraga Ave & Montgomery St	415-561-2695	Weekdays $4.50-7.25/game, weekends $6-7.25/game, shoes $4	page 154
Lucky Strike	200 King St	415-400-8260		13
Albany Bowl	540 San Pablo Ave, Albany	510-526-8818	Mon-Tue nights $1.50/game, Thur-Fri nights $1.25/game,n/a Sun $2.50/game, all other times 4-5/game, shoes $4	
AMF Southshore Lanes	300 Park St, Alameda	510-523-6767	$2-$3 / game; $4.50 for shoes	n/a
Bel Mateo Bowl	4330 Olympic Ave	650-341-2616	Weekdays until 5pm $5/game, weeknights and weekends $6/game, shoes $4	n/a
Country Club Bowl	88 Vivian Wy	415-456-4661	$4/game daytime, $5 at night, $5 on weekends. $3 for shoes.	n/a
Sea Bowl	4625 Coast Hwy	650-738-8190	Weekdays until 6pm $22/hr/lane, weeknights $27, weekends $29, shoes $4	n/a

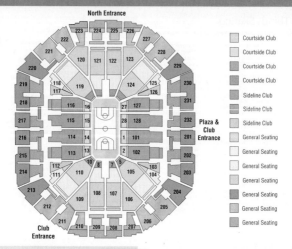

North Entrance

Plaza & Club Entrance

Club Entrance

Courtside Club
Courtside Club
Courtside Club
Courtside Club
Sideline Club
Sideline Club
Sideline Club
General Seating
General Seating
General Seating
General Seating
General Seating
General Seating
General Seating

General Information

Address:	7000 Coliseum Wy Oakland, CA 94621
Phone:	510-569-2121
Website:	www.coliseum.com
Warriors:	www.nba.com/warriors

Overview

While the Oracle Arena plays host to a variety of sporting events and concerts, its full time tenant is the Golden State Warriors, the Bay Area's down-and-out basketball team.

The Golden State Warriors began as the Philadelphia Warriors, earning the honor of being the first NBA champions in the league's inaugural 1947 season. They moved to San Francisco in 1962 and changed their name to Golden State after relocating to Oakland in 1971. The current Warriors team is led by the sharp-shooting Stephan Curry, but the history of the team is especially impressive. The Warriors can boast the NBA's first superstar in Joe Fulks, who averaged 23.2 points per game in the first season of the NBA (originally called the BBA). The only player to ever score 100 points in a single game was the Warriors' Wilt Chamberlain. One of the

best free throw shooters ever was Rick Barry, whose underhanded tosses connected 89.3 percent of the time. Impressed yet?

How to Get There—Driving

Go east over the Bay Bridge to 880 S. Take the 66th Avenue exit. Turn left at the end of the ramp and follow signs to the Arena. The Arena is located right next door to McAfee Coliseum.

Parking

North and south parking lots open two hours prior to game time. Parking fees range from $25-35 for cars and motorcycles and from $48-$85 for RV/Limos/ Buses.

How to Get There—Mass Transit

Take the Fremont BART to the Coliseum/Oakland Airport stop. AC Transit also runs buses 45, 46, 49, 56, 58, and 98 to the Coliseum BART stop.

How to Get Tickets

For Warriors season tickets, call 888-GSW-HOOP. For single game tickets or any other performances at the Arena, purchase your tickets from Ticketmaster— www.ticketmaster.com.

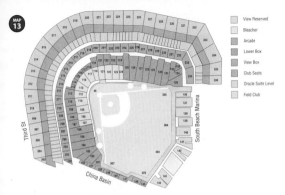

MAP
13

View Reserved
Bleacher
Arcade
Lower Box
View Box
Club Seats
Oracle Suite Level
Field Club

Third St

South Beach Marina

China Basin

General Information

NFT Map:	13
Address:	AT&T Park
	24 Willie Mays Plz
	San Francisco, CA 94107
Phone:	415-972-1800
Giants Website:	sanfrancisco.giants.mlb.com

Overview

After playing at Seals Stadium and the much-maligned Candlestick Park, the San Francisco Giants got a home they could be proud of at AT&T Park, which opened in 2000 under the name Pacific Bell Park. This 41,503-seat jewel of a stadium is a glorious throwback to the intimate ball fields of yore, and the expansive views from the top levels make in the Bay and Treasure Island. Kayakers and other boaters forgo stadium views (and increasingly hefty ticket prices) and bob around McCovey Cove, drinking beers and waiting for splash four-baggers to drop from the sky. The park is emblazoned with giants nostalgia from the iconic statue of Willie Mays to Orlando Cepeda's signature Cha Cha bowl located behind center field.

How to Get There—Mass Transit

Public transit is greatly encouraged when you're heading for the ballpark. Take the Muni Metro trains inbound (or specially marked Metro trains on game days) directly to China Basin by getting off at the Second and King Muni Metro station. You can also catch regular Muni bus routes 10 (Townsend), 15 (Third Street), 30 (Stockton), 42 (Downtown Loop), 45 (Union), or 47 (Van Ness), which will drop you within one block of the park. If you're coming from the South Bay or the Peninsula and Caltrain is your mode of transportation, the San Francisco stop at Fourth and King Streets is one block from the ballpark. Or take BART from the Peninsula or the East Bay to downtown San Francisco and transfer to the Muni N Line at the Civic Center, Powell, Montgomery, or Embarcadero stations (or, better yet, stroll along

the waterfront to the park, it's a local, albeit new, tradition). If sitting in game-day traffic is too daunting then leave your car in the East Bay and take the ferry from Alameda, Oakland, or Larkspur to the China Basin Ferry Terminal, right behind the park (and don't forget to enjoy the scenery on your way).

How to Get There—Driving

From the Peninsula/South Bay, take 1-280 N (or 101 N to I-280 N) to the Mariposa Street exit. Turn right on Mariposa Street, then left on Third Street.

From the East Bay, take I-80/Bay Bridge to the Fifth Street exit. Exit onto Harrison Street, then turn left onto Sixth Street and continue onto I-280 S. Take the first exit at 18th Street and turn left. Go over the freeway and turn left onto Third Street.

From the North Bay, take Highway 101 S/Golden Gate Bridge to the Marina Boulevard exit. Drive past Fort Mason and turn left onto Bay Street, then right onto the Embarcadero. Continue on the Embarcadero under the Bay Bridge until it turns into King Street. Turn left onto Third Street.

Parking

AT&T Park has over 5,000 parking spaces in Parking Lots A (Charter Seat Holder parking), B, and C. The lots are located on the south side of the China Basin Channel across the Lefty O'Doul Bridge from the ballpark. For season parking, call 415-972-2000.

How to Get Tickets

Individual tickets range in price from $10 to $90 and can be purchased through the Giants website.

If you're interested in season tickets, call 415-972-2298 or email seasontickets@sfgiants.com.

Oakland-Alameda County Coliseum

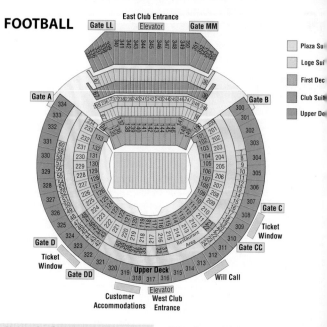

FOOTBALL

East Club Entrance

Gate LL   Elevator   Gate MM

Gate A   Gate B

Gate D   Gate C
                                    Ticket Window

Gate DD   Gate CC

Ticket Window

Customer Accommodations

Elevator
West Club Entrance

Upper Deck

Will Call

Plaza Sui

Loge Sui

First Dec

Club Suit

Upper De

General Information

Address: 7000 Coliseum Wy
                Oakland, CA 94621
Phone: 510-569-2121
Website: www.coliseum.com
A's Website: oakland.athletics.mlb.com
Raiders' Website: www.raiders.com

Overview

They used to call it the Oakland-Alameda County Coliseum. But we live in an age when corporate sponsorship dictates the majority of stadium names. So is it any surprise that Network Associates shelled out $5.8 million in 1998 to put their name on the stadium, then changed the company's name to McAfee in 2004, renaming the arena for the third time in seven years? But lo and behold, the recession took hold and now we're back to Oakland-Alameda County Coliseum. Built at an initial cost of

$25.5 million in 1966, the 1996 renovation budget ballooned from $100 million to $200 million by the time it was complete. But hey, it was money well spent. After all, the renovated Coliseum lured the Raiders back from a 12-year stint in Los Angeles. The Coliseum also plays host to the Oakland Athletics, who began in 1901 as a franchise in Philly, moved to Kansas City in 1954, and then finally to Oakland in 1968. The A's have nine World Series wins to their name, four of them as the Oakland A's. Their next win, though, may be as the Fremont A's—recently, there's been talk that the team may relocate.

How to Get There—Driving

From San Francisco, take the Bay Bridge to I-580 E toward Hayward and exit at I-980 going toward downtown Oakland. Continue on I-980, which becomes I-880 S. Exit at 66th Avenue and follow signs to the Coliseum.

BASEBALL

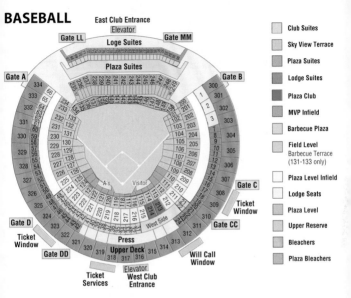

Club Suites

Sky View Terrace

Plaza Suites

Lodge Suites

Plaza Club

MVP Infield

Barbecue Plaza

Field Level
Barbecue Terrace
(131-133 only)

Plaza Level Infield

Lodge Seats

Plaza Level

Upper Reserve

Bleachers

Plaza Bleachers

Parking

There is ample parking available for fans on all sides of the Coliseum. Bus and RV parking is located in a designated lot directly south of the stadium. Parking rates range from $17-35 for cars and motorcycles and from $30-75 for RV/Limos/Buses. Lots open 2.5 hours ahead of schedule for the A's and 5 hours prior to game time for the Raiders.

How to Get There—Mass Transit

Take the Fremont BART to the Coliseum/Oakland Airport stop. AC Transit also runs buses 45, 46, 49, 56, 58, and 98 to the Coliseum BART stop.

How to Get Tickets

For Raiders season tickets, call 888-44-RAIDERS. For individual game tickets you can call the Box Office at 510-569-2121 or purchase them online from www. ticketmaster.com.

Athletics prices range from $9–$44 for individual game tickets and may be purchased through the team's official website, online at www.tickets.com, or by calling 510-762-BALL. If you're after season or group tickets, call 510-638-4627.

Legend:
- VIP Club Glass
- Sideline Club
- End/Corner Club
- Premium Glass
- Premium Lower
- Upper Rim (first row)
- Lower Reserved
- Upper Reserved
- Upper Reserved
- Upper Reserved
- Upper Reserved

General Information

Address: 525 W Santa Clara St
San Jose, CA 95113
Phone: 408-287-9200
Website: www.hppavilion.com
San Jose Sharks: sharks.nhl.com

Overview

In 1991, the San Jose Sharks paid the $50 million entrance fee to the NHL. The construction of a brand new stadium soon followed, with the San Jose Sharks playing their first game in the San Jose Arena on September 30th, 1993. Since then, this 20,000-seat arena has undergone three name changes (San Jose Arena to Compaq Center at San Jose to HP Pavilion), yet remains known locally as the Tank. Ice skating events, boxing matches, and horse shows regularly make a spectacle of themselves here, and the arena was the site for the 2007 West Regional of the NCAA men's basketball tournament. Besides athletics, the Tank plays host to a wide variety of non-sporting entertainment acts. After a long week on the job, you can blow off steam and pump your fists in the general direction of the stage while catching Slayer or the Rock and Roll Visa Championships. Circuses abound at the Tank, with cirque de somethings and Ringlings on steady rotation. But before you grab your seats for Streisand, head down to the Club Level and sample the Oven Roasted Duckling with orange-lingonberry sauce and beluga lentil pilaf at The Grill at HP Pavilion. Regardless of your reason for visiting the Pavilion, please note that no one is allowed to throw objects onto the stage or playing surface in the stands. However, there is one exception to the rule—"...when, during a hockey game, a player scores a 'hat trick'

(three goals in a game); in this case, throwing of hats is customary and has been deemed appropriate." Keep in mind that HP Pavilion cannot return the hats.

How to Get There—Driving

Take the US-101 and exit at CA-87 Guadalupe Parkway. Bear right on Guadalupe Parkway and continue until the Julian Street exit. Turn right onto West Julian Street and left on Stockton Avenue. If you take 280, take the Bird Avenue exit and continue until it becomes Autumn Street. Follow the signs to the parking lots.

Parking

There are more than 6,000 parking spaces located within a 1/2-mile radius of the Pavilion. The charge for parking ranges from $10 to $20 for most events.

How to Get There—Mass Transit

Caltrain is the best public transportation option, with the San Jose Diridon stop located right across the street from the stadium. A one-way fare from any of the stations in Zone 1 to the San Jose Diridon station in Zone 4, costs $7. VTA bus lines 63, 64, 65, 68, 180, and the DASH all stop at the San Jose Diridon Station.

How to Get Tickets

For Sharks season passes, call 408-999-5757 or check their website for order form details. Single game tickets can be purchased via ticketmaster.com and all Ticketmaster outlets including Wherehouse Music, Tower Records, Ritmo Latino, and select Rite-Aid stores.

General Information

Address: 4900 Marie P. DeBartolo Way, Santa Clara CA, 95054

Ticket Office: 415-GO-49ERS

Website: www.levisstadium.com or @levisstadium

49ers: www.49ers.com or @49ers

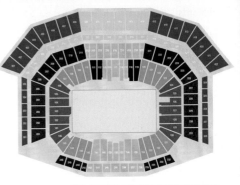

Overview

San Francisco 49ers fans are sometimes pegged a "wine and cheese" crowd, far more reserved than their rowdy Raider Nation counterparts across the Bay. While it is true the fans tailgate in style, this misnomer probably arises from jealousy over the five Super Bowl rings the Niners have amassed over the years.

One of the older West Coast major sports teams, the 49ers were founded in 1946, and played in Golden Gate Park's Kezar Stadium until 1971 when they moved to Candlestick Park. Candlestick was so named for Candlestick Point, a piece of land that juts into San Francisco Bay which used to maintain a long-billed curlew (or "candlestick bird") population. While at Candlestick, the 49ers enjoyed one of the most successful dynasties in major league sports, winning five Super Bowls with a panoply of Hall of Fame talent including Joe Montana, Ronnie Lott and Jerry Rice—some of the best players at their respective positions. Candlestick was also notorious for its foul weather, and after more than 40 years time and without a viable plan for a new stadium within the city limits, the 49ers ownership looked about 40 miles south in the town of Santa Clara for a site for a new stadium.

After a successful ballot measure in which just under 15,000 citizens opted to take on $850 million in loans, construction moved forward on the project, which in the end cost somewhere in the neighborhood of $1.2 billion. The stadium's financing hinges on the profitability of the endeavor; as long as it remains in the black, taxpayers will stay off the hook for the debt incurred building the multi-use development. And although Santa Clara has been successful so far in leveraging the facility (vis a vis luxury suite sales, personal seat licenses, and Levi's naming rights), the loans are substantial for a city of its size; if it works it will be a huge coup and if it doesn't it could be disastrous.

Levi's Stadium seats 68,500 for football with 165 luxury suites. Any new sports facility worth its salt has environmentally friendly features, and Levi's Stadium has all the requisite bells and whistles: solar panels, a green roof, reclaimed water and LEED certification all feature prominently. For all you ever wanted to know about the Bay Area's most popular sports franchise, a 20,000-square-foot 49ers Museum at the site is open daily year-round. Guided public tours are available daily year-round except for 49ers home games, major events, and some holidays.

How to Get There—Driving

From San Francisco and the peninsula, take the 101/Bayshore Fwy south to 237/Southbay Fwy east, exiting at Great American Pkwy and turning left onto Tasman Dr. From the East Bay, take 880/Nimitz Fwy south to 237/Southbay Fwy west, exiting at Great American Pkwy and turning left onto Tasman Dr.

Parking

Expect to pay at least $40 for the privilege of parking. Cash lots are limited and pre-paid passes will save money and time. Tailgating is allowed in certain lots only. Complimentary bicycle valet service is located in Red Lot 1 and Red Lot 6. Courtesy buses and carts will be available to those requiring assistance.

How to Get There—Mass Transit

Levi's Stadium is accessible via various public transportation systems. Valley Transportation Authority (VTA) light rail connects with South Bay communities, dropping off and picking up passengers at the Great America Station located on the north side of the stadium. VTA light rail also connects with Caltrain to San Francisco at Mountain View Transit Center. VTA buses also drop off and pick up close to the stadium. Altamont Corridor Express (ACE)/Capitol Corridor trains provide direct service from inland communities.

How to Get Tickets

Niners tickets can be purchased through Ticketmaster, which also runs the official aftermarket ticket exchange. For other events, such as Pac 12 football or MLS soccer, visit the Levi's Stadium website.

Billiards	Address	Phone	Fees	Map
King Kong	745 O'Farrell St	415-346-4645	$10/hr	7
Jillian's	101 4th St	415-369-6100	Before 4 pm: $8/table/hr. After 4 pm: 12/table/hr	8
Family Billiards	2807 Geary Blvd	415-931-1115	1 person: $7.25/hr:: 2 people: $12/hr.	22
Billiard Palacade	5179 Mission St	415-585-2331	1 person: $5.55/hr: 2 people: $10.75/hr.	34

If you're looking to add more cardiovascular activity to your life, a good place to start exploring your options is the San Francisco Recreation and Park Department webpage (sfrecpark.org). Here you will find information on all city-sponsored sports including tennis, volleyball, softball, lacrosse, football, and soccer. Of course, this fine city of ours prides itself on its diversity, so in addition to these more common sports, you will also find information on other activities such as bocce ball, badminton, lawn bowling, tai chi, public trampolines, and more. They've really got it all. Another semi-all-inclusive website to check out is: www.playnotwatch.com, which isn't local but will help you find a team/league/facility in and around SF nonetheless. If you are looking to join a team, go to (the god of all things San Francisco) Craigslist and search the Community section for your particular sport. If you want to expand your team sports horizons even more, consider checking out some leagues in the East Bay. Since most games are once a week or less, it's worth the short commute and gives you a host of other options. Large workplaces are also apt to hosting softball leagues. If you are a student, your school probably has intramural sports, but you're probably too busy drinking to be reading this page anyway.

One quick tip on joining any city league—it's about persistence, community, and timing. Many of the city's recreational leagues are run by the players in their spare time. If they are slow to return phone calls, or don't have a spot for you the first time you call—stick with it. The community you will find is worth the hassle of getting started.

Soccer

The San Francisco Soccer Football League (SFSFL) is one of the oldest semi-professional and amateur leagues in the nation. It is also one of the few venues in which the city's cultural diversity truly shines. Take a stroll through the Polo Fields at Golden Gate Park on a Saturday morning in July, and you'll feel like you've happened onto a World Cup opening ceremony. Games are played throughout Northern California between March and November. For more information call 415-863-8892 or visit www.sfsfl.com. Also check out All Power Indoor Soccer at 660 15th St in Oakland (510-452-1741).

Biking

Whether you prefer riding your bike on pavement or dirt, the Bay Area has what you're looking for. Even a short ride can traverse the entire city, and (depending on which route you take) will lead you up and over several challenging hills. Cross the Golden Gate for some spectacular views, and keep going into the Marin Headlands for even more great back roads and dirt trails. Not into Lycra shorts and toe clips? Pack yourself a cooler, grab some friends, and rent a bike for two, four, or even six people at Stow Lake Bike & Boat (415-752-0347) in Golden Gate Park.

Softball

With our mild climate, softball is one of the more popular league sports in the Bay Area, with leagues for every season. Activity levels range anywhere from those who bring a 6-pack to the game, to organized Sunday pick-up games, to a recreational high-level of competition. In addition to the above general info try www.sfsoftball.com for San Francisco, www.leaguelineup.com/oaklandsoftball for Oakland, 510-981-5153 for Berkeley's softball league, and Daly City Softball at Daly City Parks and Rec 650-991-8001. You don't have to be a resident of any city to play in a league there. On a related note, check out Bay Area Vintage Baseball (www.eteamz.active.com/BAVBB). The league is dedicated to preserving the style of play that was in effect between 1880 and 1890, which includes regulations, uniforms, and style. Unfortunately that era excluded women players, as does this league.

Frisbee

Played that game in college to great success and want to rekindle that special feeling? You can find all your SF Ultimate Frisbee needs at San Francisco Ultimate League or San Francisco Ultimate Club (visit: bayareadisc.org). Despite the often cold temps, work those calf muscles in a pick-up game of Beach Ultimate, played most weekends. Ultimate players are pretty hard-core and dedicated about their game, but that makes it all the more fun.

Frisbee Golf

If you are looking for a more beer-oriented Frisbee challenge, Disc Golf might be just the thing to float your boat. A world class (and non-profit) 18 hole course is located in GGP at Marx Meadow, deep in the Richmond between 25th and 30th Avenues.

Sports Arenas

If it's too foggy and cold out and/or you'd like to practice your skills, there are a few indoor arenas that have a variety of indoor team sports activities. You don't need to be a member to utilize the following places: Triple Play- 2055 Adams Ave, San Leandro, 510- 568-2255, www.tripleplayusa.com. Primarily softball and baseball batting cages as well as a small indoor basketball court and arcade games for the kid in you. Bladium Sports Complex- 800 West Tower Avenue, Alameda , 510- 814-4999, www.bladium.com. Best place for fun not under the sun. Indoor activities include basketball, soccer , football, inline hockey, lacrosse, volleyball, and climbing. You can also become a member for regular gym privileges. This place is in an old abandoned warehouse that used to be a Navy base, and while half of the base is still abandoned and unused, Bladium is hopping with action.

Gay Sports

Sports Complex (http://sportscomplex.org) organizes "Gay Games" of all kinds including swimming, cycling, softball, and track. Not only is their website a resource for finding teams and leagues, they also post news, events, and political actions affecting LGBT athletic folk.

No matter what you're into—football or badminton, SCUBA, diving, or hand gliding—the diverse topography combined with the adventurous spirit of the San Francisco people to guarantee almost anyone a good time in the great outdoors.

General Information

Airport Information: 650-821-8211
Airport Website: www.flysfo.com
Ground Transportation: 817-1717
  (Bay Area only, no area code required)
Lost & Found: 650-821-7014
Parking: 650-821-7900
Police (Non-Emergency):   650-821-7111
US Customs: 650-624-7200

Overview

This is fog city, baby, and airports and fog do not go hand in hand. With just two closely spaced runways, flights from SFO are particularly prone to weather-related delays. SFO is the fifth-largest airport in the US and the ninth-largest in the world, and serves over 40 million passengers per year. Eighty flights per day depart for Los Angeles, and 42 for New York. While other local airports have been giving SFO some stiff competition for popular destinations, SFO's streamlined security and baggage check make it far more user-friendly than Oakland's congested terminals. The newly-remodeled international terminal has earned rave reviews with its ultra-stylish design and art-filled space, and the BART connection to SFO has eased the commute for thousands of travelers.

New runways would ease congestion and delays, but the now eight-year-old runway expansion plan has been delayed. These runways would fill in 1.5 square miles of open water in the Bay—a prospect that has environmentalists worried (think churning mud, lots of nasty chemicals, dying fish). For now, the economic downturn and the resulting reduction in air traffic have the expansion on hold, but discussion is expected to heat up again when air travel increases.

How to Get There—Driving

If you're driving from San Francisco, take 101 S and get off at the SF International Airport exit. You can also take 280 south and connect to 101 via Highway 380, go south and take the SF International exit.

How to Get There—Mass Transit

There are three options for public transit to SFO, and the best option for you will depend on where you're going, how much baggage you have, and when you're leaving. BART is the most efficient, as the Millbrae line runs all the way to SFO (downtown SF to the airport is $8.25 one way), but you'll have to lug your bags. Also, the earliest train doesn't arrive at SFO until 5:30 am, which can be a problem, particularly for early morning international departures.

Caltrain runs a service from Millbrae Station to Fourth and King Streets ($5.00) and free shuttles run between the station and the airport approximately every 20–30 minutes, except on weekends. BART also offers a cross-platform transfer at Millbrae.

SamTrans runs a few bus routes out of SFO, including the KX Express bus, which provides service between San Francisco, SFO, and Palo Alto. You'd better be traveling light though, because the KX doesn't allow luggage! Route 292 is a local bus that makes many stops in the communities between San Francisco, SFO, and San Mateo. Route 397 runs an overnight "owl" service between San Francisco, SFO, and Palo Alto. Route 193 operates on a limited schedule between the Stonestown Galleria in San Francisco, Daly City BART Station, and SFO. KX Express will set you back $4, while the local buses cost $2.00.

How to Get There—Really

If you'd rather not drive and you don't relish the prospect of lugging your bags to the nearest BART station or bus stop, there are a number of shuttle services (Super Shuttle is a good one) that can get you to SFO from the city for around $20 (a bargain compared to the typical cab fare of $40). Most shuttles pick you up at your front door in plenty of time to make your flight—just be prepared to stop by a couple of other people's houses on your way to the airport.

Parking

For domestic flights departing from Terminal 1, park in Sections A/B, B, or C. Flights departing from Terminal 2 should head to Section D, and if you're going from Terminal 3, park in Sections E, F, or F/G. Rates for parking are $2 for 20 minutes, $36 maximum for the first 24 hours, and $35 maximum for each additional day.

If your destination is abroad, use Garage A for Air France, AirTran, Alaska Airlines (Mexico flights), British Airways, Cathay Pacific, China Airlines, Japan Airlines, KLM, Korean Air, LACSA, Northwest (International), Philippine Airlines, TACA, and Virgin Atlantic. Garage G serves AirChina, ANA, Asiana, EVA, Lufthansa, Mexicana, Singapore Airlines, and United (International). Parking costs $2 per 20 minutes and $28 per 24-hour period.

For two hours of free parking in any terminal garage, you need to spend $20 at participating shops and restaurants in the International Terminal to have your ticket validated. You can also print out discount parking coupons via the airport website at www.flysfo.com.

If your budget doesn't cover long-term parking in the domestic lots, a cheaper alternative is the long-term lot located off the US 101/San Bruno Avenue-East exit. You can park there for up to 30 days and a free shuttle service to and from the terminals runs every few minutes. Parking costs $2 for each 20 minutes, $18 for 24 hours through day seven and $11 per 24 hours thereafter. The website offers a "seventh day free" coupon, so if you'll be there for a week, print it out and take it with you. If the long-term lot happens to be full, get a voucher to park right at the terminals for the same long-term rate!

Cabs

Typical fare from the airport to Cow Palace costs around $29. A cab from downtown will set you back roughly $37, and from the Wharf will be around $44.

Rental Cars

- **Alamo** • 650-616-2400
- **Avis** • 650-877-6780
- **Budget** • 650-877-0998
- **Dollar** • 866-434-2226
- **Enterprise** • 650-697-9200
- **Hertz** • 650-624-6600
- **National** • 650-616-3000
- **Thrifty** • 877-283-0898

Hotels

- **Best Western Grosvenor** ·
  380 S Airport Blvd, San Francisco · 650-873-3200
- **Clarion** · 401 E Millbrae Ave, Millbrae · 650-692-6363
- **Hampton Inn Airport** ·
  300 Gateway Blvd, San Francisco · 650-876-0200
- **Holiday Inn** ·
  373 S Airport Blvd, San Francisco · 650-589-0682
- **Hyatt Regency** ·
  1333 Bayshore Hwy, Burlingame · 650-347-1234
- **La Quinta Inn** ·
  20 Airport Blvd, San Francisco · 650-583-1431
- **North Travelodge** ·
  326 S Airport Blvd, San Francisco · 650-583-9600
- **Radisson San Francisco** ·
  5000 Sierra Point Pkwy, San Francisco · 415-467-4400
- **Sheraton Gateway** ·
  600 Airport Blvd, Burlingame · 650-340-8500
- **Staybridge Suites** ·
  1350 Huntington Ave, San Bruno · 650-588-0770

Terminal 1

Alaska Airlines (domestic & Canada flights)
Delta Airlines
Frontier Airlines
Hawaiian Airlines
Horizon
Midwest Airlines
Southwest
US Airways

Terminal 2

American Airlines
Virgin America

Terminal 3

United Airlines (domestic)
United Express

International Terminal

AeroMexico
Air Berlin
Air Canada
Air China
Air France
Air New Zealand
AirTran Airways
Alaska Airlines (Mexico flights)
ANA (All Nippon Airways)
Asiana
British Airways
Cathay Pacific
China Airlines
Delta (international)
Emirates
EVA Air
Japan Airlines
JetBlue
KLM
Korean Air
LACSA
LAN
Lufthansa
Philippine Airlines
Singapore Airlines
Sun Country
Swiss International Air Lines
TACA
United Airlines (international)
Virgin America (Mexico arrivals only)
Virgin Atlantic
WestJet

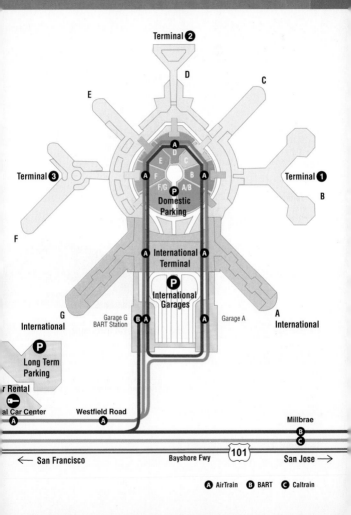

Terminal **2**

D

C

E

Terminal **3**

Terminal **1**

E
F
F/G **P** A/B
B
A **A**
Domestic
Parking

B

F

A International **A**
Terminal

P
International
Garages

G
International

Garage G
BART Station

B **A**

A

Garage A

A
International

P
Long Term
Parking

r Rental

al Car Center

A

Westfield Road

A

Millbrae

B
C

← San Francisco

Bayshore Fwy **101** San Jose →

A AirTrain **B** BART **C** Caltrain

Terminal 1

Alaska Airlines
Allegiant
America West/US Airways
ArkeFly
Delta/Delta Connection
Hawaiian
JetBlue
SATA
Spirit Airlines
United/Express
Volaris

Terminal 2

Southwest

General Information

Airport Phone:	510-563-3300
Airport Website:	www.flyoakland.com
Parking:	1-888-IFLYOAK
Lost & Found:	510-563-3982
Friendly Cab Service:	510-536-3000
Veteran's Cab Service:	510-533-1900

Overview

When Gertrude Stein visited her Oakland birthplace and couldn't find her house, the famous quote was born: "There's no there there." Today, many people start "there" to get everywhere else. Oakland International Airport houses several low-fare carriers, and patronage increases. However, while flights from Oakland are typically cheaper than those leaving from its higher-profile San Francisco counterpart, be prepared for the added toll on your sanity: chronically congested terminals (particularly Southwest Airlines Terminal 2), and security and baggage check lines can be over an hour long around the holidays. In fog, Oakland is always a faster landing than SFO.

Oakland might not be the biggest Bay Area airport, but it's rich in history. Amelia Earhart took off from Oakland on her ill-fated flight—thankfully navigation is a bit more reliable these days. The original airport at North Field was built in 1927 and is still in operation today for air racing, general aviation, and corporate jet activities. Commercial passenger and cargo jet aircraft operate from South Field, which opened in 1962. Oakland Airport is a thriving business, handling more than 10 million passengers per year and employing approximately 10,700 airport-related workers.

How to Get There—Driving

If you're coming to Oakland from San Francisco, give yourself a little extra time for possible Bay Bridge delays, especially if you're traveling during the morning or evening rush hours. Travel south on 880 and exit at Hegenberger Road. Merge onto Hegenberger Road and continue straight ahead to the airport. Use the right lane for Terminal 1/International, the economy parking lot, and cargo facilities. Use the left lane for Terminal 2, the hourly and daily parking lots, the new Park & Call Zone, and all rental car returns.

How to Get There—Mass Transit

The best way to get from San Francisco to the Oakland Airport is via the Fremont, Dublin/Pleasanton (from points north), and Richmond (from points south) BART lines. Hours of operation to the Coliseum/Oakland Airport station are Monday–Saturday, 5 am until midnight; Sunday, 8 am until midnight. From the Coliseum/Airport station, the airBART shuttle to the airport departs every 10 minutes and costs $3 for adults and $1 for those entitled to discounts. A BART extension from the Coliseum station to the airport is (and has been for several years) in the planning stages, but don't hold your breath.

If you're arriving to the area by Amtrak (Jack London Square Station), Alameda/Oakland Ferry, or BART, local AC transit Line 73 will take you right to the airport for $2.00 or $1.00 discounted fare. The line runs every 11–13 minutes between 4:56 am. and 12:06 am. Line 805 is the late-night service that runs every hour between 12:35 am. and 4:30 am.

How to Get There—Really

Avoid driving to Oakland Airport if you can—somewhat confusing signage and recent construction means about the only benefit is the view from the Bay Bridge. Instead, save yourself the money and hassle and take BART, or save yourself the hassle and time and call one of the many door-to-terminal shuttlebus services that will pick you up from anywhere in the Bay Area, usually for around $15–$20, like Supershuttle (1-800-BLUE-VAN) or BayPorter Express (1-877-467-1800).

Parking

Oakland Airport parking is logically organized by letter with Lot H accommodating hourly parking, Lot D housing daily parkers, and Lot E assigned for economy parking. All lots are $2 per 30 minutes for short-term parking; per day, Lot H is $32, Lot D is $22, and Lot E is $16. If you're picking someone up, the new Park & Call Zone offers 30 minutes free parking for those who connect with their passengers via cell phone. For real-time parking availability, call 510-633-2571

Rental Cars

- **Avis** • 510-577-6360 or 800-331-1212
- **Budget** • 800-527-0700
- **Dollar** • 866-434-2226 or 800-800-4000
- **Enterprise** • 510-567-1760 or 800-261-7331
- **Fox** • 800-225-4369
- **Hertz** • 510-639-0200 or 800-654-3131
- **National** • 510-632-2225 or 800-227-7368
- **Thrifty** • 877-283-0898 or 800-847-4389

Hotels

- **Best Western** • 170 Hegenberger Loop • 510-633-0500
- **Clarion Hotel** • 500 Hegenberger Rd • 510-562-5311
- **Comfort Inn and Suites** • 8452 Edes Ave • 510-568-1500
- **Courtyard by Marriott** • 350 Hegenberger Rd • 510-568-7600
- **Days Inn** • 8350 Edes Ave • 510-568-1880
- **Holiday Inn Express** • 66 Airport Access Rd • 510-569-4400
- **Hilton** • One Hegenberger Rd • 510-635-5000
- **La Quinta Inn** • 8465 Enterprise Wy • 510-632-8900

Terminal A

All Nippon Airlines (ANA)
American/American Eagle
Delta Air Lines
Hawaiian Airlines
JetBlue
United
US Airways
Virgin America
Volaris

Terminal B

Alaska Airlines
Southwest

General Information

General Airport Info: 408-277-4759
Airport Website: www.flysanjose.com

Overview

Located two miles north of downtown San Jose, SJC is a completely self-supporting enterprise, owned and operated by the City of San Jose. Like Oakland Airport, with low-cost airlines like JetBlue and Southwest, SJC can sometimes offer more affordable flights than SFO (if you don't mind driving a while to get there). They're working on making SJC more accessible by adding freeway routes and new interchanges. It might be a tad messy right now, but it'll get better.

How to Get There—Driving

"Do You Know the Way to San Jose?" croons Dionne, but you might not be singing along if you're stuck in the morning commute to Northern California's biggest 'burb. Silicon Valley traffic can turn the trip from San Francisco into a two-hour plus affair, so if you have to drive to or from the city, particularly during rush hours, plan for the worst.

From San Francisco, begin on I-80 W, which eventually becomes US 101 S. Stay on US 101 S and take the Highway 87 exit on the right. Take the Skyport Drive exit to the airport. If you're coming down I-880, take the Brokaw Road exit. Drive along O'Toole Avenue and make a right on East Brokaw Road, which becomes Airport Parkway.

How to Get There—Mass Transit

There are a few public transportation options that will take you close to the airport, and then you'll need to take a bus or a shuttle to the terminals. Caltrain riders should get off at Santa Clara and take the VTA Airport Flyer (Route 10) to the airport. The Route 10 bus also makes a stop at the VTA Metro Light Rail Station. From there, it's a convoluted route to get to the BART. Other options: take the light rail to the Civic Center stop and board the VTA 180 Express Bus, which will take you right to the Freemont BART stop. If you're traveling from further afield, Greyhound and Amtrak both stop roughly three miles from the airport and then you can grab a cab.

Parking

There are only two options for parking at San Jose Airport—short-term or long-term parking. If you're going to Terminal A or International Arrivals, head to the short-term parking garage, and if Terminal C is your destination, try the short term parking lot across the roadway from the terminal. Short-term parking costs $1 per 20 minutes, with a maximum daily fee of $30. For longer stays, park in one of two long-term lots on Airport Blvd, which cost $22 per day. A free shuttle is provided to and from the terminals. Call 408-277-4759 for current parking availability.

Cabs

Yellow Cab (408-293-1234) departs from Terminal A and United Cab (408-971-1111) from Terminal C. Cab fare to San Francisco Airport will set you back $82, while a longer trip to downtown SF will cost you between $110 and $120.

Rental Cars

- **Alamo** · 408-327-9633
- **Avis** · 800-831-2847
- **Budget** · 800-527-0700
- **Dollar** · 800-800-4000
- **Enterprise** · 800-736-8222
- **Fox** · 800-225-4369
- **Hertz** · 800-654-3131
- **National** · 800-227-7368
- **Payless** · 800-729-5377
- **Thrifty** · 800-367-2277

Hotels

- **Adlon Hotel** ·
  1275 N Fourth St · 408-282-1000
- **Best Western Inn Airport South** ·
  2118 The Alameda· 408-243-2400
- **Courtyard by Marriott at the San Jose Airport** ·
  1727 Technology Dr · 408-441-6111
- **Crowne Plaza San Jose** ·
  282 Almaden Blvd · 408-998-0400
- **Hilton San Jose & Towers** ·
  300 Almaden Blvd · 408-287-2100
- **Holiday Inn Express Airport** ·
  1350 N Fourth St · 408-467-1789
- **Homestead Village Guest Studios** ·
  1560 N First St · 408-573-0648
- **Hotel De Anza** ·
  233 W Santa Clara St· 408-286-1000
- **Hyatt Saint Claire** ·
  302 S Market St · 408-295-2000
- **Radisson Plaza Hotel** ·
  1471 N Fourth St · 408-452-0200
- **Travelodge—San Jose Convention Center** ·
  1415 Monterey Hwy · 408-993-1711
- **Travelodge—San Jose Sports Arena** ·
  1041 The Alameda · 408-295-0159

Overview

Parking in San Francisco is a notoriously tricky game. Imagine you could get a half hour of your day back instead of circling the neighborhood for parking. Imagine you could get an extra $100 – 200 a month in spending money instead of giving it to the Department of Parking & Transportation. Imagine you didn't have to be outraged by the escalating gas prices. All that is more than a dream with car sharing. Use one when you need one, return it when you're done, and never worry about the inevitable costs and hassles that come with owning a car. It's like renting a car, but by the hour, and without trekking to the airport for cheap rates. Reserve your car online and pick it up in the designated lot in your 'hood where the cars live. It's great when you need that couch picked up from Ikea, or help a friend move, or go on a hike in Marin. For trips longer than two days, car-sharing is not as cost-efficient as renting a car the traditional way.

Car sharing's big two are **Zipcar** and **CityCar Share**. Both are constantly offering special deals, perks, and even social events as they expand their services. If you like new cars, these fleets change often and you can pick from a variety of economical models, with an emphasis on the hybrid. They are all better alternatives to having a car in the city, unless you have a really cool car and/or a good parking situation. Gas, insurance, and maintenance are always included in all of these company's fees, so you don't have to worry about the ever-increasing price of gas. But remember these are not your cars (and many people are sharing them), so pay attention to and respect the rules, otherwise you'll have to pay later (monetarily that is).

CityCar Share is a local company (founded in· 2001 by transportation activists) and the most established operation with cars all over the Bay Area. Monthly membership fees are $45/month, and membership has its definite advantages.

Website: www.citycarshare.org
Phone: 415-995-8588 or 510-352-0323
Fees: Membership: $50/month.
    One-time security deposit: $300.
    Driving: $6.50/hour + 44¢/mile.

Zipcar is a national company trying to woo consumers with an $9.25 hourly, $0 per mile fee, as long as the mileage is "within reason." Zipcar offers two different plans, so be sure to do your research and assess your car needs before choosing one.

Website: www.zipcar.com
Phone: 415-495-7478
Address: 191 2nd Street
    San Francisco, CA 94105
Fees: Occasional Driver: $50/yr and drive from $9.25/
    hr and $69/day weekdays, $9.75/hr and $74/day
    weekends.
    Extra Value Plan: $50/month and drive from
    $8.33/hr and $62.10/day weekdays, $8.78/hr and
    $66.60/day weekends.
    All Fees: 125 "free" miles per day (and then 20¢ for
    each extra mile). One-time application fee: $25

Taxis

OK, we're not Manhattan. It's not always easy to just walk outside and grab a cab, but taxis are still the most convenient way to get around the city if you're going out drinking, or if you're heading over to North Beach or Russian Hill, where it's notoriously difficult to park and walk. For some terrible reason, it seems to cost at least $10 to go anywhere in the city and usually more.

Cabs are a pricey way to get to the airport now that BART goes directly to the SFO and Oakland Airports. But if you've got lots of bags and don't want to park or take a shuttle, splurging on a cab is the way to go.

While there are a few spots around the city where you can reasonably expect to walk outside and hail a cab (16th and Valencia, Union Street, North Beach on a weekend), for the most part you're better off calling a cab company and having them pick you up. Here are a few numbers:

Alliance	415-285-3800
American	415-614-2000
Arrow	415-648-3181
Executive	415-401-8900
Luxor	415-282-4141
National	415-648-1313
Regents	415-487-1004
Town	415-401-8900
United	415-648-4444
Yellow	415-282-3737

Fares

San Francisco Taxicab Rates of Fare (Section 1135 San Francisco Municipal Police Code):

First 1/5th mile or flag	$3.50
Each additional 1/5th mile or fraction thereof	55¢
Each minute of waiting, or traffic time delay	55¢
Airport Exit Surcharge	$2.00

For out-of-town trips exceeding 15 miles beyond city limits, the fare will be 150% of the metered rate. For trips exceeding 15 miles from San Francisco International Airport and not terminating within the city limits of San Francisco, the fare will cost 150% of the metered rate except for those trips from San Francisco International Airport traversing San Francisco going to Marin County or to the East Bay—the 15-mile limit will apply from the city limits of San Francisco as set forth above.

If traditional car rental is more your style, or you need a rental for a longer period of time, try one of the many old-fashioned car rental places in San Francisco.

Map 3 · Russian Hill / Fisherman's Wharf

Avis	500 Beach St	415-441-4186
Budget	495 Bay St	415-292-3683
Hertz	500 Beach St	415-674-8330

Map 4 · North Beach / Telegraph Hill

Dollar	2500 Mason St	866-434-2226
Enterprise	350 Beach St	415-474-9600

Map 6 · Pacific Heights / Japantown

Hertz	1644 Pine St	415-923-1119

Map 7 · Nob Hill / Tenderloin

Alamo	320 O'Farrell St	415-292-5353
Alamo	750 Bush St	415-693-0191
Avis	675 Post St	415-929-2555
City Rent-A-Car	1433 Bush St	415-359-1331
Discount Rentals	349 Mason St	415-922-1994
Dollar	364 O'Farrell St	866-434-2226
Enterprise	222 Mason St	415-837-1700
Hertz	335 Powell St	415-362-2780
Hertz	433 Mason St	415-771-2200
Hertz	500 Post St	415-771-8600
Hertz	55 4th St	415-957-9425
Hertz	950 Mason St	415-398-3944
National	320 O'Farrell St	415-292-5300
National	750 Bush St	415-693-0191
Reliable Rent-A-Car	349 Mason St	415-928-4414
Thrifty	350 O'Farrell St	415-788-8111

Map 8 · Financial District / SOMA

Budget	5 Embarcadero Ctr	415-433-3717
Enterprise	1600 Mission St	
Hertz	101 The Embarcadero	415-546-4480
National	687 Folsom St	415-882-9440

Map 11 · Hayes Valley / The Mission

Enterprise	1600 Mission St	415-522-5900
Hertz	241 10th St	415-703-0205

Map 12 · SOMA / Potrero Hill (North)

Avis	821 Howard St	415-957-9998
Enterprise	312 8th St	415-703-9000

Map 17 · Potrero Hill / Dogpatch

Rent-A-Wreck	2955 3rd St	415-282-6293

Map 21 · Inner Richmond

Enterprise	4250 Geary Blvd	415-750-2500
Hertz	3928 Geary Blvd	415-387-0136
Toyota	3800 Geary Blvd	415-750-8300

Map 27 · Parkside (Inner)

Enterprise	Winston Dr/ Stonestown Mall	415-337-9000
Enterprise	498 Winston Dr	415-242-5620

Map 33 · Ingleside

Enterprise	4050 19th Ave	415-406-1164

Map 36 · Bayview / Silver Terrace

Enterprise	445 Charter Oak Ave	415-330-0270

Alameda/Oakland Ferry

510-749-5972 · sanfranciscobayferry.com/route/hbi/sffb
The Alameda/Oakland Ferry provides commuter routes from the East Bay to San Francisco and South San Francisco, as well as direct service from Pier 41 to AT&T Park for Giants games ($4.75–$7.50 one way). You can also take it from San Francisco direct to Jack London Square in Oakland. Tickets may be purchased on board and one-way fares vary from $.75–$6.25, depending on your destination. The Alameda/Oakland Ferry provides service to Angel Island on weekends during the summer ($8.50 –$14.50 round trip, including park admission).

Angel Island-Tiburon Ferry

415-435-2131 · www.angelislandferry.com
This family-owned ferry offers an array of services, including sunset cruises (reservations recommended), whale watch cruises, and trips between Angel Island and Tiburon. These vessels may also be chartered for special occasions, such as weddings or birthday parties. Tickets from Angel Island to Tiburon cost $13.50 round trip for adults and $11.50 round trip for children 6–12 (includes park admission). Cash and checks only. The trip takes about ten minutes each way.

Blue & Gold Fleet

415-705-5555 · www.blueandgoldfleet.com
Located at Pier 41, Blue & Gold provides narrated historical tours of the Bay that last approximately one hour ($23), trips to Angel Island ($17 round trip, including park admission), ferry and bus shuttle to Six Flags Marine World ($65; includes park admission), and trips to Tiburon ($21 round trip).

Golden Gate Ferry

511, or 415-455-2000 · www.goldengate.org
Golden Gate Ferry serves Larkspur and Sausalito. The one-way fare is $8.75 to Larkspur and $9.25 to Sausalito. Receive a frequent rider discount using a Clipper card and ticket prices drop 37-46%. The Larkspur ferry also goes to AT&T Park for Giants games ($8.75 one way). Great views of San Quentin too, if you're into prisons, that is.

Alameda Harbor Bay Ferry

510-769-5172 · sanfranciscobayferry.com/route/hbi/sffb
Alameda Harbor Bay Ferries provide convenient commuter service between San Francisco and Alameda. The fare is $6.50 one way, but commuter rates and monthly passes are available at discounted rates. The monthly pass ($185) includes free AC Transit and Muni transfers. Harbor Bay Ferry also offers a river cruise up the Sacramento Delta on weekends with lunch and no-host bar. All services leave from San Francisco's Ferry Plaza.

Red & White Fleet

415-673-2900 · www.redandwhite.com
This service offers tours of San Francisco Bay narrated in eight different languages. Tickets cost $26 but are usually offered at discounted prices if you buy them on the web. Ferries depart from Pier 43 1/2.

Vallejo Baylink Ferry

707-643-3779 · www.baylinkferry.com
Makes stops at Vallejo, Fisherman's Wharf (Pier 41), and the San Francisco Ferry Building. The fare is $13 each way for adults and $6.50 each way for students and seniors. Monthly passes are available for $290, which includes Baylink ferries and Vallejo Transit buses. A ten-ride punch ticket can be purchased for $103.

Fomalhaut Ferry

Currently, this one-way ferry to Fomalhaut is under major renovation, due to serious problems with the interstellar matter converters and the rear-window defrostor. Both the Interstellar Rapid Transit Organization (IRTO) and Zetadyne, Inc. have promised to have it back in action within the next five parsecs.

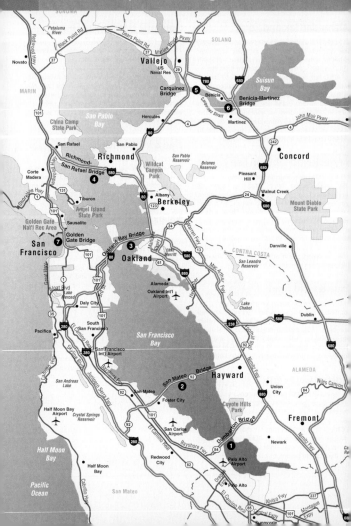

Bridges, in all their glory, are icons of San Francisco's romantic allure. The Golden Gate, the state's namesake and postcard darling, features in films from classics like *Vertigo* to sci-fi flicks like *The Core* (where it falls apart—let's not think about that one). In *So I Married an Axe Murderer*, sitting on the Bay Bridge in traffic after eating bran muffins was deemed worse than being electrocuted, and Dustin Hoffman drove across it to Berkeley (the wrong way on the upper deck!) in *The Graduate*. But don't let these star traffic conduits eclipse their lesser-known but no less hardworking counterparts: most of the seven bridges have claims to fame. The Dumbarton Bridge was the first vehicular crossing of the San Francisco Bay. The original San Mateo Bridge was the longest in the world when it was completed in 1929. Carquinez's new span was dedicated to Al Zampa, a construction worker who was instrumental in the building of four of the Bay Area bridges (and who was one of the first to have survived a fall off the Golden Gate).

The Golden Gate Bridge is California's only bridge that is not under state jurisdiction of Caltrans. It is left up to the folks at Golden Gate Bridge Highway and Transportation District to make sure the bridge's distinctive orange vermilion always sparkles. After the original coat of paint succumbed to corrosion and was replaced in 1965 by inorganic primer and acrylic topcoat, only touchups are needed once in a while. It's the most expensive bridge to cross—$6 cash or $5 if you use FasTrak. Aesthetics don't come cheap.

As Bay Area traffic balloons and overwhelms bridges built during the model T generation, most of the structures are going through rehab to incorporate the latest in steel and concrete bridge technology. The Carquinez Bridge welcomed the new westbound span in 2003, including a 12-foot-wide bike and pedestrian path (the old 1927 span will be demolished). In 2007, the Benicia-Martinez Bridge acquired a new 5-lane northbound span. The old northbound structure was converted into a 4-lane southbound span with a separate pedestrian/bike lane. The cantilever span between Oakland and Yerba Buena Island on the Bay Bridge is still under heavy construction, and will reincarnate as a suspension bridge in 2013.

FasTrak

www.bayareafastrak.org
If you own a car and drive at all, even if you only occasionally cross bridges (lets face it you'll have to eventually) it is worth getting a FasTrak. The device is free and automatically deducts from the account of your choosing as you zip past the other suckers stuck in the toll plaza traffic. Users of FasTrak also get a 15¢ discount at all other toll bridges.

		Toll	# of lanes	Bike Path?	# of vehicles/day (in thousands)	Cost in millions – original	Engineer	Length	Original Structure Completion Date
1	Dumbarton Bridge	$5	6	Yes	61	$2.5		1.6 mi	Jan 1927
2	San Mateo - Hayward Bridge	$5	6	Yes[1]	81	$70		7.0 mi	Oct 1967
3	SF - Oakland Bay Bridge	$5	10	Yes[2]	270	$77	Charles C. Purcell	8.4 mi	Nov 1936
4	Richmond - San Rafael Bridge	$5	4	No	59	$66	C. Derleth, Jr	5.5 mi	Sep 1956
5	Carquinez Bridge	$5	8	Yes	116	$4.6	Aven Hanford & Oscar Klatt	0.7 mi	May 1927
6	Benicia - Martinez Bridge	$5	6	No	94	$25		1.2 mi	Sep 1962
7	Golden Gate Bridge	$5	6	Yes	112	$35	Joseph Baermann Strauss	1.7 mi	May 1937

[1] Via AC Transit
[2] Bicycle Shuttle $1 each way
Check www.dot.ca.gov/dist4/shuttle.htm for bike shuttle schedules.

Web Resources

City of San Francisco Dept of Parking & Traffic

Address:	11 South Van Ness Ave
	San Francisco, CA 94103
Phone:	415-554-7275 (recorded info)
	415-554-9805 (administration office)
Website:	www.sfgov.org
	www.sfbaytraffic.info
	www.sfgate.com/traffic

California Dept of Transportation (Caltrans)

Traffic Hotline:	800-427-7623
Outside CA:	916-654-5266
Website:	www.dot.ca.gov

Golden Gate Bridge

Phone:	415-921-5858

Bay Bridge Traffic: www.dot.ca.gov/hq/roadinfo

Bay Area Traffic: www.traffic.511.org

Radio Traffic Info:

KGO 810 AM
KQED 88.5 FM
KALW 91.7 FM

Orientation

San Francisco sits isolated on a peninsula, physically and ideologically separated from the rest of the country. It is a great city to walk, bike and bus in—that means driving can end up being a hectic conglomeration of bold pedestrians, honking commuters, and Critical Mass bikers.

Aside from the relatively orderly layout of the avenues out in the Sunset and the Richmond, the 46 square miles of streets, lanes, alleys, and winding roads that are crammed onto the tip of the San Francisco Peninsula make it look like Jackson Pollock was on the job when they were laying out the grid. Navigating a city seven by seven miles ought to be relatively easy, but there are too many pedestrians, cars, and hills to make driving here pleasant; rush hours (7 am to 10:30 am and 3:30 pm to 7 pm) can cause some gray hair (if you didn't know your usual lane is closed or left turns are illegal). And if there's a parade or construction going on—which happens frequently—forget about trying to get Downtown, the Castro, the Mission, or any other central area for big gatherings. Icon signs and color-coded plaques mark famous tourist areas (map of Italy points to North Beach, a crab shows way to Fisherman's Wharf, and a pagoda is symbol for Chinatown).

Driving on the hills of San Francisco is a skill which takes years to master. If you drive a stick, be prepared for stop signs at the crest of very steep hills—the City will be the ultimate test of your mettle. Some intersections are so fierce you'll be airborne before you actually see the cross-street (Gough and Turk, middle lane, is a good one). And be mindful of the cable car and street car lines that run all over the City—there's plenty of pedestrian traffic as passengers board and disembark. And as long as you're staying polite, watch out for the bikers, if you cut them off don't be surprised when you hear an angry tirade of insults and a knock on the side of your car. (Conversely, if you are a biker, this increases your intimidation factor.) There are some designated bike lanes, but often they will be sharing lanes with you and your car. Remember, it's California law to share the road.

Bridges

The Golden Gate Bridge, which connects the city to Marin County in the north, and the Bay Bridge, which runs through Treasure Island and the into Oakland/Berkeley in the east,

can be either smooth sailing or a grid-locked mess. With the ongoing Bay Bridge construction and new configuration of exits on the San Francisco side, there is almost always traffic, but on the off-chance that there's not, kick back and enjoy the views. On weekends, particularly if the weather is good, the Golden Gate is usually packed with residents fleeing the city for Marin. The Bay Bridge tends to back up most during weekday rush hours and Friday and Saturday nights. Check local traffic reports on www.511.org for up-to-the-minute bridge traffic updates.

Major Freeways

Hwy 101: Runs north to south from the Oregon border to Los Angeles.

I-280: Runs parallel and just to the west of Highway 101. This route tends to be less crowded than the 101, and the scenery is a bit easier on the eyes. On the south end, it becomes I-680 in San Jose where it wraps around the east side of the bay.

Hwy 1: Like a wayward lover, this pretty bit of road merges briefly with Highway 101 as they cross the Golden Gate Bridge together, then ambles off on its own again. Hwy 1's scenic, winding route is one of the prettiest in the nation—but don't drive it if you're in a hurry. Parts of the picturesque Pacific Coast Highway (PCH as they call it in LA) are treacherous, twisty and overlook some of the most iconic cliffs of the California the coast. The road is most often characterized by two snaking lanes, impressive vistas and double arched bridges.

I-80: Runs north-south through Berkeley and connects the East Bay with San Francisco via the Bay Bridge. Continues east to Sacramento and is a major thoroughfare to destinations in the Sierras.

I-580: Connects the East Bay with I-5 and I-80, which runs through the Central Valley and provides the fastest route south to Los Angeles. Be warned: the 390-mile, six-to-seven-hour drive isn't scenic (although you'll reach the grapevine which takes you into Los Angeles county), but it's the quickest and most direct way down. And you can always stop at Harris Ranch for a mid-trip burger (that is if the cow smell isn't too much to handle).

Major Construction Projects & Alternate Routes: The new six-lane Octavia Boulevard was completed in early 2006 and has been a blessing to anyone living west of Van Ness, providing a quick route off Oak and onto Fell. The new exit replaces the Fell Street off-ramp which closed some years back and forced Mission Street to function as the last Central Freeway exit. The area around the western end of the Bay Bridge is undergoing major exit reconfiguration, so watch out for signs or else you might easily be swept away onto the wrong off-ramp.

Drivers wishing to avoid Central Freeway congestion can use alternate surface street routes, or I-280. If you're coming into the city from the Bay Bridge (I-80), use the Harrison Street, Fremont Street, Fifth Street, or Ninth Street exits. Do not get off too early during rush hour or you'll hit downtown traffic, not to mention the one-way obstacles surrounding Market Street. For easy access to the Marina from Market, Franklin is a quick route, as is Gough for easy access in the opposite direction. If you're coming into the city from the Peninsula on the South Bay on Highway 101 and see a nasty-looking back up, get off at Cesar Chavez or Vermont Street in Potrero Hill. Otherwise use the Ninth Street exit on US 101, or the Seventh Street exit on I-80 as alternatives to Mission Street. You can also take the I-280 and exit at Sixth Street to reach downtown San Francisco, the Richmond district, or the Western Addition. If you can only stop once, make sure to visit Big Sur for its expansive views, majestic beaches, and beautiful state parks.

Parking Stickers & Permits

f you live in an established Residential Permit Parking (RPP) area (identified by a sign displayed on your block), then you need a parking permit. The only catch is that even some metered streets are RPPs, and there aren't always signs posted. Your only real hope is to call one of the phone numbers listed below. If you reside in the area, you can get an application for a permit by calling 415-503-2020, by downloading it from www.sfgov.org, or by visiting the 1380 Howard Street office. (Unless you're in the business of wasting time, this should always be your last resort.)

Department of Parking & Traffic
Residential Parking Permit Office (RPP)
Address: 11 South Van Ness Ave
              San Francisco, CA 94103
Phone: 415-503-2020 or 415-554-5000
              (recorded info)

Enforcement Division
Address: 505 Seventh St
              San Francisco, CA 94103
Phone: 415-553-1631

Traffic Engineering Division
Address: 25 Van Ness Ave, Ste 345
              San Francisco, CA 94102
Phone: 415-554-2339

Tickets, Towing, and Other Bad Things

f your life suddenly turns into *Dude, Where's My Car?*, chances are you've been towed. Here are some phone numbers (and options) you need to know about:

Department of Parking & Traffic
Tow Line: 415-553-1235
(basic information)
Tow Desk: 415-553-1239 or 553-1240
(if you're not sure your car has been towed)
SF Police: 415-553-0123
(to report a stolen vehicle)
To protest a towing: 415-255-3967
(Hearing Division)
If the SFPD towed your car: 415-553-1619
If your car is booted: 415-553-1634
(Boot-removal fee is $75)

Getting Your Car Back
City Tow (Towing yard):   415-865-8200
Location of yard: 415 Seventh St, at Harrison
City Tow offices: 11 S Van Ness Ave
SFPD Towing: 850 Bryant St, Rm 154

For Parking Citations and Hearings
Address: 11 South Van Ness Ave
             San Francisco, CA 94103
Phone: 415-255-3900 (citations/permits)
             415-255-3964 (hearings)
             415-255-3999 or 800-531-7357
             (citation telephone payment)
Hours: Mon–Fri 8 am–5 pm

Parking Meters

Meters usually operate Monday–Saturday, 9 am–6 pm, but in some areas the hours start as early as 7 am and run to as late as 9 pm (just be sure you check your meter). On Port property (Including Fisherman's Wharf), meters also operate on Sundays and holidays. Remember that parking time limits are still enforced even if a meter is broken.

Hourly Rates for Selected Areas:
Downtown: $3.50 hourly/70¢ for motorcycles
Downtown Periphery: $3.00 hourly/60¢ motorcycles
Fisherman's Wharf: $3.00 hourly/60¢ motorcycles
All other areas: $3.00 hourly/60¢ motorcycles

Curb Colors

A handy guide to the curb palette:

Green: Limited time parking—ten minutes 9 am–6 pm, Mon–Sat.
Yellow: Commercial loading and unloading; vehicles with commercial plates may park up to 30 minutes from 9 am–6 pm Mon–Sat. Some yellow zones are restricted to trucks with commercial plates only. Violators will be towed. Usually accompanied by a sign; check for hours of enforcement.
Blue: Parking for vehicles with special disabled person plates or placards only. Always enforced; violators will be fined $275.
Red: No parking at any time. Vehicles in bus stops will be towed and subject to $250 additional fine.
White: Passenger loading zone (usually in front of churches, restaurants, hotels, etc.). Vehicles may not be left unattended for any length of time during enforcement hours; attended vehicles may stand for up to five minutes. Hours of enforcement may be painted on the curb or posted on a sign. If not, check to see if the business in front of the white zone appears to be in operation.
Brown: A dog just pooped here, so watch out when getting out of your car.

Street Cleaning

San Francisco streets are swept on a rotating weekly schedule between the hours of 6 am and 3 pm. Unless a posted sign says "Every day including holidays," the following holidays are exempt from street cleaning:

• New Years Day
• Martin Luther King Jr's Birthday
• Presidents' Day
• Memorial Day
• Independence Day
• Labor Day
• Columbus Day
• Veterans' Day
• Thanksgiving and Day after Thanksgiving
• Christmas Day

Transbay Terminal

Address:	425 Mission St
	San Francisco, CA 94105
Phone:	415-495-1569, or 415-495-1575

The massive Transbay Terminal redesign project now underway is at once a utopian vision and an urban planner's nightmare. It's slated to cost billions and will attempt to tackle major structural issues, such as running transit lines under an already-developed city. But the new six-story modern building will, supposedly, become a center for a green transit system streaming into downtown from all corners of the Bay Area and even from the Central Valley, electrifying trains and cutting many commutes times nearly in half. For now, all we can do is hold our breath: it's not going to be affecting our lives for the better any time soon.

AC Transit

Phone:	510-891-4777
	510-891-4706 (Lost & Found)
Website:	www.actransit.org

Carrying 230,000 riders daily to and from 15 communities, the Alameda-Contra Costa Transit District runs a fleet of 700 buses. Most of the vehicles can accommodate two bikes on a front-mounted rack, and all are wheelchair-accessible. AC Transit operates more than 70 local East Bay routes, as well as almost 30 transbay lines, which offer a convenient ground alternative to commuting into the city by BART. From East Bay destinations to the Transbay Terminal, the fare is $4.20 with a free transfer. Within the East Bay, you'll want to save your quarters to pay $2.10 (and 25¢ for a transfer good for 1.5 hours). Frequent riders can buy a monthly pass on their clipper card for $80 and then swipe on board (the pass costs just $15 for riders under 17). NextBus Internet and satellite tracking technology is supposedly on the way, so you'll know when the next bus will arrive. For routes and schedules, AC Transit website and TripPlanner (www.transitinfo.org) are both very useful. Fun places to go on AC Transit from SF: the 19th-century estate Ardenwood Historic Farm in Fremont, where you can learn about the horse-to-mechanic power agricultural transition, or a planetarium show at the Lawrence Hall of Science in Berkeley.

Golden Gate Transit

Phone:	415-455-2000;
	415-257-4476 (Lost & Found, buses
	415-925-5565 (Lost & Found, ferries
Website:	www.goldengate.org

Golden Gate Transit serves the North Bay passac from San Francisco into Marin and Sonoma counti by land (bus) and water (ferries), and operates usin ten fare zones. The cash-only fares range from $4.2 to $11.25, depending how many zones you cross your commute. Commuters can purchase a ticke book for up to 20% discount (50% youth and senio discounts also exist). Transfers from bus to ferry a free, and you can even ride Muni for free with transfer from a GGT ferry (but not from a GGT bu Bikes are welcome on front-mounted racks, availabl on most buses. Special event and discount purcha locations can be found on the GGT website. Fu places to go on GGT from SF: Muir Woods on a fre "route 66" shuttle departing Marin City on weeken between Memorial Day and Labor Day; Stinso Beach/Bolinas and Point Reyes via the West Mar Stagecoach departing Marin City; back to the Nor Bay by ferry after music and sports events at AT& Park.

SamTrans

Phone:	800-660-4287
Website:	www.samtrans.com

San Mateo County Transit District is mostly for trav within the county, but also serves destination around Palo Alto and San Francisco, including special service for wheelchairs. SamTrans fares rang from $2.00 for local travel to $5 for express commut service. Monthly passes for unlimited travel can b as expensive as $165. But, for traveling locally onl monthly passes cost $64. All SamTrans buses wi front-mounted racks can carry two bikes, and ca take on two more inside the bus (if it is not crowde Special event and discount purchase locations ca be found on the SamTrans website. Fun places go on SamTrans from SF: back to the Peninsula fro Bay2Breakers on a special "participant bus" that hol your stuff during the race; or to Año Nuevo Sta Reserve near Santa Cruz during seal mating season

Greyhound

Phone: 415-495-1569
            415-495-1555 (Baggage)
Website: www.greyhound.com

Never taken Greyhound? It's exactly what you've heard it to be: sporadically on time, habitually uncomfortable, and always an "interesting" ride. Seating is on a first-come, first-served basis, so if you don't hurry to get that window seat next to the little Southern lady with '50s-style hair, you might end up next to another colorful character or two. In comparison, you'll probably appreciate the old lady's perfume over other scents for the duration of your ride. Greyhound offers service between major cities and goes through little towns on the way. Nonetheless, most of us prefer other modes of transportation, and in 2004 Greyhound cut service to over 60 destinations across California, rural and suburban both, due to decreasing revenues.

A standard one-way fare from San Francisco to Los Angeles costs around $50, which is cheaper than flying on most days, but it is also about a ten-hour bumpy ride. The cheap fares also explain the clientele. If you think a cool beer will make the ride more bearable, so does everyone else. Though alcohol is not allowed on the bus, many patrons take care of the matter prior to boarding. A pillow and earplugs can become more precious than gold if you board a bus from San Francisco to Seattle, after paying the $82 fare by credit card online or at the station's ticket office (save more when you reserve seven days in advance): Greyhound will creep up the coast for one day and eight hours straight.

Still excited about traveling America's scenic highways and country by-ways by Greyhound? Head over to the Bay Area hub at the Transbay Terminal or find out about select buses that stop at the Ferry Building, Caltrain depot, and the Airport from the website. And don't forget the TP.

Greyhound also provides a Package Express service for commercial and personal shipping needs from the Transbay Terminal (so while your college textbook collection travels securely by bus to your parents' basement in Minnesota, you can enjoy the comfort of staying home in San Francisco).

Green Tortoise Adventure Travel

www.greentortoise.com

Green Tortoise Adventure Travel offers another option for long-distance bus travel for college kids and adults who don't mind an alternative experience. The company has been transporting folks to exciting destinations like Mardi Gras, Burning Man, and the Mayan trail in Mexico, among others, for many years, and having fun on the way. They also run hostels in San Francisco and Seattle, and are devoted to bringing together "beautiful places, great food, and sociable people" for a gratifying traveling experience.

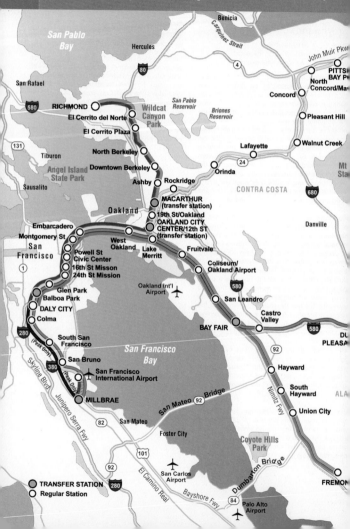

General Information

Mailing Address: PO Box 12688
                  Oakland, CA 94604
Phone: 415-989-2278
Website: www.bart.gov
Hours: Mon–Fri: 4 am–midnight;
                  Sat: 6 am–midnight;
                  Sun: 8 am–midnight.

Overview

The Bay Area Rapid Transit system (BART) evolved in order to ease congestion on the Bay Bridge that followed the post-war influx of people and automobiles to the Bay Area. The proposed solution was an underwater tube devoted solely to high-speed electrical trains. After years of researching, planning, and gaining public approval, the Transbay Tube structure was completed in August 1969. Constructed in 57 sections and sitting as deep as 135 feet beneath the surface on the bay floor, the $180 million structure took six years to design and less than three years to construct. Today, the BART system provides efficient train transit between San Francisco and the East Bay cities and suburbs of Contra Costa and Alameda counties.

Tickets & Fares

BART fares are calculated based on distance traveled. You can determine the cost of your trip by using the BART Fare Calculator or one of the fare charts located at each station. The minimum is $1.75 and the maximum is $11.05. Children under four ride for free. All vending machines accept nickels, dimes, quarters, $1, $5, and $10 bills. If you place more money on the ticket than is needed for the ride, the ticket can be used for several trips. Discount tickets for seniors, children, students and persons with disabilities are sold online, through the mail, and at select retail vendors throughout the San Francisco Bay Area. Check online for vendor locations and discount rates. Participate in the re-chargeable ticket EZ Rider program, and never buy another BART ticket at the machines again! Or better yet, purchase a Clipper card for an all-in-one transit pass that can be used to ride any participating transit system in the Bay Area.

To enter the BART system, insert your ticket into the fare gate. The ticket will be returned to you, and then the fare gate will open. Use the same ticket when you exit the station. The correct fare will automatically be deducted, and a ticket with any remaining value will be returned to you. Money can be added to your card using the Addfare machines.

Lost & Found

The Lost & Found office is located at the 12th Street City Center Station in Oakland near the 14th Street exit. Hours: Mon, Wed, Fri: noon–2 pm and 3 pm–6 pm. Call 510-464-7090 for more information.

Parking

Customers parking at Daly City, Colma, South San Francisco, San Bruno, and Millbrae Stations will be required to pay a daily ($1–$2) or monthly parking fee (between $30 and $115.50 depending on the station). There is a 24-hour limit to all parking, but Daly City and all East Bay BART stations offer additional long-term parking.

Seniors & People with Disabilities

All BART stations have escalators and elevators. All trains have a sign located above some seats suggesting that passengers make those seats available to seniors and persons with disabilities. Specific C2 cars have flip-up seats, which are near each set of doors, to allow room for wheelchairs. All restrooms are designed to be wheelchair accessible.

Bicycles & Pets

Bikes abide by enforced rules on the trains: no bikes in packed commuter rush hour trains, no bikes in the the first car of any train, no bikes on moving escalators; no riding in the station. Otherwise, bikes can be taken on any train—and the newly updated BART schedule in all stations indicates which trains are off-limits. Also no gas-powered vehicles (mopeds, scooters) are permitted. If you chain your bike to a pole, fence, or railing in any BART station, it'll probably be removed while you're gone—use the bike parking cages inside the station.

Pets are only allowed if they are in carrying cases, but service animals (guide dogs, police dogs, magician's assistant, etc.) can always ride, especially if they can talk.

Third Street Light Rail

In 2006, a new, extensive line known as the Third Street Light Rail Project opened running south from the current Caltrain depot station along 3rd Street. It is a modern light rail line, like the Embarcadero extension, and runs all the way to the south border of the city. At its north end, the line passes through older industrial areas that have become more residential in the aftermath of the city's late-90s real estate boom; at its center, it runs through some of San Francisco's most economically depressed areas, and planners hope that it will improve the prospects of those neighborhoods. This extension is served by a new line, the T-Third. After initial mechanical complications and scheduling mishaps which often screamed "debacle" in newspaper headlines, Muni has supposedly brought the T-Third up to a serviceable level. It is still affectionately called the "T-Turd" by patrons, a colloquialism which needs no explanation.

Expansion

The Great Recession hit public transit hard. The glories of new downtown stations were trumped by the realities of a huge budget shortfall. In classic Muni fashion, the result affected service, with requisite fare hikes and service cuts that eliminated some lines all together.

In 2010, planners broke ground on an ambitious new project dubbed the Central Subway. This line will head north and west from the Caltrain depot and quickly pass underground into a new subway tunnel. The line will pass under the current Metro tunnel, with a transfer station at Montgomery, then turn due north with stops at Union Square and Chinatown. Though the line would be relatively short, it would provide service to areas of downtown currently somewhat isolated from the Metro network, as well as a springboard for future expansion. Planners hope that the Central Subway will be completed by 2019. Planners are also eyeing two more underground stations at North Beach and Fisherman's Wharf, although with no firm plans for the foreseeable future.

Many activists have sharply criticized these long-term plans as catering to the needs of visitors at the expense of city residents, asserting that Muni resources would be better spent on a seventh light rail line running along (or under) Geary Boulevard into the densely populated Richmond District. Well, something is better than nothing, folks—just ask the people in places like LA and Dallas.

The Owl

The Muni system operates 24 hours a day with the aid of its late-night Owl service. After the stations close, the Owl takes flight from 1 am to 5 am every thirty minutes on 10 lines throughout the city, replacing Muni streetcar service with a fleet of buses. It sounds like a good idea in theory, 24-hour bus service all over the city. But nightrider beware… waits between these buses are frequently well over what the hypothetical 30 minute schedule predicts. The buses run on lines 5, 14, 22, 24, 38, and 108 (Treasure Island and Yerba Buena Island), and duplicate service along the L and N lines as well. The 90 and 91 Owl lines are night-only; the 91-Owl is actually the longest route in the Muni system at 24.1 miles one-way, combining several other routes into one looping and winding trip through late-night SF's variegated display.

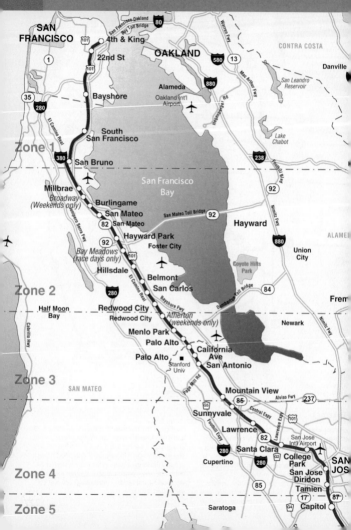

General Information

Mailing Address: 1250 San Carlos Ave
PO Box 3006
San Carlos, CA 94070-1306

Phone: 800-660-4287

Website: www.caltrain.com

Overview

Caltrain provides a fast, reliable alternative to one of the Bay Area's most stressful activities—driving. The system runs local and express trains between 32 stations along the peninsula from San Francisco to Gilroy, with connections to San Francisco and San Jose International Airports. Free shuttles are also available between several stations and surrounding office and residential areas—the Caltrain website provides links to detailed schedules and maps. Caltrain is also the best way to get to Giants games—the San Francisco station at Fourth & King is just one block from AT&T Park. Extra trains run before and after baseball games.

Schedules & Fares

Caltrain offers daily service between San Francisco and San Jose, with extended service to Gilroy during peak weekday commute hours. During these times, Caltrain runs only "Baby Bullet" express and limited-stop trains on a staggered schedule, with timed connections to all other stations. Baby Bullet trains travel from San Francisco to San Jose in one hour, limited-stop trains in just over an hour; specific stops for either line vary according to departure time. Local trains make all stops and operate during non-peak hours and on weekends.

Fares range from $3 to $13 depending on distance traveled, and must be paid before boarding. Conductors check for tickets frequently, so fare-jumping is never advisable. All stations have ticket vending machines, which take cash and major credit cards. Monthly, daily, and 10-ride passes are available.

Airport Connections

Connections are available from Caltrain to both San Francisco and San Jose International Airports. BART operates a shuttle train every 15 minutes between Caltrain's Millbrae station and SFO. Tickets for the shuttle cost $4.05 and must be purchased before boarding.

The SJC Airport Flyer (Rte 10) shuttles passengers between the Santa Clara Caltrain Station and San Jose International Airport. The Airport Flyer is free and operates daily between 5:30 am and midnight. Buses operate every ten minutes on weekdays and every fifteen minutes on weekends.

Parking

All-day parking (24-hour limit) is available at most Caltrain stations for $5.00. Stations south of San Jose Diridon offer free parking. Palo Alto, San Jose Diridon, and other select stations charge higher rates on some evenings. The Millbrae Station lot is reserved for customers with a monthly parking permit until 10 am. After 10 am, anyone can pay to park. Monthly parking permits may be purchased along with monthly train tickets from ticket vending machines, at staffed stations, or through the Ticket-By-Mail program (forms available online).

Lost & Found

The San Francisco and San Jose Diridon stations collect lost articles. To check for an item, call 415-546-4482 for San Francisco or 408-271-4980 for San Jose.

Seniors and People with Disabilities

Discounts on one-way tickets and monthly and 10-day passes are offered to seniors and the disabled. Most, but not all, Caltrain stations are wheelchair-accessible. Check the website for a list of accessible stations. All trains offer priority seating for seniors and people with disabilities, and parking fees at Caltrain stations are waived for vehicles displaying DMV-issued Disabled Person (DP) plates.

Bicycles

Bikes are allowed on all trains at all times, provided there is enough space. The regular trains can accommodate up to 32 bikes, and some are equipped to handle 64 bikes if a second bike car is added; Baby Bullet trains have limited space, and allow only 16 bikes on board per car. The bike car on each train is located at the northern-most end of the train (the end closest to San Francisco) and is clearly marked with a black and yellow bike sticker. Bike lockers are available at 27 Caltrain stations, and cost $33 per six-month rental term, plus a $25 refundable key deposit. Fridays, the 5:48pm train from Mountain View station is the Bike Party Car. Bring snacks and drinks to share! TGIF.

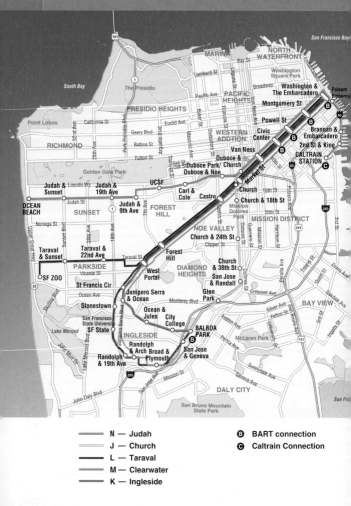

N — Judah
J — Church
L — Taraval
M — Clearwater
K — Ingleside

B BART connection
C Caltrain Connection

General Information

Website: www.sfmta.com
Mailing Address: 949 Presidio Ave, #243
             San Francisco, CA 94115
Phone: 415-554-6999 (recorded hotline)
             415-673-6864 (voice operator)
Lost & Found: 415-923-6168

Overview

Muni mirrors the city it serves. Unfortunately, "boisterous individualism" isn't necessarily a good thing when it comes to public transportation. However, steps have recently been made to get Muni running a little bit better. Digital scrolls at the major stops that tell you when the next train or bus will arrive make the ride more predictable. You can also time your morning walk by checking www.nextbus.com before you leave the house. This feature is still working the kinks out, but in general it is accurate within a few minutes before actual arrival. Would-be Muni riders who don't have this GPS technology at hand should know that it is not uncommon for buses to be 10–20 minutes late in off-peak hours. In peak hours, the system works. The five train lines (J,K,L,M,N) of the Muni Metro are more reliable than the numbered buses. Muni will always get you there eventually, but be wary when making plans that include this sometimes ornery player in the transportation scene. A new line of hybrid electric buses is now servicing Haight-Sunset part of the city: though diesel-gan, they have fewer emissions and consume 19% less fuel.

Hours

Muni operates 24 hours on the following lines: L Taraval, N Judah, 5 Fulton, 14 Mission, 24 Divisadero, 38 Geary, 90 San Bruno Owl (a combination of routes 9 San Bruno and 47 Van Ness), 91 Owl (a combination of routes K Ingleside, 15 Third Street, 30 Stockton, and 28 19th Avenue), and 108 Treasure Island. All night "owl" services operate every 30 minutes, with the exception of route 108. All other Muni lines run 5 am–1 am Monday through Friday. On these lines, service begins at 6 am on Saturdays, and 8 am on Sundays.

Fares & Tickets

For buses, Metro, and historic streetcars, adults pay $2.00, seniors and youth pay 75¢, and children four and under ride free. Exact fare is always required, as drivers cannot provide change. Transfers are available and are generally good for 90 minutes from time of issue. Monthly passes are also available for $64 (ages 18–64) and $22 (everyone else).

There are three cable car lines still running. The two most popular are the Powell-Mason and the Powell-Hyde. They both start at Hallide Plaza (Powel and Market) and go to Mason and Hyde at the waterfront, respectively. The third line runs up California Street from Market to Van Ness. The fare is $5 each way. Transfers are not given or accepted on cable cars, so flash your fast pass for a free ride.

Speed up your trip by boarding at any door of any Metro streetcar when you have proof of payment. Your valid Muni pass, passport, ticket, or transfer is your proof of payment. Keep it for your entire ride on all five Muni Metro lines, including anywhere inside the fare gates and on the platforms at the

Muni Metro subway stations, from the Embarcadero Station to the West Portal Station. Muni Fare Inspectors may ask you for proof of payment and if you don't have it, you risk getting a citation for up to $500.

Safety

Smoking, eating, drinking, littering, or playing sound equipment without earphones is not allowed on Muni vehicles or at Metro stations. Under Muni regulations, passengers are not allowed to put their feet on the seats and children (and adults) are not allowed to stand on the seats.

Between 8:30 pm and 6:30 am, additional passenger stops will be made for people waiting for a transit vehicle, or for passengers on a transit vehicle at their request, at the nearside corner of any street intersection located between the regular stops.

Working dogs, including guide dogs, signal dogs, and service dogs may ride free at any time. These dogs do not have to be muzzled, but must be leashed. People boarding with an animal that is not a working dog must pay the same fare for the animal as they do for themselves. Non-service animals are allowed to ride on Muni vehicles from 9 am to 3 pm and between 7 pm and 5 am on weekdays, and all day on Saturdays, Sundays, and holidays. Only one animal may ride per vehicle. Dogs must be muzzled and on a short leash or in a closed container, and all other animals must be carried in closed containers.

Airport Connections

Muni does not serve the San Francisco International Airport. The airport is located 14 miles south of downtown San Francisco, in San Mateo County. For public transit information to the airport, check out our BART and Caltrain pages.

Seniors and People with Disabilities

Most Muni vehicles are fully accessible to the elderly and handicapped. Cable cars are not wheelchair accessible. All of the underground stations are easy to get to by elevator, escalator (except for Forest Hill, which has no escalators, and West Portal, which has ramps), or stairs. If you're using Muni elevators, you might want to wear a surgical mask—the lifts are not always clean, and the aroma inside the elevators can be less than welcoming.

Bicycle Rules

All newer trolley and diesel Muni buses are equipped with bike racks. The only lines that might not have a bike rack are the 6-Parnassus and 41-Union vehicles, though on other routes, if an older vehicle is used, you might have to wait for the next bus to load up your bike. There are racks on the front of the buses that fit two bikes per bus. If a Muni vehicle does not have a bike rack, then bikes are not allowed. Metro vehicles, historic streetcars, and cable cars do not have bike racks.

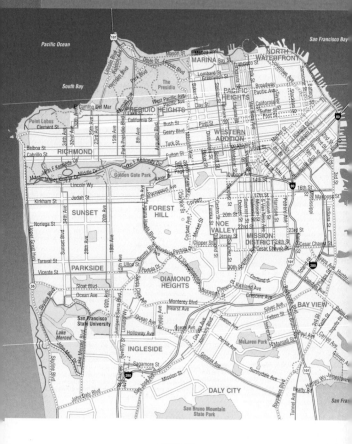

——	bike path
——	wide road
·········	bikes and cars share road
——	bike lane

Biking Information

San Francisco's many bicycle subcultures all have one thing in common: the hills, the hills! Whether you're a messenger who rides for a living, a cyclist who rides for distance, a commuter who rides for exercise, or if you're just taking your vintage cruiser out for a spin on the weekends, we all have to do the climbs. The city's landscape profile bestows grueling physical trials, like fighting gravity on a fixie out of the Presidio. Sharing the road can also be a challenge: weaving through the morning rush hour commute along Market Street is reminiscent of a videogame (except for the multiple lives part). Many San Franciscans do it every day. The non-profit Bike Coalition (SFBC for short: 415-431-IKE, www.sfbike.org) has been working for more than two decades to improve cycling conditions. Among other things, it's achieved legislation for mandatory bike racks in parking garages, as well as new bike lanes all over town, and a citywide marked bike route system that makes it easy to get around even without a map. Its "Bike to Work Day" event strives to promote commuting by bicycle, and makes converts of many drivers each May.

On the last Friday of every month, Critical Mass (www.sfcriticalmass.org) takes over the streets. Downtown dwellers in the know are aware that to get to where they are going, they should cross Market Street before 6:30 pm. This is when hundreds of bikers assert the right of way in traffic (letting buses get through), as the fifteen year-old tradition celebrates alternative, environmentally-friendly modes of transportation (and not mayhem, as some angered drivers assume). Your bike needs help? Thrifty bikers or fans of DIY should check out the Bike Kitchen (www.bikekitchen.org), in their new space at 19th and Florida, repair co-op on Tuesday and Thursday nights and Saturday afternoons: the volunteer mechanics won't fix it for you, but they'll show you how to do it ($5 per visit or $40 per year membership for use of tools and services).

Where to Ride Bikes

Within city limits, scenic rides abound. The best route to the beach is "The Wiggle," which skirts around the grades and provides a hill-free ride to Golden Gate Park. Email bicycle@sfgov.org for a free bike map and know which routes are for you, based on hill grade and bike route signs. Some bike shops in town host monthly or weekly rides, a great opportunity to adopt new trails and meet like-minded folk. Favorites remain the city loop, encompassing the Embarcadero, Ocean Beach, and the Daily City border; Golden Gate Park loop; and the classic ride over the Golden Gate Bridge to destinations in Marin County. A great resource with maps is the SF Mountain Biking website (www.sfmtb.com). Check our Buses pages (p. 234) for bikes onboard rules for mass transit systems—almost every bus in the Bay Area now has bike racks on the front. Just remember that for every short-of-breath climb, there will be a downhill you'll descend with wind in your helmeted hair. Have fun! Rider beware: it is known that people steal bikes off the front of buses at red lights, lock up and keep an eye out.

Beyond city limits, hundreds of miles of bike-friendly roads weave a network through the North and the East Bay, uncovering gorgeous views and sunny skies, a welcome escape from city fog. If you can't ride out there, take public transit. BART-accessible mountain biking is at Joaquin Miller Park near Fruitvale Station or Mount Diablo near Walnut Creek and Pleasant Hill Stations. BART-accessible road biking is in the Berkeley and Oakland hills and around Mount Diablo off the Walnut Creek Station. Check the Bicycle Rules section on our BART pages and be aware of the regulation prohibiting bikes on BART during rush hour. To get to South Bay's regional parks, take Caltrain: it has room for 32 bikes per train, but only 16 on the Baby Bullet Express trains. Blue & Gold, Alameda/Oakland, Golden Gate, and Vallejo/Baylink ferries accommodate bikes onboard.

Bike Shops

- **American Cyclery** • 510 Fredrick St • 415-664-4545
- **American Cyclery Too** •
  858 Stanyan St • 415-876-4545
- **Avenue Cyclery** • 756 Stanyan St • 415-387-3155
- **Big Swingin' Cycles** •
  2260 Van Ness Ave • 415-441-6294
- **Bike & Roll** • 899 Columbus Ave • 415-229-2000
- **The Bike Hut** •
  Pier 40 Embarcadero & Townsend • 415-543-4335
- **The Bike Kitchen** •
  650H Florida Street • 415-255-2453
- **Bike Nook** • 3004 Taraval St • 415-731-3838
- **Blazing Saddles Bike Rental** •
  2715 Haight St • 415-202-8888
- **Box Dog Bikes** • 494 14th Street • 415-431-9627
- **City Cycle** • 3001 Steiner St • 415-346-2242
- **DD Cycles** • 4049 Balboa St • 415-752-7980
- **Fresh Air Bicycles** •
  1943 Divisadero St • 415-563-4824
- **Freewheel Bicycle Shop** •
  914 Valencia St • 415-643-9213
- **Freewheel Bicycle Shop** •
  1920 Hayes St • 415-752-9195
- **Mojo Bicycle Café** • 639 Divisadero Street •
  415-440-2338
- **Noe Valley Cyclery** • 4193 24th St • 415-647-0886
- **Nomad Cyclery** • 2555 Irving St • 415-564-2022
- **Ocean Cyclery** • 1935 Ocean Ave • 415-239-5004
- **Pedal Revolution** • 3085 21st St • 415-641-1264
- **PUBLIC BIKES** • 123 S Park St San Francisco •
  415-896-0123
- **Refried Cycles** • 3804 17th Street • 415 - 621-2911
- **Roaring Mouse Cycles** •
  1352 Irving St • 415-753-6272
- **Road Rage Bicycles** •
  1063 Folsom St • 415-255-1351
- **Sports Basement** • 1415 16th St • 415-437-0100
- **Sports Basement** •
  610 Mason Str (the Presidio) • 415-437-0100
- **Valencia Cyclery** •
  1065 and 1077 Valencia St • 415-550-6600

Overview

Just when you thought it was safe to pencil in that all-important date, check again because San Franciscans can almo_ always find an excuse to celebrate. Taking cues from many different ethnic and cultural sectors of the community, the next 365 days are chock full of events dedicated to voices mingling, laughter erupting, minds overflowing, and bootie_ shaking. The arts often motivate the annual festivals, but revelry for the hell of it never hurt anyone, either. Wherever you_ merrymaking takes you throughout town, good food and drink are sure to be close by. So party on!

January
- **San Francisco Sketchfest** · www.sfsketchfest.com · Improv, stand-up, one-man shows, and musical comedy from a mix of amateu_ and comic celebrities.

February
- **Chinese New Year Celebration & Parade** · www.chineseparade.com · The largest and longest-running Chinese Parade in th_ country. Sponsored by Southwest Airlines.
- **San Francisco Bluegrass & Old Time Festival** · www.sfbluegrass.com · Break out your banjo.

March
- **St. Patrick's Day Parade** · www.uissf.org ·160-years-old and still getting drunk with the best of us.
- **CAAMFest** · www.caamedia.org · Showcasing the Bay Area's vibrant Asian American community through film, food, music, an_ digital media.
- **Noise Pop** · www.noisepop.com · The most promising independent and local musicians take over the city's venues.

April
- **Cherry Blossom Festival** · www.nccbf.org · Celebrating nature and Japanese culture.
- **International Beer Festival** · www.sfbeerfest.com · If the neighborhood bars don't cut it anymore, sample over 300 brews fron_ around the world instead.
- **San Francisco International Film Festival** · www.festival.sffs.org · The stars come out for this one…get your tickets early.

May
- **Cinco de Mayo Celebration** ·www.sfcincodemayo.com · See the Mission in all of its glory. Most definitely not to be missed.
- **ING Bay to Breakers** · www.baytobreakers.com · Run the 12K naked or strap a keg to your back. Either way, you won't be alone_ Better yet, watch the insanity from the sidelines.
- **Carnaval Celebration** · www.carnavalsf.com · Cinco de Mayo with a lot more skin and sin.
- **Mission Creek Music & Arts Festival** · www.mcmf.org · Multi-venue indie music and experimental art explosion.

June
- **Escape from Alcatraz Triathlon** · www.escapefromalcatraztriathlon.com · Grueling 1.5-mile swim, 18 mile bike ride, and 8 mil_ run—all commencing in the frigid waves surrounding the Rock.
- **Haight Ashbury Street Fair** · www.haightashburystreetfair.org · Haight. Hemp. Hippies. Hordes.
- **North Beach Festival** · http://www.sresproductions.com/north_beach_festival.html · Outdoor festivities in the city's famed Littl_ Italy.
- **San Francisco Gay & Lesbian Film Festival** · www.frameline.org/festival · Queer cinema at its most intriguing. Just in time fo_ Pride.
- **San Francisco Design Week** · http://sfdesignweek.org · Follow the designer within for a week of Fashion, Architecture_ Advertising, Urban-planning and more! Organized by AIGA San Francisco.
- **San Francisco Gay Pride Week** · www.sfpride.org · Somewhere over the rainbow is here. Come see for yourself.
- **San Francisco's Union Street Eco-Urban Festival** · http://www.unionstreetfestival.com · Meet up in the Marina for an eco-chi_ weekend.
- **Stern Grove Festival** · www.sterngrove.org · Free live music and performances throughout the summer. Jam among th_ redwoods.

July
- **SF Silent Film Festival** · www.silentfilm.org · Check out the festival at the Castro Theatre, built in 1922 to screen silent films.
- **Fillmore Jazz Festival** · www.fillmorejazzfestival.com · Everybody likes jazz, especially when it's free.
- **San Francisco Jewish Film Festival** · www.sfjff.org · Thirty years and running. You'd really have to be meshuga to miss it.
- **Up Your Alley Fair** · www.folsomstreetfair.com/alley · Warning: the alley party makes the Folsom Street Fair seem PG.

August
- **Nihonmachi Street Fair** · www.nihonmachistreetfair.com · Celebration of the Asian and Pacific American community in Japantown_
- **Outside Lands Festival** · www.sfoutsidelands.com · Massive music and arts festival with headliners reminiscent of Lollapalooza'_ glory years.
- **San Francisco Zine Fest** · www.sfzinefest.com · Two-day conference for do-it-yourself publishers.

September
- **Comedy Day** · www.comedyday.com · Five hours, 30 comedians, all free, some funny. Have a hoot in Golden Gate Park.
- **San Francisco Fringe Festival** · www.sffringe.org · Release your inner freak (or at least see what some of the best freaky artist_ are up to). If you've got time on your hands, they're always looking for volunteers.
- **Opera at the Ballpark** · www.sfopera.com/simulcast · Arias aplenty, and a blanket for two.
- **Folsom Street Fair** · www.folsomstreetfair.com · Not your mother's street fair—this is all whips, chains, and leather, baby.

October
- **Castro Street Fair** · www.castrostreetfair.org · Shop in the sun under the Big Rainbow flag.
- **Hardly Strictly Bluegrass Festival** · http://www.strictlybluegrass.com · From old timey legends to knee-slappin' newcomers, this_ free festival in Golden Gate Park will get you back to your roots.
- **Marin Italian Film Festival** · www.italianfilm.com · A bit of recent Italian cinema across the Golden Gate every Saturday nigh_ through October (and a little bit of November, too).
- **San Francisco Open Studios** · www.artspan.org · A scavenger hunt for the best local artists. Bring your street map (or your NFT, silly)_
- **Treasure Island Music Festival** · www.treasureislandfestival.com · Indie favorites play music on that island in the middle of the Bay.
- **Fleet Week** · www.military.com/fleetweek · Spectacular weekend event celebrating the armed forces, featuring the Navy's famous_ Blue Angels.

October—*continued*

Litquake · www.litquake.org · Get a dose of SF's literary scene. Advisors include Dave Eggers and Lawrence Ferlinghetti.
San Francisco LovEvolution · www.sflovevolution.org · The spirit of Berlin's Love Parade unleashed at the Civic Center and streets of downtown.

November

Dia de los Muertos (Day of the Dead) · www.sfmission.com/dod · Come purge all your Catholic demons.

Monthly

Critical Mass · www.sfcriticalmass.org · Mobs of cyclists show support for their eco-friendly mode of transportation the last Friday of each month.

Overview

The roughly 47 square miles that comprise the city of San Francisco contain a collection of diverse and lively neighborhoods—not to mention people. Now that you're here, there are some things you should know. Although many of the city's nicknames annoy residents, you'll still hear the following used from time to time: Fog City, Frisco (mostly from out-of-towners), Baghdad By the Bay, San Fran Disco, Sam Clam's Disco, the City by the Bay, Ess Eff, Golden Gate City, and often simply the City. The city counts 43 hills with names—and a whole lot more without. The official flower is the dahlia, the city's namesake is St. Francis of Assisi, the city colors are black and gold, and the tallest building is the 853-foot Transamerica Pyramid. We could go on and on with the mindless trivia, but we know you're busy. We'll just stick to the stuff every San Franciscan should have at their fingertips. With so much juicy history and cultural intrigue, it's hard to reduce San Francisco to facts and figures, but what the hell—we're going to try.

Population

San Francisco city population:	808,977	
Area (square miles):	46.69	
(source: U.S. Census Bureau, State and County QuickFacts)		
Gender		
Male:	362,869	50.5%
Female:	356,208	49.5%
Age		
Median:	39.4 years	
Under 18:	108,695	14.7%
Ages 18–64:	610,407	84.9%
Age 65 and Over:	105,176	14.6%
Race		
One race:	699,514	97.3%
Caucasian:	382,220	53.2%
Asian:	238,133	33.1%
African-American:	46,779	6.50%
American Indian/Alaskan Native:	2,098	0.30%
Native Hawaiian/Pacific Islander:	2,726	0.40%
Hispanic or Latino:	98,891	13.8%
Two or more races:	19,563	2.7%
Some other race:	27,558	3.8%

*All numbers from U.S. Census Bureau, 2005 American Community Survey, unless otherwise noted

Useful Phone Numbers

Emergencies	911
Traffic Information	511
PG&E	800-743-5000
Comcast Cable	800-266-2278
AT&T	800-228-2020
City Hall	415-554-4933
Police Department (Non-Emergencies)	415-553-0123
Fire Department	415-558-3200
Department of Elections	415-554-4375
Department of Motor Vehicles	800-777-0133
Department of Parking & Traffic	415-554-9811
Department of Public Works	415-554-6920
SF Rent Board	415-252-4600

Essential San Francisco Movies

Greed (1925)
The Thin Man (1934)
San Francisco (1936)
The Maltese Falcon (1941)
Dark Passage (1947)
The House on Telegraph Hill (1951)
Vertigo (1958)
Flower Drum Song (1961)
Point Blank (1967)
The Graduate (1967)
Bullitt (1968)
Dirty Harry (1971)
Harold and Maude (1971)
Play Misty for Me (1971)
Play it Again Sam (1972)
The Towering Inferno (1974)
The Conversation (1974)
High Anxiety (1977)
Invasion of the Body Snatchers (1978)
Foul Play (1978)
Time After Time (1979)
Chan Is Missing (1982)
Presidio (1988)
So I Married an Axe Murderer (1993)
Mrs. Doubtfire (1993)
The Joy Luck Club (1993)
The Rock (1996)
Romeo Must Die (2000)
Haiku Tunnel (2001)
The Wedding Planner (2001)
Pursuit of Happyness (2006)
Zodiac (2007)
Medicine for Melancholy (2008)
Milk (2008)
Star Trek (2009)
The Five-Year Engagement (2012)

Essential San Francisco Songs

"I Left My Heart in San Francisco" — Tony Bennett
"San Francisco" — Judy Garland
"Dock of the Bay" — Otis Redding
"Frisco Blues" — John Lee Hooker
"San Francisco Days" — Chris Isaak
"Lights" — Journey
"San Francisco" — Scott McKenzie
"We Built This City" — Starship
"San Francisco (You've Got Me)" — Village People
"Little Boxes (Ticky Tacky)" — Pete Seeger
"The Great Night" — Chris Adrian

Essential San Francisco Books

The Maltese Falcon, by Dashiell Hammet. Sam Spade, in perhaps the most famous noir detective story.

Tales of the City, by Armistead Maupin. Seven-volume series about San Francisco in the 1970s and beyond.

The Works of Philip K. Dick, by Philip K. Dick. The man who gave us Blade Runner set nearly all his novels and stories in the Bay Area.

Flower Drum Song, by C.Y. Lee. A young Chinese immigrant strives to make it in San Francisco's Chinatown.

McTeague, by Frank Norris. An unnerving, realistic portrayal of a crazed dentist in 19th-century San Francisco.

Our Lady of Darkness, by Fritz Leiber. Wonderfully creepy supernatural thriller that pays loving homage to the city.

Bombardiers, by Po Bronson. Perhaps "the" novel of the dot-com boom.

Lonesome Traveler, by Jack Kerouac. The famous Beat wanders around San Francisco, and elsewhere.

The Mayor of Castro Street, by Randy Shilts. Novelisti report about the assassinations of Mayor Georg Moscone and Supervisor Harvey Milk.

Golden Gate, by Vikram Seth. A novel in vers about the lives and loves of '80s-era San Francisc singles.

The Joy Luck Club, by Amy Tan. Four immigrar families mingle generations of memories.

A Rush of Dreamers, by John Cech. A novel base on the life of real-life eccentric Joshua "Empero Norton in 19th-century San Francisco.

A Heartbreaking Work of Staggering Genius, by Dav Eggers. A cult hit based on the author's life in Sa Francisco during the 1990s.

Daughter of Fortune, by Isabel Allende. Largely set i the Gold Rush era, this tale of entwined lives paint a portrait of San Francisco in its infancy.

China Boy, by Gus Lee. Semi-autobiographica account of growing up Chinese American in th 1950s.

The Confessions of Max Tivoli, by Andrew Sean Gree Musings of love, time, and humanity at the turn c the 20th century.

San Francisco Timeline

A timeline of significant events in San Francisco's history (by no means complete).

Circa 1000 BC: Ohlone people construct villages in marshlands and along creeks, where they live until Spanish explorers arrive.

1542: Juan Rodriguez Cabrillo discovers the Farallones.

1575: Sebastian Rodriguez Cermeno claims Drake's Bay for Spain and names it Puerto de San Francisco.

1579: Sir Francis Drake claims Drake's Bay for England and names it Nova Albion.

1769: The Golden Gate is discovered by Jose Francisco Ortega and Don Gaspar de Portola.

1776: The Presidio and Mission Dolores are founded.

1835: Yerba Buena is founded.

1846: Yerba Buena is renamed San Francisco by Washington A. Bartlett, Chief Magistrate.

1848: Gold is discovered!

1850: San Francisco County is officially created.

1850: The City of San Francisco is incorporated.

1850: Transbay ferry service begins.

1852: Domingo Ghirardelli opens his chocolate company.

1853: California Academy of Sciences is founded.

1856: The Consolidation Act of 1856 combines the City and County of San Francisco.

1858: Sutro & Co. is founded by Gustav, Charles, and Emil Sutro. It is the oldest investment banking firm in San Francisco.

1859: The highly eccentric Joshua A. Norton declares himself Emperor of the United States

1861: Fort Point is completed.

1864: Mark Twain visits San Francisco and writes for *San Francisco Daily Morning Call*.

1865: San Francisco is hit with a great earthquake on October 8th.

1868: San Francisco is damaged by another severe earthquake on October 22nd at 7:53 am.

1868: Charles and M.H. De Young launch *The Daily Morning Chronicle*.

1868: The San Francisco SPCA is founded.

1869: The first westbound train reaches San Francisco on September 6th.

1870: California Legislature creates Golden Gate Park.

1873: Jacob Davis and Levi Strauss patent and begin selling jeans.

1873: Andrew S. Hallidie's cable car system begins public service.

San Francisco Timeline—*continued*

875: Pacific Stock Exchange opens.

880: The highly eccentric Joshua A. Norton drops dead on California Street. Between 10,000 and 30,000 people reportedly attended his funeral.

883: The infamous Black Bart (Charles Boles) is arrested and sentenced to 6 years at San Quentin for robbing Wells Fargo stagecoaches.

892: The Sierra Club is founded and John Muir is elected president.

892: US Quarantine Station opened on Angel Island.

898: The Ferry Building is built.

906: The Great Earthquake strikes on April 18 at 5:12 am, magnitude 8.25, and lasts 49 seconds. The Great Fire that follows destroys 28,000 buildings, killing 3,000, and leaving 225,000 homeless.

910: Angel Island opens.

915: Bernard Maybeck's Palace of Fine Arts is built to host the Panama Pacific International Exposition.

915: James Rolph dedicates the new City Hall.

923: Lombard, "the crookedest street in the world," is built.

923: Golden Gate Park and the Steinhart Aquarium open to the public.

929: The Great Highway and Ocean Beach Esplanade are completed.

933: Coit Tower on Telegraph Hill is completed.

933: The San Francisco Ballet is founded.

935: The San Francisco Museum of Art opens.

936: The Bay Bridge officially opens to the public on November 12th.

937: The Golden Gate Bridge officially opens to pedestrian traffic on May 27, and to vehicular traffic the next day.

945: World War II ends.

954: San Francisco International Airport opens.

955: Allen Ginsberg reads "Howl" at the Six Gallery.

960: Candlestick Park opens.

966: Beatles play last live concert at Candlestick Park.

967: The Summer of Love draws thousands to Haight-Ashbury.

968: Zodiac Killer kills first victim in the Bay Area.

968: Alcatraz occupied by Native Americans.

970: Jim Jones starts People's Temple in San Francisco.

1972: The Transamerica Pyramid officially opens.

1972: BART carries first passengers.

1976: George Moscone elected mayor.

1977: Harvey Milk is elected supervisor and becomes the country's first openly-gay elected official.

1978: Supervisor Dan White assassinates Mayor George Moscone and Supervisor Harvey Milk. Dianne Feinstein becomes mayor.

1979: White Night Riots erupt after Dan White's sentencing.

1988: Art Agnos elected mayor.

1989: A severe earthquake (the Loma Prieta, also known as the World Series Quake) hits the San Andreas fault on October 17 at 5:04 pm, causing extensive damage in and around San Francisco and the collapse of part of the Bay Bridge.

1992: Frank Jordan elected mayor.

1995: The Grateful Dead's Jerry Garcia dies.

1996: Willie Brown elected mayor.

2000: SBC Park (originally Pacific Bell Park) opens.

2001: The dot com investment bubble bursts, severely damaging San Francisco's economy and thousands lose their jobs.

2004: Gavin Newsom elected mayor.

2004: San Francisco becomes the first city to issue same-sex marriage licenses.

2005: SBC Park changes its name, once again, to AT&T Park.

2008: Controversial Proposition 8 passes, eliminating same-sex couples' right to marry.

2010: Judge overturns Proposition 8.

2010: the San Francisco Giants win the World Series

2011: City's Happy Meal ban goes into effect; McDonald's skirts law by charging ten cents for toys and donating money to local Ronald McDonald House.

2012: After a lackluster 2011 season, the Giants return to glory and beat the Detroit Tigers in four straight to secure the franchise's seventh World Series title.

2014: World Series MVP Madison Bumgarner leads Giants to third championship in five years.

2015: Golden State Warriors defeat LeBron James and the Cavaliers and win first NBA championship in 40 years.

Overview

According to San Francisco's Animal Care and Control Department, there were an estimated 120,000 dogs in the city in 2007. In the city's upscale Marina neighborhood, for instance, where pooches outnumber strollers, dogs have free reign of its streets and waterfront parks. And it makes sense too: living in San Francisco is pricey, and raising a pooch is much easier than a kid—and perhaps more fashionable. With their ability to accompany you on your morning coffee run, or wait patiently for you at home while you're hittin' the bar, dogs are where it's at. Boasting trendy dog hotels, established pet cemeteries and services, and an eco-friendly plan to convert pet waste into fuel, San Francisco is simply an urban playground for canines. The San Francisco Recreation and Park Department is in the midst of a 10-year, $400 million capital plan for the development and renovation of the city's parks. And thanks to the growing strength and influence of pet-owning communities and programs recommended by the Dog Advisory Committee in 2002, considerations are underway to include more off-leash dog facilities. More informally, dogs are welcome at many restaurants and cafés with outdoor seating areas, in many stores, and can even be seen at a bar (with its drinking bowl, of course). Decent, often hip pet stores are easily found in most neighborhoods. If you're looking to adopt a new poochie, contact a shelter or one of the many local dog rescue organizations: www.hopalong. org, www.badrap.org, www.homeatlastrescue.org, www. milofoundation.org.

For questions regarding off-leash dog policy, contact the San Francisco Recreation and Park Department at 415-831-2700 or www.sfrecpark.org/parks-open-spaces/dog-play-areas-program. Other good local dog websites include www.sfdog.org, and www.sfspca.org.

Alamo Square Park

Along Scott Street between Hayes and Fulton Streets. The western half of the park is an open playground for dogs to romp off-leash. Come see the Victorian houses known as the "Painted Ladies" with your little tramp.

Alta Plaza Park

Bordered by Jackson, Clay, Steiner, and Scott Streets. This on-leash dog park with some designated off-leash areas hosts the Original Pug Sunday in San Francisco on the first Sunday of every month at the top of the park's hill. At these gatherings, which take place between 1 pm and 4 pm, there can be up to 50 pugs in the park at one time. When it comes to pugs, it seems these pups prefer the Alta Plaza Park.

Bernal Heights

At the top of the hill bounded by Bernal Heights Boulevard, there's a doggie utopia of off-leash frolicking. The park is such a haven for canines that humans without puppy pals are a rare breed indeed.

Buena Vista Park

Located at Buena Vista Avenue and Central Avenue, Buena Vista is Spanish for "great view." This park truly does offer a spectacular view of the city for the many dog walkers who swarm the park, with some off-leash areas.

Corona Heights

Field area next to Randall Museum at Roosevelt Way and Museum Way. The Randall Museum Dog Run is taken over by smaller, off-leash dogs for the Chihuahua Cha Cha held on the first Sunday of every month at noon. It's the only time that Corona and Chihuahuas should ever be mixed.

Dolores Park

The off-leash doggie area is located south of the tennis courts between Church and Dolores Streets. This beautifully renovated park is actually built on top of a cemetery, but don't worry about your dog digging up any bones. Nobody's been buried there since 1894.

Glen Canyon

Hiking with your dog has never been easier. Many residents are amazed to discover that they can roam freely with their canine companions along scenic trails, past jutting rock outcroppings and little streams—all without leaving the city. Dogs are allowed off-leash. The park's main entrance is at Bosworth Street and O'Shaughnessy Boulevard in the Glen Park neighborhood, but you can also pick up trails at the back of Christopher Playground Park, which is behind the Diamond Heights shopping center (the one with the Safeway). The trails down to the canyon's floor are steep and narrow at times, but offer a gorgeous view that's well worth the knee strain.

Golden Gate National Recreation Area

Starting at the coastline south of San Francisco and stretching for 76,500 acres to the area north of the Golden Gate Bridge, this dog-friendly recreation area includes many San Francisco parks and beaches, some with off-leash areas. In June 2005, a San Francisco judge affirmed off-leash rights in certain sections of the GGNRA. Visit www.nps.gov/goga/parkmgmt/pets.htm for complete, updated information about where your pooch can roam free.

Golden Gate Park Dog Runs

Golden Gate Park has four off-leash areas: a southeast section bounded by Lincoln Way, King Drive, and 2nd and 7th Avenues; a northeast section at Stanyan and Grove Streets; a south-central area bounded by Kind Drive, Middle Drive, and 34th and 38th Avenues; and a fenced training area in the north-central area near 38th Avenue and Fulton Street.

Lafayette Park

The off-leash dog section is located on the corner of Gough and Sacramento. This area is unfenced and bordered by busy streets, so be careful with that long-distance tennis ball fetch.

Lake Merced

This is like San Francisco's largest body of water and an oasis for large dogs to cool down. The official off-leash area is at the North End, at Lake Merced and Middlefield Drive. However, not all of the area is open to doggies. The area to the south by the cement bridge is where your furry friend can take a dip.

McLaren Park

This is a nicely wooded park popular with children and picnickers, so you may not want to let your dog wander off. The official off-leash area is at the top of the hill bounded by Shelly Drive and Mansell Avenue.

Mountain Lake Park

8th Avenue and Lake Street. A strong, local dog community utilizes this off-leash park, which features a canine water fountain at 9th Avenue.

Panhandle

Though those driving past the panhandle see it as the beginning of Golden Gate Park, it is a haven for those who live in the nearby neighborhoods. The park, which is one block wide between Fell and Oak Streets and almost eight blocks long (between Baker and Stanyan), is a great place to exercise yourself or your dog. While it's not a sanctioned off-leash area, you can find dogs roaming free of their leashes at any given time. If your dog likes to chase bicycles or runners, stay clear of the two paths on either side of the park.

Pine Lake Park

Adjacent to Stern Grove, this park has a small lake at the west end of the park. Swimming is not allowed, but there's always the muddy shore for wallowing. This is supposed to be an on-leash park, but you'll notice quite a few puppies roaming free.

St Mary's Park

Located at Murray Street and Justin Drive. This park has a recreation center with a fenced-in dog park on the lower tier below the playground, including canine water fountains.

Walter Haas Playground

A fenced-in, double-gated dog park with doggie drinking fountains sits at the top of this Diamond Heights park and playground area. Located at the intersection of Diamond Heights Boulevard and Gold Mine Drive, the park is moderate in size and, consequently, a popular choice for smaller dogs, though larger dogs are also frequent visitors. This is a good park to choose if you need an after-dark option. It's clean, safe, and outfitted with a red, sandy base instead of grass or dirt.

Beaches

San Francisco has a handful of dog-friendly beaches. However, owners should be aware that most of the time dogs are required to remain on their leashes, unless signs specify otherwise.

Baker Beach, which is located in the Golden Gate National Recreation Area between Lincoln Boulevard and Bowley Street, near the south end of the Golden Gate Bridge. Baker Beach is dog-friendly and is one of the areas recently designated an off-leash beach in a June 2005 court decision.

Crissy Field, another area recently confirmed as an off-leash frolicking ground, is one of the most picturesque beaches in the city. Located in the Presidio at 603 Mason Street at Halleck Street, Crissy Field has panoramic views of the Golden Gate Bridge, Alcatraz, and Marin County. Water dogs can paddle far in the usually calm waters, while non-swimmers can trot down the coastline from the East Beach to Fort Point leash-free. The grass field is also leash-free as long as dogs are under voice control.

Fort Funston/Burton Beach is very popular with dogs and their owners. This beach features trails that run through the dunes, and a water faucet/trough for thirsty K-9s at the Skyline Boulevard and John Muir Drive parking lot. Though you'll probably see many dogs running off-leash, beware that you will be ticketed if caught by the authorities.

Ocean Beach is 4 miles long and runs parallel to the Great Highway. The beach has a mix of off-leash and leash-required areas. Dogs must be on-leash on Ocean Beach between Sloat Boulevard and Fulton Street. Dogs may be off-leash north of Fulton to the Cliff House and south of Sloat for several miles.

Other Dog Play Areas to Explore

Douglass Park · 26th St & Douglass St
Duboce Park · Steiner St & Duboce Ave
Esprit Park · 22nd St. and Tennessee St.
Eureka Valley Park ·19th St & Collingwood St, east of the baseball diamond
McKinley Square Park · San Bruno Ave & 20th St, on the western slope
Potrero Hill Mini-Park · 22nd St & Arkansas St
Upper Noe Park · Day St & Sanchez St

Overview

If there was an unofficial gay capital of the world, San Francisco rivals all major cities for such a title. In 2004, Mayor Gavin Newsom allowed more than 4,000 gay and lesbian couples to legally wed, transforming the steps of City Hall into an altar and turning the Civic Center into a place of celebration. The State Supreme Court eventually nullified the marriage licenses, but the act of the mayor reminded the rest of the world that the City by the Bay has remained a leader in the fight for equal rights. And although the gay rights movement suffered a major defeat as California voters passed Prop 8—approving a ban on same-sex marriages—the community continues to fight for equality. Recent films such as Milk, the biopic about Harvey Milk, the openly gay politician and city's champion of gay rights in the 1970s, reflect the pride and spirit of San Francisco's LGBT community, which continues to grow strong.

Sunny weekends on Castro Street are alive with buff, tanned men in tank tops, while the Mission is home to the girls. While the Castro is man-ville and the Mission might be girl-ville, LGBT families gravitate towards Noe Valley and Bernal Heights in San Francisco, and the Rockridge, Piedmont Ave, and Laurel districts of Oakland. Make no mistake, the LGBT community isn't somewhere, they are everywhere, as are bi-sexual, bi-curious, transsexual, and outside-the-box gender creative folks. The only thing you can be sure of is that every bar or club is "mixed." If you can think of it, you can find it in San Francisco. Don't be afraid to ask.

Annual Events

- **San Francisco Pride**, end of June—www.sfpride.org, 415-864-0831
- **Lesbian and Gay Film Festival**, usually held in June each year—www.frameline.org/festival/, 415-703-8650
- **National Queer Arts Festival**, June— www.queerculturalcenter.org
- **Up Your Alley Fair**, end of July— www.folsomstreetfair.com/alley, 415-777-3247
- **Drag King Contest**, usually August— www.sfdragkingcontest.com
- **Castro Street Fair**, usually in October— www.castrostreetfair.org, 415-841-1824
- **Folsom Street Fair**, usually in September— www.folsomstreetfair.com, 415-777-3247

Bookstores

- **Books Inc**, 2275 Market Street, 415-864-6777— www.booksinc.net. This general bookstore is located in the Castro and has a decent selection of gay and lesbian books.
- **Modern Times**, 888 Valencia Street, 415-282-9246—www.mtbs.com. In the Book Buzz section of their website, Seeley's Starter List for Transgender and Queer Issues sits comfortably amongst Monthly Staff Picks, Children's Books, and Ideal Books for a Lazy Sunday. Located in the Mission.
- **City Lights Bookstore**, 261 Columbus Avenue at Broadway, 415-362-8193—www.citylights.com. In North Beach, Lawrence Ferlinghetti's City Lights Bookstore has an excellent selection of fiction, including many foreign titles. Queer beats include Ginsberg, Kerouac, Burroughs, Orlovsky, and bi-fave Diane DiPrima.

Websites

- **Craigslist**—www.craigslist.org General community site with heavily trafficked "men seeking men" and "women seeking women" sections, as well as "casual encounters" for those who need it now and "missed connections" if you are intent on chasing fate
- **Bay Area Bisexual Network**— www.bayareabisexualnetwork.org An online resource and network for the multicultural bisexual community.
- **Dykealicious**—www.dykealicious.com Blog, calendar, and listings for upcoming lesbian-related events.
- **TransBay**—www.transbay.org Everyone means everyone. Bay Area resource for those who transcend the gender assigned at birth.
- **Out in San Francisco**—www.outinsanfrancisco.com Read your homoscope (ugh, sorry) and plan accordingly.
- **SFgate**—www.sfgate.com/eguide/gay The gay and lesbian section of the sfgate.com website with local stories and extensive reviews of nightlife venues.
- **SF Gay**—www.sfgay.org Powered by the popular website SF Station, this online resource lists events and news for the entire LGBT community.
- **SF Queer**—www.sfqueer.com Queer event listings, Tweets, and a sampling of LGBT-related links.

Publications

- **The Bay Area Reporter**—www.ebar.com Weekly newspaper for San Francisco's lesbian, gay, bisexual, transgender, queer, and questioning community. Look for it on Thursdays.
- **The Bay Times**—www.sfbaytimes.com Free weekly newspaper with extensive arts and entertainment listings.
- **The Bay Guardian**—www.sfbg.com SF's major (and free) alternative weekly with all of the news, entertainment, and events the Gay, er, Bay Area has to offer.
- **Frontiers Magazine**—www.frontierspublishing.com Biweekly publication for the LGBT community. Based in Southern California, but relevant for all California readers.
- **Girlfriends Magazine**—www.girlfriendsmag.com Lesbian culture, politics, and entertainment.
- **Odyssey Magazine**—www.odysseymagazine.net Online source for gay nightlife, news, entertainment, and celebrity gossip.
- **San Francisco Spectrum**—www.sfspectrum.org Offers community news and entertainment listings, as well as columns for specific LGBT communities (bears, leather, etc.).
- **Passport Magazine**—www.passportmagazine.com Gay and lesbian travel magazine.
- **Gaypocket San Francisco**—www.gaypocketusa.com A small, free quarterly available at gay-frequented businesses.

Health Centers and Support Organizations

- **Asian & Pacific Islander Wellness Center,** 730 Polk St, 4th Fl, San Francisco, CA 94109, 415-292-3400—www.apiwellness.org. HIV-related and general health services for the Asian LGBT community.
- **California AIDS Hotline**—800-367-AIDS—www.aidshotline.org
- **CUAV (Community United Against Violence)**, 170A Capp St, San Francisco, CA 94110 , 415-777-5500, 24-hour support line: 415-333-HELP—www.cuav.org. CUAV offers counseling and legal assistance for victims of hate crimes and domestic violence, as well as education programs and programs for queer youth.
- **Gay and Lesbian Medical Association**, 459 Fulton St, Ste 107, San Francisco, CA 94102, 415-255-4547—www.glma.org. A 501(c)3 non-profit organization working to end homophobia in health care. If you're looking for a gay, lesbian, bisexual, transgender, or LGBT-friendly chiropractor, dentist, therapist, or doctor, they have an online referral service and will point you in the right direction.
- **Gay Health Care in San Francisco**, 45 Castro Street, Ste 402, San Francisco, CA 94114, 877-693-6633—www.ownemed.com. Bill Owen, MD's practice places emphasis on the primary health care of adults. As a gay doctor, Bill has a special focus on primary care of gay men and lesbians, including patients with HIV/AIDS.
- **San Francisco LGBT Community Center**, 1800 Market St, San Francisco, CA 94102, 415-865-5555—www.sfcenter.org. The 35,000-square-foot facility is referred to simply as the Center, and supports the needs of all LGBT individuals. Health, wellness, arts, culture, social activities, job skill development, events, and resources. Very community-oriented, staffed with more than 100 volunteers.
- **LYRIC (Lavender Youth Recreation and Information Center)**, 127 Collingwood St, San Francisco, CA 94114, 415-703-6150—www.lyric.org. Youth Talkline: 800-246-PRIDE. Peer-based education, advocacy, recreation, information, and leadership for queer youth, 23 and under.
- **Magnet**, 4122 18th St., CA, 94114—http://www.magnetsf.org —A health clinic, art gallery and lounge, all supporting the physical, mental and social wellness of gay men.
- **Rainbow Flag Health Services**, 510-521-7737—www.gayspermbank.com. A bank that provides known-donor insemination, Rainbow Flag Health Services actively recruits gay and bisexual sperm donors.
- **Pacific Reproductive Services**, 444 De Haro St, #222, San Francisco, CA 94107, 415-487-2288—www.pacrepro.com —Fertility center for women planning alternative families.
- **San Francisco AIDS Foundation**, 995 Market St, #200, San Francisco, CA 94103, 415-487-3000—www.sfaf.org—A leader in the fight against AIDS, the foundation seeks to educate and provide services for people living with the disease. Co-produces the AIDS Ride from SF to LA every June.
- **New Leaf**, 103 Hayes St, San Francisco, CA 94102, 415-626-7000—www.newleafservices.org. Providing mental health and substance abuse counseling, as well as social support for LGBT individuals and families.
- **National Center for Lesbian Rights**, 870 Market St, Suite 370, San Francisco, CA 94102, 415-392-6257—www.nclrights.org. NCLR is a non-profit law firm headquartered in San Francisco. Offers free legal advice.
- **Team San Francisco**, www.teamsf.org. Find a recreational league or participate in an upcoming athletic event.

Places of Interest

- **Castro Theatre** • 429 Castro St, 415-621-6120 • Built in 1922, this is a historic movie palace that shows popular, special interest flicks and is home to the gay and lesbian film festival. www.thecastrotheatre.com
- **Dolores Park** • Dolores St (between 18th and 20th) • With one of the city's warmest microclimates, the park is also known as Dolores Beach. Gaze at the boys on Speedo row or take a cute dog to spark conversation. The Dyke March during Pride starts here, and there are often speakers and activities.
- **Good Vibrations** • 603 Valencia St, 415-522-5460 • Co-operatively owned sex toy institution. www.goodvibes.com
- **North Baker Beach** • Sunbathe naked or simply avoid shrinkage from the freezing winds off of the Bay.
- **Q Comedy** • 1519 Mission St, 415-541-5610 • 2nd Mondays at the LGBT center showcase queer comedy. And yes, gay stand-up is funnier than straight humor. www.qcomedy.com
- **QCC** (The Center for Lesbian, Gay, Bi, Transgender Art and Culture) • Queer comedy event listings in San Francisco.
- **Rainbow Grocery** • 1745 Folsom St, 415-863-0620 • While not all lesbians are granola-crunching, soy-slurping vegans who shop at co-ops, many are. The best place in the city for natural, organic, and healthy food at reasonable prices. www.rainbowgrocery.com
- **White Horse Inn** • 6551 Telegraph Ave, 510-652-3820 • This spot is the second oldest gay bar in the nation. It may be in the East Bay, but its history is reason enough to make the trek across the bridge. www.whitehorsebar.com
- **The Women's Building** • 3543 18th St, 415-431-1180 • One stop shop for women gay and straight to tap into the best resources San Francisco has to offer. This place is practically a landmark. You'll be smarter leaving than when you arrived. www.womensbuilding.org

Venues

Lesbian	Address	Phone
El Rio (4th Saturday)	3158 Mission St	415-282-3325
Endup (Saturday)	401 6th St	415-357-0827
Harveys (2nd and 4th Tuesday)	500 Castro St	415-431-4278
Lexington Club	3464 19th St	415-863-2052
Medjool	2522 Mission St	415-550-9055
Wild Side West	424 Cortland Ave	415-647-3099

Gay	Address	Phone
440 Castro	440 Castro St	415-621-8732
1015 Folsom	1015 Folsom St	415-431-1200
Asia SF	201 Ninth St	415-255-2742
Aunt Charlie's Lounge	133 Turk St	415-441-2922
Cinch Saloon	1723 Polk St	415-776-4162
Divas	1081 Post St	415-928-6006
Edge	4149 18th St	415-863-4027
Endup (Asian LGBT, Saturday)	401 6th St	415-357-0827
Esta Noche	3079 16th St	415-861-5757
Harvey's (Gay comedy, Tuesday)	500 Castro St	415-431-4278
Hole in the Wall Saloon	1360 Folsom St	415-431-4695
Pink	2925 16th St	415-431-8889
Lone Star Saloon	1354 Harrison St	415-863-9999
The Lookout	3600 16th St	415-703-9750
Marlena's	488 Hayes St	415-864-6672
Martuni's	4 Valencia St	415-241-0205
Midnight Sun	4067 18th St	415-861-4186
Moby Dick	4049 18th St	415-861-1199
Mix	4086 18th St	415-431-8616
N Touch Bar	1548 Polk St	415-441-8413
Powerhouse	1347 Folsom St	415-552-8689
QBAR	456 Castro Street	415-864-2877
SF Badlands	4121 18th St	415-626-9320
Twin Peaks Tavern	401 Castro St	415-864-9470

Mixed	Address	Phone
The Café	2367 Market St	415-861-3846
Café Du Nord	2170 Market St	415-861-5016
Club Eight	1151 Folsom St	415-431-1151
The Deco Lounge	510 Larkin St	415-346-2025
Eagle Tavern	398 12th St	415-626-0880
El Rio	3158 Mission St	415-282-3325
Lucky 13	2140 Market St	415-487-1313
Lush Lounge	1092 Post St	415-771-2022
The Mint	1942 Market St	415-626-4726
Pilsner Inn	225 Church St	415-621-7058
Phone Booth	1398 S Van Ness Ave	415-648-4683
Stray Bar	309 Cortland Ave	415-821-9263
The Stud Bar	399 9th St	415-252-7883
Trax	1437 Haight St	415-864-4213
Truck	1900 Folsom St	415-252-0306

Overview

Raising your kids in San Francisco gives them—and you—boundless opportunities for learning and playing. Or learning while playing. Or learning about playing (after all, it's a lost art). Whatever—the point is that the city offers enough interesting, cultural, and just plain fun options that you'll never be at a loss for things to do.

The Best of the Best

- **Coolest Place to Cool Down:**
Toy Boat Dessert Café (401 Clement St, 415-751-7505) So maybe we don't get your typical summer weather. That doesn't mean you can't take your kids out for a cool treat. The walls of this ice cream parlor are lined with little plastic cartoon toys, and a coin-operated horse ride will distract the antsy ones while you wait in line.

- **Spookiest Hike:** Lands End
(El Camino del Mar, 415-561-4323) If your kids have a "been there, done that" attitude about the 4.5-mile Coastal Trail, spice things up with a "Shipwrecks of the Golden Gate" tour. Park rangers lead visitors on monthly hikes when low tide allows a glimpse at the remains of the unfortunate, resting in the watery waters below. Call the Visitor's Center for times. Yaaaar.

- **Funnest Park:** Adventure Playground
(160 University Ave, Berkeley Marina, Berkeley, 510-981-6720) Kids hammering on everything in the house? See a future architect in your Lego maker? Take them to this fenced-in, carpentry fun-for-all to exorcise those demons. They can check out tool and wood to add to the existing kid-built shacks in the park or start their own. It's free for four children or less if they are accompanied by an adult, while groups must make reservations. Don't forget to wear sturdy shoes!

- **Neatest Museum:** Children's Creativity Museum
(221 Fourth St, 415-820-3320, www.zeum.org) One of the coolest museums in town, this interactive arts mecca that imaginative kids and their families will enjoy. Children are encouraged to try their hand at such jobs as television producer and cartoon animator, as well as experiment with other art media. There's also a 200-seat theater for live performances produced by the American Conservatory Theater. And if the kids run out of ideas, you can hop over to the bowling alley or ice-skating rink. (Admission $11; kids 2 and under are free)

- **Best Out-of-the-Way Place to Find Project Goodies:**
Scroungers Center for Reusable Arts Parts (SCRAP) (801 Toland St, 415-647-1746, www.scrap-sf.org) Fabric, wood, plastic, glass, cardboard and tile—you can find the weird and wonderful in this bargain-hunter's treasure trove that will inspire your children's creativity and teach a great lesson in recycling while they're at it.

- **Brainiest Place to Expand Your Mind:**
San Francisco Public Library (415-557-4400, http://sfpl4.sfpl.org) There's always something exciting going on at one of the 27 branch libraries and the expansive Main Library downtown, from magic shows and opera to art exhibits and readings. Or just get lost in the stacks. It's free! It's educational!

Parks for Playing

Oh plaaaaaymate, come out and play with me…

- **Bernal Heights Playground and Recreation Center**
(Cortland St & Moultrie St) This playground features updated equipment with benches and picnic tables nearby for the weary. A rec center next to the park has programs for tots, teens, and adults.

- **Cow Hollow Playground**
(Baker St & Miley St) This small, sand-covered, fenced-in park is ideal for babies to 6-year-olds and is just a short walk from Union Street shopping if anyone (say, you) is getting restless.

- **Crocker Amazon Playground**
(Geneva Ave & Moscow St) A large play area with updated, brightly colored plastic equipment. If yours are more inclined towards organized sports, you'll find six ball fields, tennis courts, and a bocce court nearby.

- **Duboce Park**
(Duboce Ave & Scott St) Perched on one end of a grassy knoll, this recently renovated fenced-in playground provides kids ages 3 to 9 with a balance beam, climbing wall, slides, and fountain. The surrounding field is great for flying kites, playing tag, and watching the dog dance.

- **Garfield Playground & Pool**
(26th St & Harrison St) A large playground for kids 2 & up replete with the regular sandbox and climbing structures, plus a public pool (adults: $4, kids: $1, call for schedule: 415-695-5001) for those hot summer days. There's also a ball field and game courts nearby.

- **Golden Gate Park**
(Fulton St & Lincoln Wy) Within more than 1,000 acres of parkland are tennis courts, casting ponds, the Conservatory of Flowers, boating, and a carousel ($2/ride). The city's biggest playground is also here, the recently remodeled (and aptly named) Children's Playground, off Kezar Drive, with a huge concrete slide and climbing structures for those 3 & up.

- **Hamilton Pool/Raymond Kimball Playground**
(Geary Blvd & Steiner St) This playground provides a sand play area, a gym, green space, a pool (adults: $4, kids: $1, call for schedule: 415-292-2001), climbing structures, and ball fields for children aged 2 to 12.

- **Holly Park** (Park St) The wooden-structured play-ground is fun for kids of all ages, and the nearby tennis court, ball field, and basketball court provide something for everyone to enjoy. Steep, grassy hills give ample opportunity for rolling down and climbing back up.

- **Julius Kahn Park** (W Pacific Ave & Maple St) Known as "JK," this park has a well-maintained playground for well-maintained children featuring two fenced-in sandy areas: one for babies and toddlers, the other for older kids. Both feature climbing structures, swings, and slippery slides.

- **McKinley Square** (20th St & Vermont St) A park on Potrero Hill with great views, a playground, and sandbox (bring your own buckets). There's also a grassy area where you can run around and kick a ball. The weather is usually sunny here, so don't forget a hat and sunscreen.

- **Moscone Recreation Center** (Chestnut St & Laguna St) A small park full of activity: four baseball diamonds, two tennis and basketball courts, a gym, two putting greens, and a shiny new playground for kids up to 12 years old.

- **Mountain Lake Park** (Lake St & 8th Ave) Great for kids of all ages, this park provides a sandy play area with two slides, swings, climbing structures, hiking trails, and a small beach with assorted (and sometimes cranky) fowl for feeding. Basketball and tennis courts, as well as soccer/baseball fields are also close by.

- **West Portal Playground** (Lenox Wy & Ulloa St) A newly refurbished rec center and added picnic tables put the perfect touches on this park above the Muni tunnel (a great diversion for young trainspotters). Climbing structures, swings, and an adjacent playing field almost make kids forget about the fog rolling through.

Museums with Kid Appeal

- **Asian Art Museum** (200 Larkin St, 415-581-3500, www.asianart.org) One of the largest collections in the West dedicated to Asian art and culture, this museum next to the public library's main branch offers interactive family programs, from storytelling, performances, yoga, and art projects. Family activities are free with museum admission, while kids 12 and under are always free.

- **Exploratorium** (Pier 15 - Embarcadero at Green St, 415-528-4444, www.exploratorium.edu) Hands-on exhibits that encourage children and their parents to explore the natural and scientific world around them make this one of the best science museums in the city. Make a reservation for the Tactile Dome, a network of tunnels and slides that you must crawl through in complete darkness. (Adults (18-64), $25; Youth (6–17), Students, Seniors (65+), and Teachers, $19; kids 5 and under are free)

- **California Academy of Sciences / Steinhart Aquarium** (55 Music Concourse Dr, 415-379-8000, www.calacademy.org) The newly reopened Academy, in a state-of-the-art sustainable facility, is the greenest museum in the world. Located across from the DeYoung Museum, it offers the whole universe under one roof: an aquarium, planetarium, rainforest, coral reef, and living roof. (Adults: $24.95; students/kids 12-17: $19.95; kids 7-11: $14.95; kids 6 and under: free; free the third Wednesday of the month)

- **Bay Area Discovery Museum** (East Fort Baker, 557 McReynolds Rd, Sausalito, 415-339-3900, www.baykidsmuseum.org) Located just across the Golden Gate Bridge, this museum for younger kids lets them play and use their bodies to their heart's content. In addition to changing exhibits, kids love Lookout Cove—it's got a shipwreck, Crow's Nest, tidepools, and a model of the Golden Gate Bridge to play on. All hands-on fun! (Adults: $10; kids 1 and up: $8)

- **Cartoon Arts Museum** (655 Mission St 415-227-8666, http://cartoonart.org) Located in downtown San Francisco's Yerba Buena cultural district, the museum features over 6,000 pieces of original and cartoon and animation art, including editorial cartoons, comic books, graphic novels, anime, Sunday funnies and Saturday morning cartoons. Fun for kids and adults, the museum offers countless events and educational experiences such as book signings, lectures, cartooning classes and workshops.

- **Musee Mecanique** (Pier 45, The Embarcadero & Taylor St, 415-346-2000 www.museeemecanique.org) If it's tough dragging your kids out of the video arcade, take them to see the largest private collection of antique carnival coin-operated machines, including the spooky old fortune-teller booths and the landmark "Laffing Sal." Admission is free, but don't forget the quarters.

- **Randall Museum** (199 Museum Wy, 415-554-9600, www.randallmuseum.org) This small, city-run, interactive museum with a focus on area wildlife offers several affordable art and science classes for kids and their families, weekly art programs, and a theater that features family-friendly films and live performances. All exhibits—including a small room with 100 rescued wild animals—are free.

- **Ripley's Believe It or Not Museum** (175 Jefferson St, 415-202-9850, http://sanfrancisco.ripleys.com) Features a walk-through kaleidoscope tunnel and such oddities as a shrunken human torso once owned by Ernest Hemingway. If your child is into the weird and occasionally grotesque, they'll take to this place. (Ages 13 and up: $14.99; kids 5–12: $8.99)

- **USS Pampanito** (Pier 45, 415-775-1943, www.maritime.org) A WWII fleet sub built in 1943, the USS Pampanito sank six Japanese ships, damaged four others, and narrowly escaped destruction twice herself. A self-guided audio tour takes you from the gun decks and periscope all the way down to the torpedo room, where some men had to sleep. Not for the claustrophobic or very young. (Adults: $9; kids 6-12: $4; kids under 6: free; self-guided tour: $2)

And Some Other Distractions

- **Jewish Community Center of San Francisco** (3200 California St, 415-292-1200, www.jccsf.org) The center provides educational, social, cultural, and fitness programs to the community and is open to all; it has wonderful programs for kids. Choose from art, music, theater, gymnastics, dance, yoga, and sports of all types. The JCC will keep you and your kids busy and healthy. Class schedules and costs are on their website.

- **Yerba Buena Ice-Skating Center** (750 Folsom St, 415-820-3532, www.skatebowl.com) An NHL-sized ice skating rink in Yerba Buena Gardens where your children can live out their hockey and figure skating fantasies. The center offers skating events, parties, and instruction. (A bowling alley is also part of the complex.) Check website for public session schedules. (Adults: $8; kids up to age 12: $6.25 seniors (over 55):$5.50; skate rental: $3)

Outdoor *and* Educational

It's time for some outside stimulation—the Learning Channel isn't quite cutting it anymore.

- **San Francisco Zoo** (1 Zoo Rd, 415-753-7080, www.sfzoo.org) The Zoo houses more than 250 species of animals and birds on its grounds. Exhibits not to miss: the Australian Walkabout full of kangaroos and koalas, the Lemur Forest with an elevated walkway that puts you on eye-level with the animals, and the Hearst Grizzly Gulch with its 20,000-gallon pool and heated rocks. (Adults: $12/locals, $15/non-locals; kids 4–14: $5.50/locals, $9/non-locals; kids 3 and underfree; free the first Wednesday of the month)

- **San Francisco Fire Engine Tours & Adventures** (415-333-7077, www.fireenginetours.com) Aspiring firefighters will absolutely love this tour, seated high atop a classic red 1955 Mack Fire Truck. The open-air expedition requires all participants to dress in an authentic fireman's uniform (provided) and lasts 75 minutes, taking guests on a ride throughout the city. The tour ends back at the century-old firehouse with a talk on fire safety and the history of the SFFD. The tour leaves from the Cannery on Beach Street and Columbus Avenue. Call for current rates and to make a reservation. (Adults: $45; teens 13–17: $30; kids under 12: $25)

Some Great Places to Make Art

- **Sharon Art Studio** (Golden Gate Park, 415-753-7004, www.sharonartstudio.org) Located in Golden Gate Park, next to Children's Playground and opposite the carousel, the Sharon Art Studio is one of the city's best deals, offering affordable art classes for children 5 and up. Check the website for class schedules, and register early because they fill up quickly.

- **Center for Creative Exploration** (300 Chenery St, 415-333-9515, www.ccesf.org) Come paint! Providing a nonjudgmental environment where curiosity and exploration can flourish, the Center offers weekly painting classes where children 6 and up can get their creative juices flowing. Check the website for class schedules and costs; scholarships are available.

- **San Francisco Children's Art Center** (Fort Mason, Bldg C, 415-771-0292, www.childrensartcenter.org) Empowering children through creative exploration! Put on your smock and get messy. Art and painting classes for kids ages 2 to 10 taught in an open studio environment where creativity and visual expression are encouraged. Call ahead for a drop- in class to see what it's all about. You can have an ARTrageous birthday party here, too.

- **Stretch the Imagination** (2509 Bush St, 415-922-0104, www.stretchtheimagination.com) Kids can express their inner creativity with art, yoga, and music.

- **SFMOMA** (151 Third St, 415-357-4000, www.sfmoma.org) Help your child find his inner Cubist! This world-class museum offers Target Family Days three times a year, as well as Family Studio programs, where kids and adults explore connections between art and their own creative genius. Activities such as book readings, film screenings, gallery tours, and hands-on art projects are included. Held on the first and third Sunday of every month.

Best Places to Spin Your Wheels

- **Golden Gate Park** (415-831-2700, www.parks.sfgov.org/) JFK Drive in the park is closed to cars on Sundays, so put on your helmet and ride your bike, or lace up those skates and go, go, go.

- **Golden Gate Promenade** (Marina/Presidio, www.nps.gov/goga) Right along the water in the Marina, this is a beautiful place to take the kids to bike, skate, or scooter. The 3.5-mile path goes from Aquatic Park through Crissy Field to Fort Point. You can stop and play on the beaches or grassy meadows, or have a snack at one of the many beautifully landscaped picnic areas.

Where to go for additional information: www.gocitykids.com

General Information · **Media**

Television

2	KTVU	(FOX)	www.ktvu.com
4	KRON	(Independent)	www.kron.com
5	KPIX	(CBS)	www.kpix.com
7	KGO	(ABC)	www.abc7news.com
9	KQED	(PBS)	www.kqed.org
11	KNTV	(NBC)	www.kntv.com
14	KDTV	(Univision)	www.univision.net
20	KOFY	(Independent)	www.yourtv20.com
26	KTSF	(Independent)	www.ktsf.com
28	KFTL	(HSN)	www.kftl.com
44	KBCW	(CW)	http://cwbayarea.com
48	KSTS	(Telemundo)	www.telemundo.com
50	KFTY	(Clear Channel)	www.kfty.com
54	KTEH	(PBS)	www.kteh.org
60	KCSM	(PBS)	www.kcsm.org
65	KKPX	(i)	www.ionmedia.tv

AM Stations

560	KSFO	Talk
610	KEAR	Religious
680	KNBR	Sports
740	KCBS	News
810	KGO	News/Talk
910	KNEW	Talk
960	KKGN	Liberal Talk
1010	KIQI	Spanish Talk
1050	KTCT	Sports
1100	KFAX	Religious
1260	KSFB	Religious
1450	KEST	Personal Growth, Multicultural
1550	KYCY	Talk, Sports

FM Stations

88.5	KQED	News/Public Radio/NPR
89.5	KPOO	Variety
90.1	KZSU	Eclectic/Independent
90.3	KUSF	Alternative Music
91.1	KCSM	Jazz
91.7	KALW	News/Public Radio/NPR
92.7	KNGY	Dance Top 40
93.3	KRZZ	Spanish
94.1	KPFA	Community/Variety
94.9	KYLD	Urban top 40/Commercial Hip-hop
95.7	KBWF	Country
96.5	KOIT	Light Rock
97.3	KLLC	Adult Contemporary
98.1	KISQ	R&B/Classic Soul/Disco
99.7	KMVQ	Urban Top 40/Pop/R&B
101.3	KIOI	Adult Contemporary
102.1	KDFC	Classical
103.7	KKSF	Smooth Jazz
104.5	KFOG	Adult Contemporary Rock
105.3	KITS	Modern Rock
106.1	KMEL	Urban contemporary/Hip-hop
106.9	KFRC	Oldies/Classic Hits
107.7	KSAN	Classic Rock

Magazines

7x7 · www.7x7sf.com · Monthly glossy with coverage on food, design, and fashion in the Bay Area.

Bark · www.thebark.com · Bi-monthly magazine of musings on modern dog culture.

Bitch · www.bitchmagazine.org · Print magazine and evolving website devoted to feminist analysis and media and pop culture criticism.

Common Ground · www.commongroundmag.com · Publication focused on alternative health, social consciousness, and sustainable living.

Curve · www.curvemag.com · Nationally distributed, cutting-edge lesbian culture magazine printed 10 times a year.

Dwell · www.dwell.com · Glossy focused on fresh, contemporary home architecture and design printed 10 times a year.

Earth Island Journal · www.earthisland.org/journal · Quarterly magazine devoted to environmental activism, sustainability, and grassroots campaigns. Based in Berkeley.

Edible San Francisco · www.ediblesanfrancisco.net · Quarterly rag dedicated to the finest local food and drink.

Edutopia · www.edutopia.org · The George Lucas Educational Foundation's publication on innovation and trends in K-12 public education.

Hyphen · www.hyphenmagazine.com · Nonprofit, all-volunteer-staff magazine on Asian American culture, politics and social issues.

Mother Jones · www.motherjones.com · Progressive, investigative, and social justice reporting on news, politics, and culture. National bi-monthly magazine and comprehensive website.

Nob Hill Gazette · www.nobhillgazette.com · Monthly magazine with a focus on local charity and society events for the city's upscale Nob Hill neighborhood.

PLANET · www.planet-mag.com · Independent culture and lifestyle mag of art, fashion, music, travel, and design with a global slant.

ReadyMade · www.readymademag.com · The DIY lifestyle magazine for the hip, resourceful, and crafty. Published six times a year.

Red Herring · www.redherring.com · Reflective of the Silcon Valley set, the publication covers trends and innovation in technology and business.

San Francisco Downtown · www.sfdowntown.com · Free lifestyle, business, and entertainment monthly.

San Francisco Magazine · www.sanfran.com · Monthly city-centric glossy.

Sierra · www.sierraclub.org · Sierra Club's bi-monthly magazine.

SOMA · www.somamagazine.com · Glossy monthly featuring high-end fashion, art features, and interviews.

Thrasher · www.thrashermagazine.com · The authority on skateboarding culture. Monthly.

Wired · www.wired.com · Conde Nast's monthly glossy on technology, science, and intelligent pop culture.

Newspapers

Asian Week · www.asianweek.com · News for SF's Asian community.

Bay Area Business Woman · www.babwnews.com · Business and lifestyle newspaper for female professionals and business owners.

Bay Area Reporter · www.ebar.com · News for gay and lesbian community.

Central City Extra · www.studycenter.org/test/cce · Progressive community news for the Tenderloin, Civic Center, and Sixth Street neighborhoods.

East Bay Express · www.eastbayexpress.com · East Bay version of the *Guardian* and the *Weekly*.

El Tecolote · www.eltecolote.org · Bi-weekly, bilingual newspaper for the Mission District.

Frontlines · www.sf-frontlines.com · Progressive news

Haight-Ashbury Beat · www.haightbeat.com · Independent neighborhood publication distributed to Upper Haight residents and businesses.

J · www.jewishsf.com · News for Bay Area Jewish community.

Marina Times · 2161 Union St · 415-931-0515 · Independent community newspaper.

Mission Dispatch · www.missiondispatch.org · Community news for the Mission District.

The New Fillmore News · www.newfillmore.com · Independent community newspaper.

The Noe Valley Voice · www.noevalleyvoice.com · Independent community newspaper.

North Beach Journal · Independent community newspaper.

The Oakland Tribune · www.oaklandtribune.com · Daily covering general news for Oakland, Berkeley, Richmond, and the surrounding areas.

Potrero View · www.potreroview.net · Independent community newspaper.

Richmond Review/Sunset Beacon · www.sunsetbeacon.com · Community publications serving the Richmond and Sunset districts on the west side of SF.

San Francisco Bay Guardian · www.sfbg.com · Alternative, progressive news and features.

San Francisco Bay View · www.sfbayview.com · National newspaper for the African American community.

San Francisco Business Times · http://sanfrancisco.bizjournals. com · Bay Area business news.

San Francisco Chronicle · www.sfgate.com · Major daily newspaper.

San Francisco Examiner · www.sfexaminer.com · Free, daily, tabloid-format newspaper.

San Francisco Weekly · www.sfweekly.com · Alternative, progressive news and features.

San Jose Mercury News · www.mercurynews.com · Major daily newspaper of San Jose and Silicon Valley.

San Francisco Spectrum · www.sfspectrum.com · Online newspaper for LGBT readers

Street Sheet · www.cohsf.org/streetsheet · Publication of the Coalition on Homelessness.

Western Edition · www.thewesternedition.com · Community news for Alamo Square, Hayes Valley, the Fillmore, Japantown, and the Panhandle.

Websites

www.notfortourists.com—THE San Francisco source. Mmhmm, that's right.

www.onlyinsanfrancisco.com—The official Convention & Visitors Bureau site—loads of useful information.

www.craigslist.org—Easily the most popular site for hooking up in San Francisco, whether that means hooking yourself up with a new job, a new apartment, news about what's going on, or a hot, new date.

www.dailycandy.com/san-francisco/ - For the fashionable, the fun, and the foodie

http://litseen.com/ - A daily calendar of literary events around the city

www.missionmission.org/ - From the absurd to the informative, this Mission-centric blog has the latest on events, up-to-the-minute happenings on the street and pure hipster silliness

www.sfstation.com—An entertainment-oriented city guide that offers a calendar of events, info on clubs, music, film, special events, literary happenings, and the like.

www.sfgate.com—The *San Francisco Chronicle's* site—news about San Francisco and the Bay Area, as well as national news, classifieds, weather and traffic updates.

www.sfist.com/ - Great source for local news and events

http://SF.funcheap.com/ - SF. Fun. Cheap. Need we say more?

www.sanfrancisco.com—Guide to hotels, restaurants, events, nightlife, jobs, and real estate.

www.sanfrancisco.citysearch.com—Comprehensive, up-to-date listings of restaurants, clubs, and other entertainment venues. Includes ratings of popular hot spots, photos of each venue, and links to related sites.

http://sanfrancisco.going.com—Social networking fused with Bay Area event listings.

http://cityguide.aol.com/sanfrancisco—AOL's City Guide to San Francisco. Coverage of select events, music, arts, restaurants, and bars in the Bay Area.

www.sfist.com—Bay Area news and gossip blog.

www.sfusualsuspects.com—Daily political news and analysis.

http://sf.flavorpill.net—Weekly selection of off-beat, artsy shows, music events, and literary readings chosen by its staff.

www.tastingtable.com/shortlist/sf/all - Daily updates on the latest in food culture

www.yelp.com—Popular site with peer reviews on just about every restaurant, bar and business in town.

Reference Books

Herb Caen's San Francisco: 1976-1991, by Herb Caen and Irene Mecchi (Chronicle Books, 1992) The late *Chronicle* columnist's best pieces about the city he loved.

San Francisco Then & Now, by Bill Yenne (Thunder Bay Press, 2003) Collection of historical and contemporary photographs of the city's neighborhoods and landmarks.

Streets and San Francisco: The Origins of Street and Place Names, by Louis K. Loewenstein and Penny Demoss (Wilderness Press, 1996) The stories behind the city's streets and landmarks.

The Barbary Coast: An Informal History of the San Francisco Underworld, by Herbert Asbury (Thunder's Mouth Press, 2002) San Francisco has always had its share of sin—here's a tour of the city's darker side.

Stairway Walks in San Francisco, by Adah Bakalinsky (Wilderness Press, 2006) The sixth edition of this popular guidebook lists just about all of the city's stairway walks, from the well-known to the hard-to-find.

Infinite City: A San Francisco Atlas, by Rebecca Solnit (University of California Press, 2010) An imaginative atlas of the city, illuminated by twenty-two maps, exploring the urban landscape of SF through thematic, historic and cultural lenses.

Imperial San Francisco: Urban Power, Earthly Ruin, by Gary A. Brechin (University of California Press, 2001) A study of the rich and powerful who helped make San Francisco.

Reclaiming San Francisco History: History, Politics, Culture: A City Lights Anthology, edited by James Brook, Chris Carlsson, and Nancy J. Peters (City Lights Books, 1998) A collection of essays about San Francisco's history.

San Francisco Secrets: Fascinating Facts about the City by the Bay, by John Snyder (Chronicle Books, 1999) A collection of city factoids perfect for the trivia-obsessed.

San Francisco Bizarro, by Jack Boulware (St. Martin's, 2000) An insider's guide to some of the strangest incidences in SF's counterculture history.

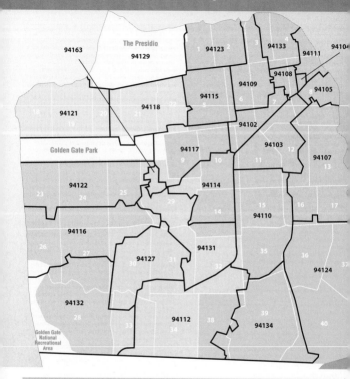

Post Offices

	Address	Phone	Map
18th Street Station	4304 18th St	415-431-2701	10
Bayview Station	2111 Lane St	415-822-7157	40
Bernal Heights Finance Station	189 Tiffany Ave	415-550-7538	35
Brannan Street Finance	460 Brannan St	415-536-6413	8
Bryant Street Station	1600 Bryant St	415-431-3720	11
Chinatown Station	867 Stockton St	415-433-1202	7
Civic Center Box Unit / Pacific Center	101 Hyde St	415-563-7284	7
Clayton Street Station	554 Clayton St	415-621-5816	9
CPU University of SF	2299 Golden Gate Ave	415-462-2525	22
CPU World Pioneer	2830 24th St	415-282-6838	15
Diamond Heights Finance	5262 Diamond Heights Blvd	415-641-0158	32

General Information • **Post Offices / Police**

Post Offices—*continued*

	Address	Phone	Map
Excelsior Finance Station	15 Onondaga St	415-334-1057	38
Federal Building	450 Golden Gate Ave	415-487-8981	7
Fox Plaza Finance Station	1390 Market St	415-931-1053	11
Gateway Station	1 Embarcadero Ctr	415-956-5296	8
Geary Station	5654 Geary Blvd	415-665-1355	20
Golden Gate Station	3245 Geary Blvd	415-751-9739	22
Irving Street Postal Store	821 Irving St	415-759-6652	25
Lakeshore Plaza Station	1543 Sloat Blvd	415-564-0258	27
Macy's Union Square Station	170 O'Farrell St	415-956-0131	7
Marina Green Retail Store	3749 Buchanan St	415-440-4390	2
Marina Station	2055 Lombard St	415-351-1875	2
McLaren Station	2755 San Bruno Ave	415-467-5026	39
Mission Station	1198 S Van Ness Ave	415-648-0155	15
Noe Valley	4083 24th St	415-821-3863	14
North Beach (Carrier) Station	2200 Powell St	415-986-3494	4
North Beach (Finance) Station	1640 Stockton St	415-362-3128	4
Parkside Station	1800 Taraval St	415-759-0150	27
Pine Street Station	1400 Pine St	415-351-2435	7
Potrero Retail Store	1655 Bryant St	415-861-8130	11
Presidio Station	950 Lincoln Blvd, Bldg 210	415-563-0126	page 154
Rincon Finance	180 Steuart St	415-896-0762	8
San Francisco P+DC	1300 Evans Ave	415-550-5005	37
Steiner Street Station	1849 Geary St	415-931-1053	5
Sunset Finance Station	1314 22nd Ave	415-759-6381	24
Sutter Street Postal Store	150 Sutter St	415-765-1761	8
Visitacion Station	68 Leland Ave	415-333-4629	39
West Portal Station	317 West Portal Ave	415-759-0158	30

Police

	Address	Phone	Map
Bayview Police Station	201 Williams Ave	415-671-2300	40
Central Police Station	766 Vallejo St	415-315-2400	4
Ingleside Police Station	1 John Young Ln	415-404-4000	34
Mission Police Station	630 Valencia St	415-558-5400	11
Northern Police Station	1125 Fillmore St	415-614-3400	5
Park Police Station	1899 Waller St	415-242-3000	9
Richmond Police Station	461 6th Ave	415-666-8000	21
Southern Police Station	850 Bryant St	415-553-1373	12
Taraval Police Station	2345 24th Ave	415-759-3100	27
Tenderloin Police Station	301 Eddy St	415-345-7300	7

Hospitals

From the top-ranked **UCSF Medical Center at Parnassus (Map 29)** to the smaller, community-based facilities like **Chinese Hospital (Map 7)**, San Francisco is a good place to get sick or hurt yourself, if you insist.

If you have to visit a hospital in a hurry, it's obviously best to know where to go. As a quick reference, this is a list of the largest hospitals with ERs open to the general public. We recommend going to the map page for your neighborhood to see the location of these and all hospitals in your area.

Emergency Rooms	Address	Phone	Map
California Pacific Medical Center California Campus	3700 California St	415-600-6000	22
California Pacific Medical Center Davies Campus	Castro St & Duboce St	415-600-6000	10
California Pacific Medical Center Pacific Campus	2333 Buchanan St	415-600-6000	6
California Pacific Medical Center St. Luke's Campus	3555 Cesar Chavez St	415-600-6000	15
Chinese Hospital	845 Jackson St	415-982-2400	7
Kaiser Permanente Medical Center	2425 Geary Blvd	415-833-3300	5
San Francisco General	1001 Potrero Ave	415-206-8000	16
San Francisco VA Medical Center	4150 Clement St	415-221-4810	18
St Francis Memorial	900 Hyde St	415-353-6000	7
St Luke's	3555 Cesar Chavez St	415-647-8600	35
St Mary's Medical Center	450 Stanyan St	415-668-1000	9
UCSF Medical Center at Parnassus	505 Parnassus Ave	415-476-1000	29

Other Hospitals	Address	Phone	Map
Laguna Honda Hospital and Rehabilitation Center	375 Laguna Honda Blvd	415-759-2300	25

Libraries

While the Main branch in Civic Center has a good reference section, thousands of tomes, and a bookstore and a café, the local neighborhood branches hold many of the literary treasures themselves. For special collections, check out Chinatown branch for titles in Asian languages, and the Eureka Valley branch for LGBT literature. : But running all over town is unnecessary: the online catalog and request system allows you to transfer an item from one library to the branch in your neighborhood.

Library	Address	Phone	Map
Anza Branch Library	550 37th Ave	415-355-5717	19
Bayview / Linda Brooks-Burton Branch Library	5075 3rd St	415-355-5757	36
Bernal Heights Branch Library	500 Cortland Ave	415-355-2810	35
Chinatown Branch Library	1135 Powell St	415-355-2888	7
Eureka Valley / Harvey Milk Memorial Library	1 José Sarria Ct	415-355-5616	10
Excelsior Branch Library	4400 Mission St	415-355-2868	38
Foundation Center, San Francisco	312 Sutter St	415-397-0902	8
Glen Park Branch Library	2825 Diamond St	415-337-4740	32
Golden Gate Valley Library	1801 Green St	415-355-5666	2
Helen Crocker Russell Library	9th Ave & Lincoln Wy	415-661-1316	25
Ingleside Branch Library	1298 Ocean Ave	415-355-2898	33
Library & Center for Knowledge	530 Parnassus Ave	415-476-2334	29
Marina Branch Library	1890 Chestnut St	415-355-2823	2
Mechanics' Institute Library	57 Post St	415-393-0114	8
Merced Branch Library	155 Winston Dr	415-355-2825	30
Mission Bay Branch Library	960 4th St	415-355-2838	13
Mission Branch Library	300 Bartlett St	415-355-2800	15
Noe Valley Branch Library	451 Jersey St	415-695-5095	14
North Beach Branch Library	2000 Mason St	415-355-5626	4
Ocean View Branch Library	345 Randolph St	415-355-5615	33
Ortega Branch Library	3223 Ortega St	415-504-6053	23
Park Branch Library	1833 Page St	415-355-5656	9
Parkside Branch Library	1200 Taraval St	415-355-5770	27
Portola Library	2450 San Bruno Ave	415-355-5660	39
Potrero Library	1616 20th St	415-355-2822	16
Presidio Branch Library	3150 Sacramento St	415-355-2880	5
Richmond Branch Library	351 9th Ave	415-355-5600	21
San Francisco Law Library	401 Van Ness Ave	415-554-6821	7
San Francisco Main Library	100 Larkin St	415-557-4400	7
Sunset Branch Library	1305 18th Ave	415-355-2808	25
Sutro Library	480 Winston Dr	415-731-4477	27
United Irish Cultural Center	2700 45th Ave	415-661-2700	26
Visitacion Valley Library	45 Leland Ave	415-355-2848	39
West Portal Branch Library	190 Lenox Wy	415-355-2886	30
Western Addition Branch Library	1550 Scott St	415-355-5727	5

Overview

There is no shortage of landmarks in San Francisco, from the very recognizable sights to the tucked-away treasures known only to locals. On any day, you can find something new to explore, whether you want to be in the center of the action or away from the commotion.

Great Architecture

The **Sentinel Building (Map 8)**, a.k.a. the Coppola Building, is a beautiful and distinctive green copper Flatiron. The ultra-modern design of the new **DeYoung Museum in Golden Gate Park (Golden Gate Park)**, seems to inspire either love or hate from city residents——stroll around the copper-skinned walls and twisting observation tower and decide for yourself. The **Roos House (Map 22)** in Pacific Heights shows off Bernard Maybeck's style. For a touch of modernism, check out **St. Mary's Cathedral (Map 6)** with its washing machine component-shaped cross. More churches in classic styles include the grand **Grace Cathedral (Map 7)** and **St. Peter and Paul's Church (Map 4)**. Moreover, the city's trademark is its ornate Victorian and Edwardian homes from the early 20th century that can be found all over town. The **Transamerica Pyramid (Map 8)** defines our skyline and we'd love to get access to the little room on top one day.

Great Public Buildings

The **Palace of the Legion of Honor (Map 18)**, in its breathtaking setting overlooking the **Golden Gate Bridge (The Presidio)**, is a beautiful Beaux Arts copy of its namesake in Paris at 3/4-scale. **City Hall (Map 7)** also belongs with Beaux Arts French Renaissance architecture and is arguably one of the finest public buildings in the world.

Great Outdoor Spaces

The **Presidio (The Presidio)**, is an entryway to the vast expanse of Marin County over the Golden Gate Bridge, complete with a chapel, a bowling alley, and a campground. Angel Island is a nice way to get out on the Bay by ferry—you can even take your bike. **Alamo Square (Map 10)** has postcard-worthy views of Victorian homes juxtaposed against the backdrop of skyscrapers, and **Dolores Park (Map 10)** is perfect for people and their dogs; enjoy a game of tennis in both spaces. Favorite neighborhood hilltop parks with amazing views include **Alta Plaza Park (Map 5)** in Pacific Heights, **Buena Vista Park (Map 9)** in the Haight, **Bernal Hill** in Bernal Heights, and **Corona Heights (Map 10)** in the Castro. **Crissy Field's (The Presidio)** beaches, running trail, and picnic areas make it a beautiful place to escape the hustle and bustle of our amazing city. But of course, there is no contest with **Golden Gate Park (Golden Gate Park)**, with its 1,013 acres of verdant green space built on what were barren sand dunes only 100 years before. Along with miles of bike trails and acres of sports fields, it is home to the De Young Museum, the Conservatory of Flowers, and the Japanese Tea Gardens.

Great Obscure Landmarks

Visit the **Official City Tree (Golden Gate Park)**, the **Golden Gate Fortune Cookie Company (Map 7)**, or the **"Shoe Garden" (Map 10)** in Alamo Square for a dose of the random historic. Roam around town and discover the dozens of murals by local artists depicting city history and culture—**Balmy Alley in the Mission (Map 15)** is a good place to start.

Overrated Landmarks

Ghirardelli Square (Map 3) and the old brick **Del Monte Cannery (Map 3)** environs are basically crowded malls chock full of tourist shops. **Fisherman's Wharf (Map 3)** is, without a doubt, the city's most popular tourist trap. But, if you've never had clam chowder in a bread bowl there, be a tourist for an hour and enjoy a bowl with some people-watching on the pier.

As a major destination for both business and pleasure, San Francisco has a wide range of hotels to choose from. Obviously, these listings will be of limited use to San Franciscans, but knowing a thing or two about the local hotel scene can be useful, indeed.

With this knowledge you can weigh in on cocktail conversations about trendy hotspots such as **Hotel Vitale (Map 8)** and steer visiting friends, family, and colleagues into accommodations that match their budgets and sensibilities. After all, you wouldn't want to land your 85-year-old auntie from Cowtown, USA smack dab in the middle of the Tenderloin and your party-hearty younger bro in a buttoned-up hotel in Pacific Heights. 'Nuff said.

For the high rollers in your life, classic luxury resides at the **Palace (Map 8)**, **Ritz-Carlton (Map 7)**, **Four Seasons (Map 8)**, **Mandarin Oriental (Map 8)**, and **Hotel Nikko (Map 7)**. Upscale accommodations steeped in local history abound on Nob Hill, where you'll find the **Fairmont (Map 7)**, a favorite lodging option among US presidents; the **Huntington Hotel (Map 7)**, home of the famous Big 4 Restaurant; and the **Intercontinental Mark Hopkins (Map 7)**, with its Top of the Mark lounge offering unparalleled city views. When your jet-setting, trend-watching friends descend upon the city, send them to the **W (Map 8)** just south of Market, or to Ian Schrager's **Clift Hotel (Map 7)**, where the visually arresting Redwood Room lounge draws many a well-heeled San Franciscan on weekend nights. If they're hip but slightly grungy, the **Phoenix Hotel (Map 7)** or the **The Hotel Tropicana (Map 11)** should fit the bill. If their main place of interest is the Castro, try the classic **Beck's Motor Lodge (Map 10)**. For visitors who plan to spend time in Marin, book your stay the **Inn at the Presidio**, a brand new luxury hotel, a stone's throw from the Golden Gate Bridge.

The city also plays host to a bevy of boutique hotels and bed and breakfasts, each with their own unique style and offerings. Love art? Downtown's **Hotel Triton (Map 8)** and **Hotel Des Arts (Map 8)** feature permanent and temporary art installations from local and well-known artists. **Hotel Monaco (Map 7)** welcomes guests with pets, and will even provide a goldfish companion for visitors who've left their furry friends at home. Other top boutique hotels include **Hotel Majestic (Map 6)** and **Hotel Drisco (Map 5)** in Pacific Heights, as well as downtown's **Campton Place (Map 8)**, **Harbor Court (Map 8)**, and **Prescott (Map 7)** hotels. San Francisco, the land of the Victorian, also has a number of beautiful, quaint, well-placed bed and breakfasts. Two fine B&B choices are: the undiscovered **'A Country Cottage' (Map 11)** and the historic **Red Victorian Bed and Breakfast (Map 9)**. Do your own searching at www.bedandbreakfast.com for the plethora of other B&B's in this city.

For the budget-conscious, the **Holiday Inn Golden Gateway (Map 6)**, **Marriott's Courtyard Downtown (Map 8)**, and **Hyatt Fisherman's Wharf (Map 3)** offer solid accommodations and amenities. And for your granola-eatin' cousin backpacking across the country, hostel choices include **the Green Tortoise (Map 8)** and **Hostelling International (Map 7)** with locations downtown, at the Civic Center, and at Fisherman's Wharf. Whatever you choose, remember that the rates indicated here are estimates and subject to change. For deals, check out one of the many hotel accommodation websites (Hotels.com, Priceline, Hotwire, Travelocity, Kayak.com, etc.) to get the best rates. Prices are generally highest during holidays, summer months, and special events like the Gay Pride Parade (June). Not all hotels have star ratings, and those that do are sometimes inaccurate. Room rates are usually a pretty good indication of hotel quality. Be aware that overnight parking fees at many city hotels can exceed $30/day. Lastly—if you are looking for good rates, great amenities and the best locations, try Craigslist's 'Vacation Rentals' section. Normal people like you and me will rent their apartment out by the night/week/month if they know they are going to be out of town and sometimes these are the best kinds of housing situations as long as there is a smidgen of mutual trust between both parties.

Like most cities, San Francisco has an over-abundance of S.R.O hotels—this stands for Single Room Occupancy, otherwise known as a residential hotel. Some are totally respectable places to live if you can't afford an apartment, some have vibrant communities, some are owned and re-habbed by non-profit organizations to make them livable places for seniors and those with life-challenges, and some are bathroom-down-the-hall-dimly-lit places where people on the fringes of society go to die. Chances are that you, Not For Tourist reader,

probably do not want to be living in one or sending your friends/parents/relatives to stay in one. Thankfully, most of the places listed in this guide are not SRO hotels. The most concentrated area of these are in the Tenderloin and South of Market area. You can tell by the per week/per month offers and also by the kind of people who hang out outside, or the kinds of things hanging in the windows. Since we can't spend a month going to every single one of these places, we'll leave it up to you to decide for yourself.

Hotel	Address	Phone	Rate $	Map
Hostelling International - Fisherman's Wharf	240 Fisherman's Wharf	415-771-7277	$	2
Hyatt at Fisherman's Wharf	555 North Point St	415-563-1234	$$	3
Hotel Drisco	2901 Pacific Ave	415-346-2880	$$	5
Holiday Inn Golden Gateway	1500 Van Ness Ave	415-441-4000	$$	6
Majestic Hotel	1500 Sutter St	415-441-1100	$$	6
Mark Hopkins InterContinental	1 Nob Hill	415-392-3434	$$$	7
Phoenix Hotel	601 Eddy St	415-776-1380	$$$	7
Prescott Hotel	545 Post St	415-563-0303	$$$	7
Ritz-Carlton San Francisco	600 Stockton St	415-296-7465	$$$$$	7
Hostelling International - Downtown	312 Mason St	415-788-5604	$	7
Hostelling International - City Center	685 Ellis St	415-474-5721	$	7
Hotel Monaco	501 Geary St	415-292-0100	$$$	7
Hotel Nikko San Francisco	222 Mason St	415-394-1111	$$$$	7
The Huntington Hotel	1075 California St	415-474-5400	$$$	7
Taj Campton Place	340 Stockton St	415-781-5555	$$$$	7
Clift Hotel	495 Geary St	415-775-4700	$$$$	7
Fairmont San Francisco	950 Mason St	415-772-5000	$$$$	7
Four Seasons Hotel SF	757 Market St	415-633-3000	$$$$$	8
Green Tortoise Hostel	494 Broadway St	415-834-1000	$	8
Harbor Court Hotel	165 Steuart St	415-882-1300	$$$	8
Courtyard San Franisco Downtown	299 2nd St	415-947-0700	$$$	8
Hotel Vitale	8 Mission St	415-278-3700	$$$$	8
Hotel Des Arts	447 Bush St	415-956-3232	$$	8
Triton Hotel	342 Grant Ave	415-394-0500	$$$$	8
W San Francisco	181 3rd St	415-777-5300	$$$$	8
Palace Hotel	2 New Montgomery St	415-512-1111	$$$	8
Red Victorian Bed, Breakfast & Art	1665 Haight St	415-864-1978	$$	9
Beck Motor Lodge	2222 Market St	415-621-8212	$$	10
Country Cottage	5 Dolores Terrace	415-899-0060	$$	10
The Hotel Tropica	663 Valencia St	415-701-7666	$$	11
Inn at the Presidio	42 Moraga Ave	415-800-7356	$$$$	Presidio

From the strange to the bold, San Francisco's museums are on the cutting edge. The city has several major destination museums, as well as smaller ones devoted to singular, sometimes peculiar, subjects (think tattoos and cartoons). In addition to museums focusing on ethnic cultures and art, the city has several interactive museums where tactile experience is as important as the objects on display. Of the art museums, the four "biggies" are the **San Francisco Museum of Modern Art (SFMOMA)** (Map 8), the **California Palace of the Legion of Honor** (Map 18), the **De Young (Golden Gate Park)**, and the **Asian Art Museum** (Map 7). In addition to the "big four," the **Yerba Buena Center for the Arts** (Map 8), in close proximity to SFMOMA, has hosted an increasing number of significant exhibits in the last several years.

SFMOMA began its life in 1935 as the first museum on the West Coast dedicated solely to modern and contemporary art. Back then, it was known as the San Francisco Museum of Art, and it was not until 1975 that the word "modern" was added to its name. In the late '80s the museum began expanding its exhibitions program. Today it offers a wealth of exhibits and public programs. Until early 2016, the SFMOMA building is closed for expansion but is offering pop up exhibitions and events around the city until then. Visit: www.sfmoma.org/exhib_events for more information.

The **Legion of Honor**, is a gorgeous Beaux-Arts building located within a picturesque setting in the Richmond District's Lincoln Park. Funded by Alma de Bretteville Spreckels to honor the soldiers who died in World War I, the museum is a three-quarter-scale copy of the Palais de la Légion d'Honneur in Paris and was completed in 1924. Today it houses Rodin sculptures, including "The Thinker," European decorative arts and paintings, ancient art and artifacts spanning 4,000 years, and a large prints and drawing collection. Admission is free on the first Tuesday of every month, although special exhibition fees still apply. When you go, consider adding a hike through the neighboring golf course out to Lands End. The ocean views are not to be missed.

Founded in 1895, the **de Young** in Golden Gate Park is the city's oldest museum. Its collection includes American painting, decorative arts and crafts, arts from Africa, Oceania, and the Americas, and Western and non-western textiles. The museum reopened after major renovations in 2005, featuring a public sculpture garden, children's garden, and exquisite landscaping. The state-of-the-art facility, with a stunning Post-Modern design by Herzog & de Meuron (check out the observation level) is covered in a copper façade to gain a rich patina over time that will blend into the natural environment. For an evening excursion, try the Friday Night series which features lectures, performances, and live music. Food items, beer, wine, and specialty cocktails are available for purchase in the Café.

The **Asian Art Museum** opened in 1966 in a wing of the de Young to house part of Avery Brundage's vast collection of Asian art. With more than 17,000 objects, this museum has one of the biggest Asian art collections in the country. In 2003, the museum moved to its current home in the former Main Library in the Civic Center. The Asian Art Museum holds an enormous collection that spans 6,000 years and covers the major traditions of Asian art and

culture. Admission is free on the first Sunday of every month and discounted on Thursday evenings from 5 pm to 9 pm for MATCHA, a happy hour event featuring DJ music, tours, performances, and a cash bar.

The Asian Art Museum may be the largest city museum devoted to one cultural diaspora, but it's certainly not the only one. Founded in 1975, the **Mexican Museum** (Map 2) at Fort Mason Center has a permanent collection of over 12,000 Mexican, Mexican-American, Chicano, and Latino art and cultural objects. When construction of the museum's new building in the Yerba Buena Center for the Arts is complete, the museum will relocate to the SOMA neighborhood. Call first to make sure it's open.

San Francisco is also home to **Museo Italo Americano** (Map 2) in Fort Mason, was the first museum in the country devoted exclusively to Italian and Italian-American arts and artists. The **Museum of the African Diaspora** (Map 8) examines the origins, movement, adaptation, and transformation of people of African descent. The museum showcases the works of African-American artists and features exhibits on Africa, African culture, and the African-American experience. The stylish interior coupled with interactive exhibits make this one of the most exciting recent addition to the city's museum circuit. The **Chinese Historical Society of America Museum and Learning Center** (Map 7) offers exhibits, library facilities, and programs on Chinese history and culture in America. **The Contemporary Jewish Museum**'s Daniel Libeskind designed space (Map 8) presents exhibitions and programs that explore contemporary perspectives on Jewish culture, history, and ideas.

For a museum trek that's a little out of the ordinary, consider visiting the **Cartoon Art Museum** (Map 8) or the **Tattoo Art Museum** (Map 4). If you dare, you can brave Fisherman's Wharf for several museums popular with tourists but still worth a visit. The **Musee Mecanique** (Map 7) at Pier 45 houses one of the world's largest collections of antique arcade machines, hand-cranked music boxes, and other mechanical musical instruments, plus rare finds like toothpick art made by inmates at San Quentin. The nearby **Ripley's Believe It or Not!** (Map 3) museum offers 18 galleries and over 10,000 square feet of weird, mind-bending illusions and unbelievable exhibits such as shrunken heads and a mirror maze. Also at the Wharf, the **Wax Museum** (Map 4) is filled with eerily lifelike versions of your favorite celebs, like Nicole Kidman, Angelina Jolie, and Lance Armstrong.

For lessons in San Francisco's history, there are several museums document elements of the city's past. Check out the **Fire Museum** (Map 5) for papers and artifacts detailing San Francisco fires, firefighters, and tools from 1849 onward. Tour restored ships and speak with knowledgeable National Park Service employees at the **Maritime Museum** (Map 3) at Fisherman's Wharf. The **Cable Car Museum** (Map 7), the **Wells Fargo Museum** (Map 8), and the **San Francisco Museum & Historical Society** exhibition spaces in City Hall's South Light Court (Map 7) and at (Map 3) are also good places to brush up on city history. Perhaps San Francisco's most spectacular history museum is in **The Old Mint**, a national landmark with 17 galleries and wonders to orient visitors to the Bay Area.

Take a kid or be one at Dr. Frank Oppenheimer's **Exploratorium (Map 1)**. The museum has hands-on exhibits and demonstrations focusing on science, art, and human perception—you can touch and play with everything. Don't miss the Tactile Dome (make a reservation), where you crawl around in total darkness using only your sense of touch to guide you. Pack a picnic and enjoy the fairytale-like building and lush gardens. Another science-friendly city favorite is the **California Academy of Sciences (Map 25)**. Cal Academy houses a natural history museum, the Steinhart Aquarium, and the Morrison Planetarium. Be sure to explore Cal Academy's Living Roof, a 4.5 acre rooftop designed by Renzo Piano to accommodate a living tapestry of native plant species. The rooftop's seven undulating green hillocks pay homage to the iconic topography of San Francisco. The free

Randall Museum (Map 10) offers a hands-on approach to exploring the sciences with both indoor and outdoor exhibits on nature, the environment, and live animals. Another fun place to take the kids is the **Children's Creativity Museum**, an interactive art and technology center in Yerba Buena Gardens. Exhibits allow kids to work with computer programs, sound equipment, and other tools to produce their own creations.

For everything you ever wanted to know about San Francisco, check out the Virtual Museum of the City of San Francisco at www.sfmuseum.org.

Museum	Address	Phone	Map
Asian Art Museum	200 Larkin St	415-581-3500	7
The Beat Museum	540 Broadway St	800-537-6822	4
California Academy of Sciences	55 Music Concourse Dr, Golden Gate Park	415-379-8000	25
Cartoon Art Museum	655 Mission St	415-227-8666	8
Children's Creativity Museum	221 4th St	415-820-3320	12
Chinese Culture Center of San Francisco	750 Kearny St, 3rd Fl	415-986-1822	8
Chinese Historical Society of America	965 Clay St	415-391-1188	7
Contemporary Jewish Museum	736 Mission St	415-355-7800	8
De Young	50 Hagiwara Tea Garden Dr	415-750-3600	pg 153
Exploratorium	Pier 15	415-528-4444	4
GLBT History Museum	657 Mission St, Ste 300	415-777-5455	8
Haas-Lilienthal House	2007 Franklin St	415-441-3004	6
Legion of Honor	100 34th Ave	415-750-3600	18
Mexican Museum	Ft Mason Ctr, Bldg D	415-202-9700	2
Mission Dolores	3321 16th St	415-621-8203	10
Musee Mecanique	Pier 45 at the end of Taylor St	415-346-2000	3
Museo Italo Americano	Ft Mason Ctr, Bldg C (entrance at Marina Blvd & Buchanan St)	415-673-2200	2
Museum of Craft & Folk Art	51 Yerba Buena Ln	415-227-4888	8
Museum of the African Diaspora	685 Mission St	415-358-7200	8
Museum of Performance & Design	893 Folsom St	415-255-4800	6
Museum of Vision	655 Beach St	415-561-8502	3
National Japanese American Historical Society	1684 Post St	415-921-5007	6
National Maritime Museum	900 Beach St	415-561-6662	3
Octagon House	2645 Gough St	415-441-7512	2
Randall Museum	199 Museum Wy	415-554-9600	10
Ripley's Believe It or Not! Museum	175 Jefferson St	415-771-6188	3
Russian Center	2450 Sutter St, 4th Fl	415-921-7631	5
San Francisco Fire Museum	655 Presidio Ave	415-563-4630	5
San Francisco Museum of Craft & Design	550 Sutter St	415-773-0303	5
San Francisco Railway Museum	77 Steuart St	415-974-1948	8
Sculpture Garden at Recology San Francisco	501 Tunnel Ave	415-330-1415	40
SFMOMA	151 3rd St	415-357-4000	8
Society of California Pioneers	300 4th St	415-957-1849	12
Tattoo Art Museum	841 Columbus Ave	415-775-4991	4
The Wax Museum	145 Jefferson St	800-439-4305	4
Wells Fargo History Museum	420 Montgomery St	415-396-2619	8
Yerba Buena Center for the Arts	701 Mission St	415-978-2787	8

General Information

NFT Map: 8
Address: 151 Third St
                 (between Mission and Howard Sts)
                 San Francisco, CA 94103
Phone: 415-357-4000
Website: www.sfmoma.org
Hours: Mon–Tues & Fri–Sun: 11 am–5:45 pm;
                 Thurs 11 am–8:45 pm.
                 Closed Wednesdays, Thanksgiving,
                 Christmas, & New Year's Day. Open from
                 10 am Memorial Day through Labor Day.
Entry: $18 for adults, $13 for seniors,
                 $11 for students, free for children
                 12 and under, free admission on
                 the first Tuesday of each month,
                 half-price admission Thursday evenings
                 6 pm–8:45 pm.
                 Note that the museum stops selling
                 tickets 45 minutes prior to closing.

Overview

[Note: Until early 2016, the SFMOMA building is closed for expansion but is offering top exhibitions and events around the city until then. Visit: www.sfmoma.org/exhib_ events for more information.]

How about sharing your midday with Mondrian? Or taking an afternoon break with Diebenkorn? For those who work downtown, the San Francisco Museum of Modern Art (SFMOMA) offers an easy-to-reach oasis of calm and creativity. When it opened in 1935 (in another location and without the "modern" in its name) under the direction of Grace L. McCann Morley, it was the first museum on the West Coast devoted solely to 20th-century art. In January 1995, SFMOMA opened a new museum facility in the burgeoning South of Market district, designed by renowned Swiss architect Mario Botta. Across the street from Yerba Buena Center, the SFMOMA is the centerpiece of a growing cluster of downtown and SOMA-area museums, with a permanent collection of more than 27,000 works.

The extensive painting and sculpture collection contains creations by distinguished artists such as Jackson Pollock and Henri Matisse and includes genres such as American Post-Minimalism, German Expressionism, and Fauvism. It also showcases the work of San Francisco Bay Area artists such as David Park and Wayne Thiebaud. More than 50 years ago, the museum was one of the first to recognize photography as an art form. Today, its Department of Photography has international stature. SFMOMA has a state-of-the-art education center adjacent to the permanent collection galleries on the second floor. Alongside the permanent collection, SFMOMA's temporary exhibitions often draw both crowds and accolades (check website for current and upcoming exhibitions). The SFMOMA library, open by appointment only, comprises more than 60,000 catalogued items, including monographs, exhibition catalogues, and 1,890 periodical titles.

Be sure to check out SFMOMA's Rooftop Garden, a 14,400 square-foot multifunctional open-air space designed by Jensen Architects, where you can ogle well-known and rare large-scale sculpture, sip a Blue Bottle Coffee latte, and take in the San Francisco skyline.

How to Get There—Driving

From the East Bay, take I-80 and exit at Fremont Street. Take an immediate left from Fremont onto Howard Street and get into the right lane. Go two blocks and turn right onto Third Street. From the Peninsula, take US 101 until it connects to I-80 and exit at Fourth Street; Fourth immediately leads onto Bryant Street. Take a left from Bryant onto Third Street and follow it until you reach the museum. From the North Bay, take US 101 to Lombard Street. Follow Lombard to Van Ness Avenue and turn right; follow Van Ness until you reach Golden Gate Avenue and turn left. Follow Golden Gate as it crosses Market Street onto Sixth Street. Turn left from Sixth Street onto Folsom Street and follow Folsom up to Third Street; turn left onto Third. Once you've arrived, you can park at the SFMOMA garage located behind the museum on Minna between Third and New Montgomery Streets or at the 5th and Mission garage.

How to Get There—Mass Transit

BART will take you to either the Montgomery Street or Powell Street Stations; both are within walking distance of SFMOMA.

Muni bus lines 9 San Bruno, 14 Mission, 15 Third, 30 Stockton, 38 Geary, 5 Fulton, and 45 Union run near the museum, and Muni Metro lines J-Church, K-Ingleside, L-Taraval, M-Oceanview, and N-Judah will take you to either Montgomery Street or Powell Street Stations.

Golden Gate Transit buses 10, 70, 80, and 101 stop at the Transbay Temporary Terminal at 250 Main Street, between Beale and Howard.

Arts & Entertainment • **Movie Theaters**

While over 35 smaller theaters have disappeared from the San Francisco cinema scene in the past 20 years, the remaining contingent still stands strong in the face of the ubiquitous multiplex. **The Clay (Map 5)** in Pacific Heights (one of the oldest theaters in San Francisco) shows a fine variety of international and specialty films. Although the Inner Richmond's historic **Bridge (Map 22)** has small screens and higher prices - showing new releases, Asian films, and "alternative world cinema." The Outer Richmond's **Balboa (Map 19)** shows first-run and art films as well as special programs on its two screens, offering a bargain matinee and occasional double features The tiny **Four Star Theater (Map 20)** caters to the large Chinese community in Outer Richmond—just like a neighborhood theater should—with weekend Hong Kong cinema, and it also offers double features and "alternative world cinema."

The three-screen **Lumiere (Map 7)** in Russian Hill plays art films you may never see anywhere else (check out the original main room; the newer two are cramped). The two-screen **Roxie (Map 11)** in the Mission wishes to remain the last gritty stronghold of independent documentaries and local shorts. The classy organ-clad **Castro Theatre (Map 10)** in the heart of the Castro prefers vintage classics to woo patrons under its 1920s-style gilded cupola. (It even has the occasional sing-along showing of the *Sound of Music*, when fans costume up to fa-so-la-ti the night away.)

The **Embarcadero (Map 8)** and **Opera Plaza (Map 6)** have a great selection of first-run international, arty, and specialty flicks. In addition to an impressive selection of Japanese films, **New People Cinema** in Japantown also screens week long runs of films from around the world, presented by the San Francisco Film Society. Originality and charm aside, for the cineplex experience, head to the **Metreon (Map 12)** south of Market (for big and comfortable everything and an IMAX screen), the multitiered **AMC Van Ness 14 (Map 6)** (housed in an old Cadillac dealership), or the **Century San Francisco Centre 9 (Map 7)** inside the new downtown Westfield mall. Just outside the city's borders is the **Century 20 Daly City**. Fandango (www.fandango.com) or Moviefone (777-FILM; www.moviefone.com) can help you beat the weekend crowds by reserving tickets in advance.

Besides the ordinary showcases, the city is home to many annual film festivals, from Jewish to LGBT, Asian to underground—even bicycle! These festivals present some of the best contemporary cinematic work year-round. Finally, let's not overlook some greats in the nearby East Bay: learn something new and culturally enriching at the **Pacific Film Archive** in Berkeley, or check out the **Elmwood Theatre**, Berkeley's best neighborhood theater, for new indie films and real butter on your popcorn.

Movie Theater	Address	Phone	Map
4-Star Theatre	2200 Clement St	415-666-3488	20
AMC Bay Street 16	5614 Shellmound St	510-457-4AMC	North Oakland
AMC Metreon 16	135 4th St	415-369-6207	12
AMC Van Ness 14	1000 Van Ness Ave	415-922-4AMC	6
Balboa Theater	3630 Balboa St	415-221-8184	19
Bridge Theater	3010 Geary Blvd	415-267-4893	22
California Theater	2113 Kittredge St	510-464-5980	Berkeley (East)
Castro Theatre	429 Castro St	415-621-6120	10
Century Empire 3	85 West Portal Ave	415-661-2539	30
Century San Francisco Centre 9	845 Market St (5th Fl of Westfield)	415-538-8422	7
CineArts at Sequoia	25 Throckmorton Ave	415-388-4862	Mill Valley
Clay Theatre	2261 Filmore St	415-267-4893	5
Elmwood Theatre	2966 College Ave	510-649-0530	Berkeley (East)
Embarcadero Theater	1 Embarcadero Ctr	415-267-4893	8
Foreign Cinema	2534 Mission St	415-648-7600	15
Four Star Theater	2200 Clement St	415-666-3488	20
Grand Lake Theater	3200 Grand Ave	510-452-3556	Downtown Oakland
Lumiere Theater	1572 California St	415-267-4893	7
Marina Theatre	2149 Chestnut St	415-345-1323	1
New People Cinema	1746 Post St	415-525-8600	6
Opera Plaza Cinemas	601 Van Ness Ave	415-771-0183	6
Pacific Film Archive	2575 Bancroft Wy	510-642-0808	Berkeley (East)
Piedmont Theatre	4186 Piedmont Ave	510-985-1252	North Oakland
Presidio Theatre	2340 Chestnut St	415-776-2388	1
Roxie	3117 16th St	415-863-1087	11
San Francisco Cinematheque	145 9th St	415-552-1990	12
Shattuck Cinemas	2230 Shattuck Ave	510-644-2992	Berkeley (East)
Sundance Kabuki Cinema	1881 Post St	415-929-4650	5
UA Emerybay 10	6330 Christie Ave	800-326-3264	North Oakland
UA Stonestown Twin	501 Buckingham Wy	800-326-3264	28
UA Vogue	3290 Sacramento St	415-221-8183	5
United Artists Cinemas 7	2274 Shattuck Ave	510-486-1852	Berkeley (East)

In search of the printed word? Although you can find your typical big-box behemoths sprinkled here and there, the city is better known for its independently owned and operated bookstores, which give personality to the many neighborhoods they serve. Their loyal clientele will argue the merits of their favorite ones, so we'll leave it up to you to choose your own bookstore focus and vibe.

General

Famed for its connection to the Beat movement during the 1950s, **City Lights (Map 8)** is often pegged as the city's best-known literary landmark. Located in the lively North Beach neighborhood, the store was opened in 1953 by poets Lawrence Ferlinghetti and Peter D. Martin, and quickly became a hub for progressive political thinkers, poets, and novelists, from Allen Ginsberg to Frank O'Hara. Today, it regularly features readings by alternative authors and poets. Be sure to visit the downstairs. Another popular venue for readings by well-known authors is **Booksmith (Map 9)** on Haight Street, with an excellent assortment of new books and a reputation for scheduling cult-hit authors and respected musicians-turned-writers. According to many in the city, the best general new and used bookstore around is Clement Street's **Green Apple Books (Map 21)**. The large store is famous for its bargain books from publisher overstock. Sadly, the oldest and largest independent bookstore in San Francisco, Stacey's, closed in 2009 due mostly to competition from the Interweb and big-box bookstores.

New & Used

Just about every neighborhood in San Francisco has a used bookstore or two, but some of our favorites are **Phoenix, Bookshop West Portal (Map 30)**, and **Red Hill Books (Map 35)**. The Mission has several independent bookstores worth visiting, including **Alley Cat Books** and **Dog Eared Books (Map 15)**. Down at Fort Mason Center is the **Book Bay Bookstore (Map 2)**, stocked with remainders and used books; sales support the city's public library system.

Art & Architecture

For books on art and design, San Francisco's museum bookstores are virtual goldmines. Not surprisingly, the **SFMOMA Bookstore (Map 8)** has an extensive collection of new art and art-related books, as does the **Asian Art Museum (Map 7)** store. At the brilliant **William Stout Architectural Books (Map 8)**, aesthetics are the raison d'etre. Titles range from the instructional to the theoretical, and span a vast array of architecture, design, and decorative arts subjects, including interior design, landscaping,

textiles, furniture, and urban planning. **Foto-Grafix Books (Map 8)** (formerly the Friends of Photography bookstore) has what many consider the best selection of photography books in the city.

Specialty

Niche bookstores also abound. Whether you're looking for Japanese comics or highly technical design books, you'll be sure to find them. **Borderlands (Map 11)** is a favorite destination among science fiction, fantasy, and horror aficionados. **Fields Book Store (Map 7)** specializes in the metaphysical, if that's your thing.

Given the city's large number of residents whose first language is something other than English, it's no surprise that there are plenty of foreign-language bookstores around. The largest Japanese bookstore in San Francisco is **Kinokuniya (Map 6)** in Japantown, carries tons of Japanese- language books and magazines, as well as a number of English-language Japanese periodicals, comics, and novels. The **European Book Company (Map 7)** emphasizes French and German texts, while **Arkipelago Philippine Books (Map 12)** stocks Filipino books and art.

If you're into Eastern thought and Buddhism, try **Eastwind Books (Map 4)** for classic and recently published new age books. Seekers of the spiritual and philosophical realms will find reading materials at **Vedanta Society Bookshop (Map 2)**, the **Zen Center Bookstore (Map 11)**, and **Browser Books (Map 5)**.

For a wide selection of politically and culturally progressive books, head to **Modern Times (Map 15)**. **Bound Together (Map 9)** has all your anarchist and subversive literary needs. **Bolerium Books (Map 11)** stocks rare and out-of-print books, posters, and ephemera on social movements.

Old sea salts love the **Maritime Bookstore (Map 3)** at the Hyde Street Pier for new nautical books. Rare book collectors can be found browsing **Thomas A. Goldwasser (Map 7)**. Two stores in the city are known for their immense inventory of African-American and black history books: **Marcus Books (Map 5)** and **Alexander Book Company (Map 8)**. **Dandelion (Map 11)** is a well-known destination for children's books, as well as fun knick knacks for the home. Find books about science and the natural world at the **California Academy of Sciences Bookstore (Map 25)** as well as the **Exploratorium Store (Map 1)**. If you're looking for books about California and its history, the **California Historical Society (Map 8)** store is where it's at.

Happy reading!

Map 1 • Marina / Cow Hollow (West)

Books Inc	2251 Chestnut St	931-3633	General new.
Exploratorium Store	3601 Lyon St	397-5673	Museum gift shop.

Map 2 • Marina / Cow Hollow (East)

The Collectors Cave	2072 Union St	929-0231	Comics, cards, collectibles.
Vedanta Society Bookshop	2323 Vallejo St	922-2323	Spiritual, metaphysical books.

Map 3 • Russian Hill / Fisherman's Wharf

Russian Hill Bookstore	2234 Polk St	929-0997	General used.

Map 4 • North Beach / Telegraph Hill

Cavalli Cafe & Imports	1441 Stockton St	421-4219	Italian books.
Eastwind Books & Arts	1435A Stockton St	772-5877	Chinese and Asian culture and medicine books.

Map 5 • Pacific Heights / Western Addition

Browser Books	2195 Fillmore St	567-8027	General.
Marcus Books	1712 Fillmore St	346-4222	African-American books.

Map 6 • Pacific Heights / Japantown

Alan Wofsy Fine Arts	1109 Geary Blvd	292-6500	Used and out-of-print art books.
Kinokuniya Bookshop	1581 Webster St	567-7625	Japanese books, English books, Asian culture, and history.

Map 7 • Nob Hill / Tenderloin

Argonaut Book Shop	786 Sutter St	474-9067	California history, the West, and Americana.
Asian Art Museum Store	200 Larkin St	581-3500	Museum gift shop.
Fields Book Store	1419 Polk St	673-2027	Metaphysical, mind-body-spirit, world religion.
Islamic Bookstore	20 Jones St	863-8005	Islamic books.
Kayo Books	814 Post St	749-0554	Vintage paperbacks from the '40s to the '70s and esoteric books of all persuasions.
Magazine	920 Larkin St	441-7737	Magazines, out-of-print, and used only.
Thomas A Goldwasser Rare Books	486 Geary St	292-4698	Rare books.
World Books	824 Stockton St	397-8473	Chinese books.

Map 8 • Financial District / SOMA

Alexander Book Co	50 2nd St	495-2992	General new.
The Book Passage	Embarcadero & Market St	835-1020	General new.
Brick Row Book Shop	49 Geary St, #230	398-0414	Rare 18th and 19th-century lit.
Camerawork Gallery & Bookstore	657 Mission St	863-1001	Photography books.
Chronicle Books	680 2nd St	369-6271	Only books published by Chronicle.
City Lights	261 Columbus Ave	362-8193	General new.
Discovery Channel Store	4 Embarcadero Ctr	956-4911	General, science.
871 Fine Arts Gallery and Bookstore	20 Hawthorne St	543-5812	Art books only.
Jeffrey's Toys	685 Market St	546-6551	Children's books.
John Windle Antiquarian Bookseller	49 Geary St, #233	986-5826	Old and rare.
Louie Brothers Book Store	754 Washington St	391-8866	Chinese books.
New China Book Store	642 Pacific Ave	956-0752	Chinese books.
Pacific Book Auction Galleries	133 Kearny St	989-2665	Book auctions of rare books, maps, manuscripts, photos.
SFMOMA Museum Store	151 3rd St	357-4035	Art, architecture, painting, photography, design.
Sino-American Books & Arts	751 Jackson St	421-3345	Chinese books.
William Stout Architectural Books	804 Montgomery St	391-6757	Architecture, design, art, landscape.

Map 9 • Haight Ashbury / Cole Valley

Booksmith	1644 Haight St	863-8688	General new.
Bound Together Anarchist Collective Bookstore	1369 Haight St	431-8355	Anarchist books.
Recycled Records	1377 Haight St	626-4075	Music, entertainment, movie books.

Arts & Entertainment • **Bookstores**

Map 10 • Castro / Lower Haight

Aardvark Books	227 Church St	552-6733	Primarily used.
Books Inc	2275 Market St	864-6777	General new.
Comix Experience	305 Divisadero St	863-9258	Comics… Only comics.
Crystal Way	2335 Market St	861-6511	Spiritual, metaphysical, recovery, yoga.

Map 11 • Hayes Valley / The Mission

Adobe Book Shop	3166 16th St	864-3936	General used, specialize in philosophy and Greek and Roman literature.
Bolerium Books	2141 Mission St, #300	863-6353	Mostly used. American social movements.
Borderlands	866 Valencia St	824-8203	Sci-fi, fantasy, horror, new/used.
California Institute of Integral Studies Bookstore	1453 Mission St	575-6100	Textbooks, spiritual-books.
Dandelion	55 Potrero Ave	436-9500	Gift shop with an extensive collection of children's books.
Forest Books	3080 16th St	863-2755	General used, poetry, eastern religion, art.
Isotope	326 Fell St	621-6543	Comics.
The Green Arcade	1680 Market St	431-6800	Eco, politics, sustainability, food and farming, urban planning books...go green!
Meyer Boswell Books	2141 Mission St, #302	255-6400	History of law.
Valhalla Books	2141 Mission St, #202	863-9250	General literature, first editions.
Zen Center	300 Page St	255-6524	Buddhist books.

Map 12 • SOMA / Potrero Hill (North)

Arkipelago Philippine Books	1010 Mission St	553-8185	Filipino books.

Map 13 • Mission Beach

Christopher's Books	1400 18th St	255-8802	Neighborhood bookshop.

Map 14 • Noe Valley

Omnivore Books on Food	3885 Cesar Chavez St	282-4712	Haven of foodie booklovers.
Phoenix Books & Records	3957 24th St	821-3477	General new and used.

Map 15 • Mission (Outer)

Alley Cat Books	3036 24th Street	824-1761	Catch up on all those literary journals.
Dog Eared Books	900 Valencia St	282-1901	General new and used.
Modern Times Bookstore	2919 24th St	282-9246	Progressive bookstore.
Nueva Libreria Mexico	2886 Mission St	642-0759	Spanish only.
Scarlet Sage Herb Co	1173 Valencia St	821-0997	Healing books.

Map 20 • Richmond

Arlekim Russian Bookstore	5909 Geary Blvd	751-2320	Russian books.
Cards and Comics Central	5424 Geary Blvd	668-3544	Comic books, collectibles.

Map 21 • Inner Richmond

Green Apple Books & Music	506 Clement St	387-2272	General interest.
Pacific Books & Arts	524 Clement St #A	751-2238	General Chinese bookstore.

Map 22 • Presidio Heights / Laurel Heights

Books Inc	3515 California St	221-3666	General new.
Dayenu Judaica	3220 California St	563-6563	Jewish books, music, and art.
USF Campus	2130 Fulton St	422-6493	General.

Map 25 • Inner Sunset / Golden Gate Heights

Amazing Fantasy	650 Irving St	681-4344	Comics
Botanical Garden Bookstore	9th Ave & Lincoln Wy	661-1316	Plant books.
California Academy of Sciences Store	55 Music Concourse Dr	379-8000	Museum gift shop.
The Great Overland Book Company	345 Judah St	664-0126	General used, California history.

Map 28 • SFSU / Park Merced

SFSU Bookstore	1650 Holloway Ave	338-2665	Textbooks, general books.

Map 30 • West Portal

Bookshop West Portal	80 West Portal Ave	564-8080	General.
Comic Outpost	2381 Ocean Ave	239-2669	Comic books, collectibles.
Mark Post, Bookseller	2555 Ocean Ave, #101	586-2363	Literature, history, art, Scottish studies. Mostly used.

Map 32 • Diamond Heights / Glen Park

Bird & Beckett Books & Records	653 Chenery St	586-3733	General new and used.

Map 35 • Bernal Heights

Badger Books	401 Cortland Ave	648-5331	New and used books to buy or trade.

Berkley (East)

Moe's Books	2476 Telegraph Ave	849-2087	Four stories of new and used books, academically inclined..

Berkley (West)

Black Oak Books	2618 San Pablo Ave	486-0698	Berkeley independent bookseller.

The Presidio

Crissy Field Warming Hut	983 Marine Dr	561-3040	Environmental/nature.

San Francisco is a drinkin' kind of town—has been since the Gold Rush, when a raucous drinker could end up falling through a trap door and into the clutches of a crimp, a nefarious type who specializes in kidnapping drunks and selling them to ships in need of sailors, a practice known as Shanghaiing. Though the drunken pirate fights have calmed down over the years, if you're looking for trouble, you can find it here. Nightlife is dynamic: old places close down, new ones pop up. Niche markets are both plentiful and eclectic here, and San Francisco has a huge assortment of bars to fulfill your every desire. Here we selected a few choice destinations to fit some of your basic bar variables.

Dive Bars

San Francisco is full of more dive bars than you can shake a broken pool cue at. We like **Trad'r Sam (Map 19)** for a grungy Richmond tiki bar, the **500 Club (Map 11)** in the Mission for shooting pool and soaking up diversity on a foggy summer night, and **Mr. Bing's (Map 8)** where you can play liar's dice (at your own risk) with Mr. Bing himself. Other good bets are the **Latin American Club (Map 15)** and Chinatown's **Buddha Bar (Map 8)**. The East Bay is also a dive bar haven, with **George Kaye's (North Oakland/Emeryville)**, Merchant's **(Oakland)** which resides largely in a hole in Jack London Square, and **Club Mallard** (752 San Pablo Ave in Albany, 510-524-8450) topping our list.

Best Beer Selection

Without a doubt, Lower Haight's **Toronado (Map 10)** wins the category prize. They pour 50 beers on tap and double that number in bottled brews. The **Mad Dog in the Fog (Map 10)** across the street has a great selection of English beers, try them out over Thursday Quiz Night. There are no shortage of great Irish bars (and Irish beers) in San Francisco, such as **Kate O'Brien's (Map 8)**, **O'Reilly's Irish Bar (Map 4)**, and **Ireland's 32 (Map 21)**. We also should mention Oakland's favorite Irish pub **McNally's (North Oakland/Emeryville)** with a solid beer selection, and The **Trappist (Downtown Oakland/Lake Merritt)** boasting one of the finest selections of Belgian brew in the Bay Area. See also locally brewed favorite **Speakeasy (Map 37)**.

Outdoor Spaces

Nothing beats those beautiful San Francisco days when the fog hasn't made it over Twin Peaks yet and you're having drinks outside on the sunny side of town. We love **The Ramp (Map 13)** and **Pier 23 (Map 4)** on the Embarcadero for their cocktails, burgers, seafood, and salads on fabulous waterfront decks. You can always catch an old movie outside at **Foreign Cinema (Map 15)**, or get drunk and eat BBQ in a gritty old junkyard turned beer garden at **Zeitgeist (Map 11)**, which, on nice days, is packed with patrons from before happy hour to the wee hours of the morning. On the other side of the Bay, Alameda's **Lucky 13** (1301 Park St, 510-523-2118) is a popular outdoor spot rain or shine for cocktails and BBQ.

Best Décor

For class and sophistication, **Slide (Map 7)** is a large, ultra-hip speakeasy with an actual slide and posh ambiance for folks who don't mind waiting in line, or try **Matrix Fillmore (Map 2)**. For funky and simple, check out the space at **The Knockout (Map 35)** or **Madrone (Map 10)**. For funky and nautical, **Spec's (Map 8)** is the place for lovers of maritime décor. For cozy and comfortable, visit **Liverpool Lil's (Map 1)** or **Balboa Café (Map 2)** (midweek only, it's anything but cozy on the weekends). For dark and romantic, try the bar at **The Big 4 (Map 7)** in the Huntington Hotel, **The Redwood Room (Map 7)**, or the **Upstairs Bar & Lounge (Map 8)** in the W Hotel.

Best Jukebox

Dalva (Map 11) has a great all-around jukebox. Rocker types have perennially awarded **Lucky 13 (Map 10)** with 'best jukebox' awards in local publications. For Louis Prima swing-era music hit **La Rocca's Corner (Map 3)** in North Beach or for Italian opera hit the **Tosca Café (Map 8)**. **Mucky Duck's (Map 25)** selection is also impressive (especially if you actually make it to the Sunset), and in addition to quirky live music, **Hemlock Tavern (Map 7)** has one of the more awesome indie and shoegazer jukes in the city.

Live Music

For live music there are historic heavy-hitters such as **The Warfield (Map 7)**, **Great American Music Hall (Map 7)**, **Bimbo's 365 (Map 3)**, **Slim's (Map 11)**, and, of course, **The Fillmore (Map 5)**—the only place where you can still get a free apple before the show and often a free poster after the show. Other venues to check out are **The Boom Boom Room (Map 5)**, **DNA Lounge (Map 11)**, **The Independent (Map 10)**, **Café Du Nord (Map 10)**, **The Elbo Room (Map 11)**, **Rickshaw Stop (Map 11)**, **Bottom of the Hill (Map 13)**, and the **Hotel Utah (Map 12)**. The **Saloon (Map 4)** has free live blues, and **Hemlock Tavern (Map 7)** and **Edinburgh Castle (Map 7)** are great spots for cheap to free local indie acts of all sorts.

If you are feeling like tapping your foot along some sit-down jazz, the best of the best come to **Yoshi's (Downtown Oakland/Lake Merritt)** in Oakland. **Rasselas (Map 5)** and **Savanna Jazz (Map 15)** are also havens for that great local sound. Also across the Bay, the **Paramount Theatre (see Landmarks for Downtown Oakland/Lake Merritt)** is one of the most historic and beautiful venues around that's grabbing some huge names of late, and **Uptown (Downtown Oakland/Lake Merritt)** is a notable new venue for various live music most nights of the week.

Sheik Yerbouti

When you're ready to get your groove on in big-n-swanky club-style, hit **Ruby Skye (Map 7)** and **1015 Folsom (Map 12)**. Both are big with the kids who like to wait in line for the traditional mega-club experience. Be sure to verify that the turntablist du jour fits your personal taste because the DJ scene here goes beyond subculture all the way to individual ecosystems. More eclectic dance hotspots include **Mezzanine (Map 7)**, **Milk (Map 9)**, **111 Minna (Map 8)**, and **Mighty (Map 12)**, and **Luka's Taproom (Downtown Oakland/Lake Merritt)** is taken over by DJ's most nights after the dinner crowds departs. For salsa, hit **Roccapulco (Map 35)** or **Café Cocomo (Map 13)**—they offer lessons three times a week for the novice. **Little Baobab (Map 11)** offers African music and cocktails made with exotic mixers like hibiscus, ginger and tamarind. And when you feel like partying after everything else shuts down, you'll probably end up at **The EndUp (Map 12)**.

Eating out is an essential part of living in San Francisco. For some, it's an obsession. For others, it's an art form. We can't wait to try a new restaurant (when we can get in) or a new type of food, and while we don't mind spending an occasional fortune in the city's most happening spots, we're also down with cramming into dives that might alarm some tourists—it's all part of dining out in our fair city. With so many distinct neighborhoods, ethnicities, and sub-cultures, it's no surprise that San Francisco brims with just about every kind of restaurant and cuisine imaginable. Hakka? Check. Yucatecan? Yep. Finding gastronomic pleasures in this city is easy. It's choosing among them that's challenging.

Eating Fresh

Vetting new restaurants is practically a competitive sport in San Francisco. Everyone wants to discover the next big culinary treasure before word hits the streets. Take **farmerbrown** (Map 7), for example. This destination for neo- soul food now attracts everyone from hipsters who've come for the swanky scene to organic foodies who appreciate the restaurant's reliance on small, local farms. **Minako (Map 11)** offers organic Japanese to patient diners, while star chef Gerald Hirogyen's **Piperade (Map 4)** serves up dreamy Basque food made from locally sourced ingredients, and **Zuni Café (Map 11)** is famous for its simple roast chicken and panzanella. Across the Bay **Tamarindo Antojería (Downtown Oakland/Lake Merritt)** continues to impress critics and patrons alike with south of the border cuisine, and **Pizzaiolo (North Oakland/Emeryville)** is a destination pizza place. Reservations at **NOPA (Map 10)** are hard to come by, and maple-laced bacon beignets and house wine blends dazzle foodies at **Frances (Map 11)**.

Eating Cheap

Can you really do this here? Mos' def'! For pizza, check out **Golden Boy (Map 4)** in North Beach, **Giorgio's (Map 21)** in the Richmond area, and the venerable **Escape From New York Pizza (Map 9)** on Haight. There's cheap Chinese food in almost every neighborhood, but we recommend **Ton Kiang (Map 20)** in Richmond, **R&G Lounge (Map 8)** near North Beach, and **Tai Chi (Map 7)** in upscale Russian Hill. Possibly the greatest Chinese experience in all the land is **House of Nanking (Map 8)** in Chinatown, where you'll consider yourself lucky to wait in line only to be rushed out, with the best fried rice you've ever eaten in between. **Primo Patio (Map 13)** is a reliably cheap and awesome Caribbean lunch spot. There is also an endless supply of Thai—try **Manora (Map 11)** South of Market and **Thep Phanom (Map 10)** in the Lower Haight. You can also get just about any type of Southeast Asian food in the Richmond area. One of our favorites is **Burma Superstar (Map 21)** on Clement Street, not far from a handful of Vietnamese pho joints.

For solid Indian on a shoestring budget, hit the popular **Naan-N-Curry chain (Maps 8, 25)**, **Shalimar (Map 7)**, or **Udupi Palace (Map 15)**. The Mission is a gold mine for Mexican and, with so many taquerias, you'll find fresh tacos and bulging burritos on every block. **La Taqueria (Map 15)** and **El Farolito (Map 15)** are city favorites.

Mediterranean fare is another way to save a buck or two. Stop by Turkish-leaning **Troya (Map 21)** on Clement for lavash sammies or **Truly Mediterranean (Map 11)** for fab falafel. For poultry fans, **Goood Frikin' Chicken (Map 35,** (yes, that's three Os) serves up a delicious version of the ubiquitous bird and American sides with Middle Eastern flair.

Eating Hip

Want to see and be seen by San Francisco's beautiful people while indulging in a truly fabulous meal? Hot spots include **Nopalito** in the Inner Sunset **(Map 25)** and by-now classic **Dosa** on Fillmore **(Map 5)**. If you find yourself in the chi-chi Marina, try **Betelnut (Map 2)** for swanky Asian small plates or make a beeline for **Mamacita (Map 1)**. Just be prepared to suck down a few cocktails while you wait for tables. In the Mission, **The Blue Plate (Map 35)**, **Foreign Cinema (Map 15)** and **Luna Park (Map 11)** are constant favorites, while new cutting-edge patisserie **Craftsman & Wolves (Map 11)** offer architectural works of sugar. In the financial district, you can mingle with business folk and locals who lunch at chic Northern Italian hotspot **Perbacco (Map 8)**. Across the Bay, the Oakland renaissance continues with **Wood Tavern (North Oakland/Emeryville)**, **Flora (Downtown Oakland/Lake Merritt)**, and **Camino (Downtown Oakland/Lake Merritt)**. For whiskey cocktails as dressy as its diners, line up for **Picán (Downtown Oakland/Lake Merritt)**, or try **Luka's Taproom (Downtown Oakland/Lake Merritt)**, where the Belgian fries are not to be missed.

Eating Brunch

Saturdays and Sundays are eggfests in the city, and there's no shortage of restaurants and cafés to choose from. So sleep late, call some friends, and step out for the best first meal of the day. Down home diners like **Chow (Map 10)** in the Castro, while **Dottie's True Blue Café (Map 7)** and the **Pork Store Café (Map 11)** are jumping almost every day of the week. Weekend warriors are willing to wait at constant favorites like **Mama's (Map 4)** on Washington Square in North Beach, Noe Valley's **Chloe's Café (Map 14)**, **Ella's (Map 5)** in Laurel Heights, and **Cole Valley's Zazie (Map 9)**. **Brenda's French Soul Food (Map 7)** wows the Tenderloin with puffy beignets, while **Outerlands (Map 23)** attracts early birds for Dutch pancakes in the Sunset district. Outside the city, **Fred's Coffee Shop (Sausalito)** serves good French toast, **Mama's Royal Café (North Oakland/Emeryville)** has hipsters out the door on weekends, while **Chop Bar (Downtown Oakland/Lake Merritt)** draws a late, casual crowd for chilaquiles and challah French toast.

Eating Old

Even though restaurant turnover continues at an astonishing rate, there are some old San Francisco eateries worth checking out, including 1867 relic **Sam's Grill (Map 8)**, **Big 4 (Map 7)** in the Huntington Hotel, the **Tadich Grill (Map 8)**, and **Swan Oyster Depot (Map 7)**. **Alfred's (Map 8)** serves up steaks and Sears Fine Foods (Map 7) still plates a mighty good breakfast. **Spenger's (Berkeley West)** still kicks it old-school across the Bay.

Eating Meat

As much as we love our locally grown, organic veggies, sometimes nothing will do but a thick slab of rare beef. Van Ness Avenue is home to several good choices for this undulgence, including **Harris's (Map 6)** and **House of Prime Rib (Map 6)**, which has been there forever and serves up good martinis and huge portions. Also worth mention on Van Ness is **Tommy's Joynt (Map 6)**, which dishes up carved turkey and roast beef to locals, tourists and the occasional celebrity (previous diners include Metallica and the late Hunter S. Thompson). Nearby, you'll find **Boboquivari's (Map 2)**, a crab and steak joint with carnival-esque décor. If you want to bring it down a notch, hit **Izzy's (Map 1)** in the Marina (order the creamed spinach and Izzy's potatoes). For upscale diners, **5A5 Steak Lounge (Map 8)** offers Japanese steaks at blue-chip prices in a Vegas-style setting. For the best BBQ, go to the East Bay, where the venerable **Everett & Jones (Berkeley West)** leads the pack, and **T-Rex (Berkeley West)** is a worthy contender.

Eating Meatless

Pretty much every San Francisco restaurant offers vegetarian options, but there are some places that cater strictly to the greens-only crowd, from **Millennium (Map 7)**, San Francisco's high-end organic vegan restaurant (even the wine is organic), to tiny **Lucky Creation (Map 7)** in Chinatown and vegan chain **Herbivore (Map 15)**, which offers soups, salads, and wraps at three locations around the Bay Area. **Greens (Map 2)** is a city favorite for its upscale vegetarian food and beautiful Bay views. Fans of Asian cuisine will find many options for meatless fare, including **Shangri-La (Map 24)** in the Sunset and **Cha-Ya (Map 11)** in the Mission.

Eating Your Wallet

If you can afford it, this is possibly the best (and easiest) way to spend your time in San Francisco. Living in this city is not cheap and neither are some of the most delicious restaurants. The following all cost a fortune, so when you get there the best thing to do is to sit back with your glass of Champagne and lap up the indulgence. **Quince (Map 8)** is the best of the best. You'll have to call at least a month ahead to get a reservation, but the experience is well worth the wait. **Spruce (Map 22)**, **Fleur de Lys (Map 7)**, **COI (Map 4)**, **Campton Place (Map 7)**, **Boulevard (Map 8)**, **La Folie (Map 3)**, and The Slanted Door (Map 8) are just a handful of other spots where you can empty your bank account, fill your belly, and enjoy every minute of it. Happy eating!

Eating Small

While few wallets stretch as far as the fanciest restaurants, most folk can afford an egg custard tart. That's why we've gone small, for specialty dishes like the famous tarts at **Golden Gate Bakery (Map 8)**, or the fried chicken sandwich at **Bakesale Betty (North Oakland/Emeryville)**. Think of these as urban orienteering, as foodies map their way around the city bite by bite: breakfast beignets from **Just For You Café (Map 17)**, tamales from the Tamale Lady at **Zeitgeist (Map 11)**, or banana cream pie at **Mission Pie (Map 15)**. Whatever your tastes, San Francisco has something tasty awaiting you—from crab salad at **Swan Oyster Depot (Map 7)** to cream puffs at **Beard Papa (Map 7)** to, uh, crab puffs at **Thanh Long (Map 23)**. Continue the culinary treasure hunt across the Oakland Bay Bridge with the huge bhatura cholle breads at **Vik's Chaat (Berkeley West)** and lemon icebox pie at **Lois the Pie Queen (North Oakland/Emeryville)**.

Eating by the Bay

Surrounded by sea on three sides, San Francisco is a wonderful place for waterfront dining. Start out west with a view of the Pacific at **Cliff House (Map 18)** or swap silverware for sandwiches at nearby **Louis' (Map 18)**, where the outlook is higher but the prices are lower. Go east for Golden Gate snapshots and vegetarian fare at **Greens (Map 2)** or order crab fresh off the boat at **Scoma's (Map 3)**, one of Fisherman's Wharf's better options. The Ferry Building is a food mecca—especially with its farmers market on Saturday—try haute Vietnamese at **The Slanted Door (Map 8)** or rotisserie sandwiches at **Cane Rosso (Map 8)**. Farther down the Embarcadero, in the shadow of the Bay Bridge, kick back with chili cheese fries and burgers at **Red's Java House (Map 8)** or super-fresh seafood at **Waterbar (Map 8)**. Past the ballpark to the south, **The Ramp (Map 13)** offers beer, brunch and burgers just a stone's throw from the shipyards. Elsewhere around the Bay, there are options aplenty, from **Fish**. in Sausalito to Sam's Anchor Café in Tiburon, a popular joint where the seafood is secondary to the skyline view across the water.

San Francisco is a city where anything can be found and everything can be enjoyed. It's a town that shines with boutiques and thrift stores alike, and even the specialist stores have something for everyone. Nothing's too strange, given that some of the most interesting spots in the city carry stuffed birds, pirate supplies, gigantic bongs and doggie shoes. Most neighborhoods have at least one street with endless retail options, both for those willing to spend some cash and those inclined to find a bargain. Whether you're a shopper on a mission or simply strolling by a storefront, here are the best places to find the basics and the not-so basics.

Clothing

Fashionistas could be lost for days inside the many trendy boutiques in town. Neighborhoods like the Fillmore and the Marina glitter with small boutiques, such as **Ambiance (Map 2)**. Hayes Valley features more high-end options, with shops boasting modern looks from new, independent designers. **Steven Alan (Map 11)** and **Azalea (Map 11)** feature classic designs, jewelry and handbags while **Reliquary (Map 6)** is a great spot for vintage wares, in addition to carefully selected new looks.

The Mission is full of hip and new designs, on the cutting edge of fashion. Check out **Voyager (Map 11)**, **The Mission Statement (Map 15)** and **Weston Wear (Map 15)** for high end, and **Dema (Map 15)** for smaller budgets. For more mainstream tastes, head to Union Square and the **Westfield San Francisco Centre downtown (Map 7)**. Just be prepared for crowds of tourists and hoards of street traffic.

For a true vintage shopping experience, head to the Haight. Check out treasures from another era at **Held Over (Map 9)**, **Static Vintage (Map 9)**, **La Rosa Vintage (Map 9)**, **Buffalo Exchange (Map 9)** and **Wasteland (Map 9)**.

In the Mission, stop by **Mission Thrift (Map 15)**, **Idol Vintage (Map 11)**, **Schauplatz (Map 11)**, **Thrift Town (Map 11)**, and **Clothes Contact (Map 11)**, where you can buy clothes by the pound. For thrift store junkies with a conscience, check out the three locations of **Out of the Closet (Maps 7, 12)**, whose threads are sold to benefit AIDS research.

Those willing to travel for jewelry, clothing and vintage trends from local designers might venture out to the **General Store** in the Outer Sunset **(Map 23)**. For style below the ankle, try **Gimme Shoes (Maps 5, 11)**, **Shoe Biz (Maps 9, 11, 14)**, **Foot Worship (Map 7)** and **Camper (Map 8)**. Fulfill your boudoir fetishes at **Dark Garden (Map 11)** to squeeze your waist with a custom corset. **Zoe Bikini (Map 11)** in the Mission is turning heads with custom swimwear designs. Accessorize with the hip custom messenger bags at **Timbuk2 (Map 11)**. If you want to get noticed, try wearing the fancy artisan jewelry at **Therapy (Map 15)**, **Claudia Kussano (Map 11)** and **Gravel & Gold (Map 15)**.

Sports

Skates on Haight (Map 9) sells and rents rollerblades, scooters, and skateboards. **FTC (Map 9)** on Haight has a great selection of skateboard gear and clothing. If you're into snowboarding and surfing when you're not on your skateboard, then check out **Purple Skunk (Map 20)** on Geary or **SFO Snowboard Shop (Map 9)** on Shrader. Before catching a wave, hardcore surfers must head to **Mollusk Surf Shop in the Outer Sunset (Map 23)**. Whether buying a bike or simply fixin' it up, check out **Freewheel (Maps 9, 15)** where you can tune up your bike, **Valencia Cyclery (Map 15)**, **Box Dog Bicycles (Map 11)** or the **Missing Link Bike Co-op (Berkeley East)**. Rustic camper types should try finding outdoor gear at the **North Face Outlet (Berkeley West)**, **REI (Map 12)**, and **Patagonia (Map 3)**. **Sports Basement** in the Potrero District is the L.L. Bean of the west, featuring everything from yoga mats to camping tents **(Map 11)**. **Lombardi's (Map 7)** in Russian Hill provides a broad range of affordable sports clothing, shoes, and goods.

Houseware

If you're looking for modern, traditional and unusual furniture, try **Artesanias Unique Home Furnishings (Map 11)**, **Monument (Map 11)** and **Harrington Galleries (Map 11)** Try hitting up some of the shops around 9th Street and Folsom and be sure to stop by **Propeller (Map 11)** for modern designs. If you are looking for a nice mattress, price the one you want at one of the chain stores, then head down to **Bedroom Outlet (Map 22)**, where the family-run store will beat any other price and give you a sweet deal and excellent service. For cheap kitchen outfitters, try **City Discount (Map 7)** on Polk or **Cliff's Variety Store (Map 10)** for design savvy, space saving, household basics. For minimalist flatware and efficient kitchen storage items, check out **Soko Hardware** in Japantown **(Map 6)**. If you're on a low-budget and you want something new, try many of the 'junk' stores on Clement Street in the Inner Richmond or Mission Street in the Mission where you can find anything you might ever need for your home, including sushi dishes, tortilla makers, and those lucky cats that wave at you for good luck. Those on a low-budget who are interested in second-hand treasures, head straight up to Bernal Heights on a Sunday morning for the **Alemany Flea Market (Map 35)**. Lastly, for high-end home and kitchen décor, visit **March** in Pacific Heights **(Map 5)**. If you have money to burn and the taste to match, head for the East Bay to Berkeley's posh 4th Street shopping district, which features numerous high-end home furnishing and kitchen supply stores, such as **The Gardener (Map 121)**.

Food

Whether you're a visitor or a resident, let's face it: San Francisco is a foodie's paradise. San Francisco's undeniably gourmet food scene strikes a perfect balance between simplicity and extravagance. This goes beyond restaurants and into the ubiquitous specialty food shop. For healthy eating, **Bi-Rite (Map 11)**, **Harvest Market (Map 10)**, **Valencia Whole Foods (Map 15)** and **Real Food (Maps 2, 7)** are good neighborhood choices, as are the larger spots such as **Trader Joe's (Maps 12, 22)** and vegetarian favorite, **Rainbow Grocery (Map 11)**, with fresh produce, bulk foods, and local products. **Berkeley Bowl (Berkeley East, Berkeley West)** is one of the original large-scale health food and organic produce grocery outlets. For those not so concerned with calories, visit one of the city's many bakeries, such as **Tartine (Map 11)**, **Liberty Cafe (Map 35)**, **Sandbox Bakery (Map 35)**, **Arizmendi Bakery (Map 15)**, **Thorough Bread And Pastry (Map 10)**, and **Noe Valley Bakery (Map 14)**. Top your loaf of bread with slices and spreads from the **24th Street Cheese Company (Map 14)** or the **Cowgirl Creamery Artisan Cheese (Map 8)** in the Ferry Building. Those with a sweet tooth ought to try gourmet ice-cream at **Bi-Rite Creamery (Map 11)**, or the unique flavors of **Humphry Slocombe (Map 15)**. The Ferry Building on the Embarcadero is a food lover's utopia, featuring specialty shops such as **Stonehouse California Olive Oil**, **Blue Bottle Coffee** and **Acme Bread (Map 8)**. Visit on weekends for free tastings as well as their extensive farmer's market on Saturdays.

Art & Photography Supplies

Running low on Cadmium Red? Use your last stick of charcoal drawing a nude? The best art stores are scattered all over the city, but **Flax (Map 11)** is the most well-known. Located on Market Street, it is the size of a small city and sells every type of art and framing supply you can imagine. **Blick Art Materials (Map 7)** is nearby and sells a variety of materials with a good paint and brush selection—they also feature an East Bay location. You can find the best selection of paper at **Paper Source (Map 5)** on Fillmore. If you're looking for photography supplies, try **Adolph Gasser (Map 8)** on Second Street, **Photographers Supply (Map 8)**, **Discount Camera (Map 8)**, **Photoworks** on Market **(Map 10)**, or **The Looking Glass (Berkeley East)**. **Pro Camera (Map 17)** on Minnesota Street is great for rental equipment. **Arch (Map 13)** in Potrero Hill is great for graphic design supplies, portfolios, and gifts. For wearable art, try **ImagiKnit (Map 10)** or **Article Pract (North Oakland/Emeryville)** for yarn.

Music

From Billie Holliday through the Grateful Dead and all the way to Green Day, the San Francisco music scene has been legendary. Accordingly, there are music shops with rare finds, nostalgia producing hits, and up and coming underground artists.

Hit up **Amoeba Music (Map 9)** on Haight for everything from new and used CDs to 78s—it's down the street from the former pads of several sixties bands and is a must for a dazed afternoon in the Haight. It's also the size of a bowling alley. Speaking of large record stores, **Rasputin (Map 7, Berkeley East)** on Telegraph Avenue offers three stories and two storefronts of new and used tunes. **Streetlight Records (Map 10)** is another great resource for new and used music. For rare vinyl, stop by **Groove Merchant Records (Map 10)** or **Jack's Record Cellar (Map 1)** in the Lower Haight. The smaller stores carry more eclectic selections and, more often than not, the staff can help you out with musical queries. Try indie shop **Aquarius (Map 15)** for a good selection and **Thrillhouse Records (Map 32)** for all your punk rock needs.

Books

San Francisco is one of the great literary cities. **City Lights (Map 8)** is the beatnik throwback essential bookstore and they'll let you have your mail sent there if you're drifting. Specialty books can be found at **Dog Eared Books (Map 15)** (new and used), **Books and Bookshelves (Map 10)** (poetry chapbooks), **Press: Works on Paper (Map 1)** (small press material), **Kinokuniya (Map 6)** (Japanese) and **Needles And Pens (Map 15)** (Art and graphic novels). Continue on to the Mission where the independent bookstore is alive and well. On 24th Street, browse through used and new titles at **Modern Times (Map 15)** or brush up on literary journals at **Alley Cat Books (Map 15)**. Valencia Street boasts **826 Valencia (Map 1)**, a spot for writing workshops that includes a pirate-themed gift store and a full collection of McSweeneys-related material. In the quaint Noe Valley you will find **Omnivore Books (Map 14)**, which carries new and vintage cookbooks and hosts food-related events. In Berkeley try the academically inclined **Moe's (Berkeley East)** for four stories of new and used books. Oakland's **Diesel (North Oakland/Emeryville)** not only has a great selection and a good atmosphere, but also hosts book and Spanish language groups. While used book stores abound, you can often find the best (if not most refreshed) selection and price at **Community Thrift Store (Map 11)**.

Pets

Where pets are more populous than kids, you can also find more pet stores than kid's stores. Most of them cater to the pampered pooch as well as having standard fare of collars, food, and the like. The **Bernal Beast (Map 35)** is less pretentious than many such shops and has a good selection at decent prices. **Best in Show (Map 10)** has a cherry-picked toy selection to keep your pup occupied and the ritzy-est of clothing to keep your little ms. or mr. in fashion, even in the Castro. **Noe Valley Pet (Map 14)** offers goods that will keep your pet both stylish and organically fed. Aside from designer pooch sweaters, **George Shop (Map 5, Berkeley West)** even has a selection of fancy baked-good items like birthday cake, donuts, etc. for your pup's special day or just for a treat.

Gifts

While a boutique might specialize in the clothes, you might find more than just an outfit as you browse. Most stores in the city can qualify as a gift store, with something unique on every shelf and hanger. **Bell Jar (Map 11)** has a grand selection of gorgeous and unusual knick-knacks, as does **Paxton Gate (Map 11)**, although it is dominated by long-expired, stuffed creatures. **The Perish Trust**

(Map 5) is a uniquely curated shop, specializing in handpicked antiques and Americana. **Good Vibrations (Map 11, 7)** is the best place to buy your significant other a sex toy, or shop for one together as a gift for your 3-month anniversary. Don't be shy. If you're looking for a classy or fun gift and want to support a good cause, try **Under One Roof (Map 10)**. Every donation or purchase goes to support 35 local AIDS service organizations. If you need to go to therapy, but don't want to deal, at least you can find some retail therapy at the store with the same name (**Therapy (Map 11)**), that also has a host of gifts like cat-butt magnets and retro-vintage signs. On weekends Telegraph Avenue near the UC Campus (**Berkeley East**)—already well-endowed with shops of all sorts—is packed with street vendors selling all manner of eclectic crafts, t-shirts, and jewelry. Or, of course, you can go to your neighborhood box store and just ask for a gift certificate.

Neighborhood Shopping

Most parts of the city satisfy any and all retail therapy needs, but the following neighborhoods have enough stores to fill a half-day of shopping activity. **Clement Street (Map 21)** in the Inner Richmond is great for the host of junk stores, where you can find cheap gloves, cheap and expensive kitchen and restaurant supplies and sushi platters, plus **Green Apple Books (Map 21)** makes it all worthwhile. **Mission Street (Map 15)** is much the same with pseudo-hardware stores, thrift stores, and household goods, cheap but often not of the best quality. **Valencia Street (Map 15)** and **Divisidero Street (Map 10)** have recently been transformed into a mecca for hip young designers, curiosity shops and boutiques. **Fillmore Street in Pacific Heights (Map 5)**, **Hayes Street** in Hayes Valley **(Map 11)**, and **4th Street** in West Berkeley (**Berkeley West**) offer the higher-end of neighborhood shopping and great window shopping. Try **Cortland Avenue** in Bernal Heights **(Map 35)**, **24th Street** in Noe Valley **(Map 14)**, and **Piedmont Avenue (North Oakland/Emeryville)** for shopping in neighborhoods with a nice mix of book, stationery, gift, pet stores, and cafés. The same can be said for the **Rockridge District** of Oakland/Berkeley along College Avenue in either direction from the Rockridge BART Station (**North Oakland/Emeryville**).

San Francisco has long been hip to an electric art scene. Even back in the dusty days of the Gold Rush, there was a strong arts tradition among pioneering groups like the **San Francisco Women Artists (Map 22)**, an organization that has managed its own gallery since the 1880s. Today the city is stocked with small art galleries that attract the diverse crowds San Francisco is known for. These galleries support the cutting-edge creations of local and emerging artists working in every medium.

Sutter and Geary Streets, near Union Square, have one of the largest concentrations of commercial art galleries in the city, and the plethora of exhibition spaces in 49 Geary are definitely worth a visit, especially the first Thursday evening of each month, when "First Thursdays" features gallery openings, free wine and snacks, and throngs of artsy SF folks to gawk at. The quirky, nonprofit, contemporary spot **Southern Exposure (Map 11)** in the Mission District is not to be missed. Edgier pieces depicting chaotic urban scenes and graffiti art come out of the **Tenderloin's White Walls Gallery (Map 7)**. Just next door is a sister art space, the **Shooting Gallery (Map 7)**, where tattoo art, erotic photography, and Japanimation have been celebrated in contemporary renderings.

Some other highlights include the **Superfrog Gallery (Map 6)**, showcasing Japanese pop culture-inspired art at New People, an arts, shopping and entertainment center for Japanese pop culture. **111 Minna Gallery (Map 8)** is a large studio that fuses fine art and live performances with a nightclub atmosphere. Housed within California College of the Arts, a forerunner in art, architecture, and design, the **CCA Wattis Institute (Map 12)** (on Wisconsin and Eighth Streets) has a reputation for putting on some of the most interesting contemporary exhibitions. The **San Francisco Center for the Book (Map 12)** on De Haro Street is also another local treasure.

Overview

Theater in San Francisco can mean anything from lavish productions straight off Broadway stages to more interactive, handcrafted performances from one artist's soul to yours. The Holy Trinity of playhouses in San Francisco may as well be represented by the **Curran (Map 7)**, **Golden Gate (Map 7)**, and **Orpheum Theaters (Map 7)**. The theaters all opened in the 1920s and are distinctive examples of the grandiose theater architecture and design. Current and future schedules and ticket sales for these theaters are available through www.shnsk.com and www.bestofbroadway-sf.com.

Long-Running Shows

Not all big productions in San Francisco are touring shows. At North Beach's **Club Fugazi (Map 4)**, *Beach Blanket Babylon* (with its ever-evolving send-ups of current events and pop culture) has been running right here in the city for over 30 years. Experiencing the wacky musical performance, complete with actors in over-the-top costumes and towering hats, is almost a rite of passage for any San Franciscan. This famous production is billed as the longest running musical revue in theater history.

The Mix

Theater-goers will find that most city theaters stage a mixture of time-honored productions and new plays. Since 1974, the **Geary Theater (Map 7)** has been owned by the American Conservatory Theater (ACT). ACT is San Francisco's highly acclaimed training institute and regional theater. ACT productions, also showcased at the **Children's Creativity Theater (Map 8)** in Yerba Buena Gardens, include classics such as *Cat on a Hot Tin Roof*, as well as new works. Expect plays from playwrights like Tom Stoppard, David Mamet, and Eugene O'Neill. Known for embracing diversity and fostering youth empowerment, the **New Conservatory Theatre Center (Map 11)** houses three theaters: the **Decker (Map 11)**, the **Walker (Map 11)**, and **Theatre Three (Map 11)**. Through its Pride Season program, the center stages multiple LGBT-themed productions each year. Other productions include solo performances, musicals, and even a few classics.

Performing Arts

The **Palace of Fine Arts Theatre (Map 1)** can hold 1,000 patrons and hosts concerts, comedy shows, and lectures in a structure that started out as a temporary structure built for the 1915 Panama Pacific Exposition. Made of wood and plaster, it began to deteriorate after the Expo. In the late 1950s, a restoration movement began, and the building was reconstructed using concrete castings. Today, the theater plays host to performance groups, concerts, film festivals, and lectures. Part of the War Memorial and Performing Arts Center in San Francisco's Civic Center area, the stage at the ornately decorated **Herbst Theatre (Map 6)** is home to a variety of annual musical productions and choral concerts, including the San Francisco Jazz Festival, as well as City Arts & Lectures presentations with authors and artists of the moment. While perhaps not as grand as the Palace of Fine Arts Theatre or the Herbst, there are many city theaters that embrace much more than staged productions. You'll find combinations of multi-disciplinary performance spaces, acting workshops, classes, youth programs, and rental space at theaters such as **The Marsh (Map 15)**, **Next Stage (Map 6)**, **ODC Theater (Map 11)**, **Intersection for the Arts (Map 11)**, **Yerba Buena Center for the Arts Theater (Map 8)**, **Victoria Theatre (Map 11)** (which happens to be the oldest operating theater in San Francisco), and **Shotwell Studios (Map 11)**.

Smaller Theaters

The city is full of small theatrical outfits boasting unique programs. Within Fort Mason Center, one can find five different venues, each catering to distinct patrons and art forms. At **Bayfront Theater (Map 2)** you'll find the BATS improv troupe making it up as they go along. Recitals and classes for budding musicians take place at the **Blue Bear School of Music Performance Hall (Map 2)** and original plays are acted upon the stages of the **Cowell Theater (Map 2)** and **Magic Theatre (Map 2)**. Even kids get in the act inside the **Young Performers Theater (Map 2)**.

You'll find more small-run, off-Broadway performances, improv, one-act plays, and even some stand-up comedy at the **The Custom Stage (Map 12)**, **Shelton Theater (Map 7)**, **Phoenix Theater (Map 7)**, **EXIT Theater (Map 7)** (host of the annual San Francisco Fringe Festival), and **Eureka Theatre (Map 8)**, which puts an emphasis on local talent and productions with social messages. Tony Kushner's *Angels In America* premiered here in 1992.

Cultural Theater

San Francisco has a variety of theaters that focus on performances of interest to specific cultural groups. Located in the Mission District, the **Brava Theatre Center (Map 15)** is the only women-owned theater in San Francisco. The primary purpose of Brava! for Women in the Arts is to produce outstanding world premieres by women of color as well as lesbian playwrights. The first US theater devoted to productions addressing LGBT issues, **Theater Rhinoceros (Map 11)** stages a five-play season each year on its main stage and maintains a smaller studio for emerging artists, workshops, and solo performances. The **Buriel Clay Theatre (Map 6)**, located inside the African-American Cultural Complex, and the **Lorraine Hansberry Theatre (Map 7)** emphasize African-American theater, artists, and performances. Another culturally-based theater organization is the **Bindlestiff Studio (Map 12)** for budding Filipino artists.

Getting Tickets

If you're short on cash, one of the best places to find advance tickets is through Goldstar Events, www.goldstar.com. This online service offers deeply discounted tickets to local events and theatrical performances. For other affordable ticket options, check out Brown Paper Tickets, at www.brownpapertickets.com, a fair-trade ticketing company with the lowest service fees in the industry, at which many smaller venues sell their tickets. Half-price tickets are on sale from 11 am to 5 pm on Tuesdays through Saturdays, and from 10 am to 3 pm on Sundays. The TIX Pavilion is located in Union Square on Powell Street, between Geary and Post. Half-price tickets go on sale at 11 am each day, and tickets for Sunday and Monday are sold on Saturday and Sunday respectively. To check which shows are discounted each day, visit www.tixbayarea.com. TIX Bay Area is a program of Theatre Bay Area, a nonprofit organization serving over 400 theater and dance companies in 11 counties. Check out their website at www.theatrebayarea.com for a comprehensive list of shows playing throughout the area. You'll also discover on their website an abundance of information about arts education, applying for CASH grants, costume rental, auditions, publications, and anything else related to the Bay Area theater scene.

Street Index

Street Index

Street Index

Street Index

Street Index

Street Index

Street Index

Street Index

Street Index

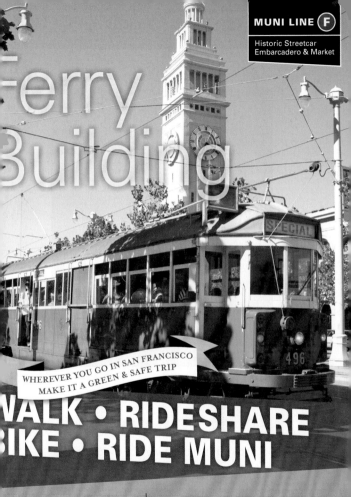

NOT FOR TOURISTS™ Guidebooks

Departures

NFT—NEW YORK CITY
NFT—BROOKLYN
NFT—LONDON
NFT—CHICAGO
NFT—LOS ANGELES
NFT—BOSTON
NFT—SAN FRANCISCO
NFT—SEATTLE
NFT—WASHINGTON DC
NFT—PHILADELPHIA

Tired of your own city?

You buy the ticket, we'll be the guide.